VIZ GRAPHIC NOVEL

X/1999™
PRELUDE

This volume contains the monthly series X/1999 #1 through #6 in their entirety.

STORY & ART BY CLAMP

English Adaptation/Fred Burke & Lillian Olsen
Touch-Up Art & Lettering/Wayne Truman
Cover Design/Viz Graphics
Senior Managing Editor/Annette Roman
Assistant Editor/Toshifumi Yoshida

Senior Editor/Trish Ledoux
Publisher/Seiji Horibuchi
Editor-in-Chief/Hyoe Narita
V.P. of Sales & Marketing/Rick Bauer

Printed in Canada

Published by Viz Communications, Inc.
P.O. Box 77010 • San Francisco, CA 94107

10 9 8 7 6
First printing, July 1996
Sixth printing, April 2002

X/1999 GRAPHIC NOVELS TO DATE

PRELUDE
OVERTURE
SONATA
INTERMEZZO
SERENADE
DUET

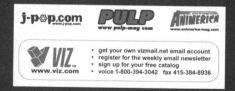

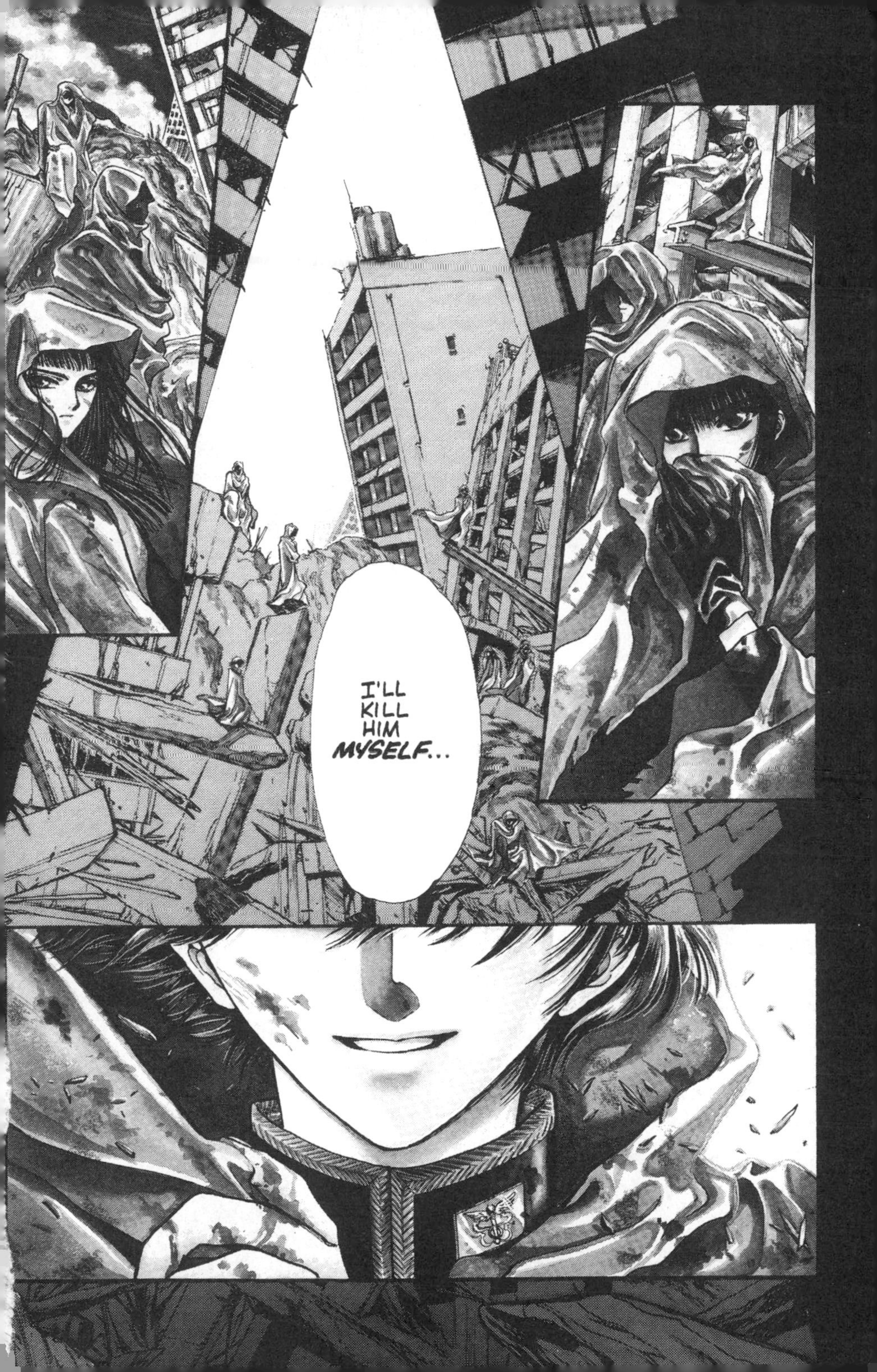
I'LL KILL HIM MYSELF...

THEIR DESTINY WAS

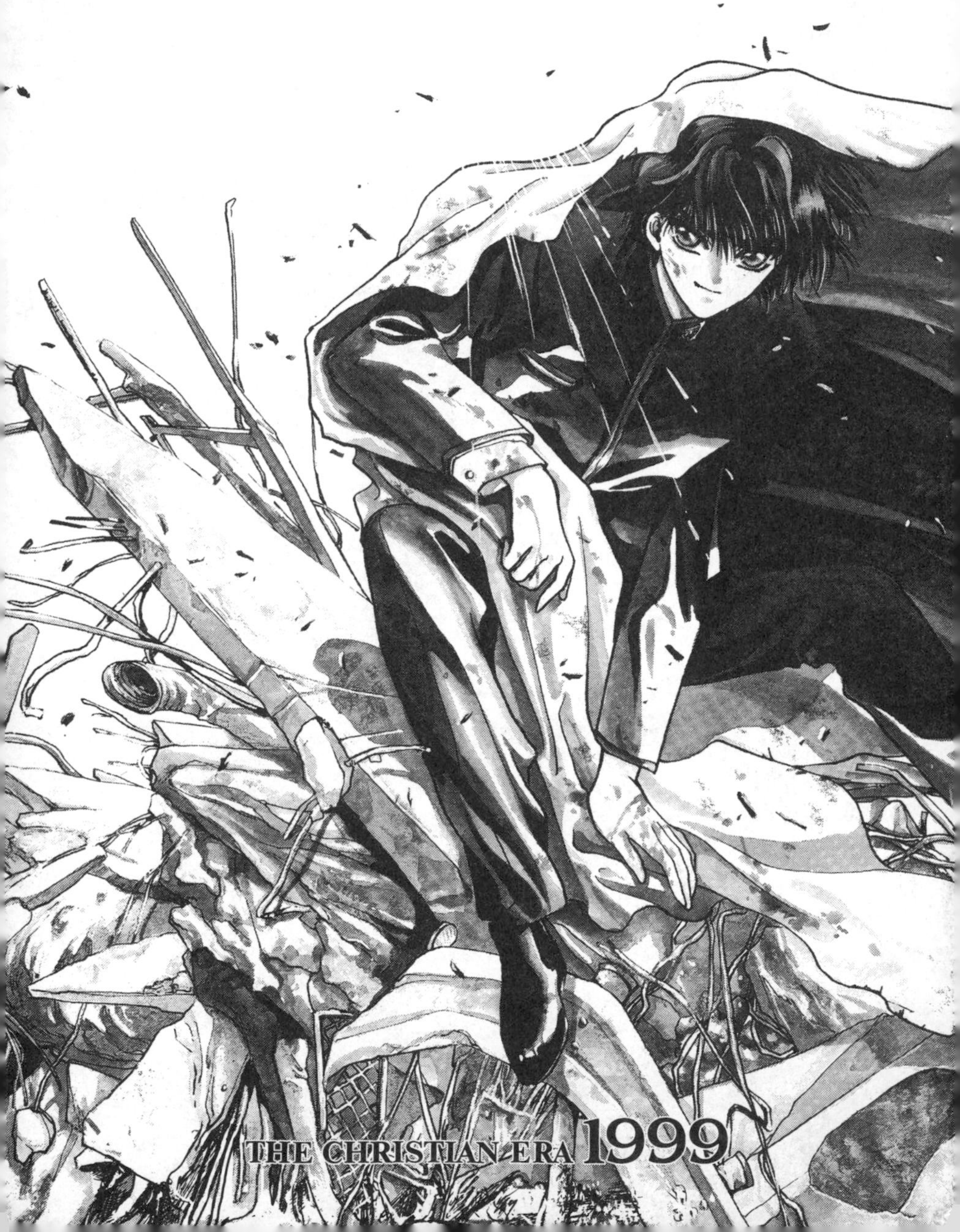
THE CHRISTIAN ERA 1999

FOREORDAINED.

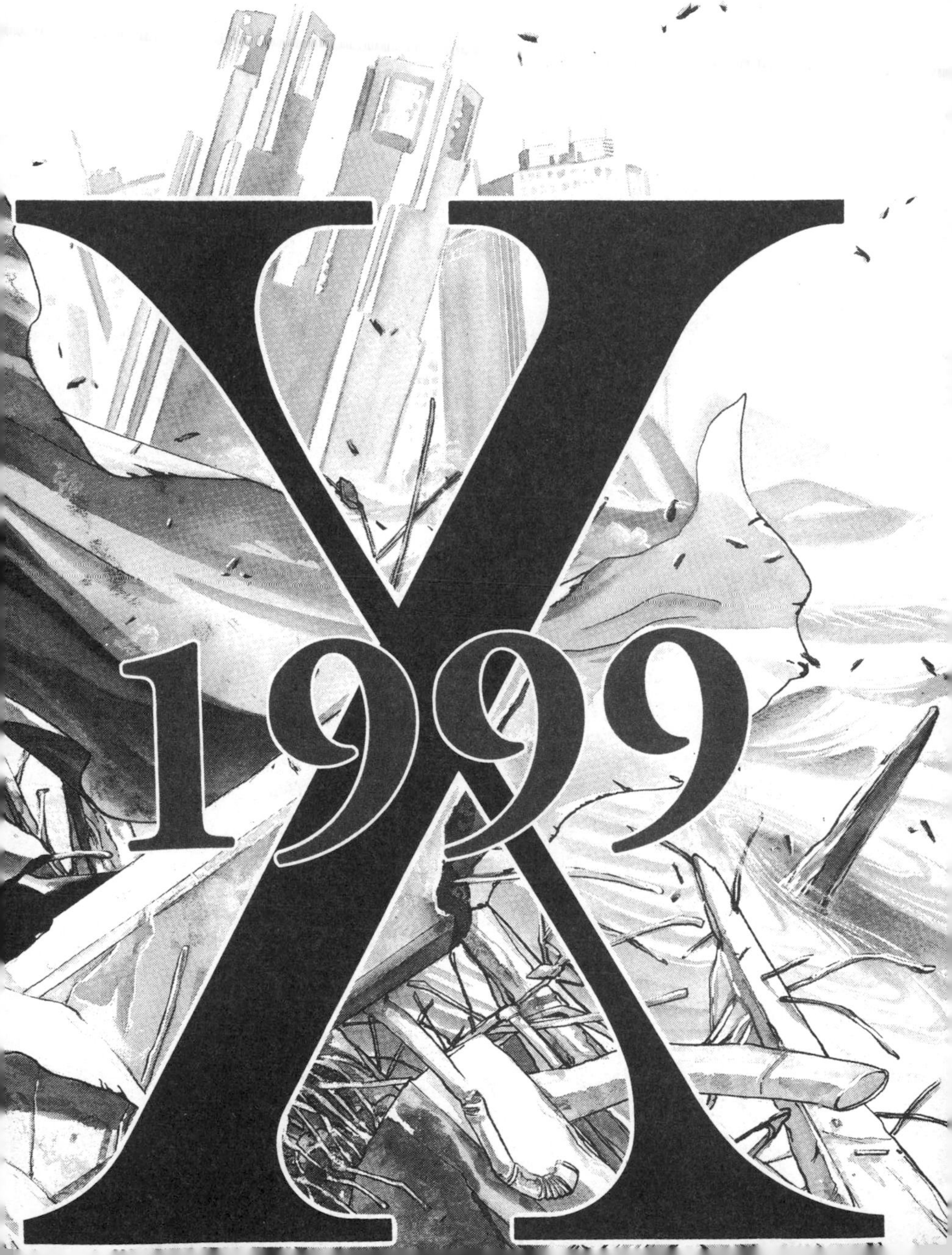
X
1999

"X/1999 demands your attention... This title is a self-contained, intellectual series that, while begrudgingly gives the reader plenty of gratuitous action and violence, manages to stand apart from that and entice readers with the beauty of its art and the seriousness of the story."

--EX: The Online World of Anime & Manga

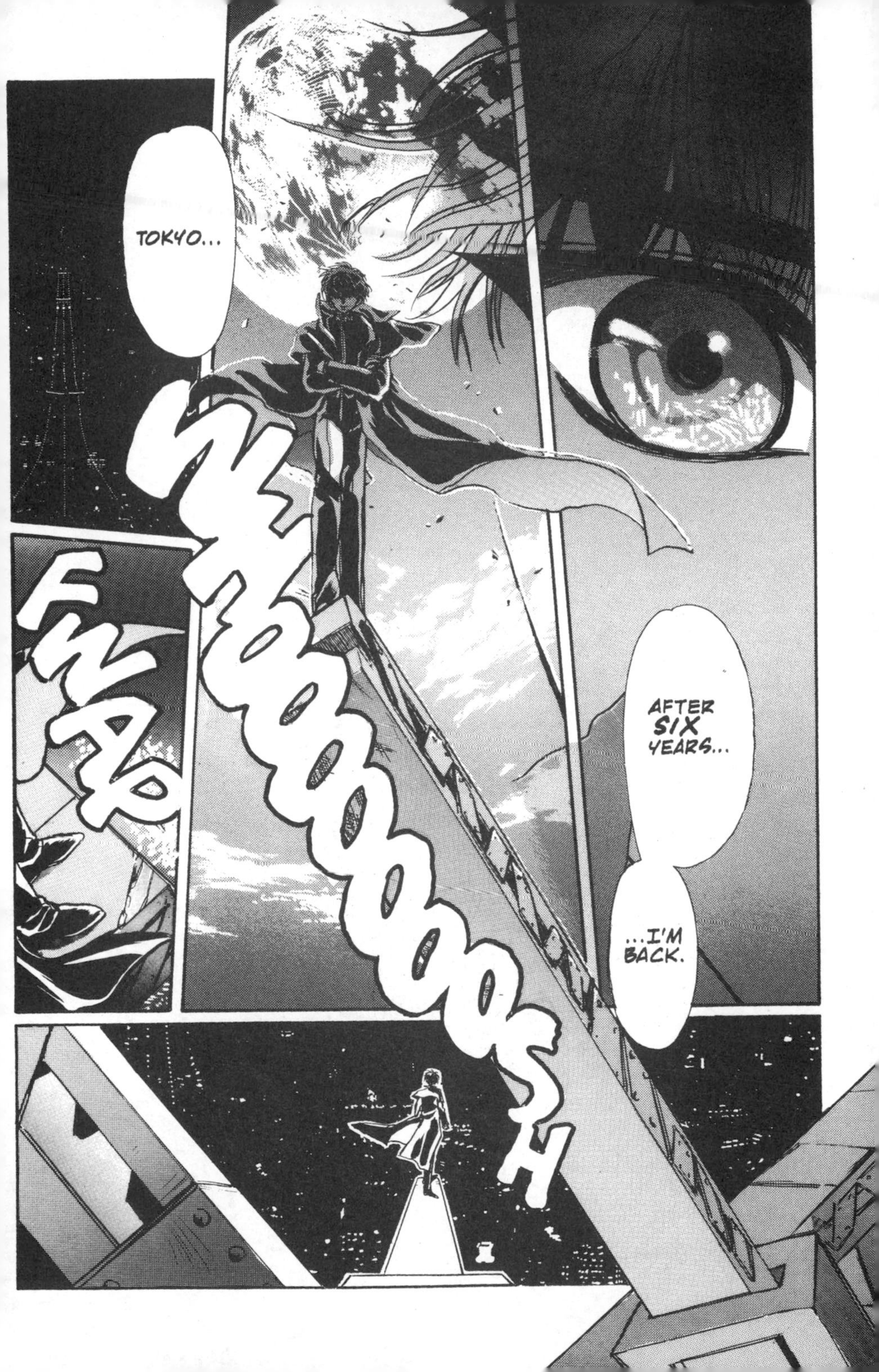
TOKYO...
FWAP
SHOOOOOOOSH
AFTER SIX YEARS...
...I'M BACK.

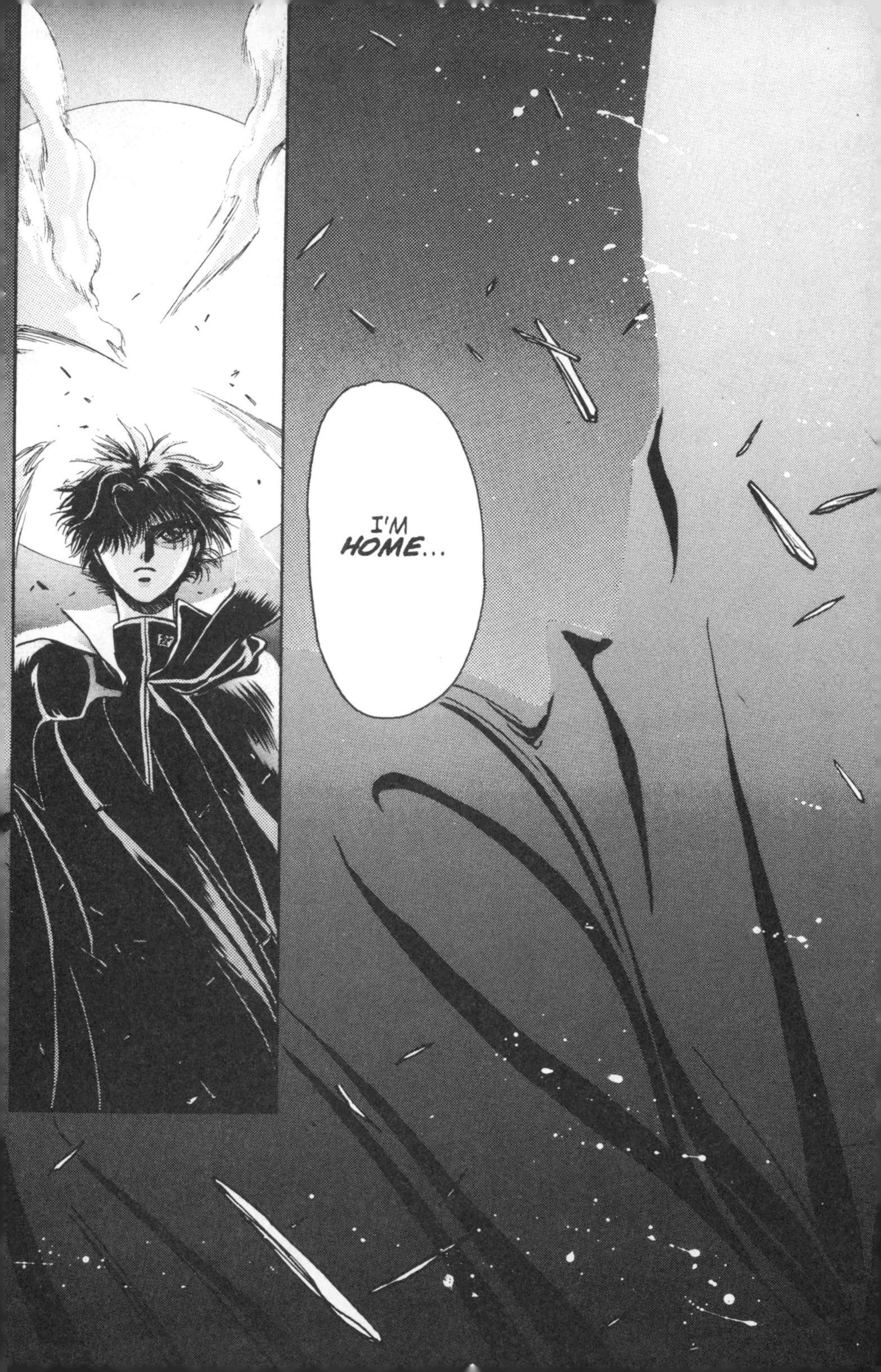
I'M HOME...

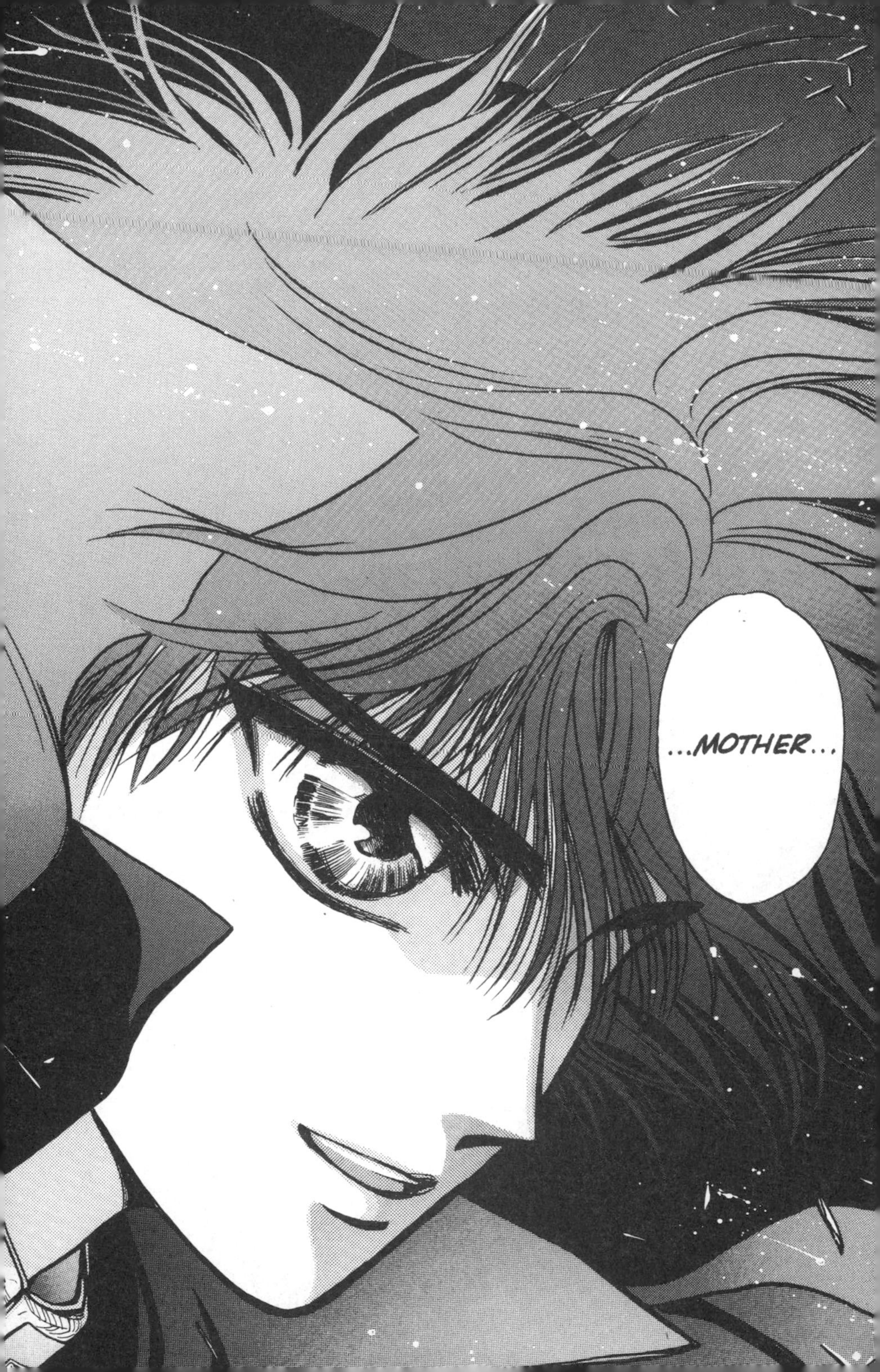
...MOTHER...

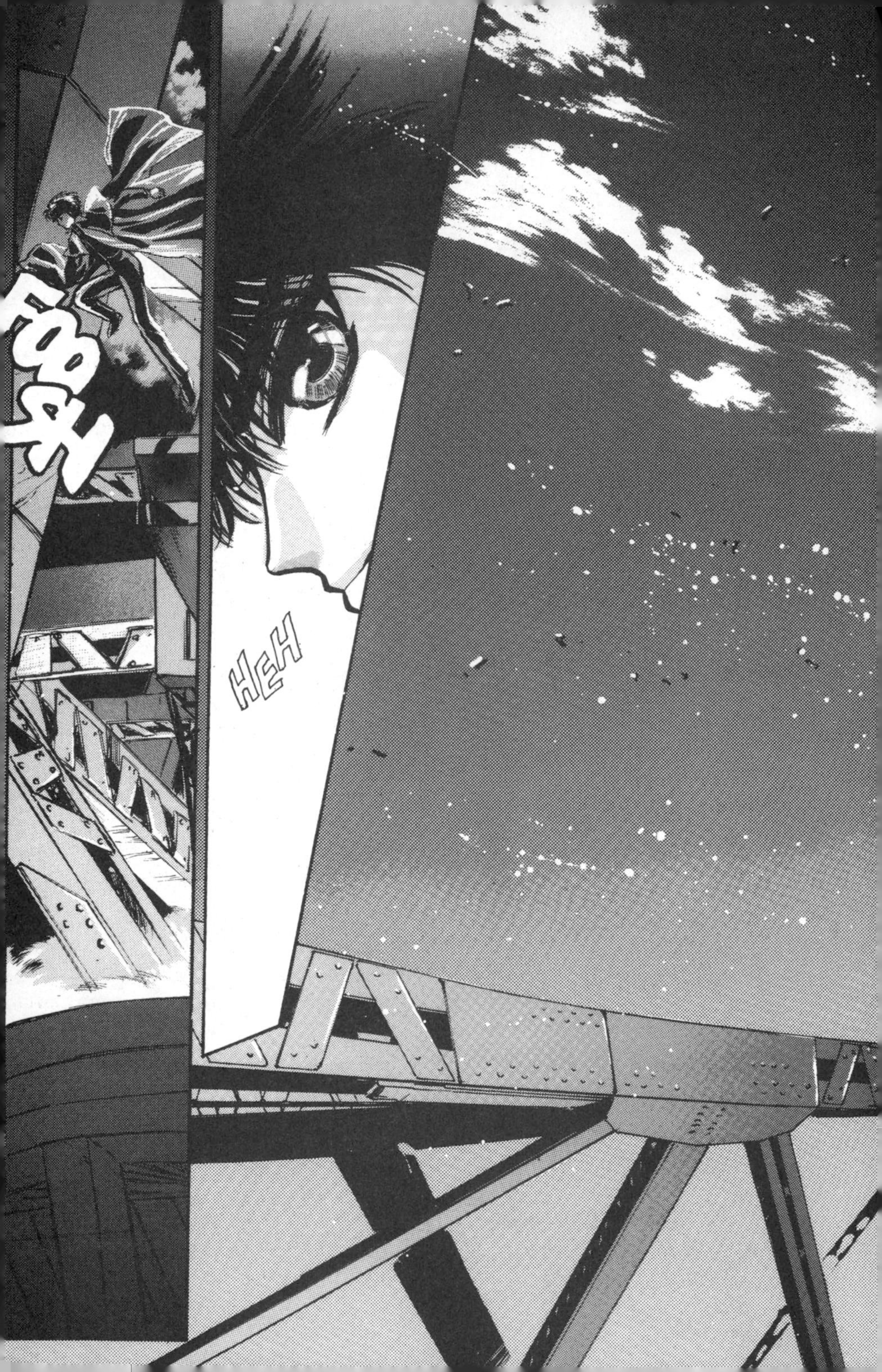
FOOSH
HEH

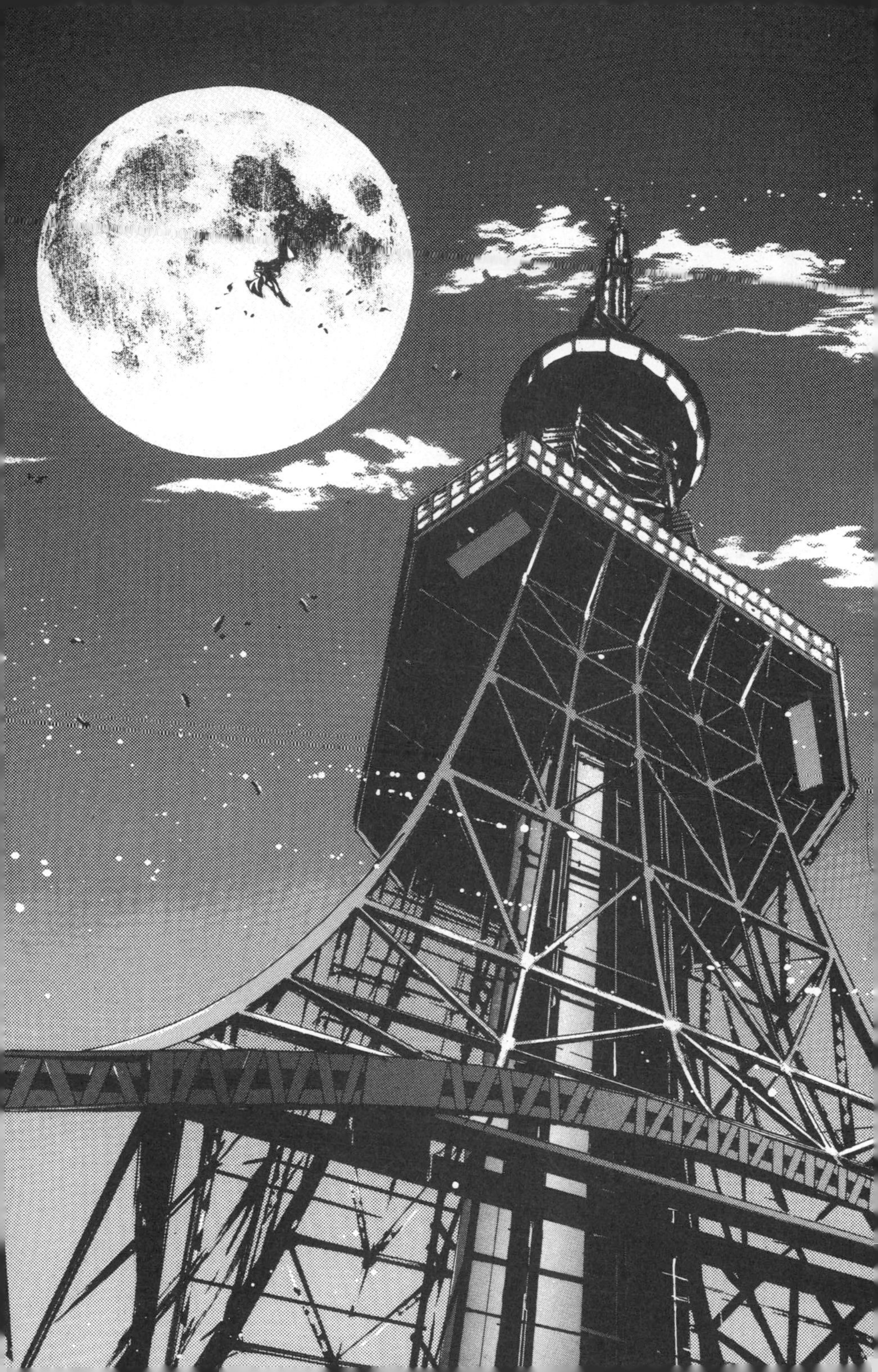

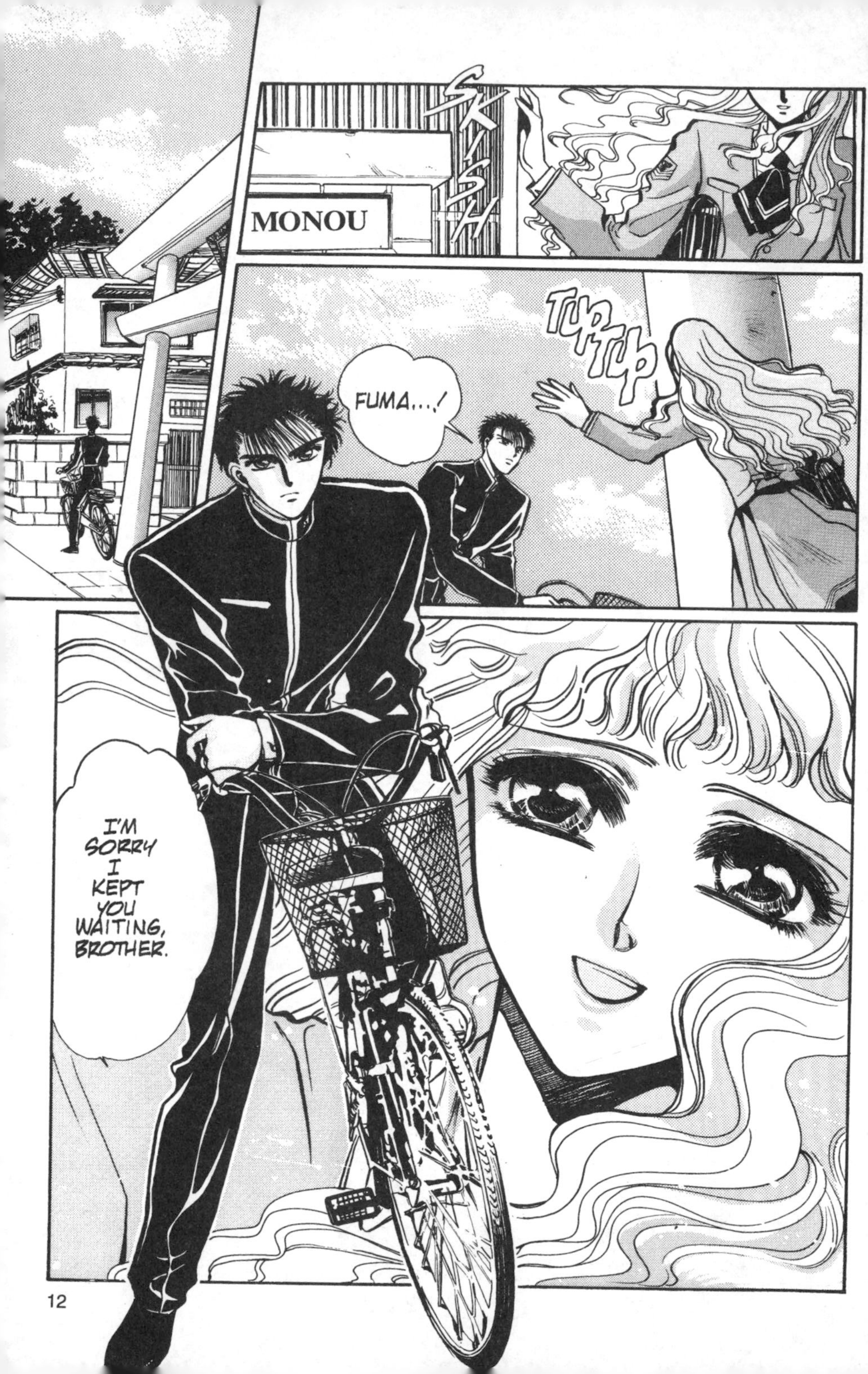

MONOU
SKISH
TUP TUP
FUMA...!
I'M SORRY I KEPT YOU WAITING, BROTHER.

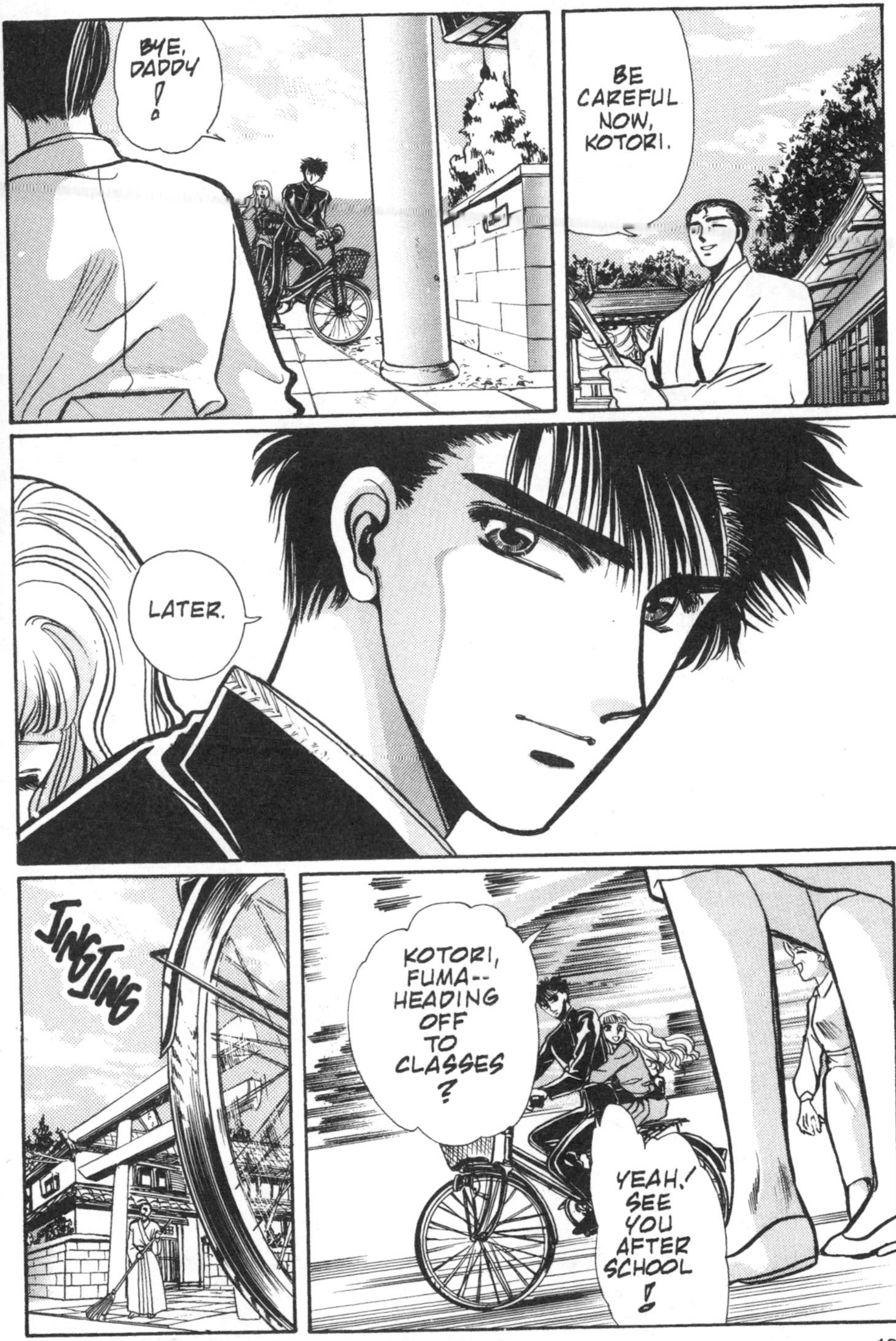
BYE, DADDY!
BE CAREFUL NOW, KOTORI.
LATER.
JINGJING
KOTORI, FUMA-- HEADING OFF TO CLASSES?
YEAH! SEE YOU AFTER SCHOOL!

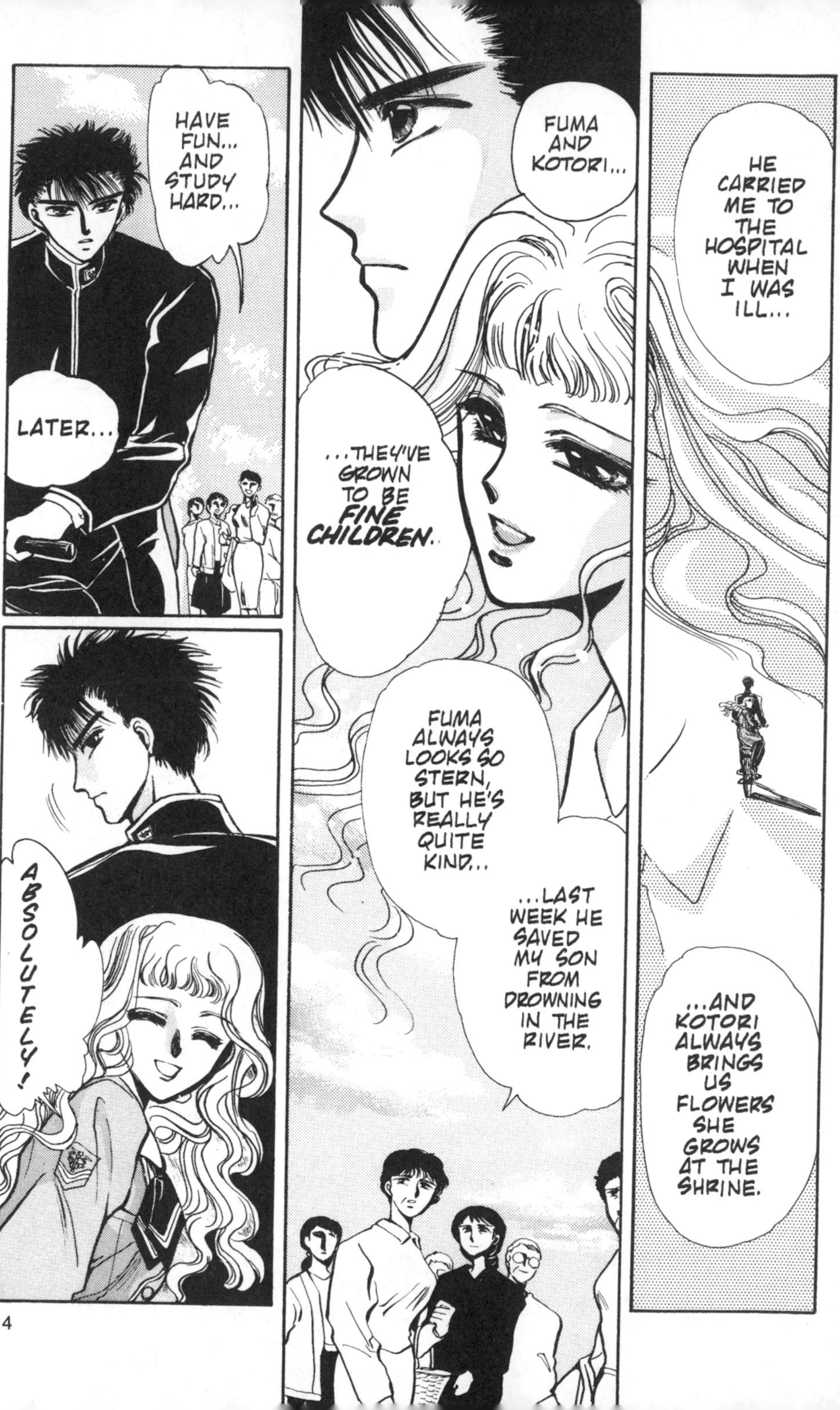
HAVE FUN... AND STUDY HARD...
LATER...
ABSOLUTELY!
FUMA AND KOTORI...
...THEY'VE GROWN TO BE FINE CHILDREN..
FUMA ALWAYS LOOKS SO STERN, BUT HE'S REALLY QUITE KIND...
...LAST WEEK HE SAVED MY SON FROM DROWNING IN THE RIVER.
HE CARRIED ME TO THE HOSPITAL WHEN I WAS ILL...
...AND KOTORI ALWAYS BRINGS US FLOWERS SHE GROWS AT THE SHRINE.

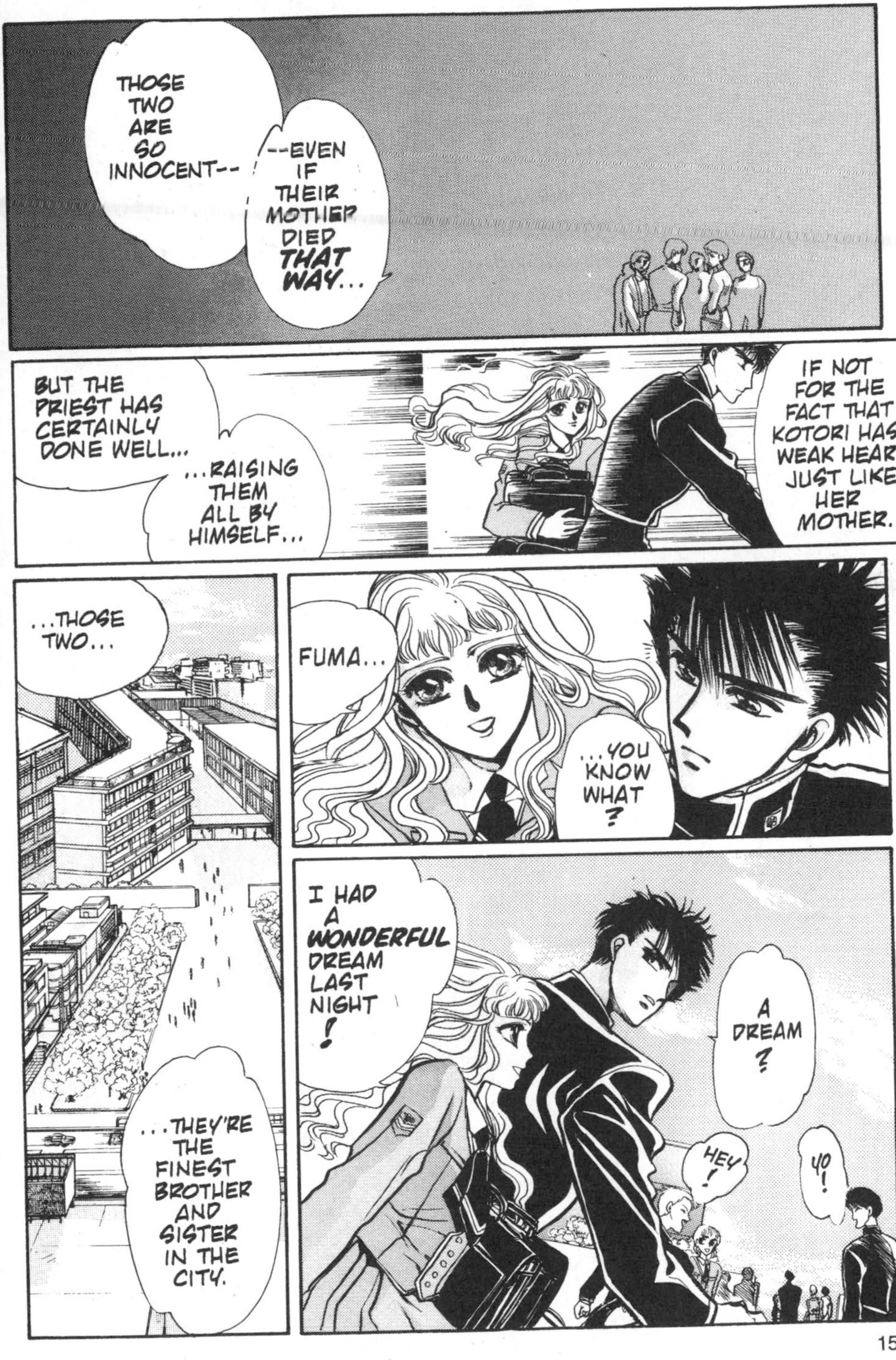
THOSE TWO ARE SO INNOCENT--
--EVEN IF THEIR MOTHER DIED THAT WAY...
BUT THE PRIEST HAS CERTAINLY DONE WELL...
...RAISING THEM ALL BY HIMSELF...
IF NOT FOR THE FACT THAT KOTORI HAS A WEAK HEART, JUST LIKE HER MOTHER...
...THOSE TWO...
...THEY'RE THE FINEST BROTHER AND SISTER IN THE CITY.
FUMA...
...YOU KNOW WHAT?
I HAD A WONDERFUL DREAM LAST NIGHT!
A DREAM?
HEY!
YO!

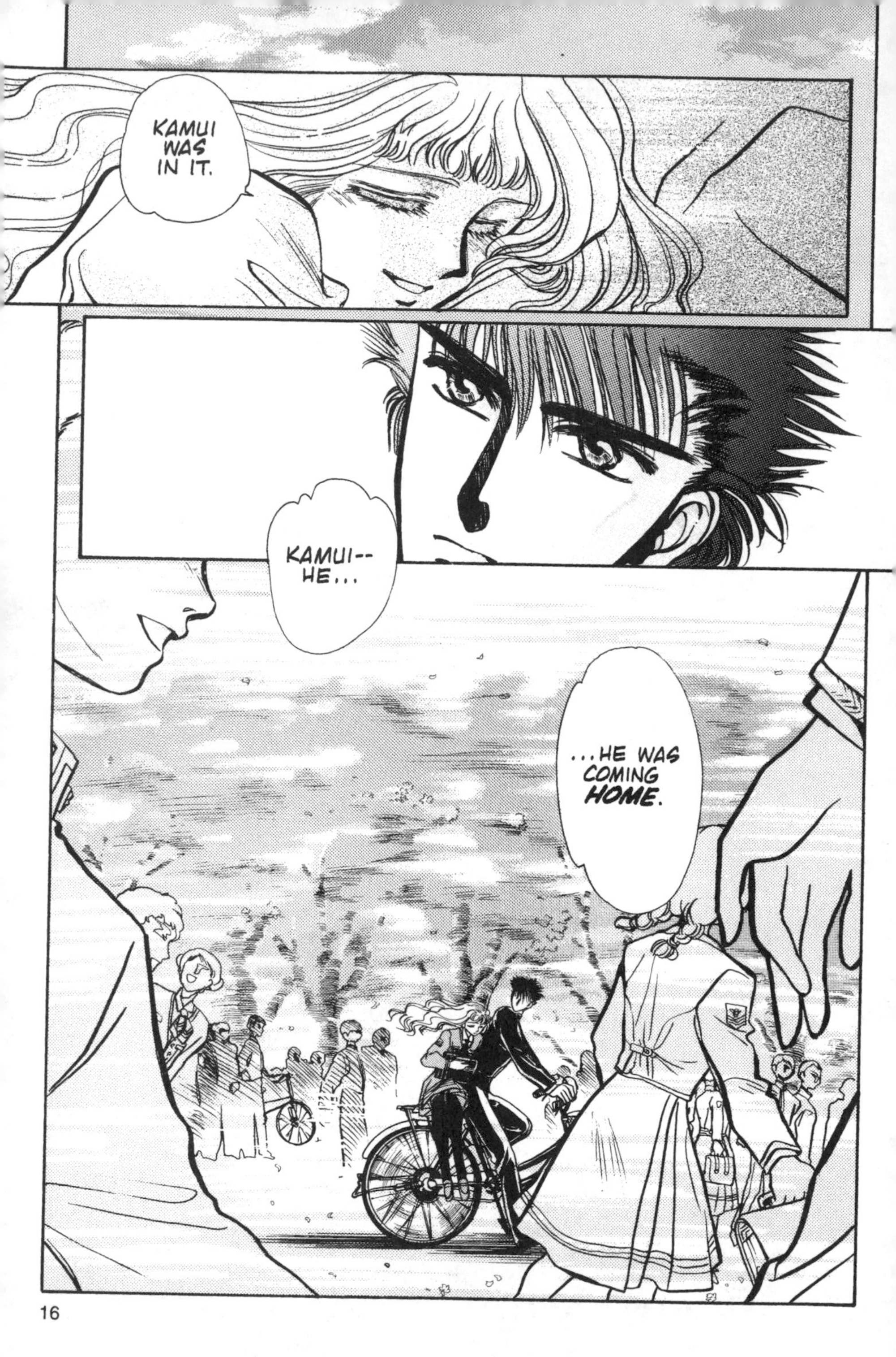
KAMUI WAS IN IT.
KAMUI--HE...
...HE WAS COMING HOME.

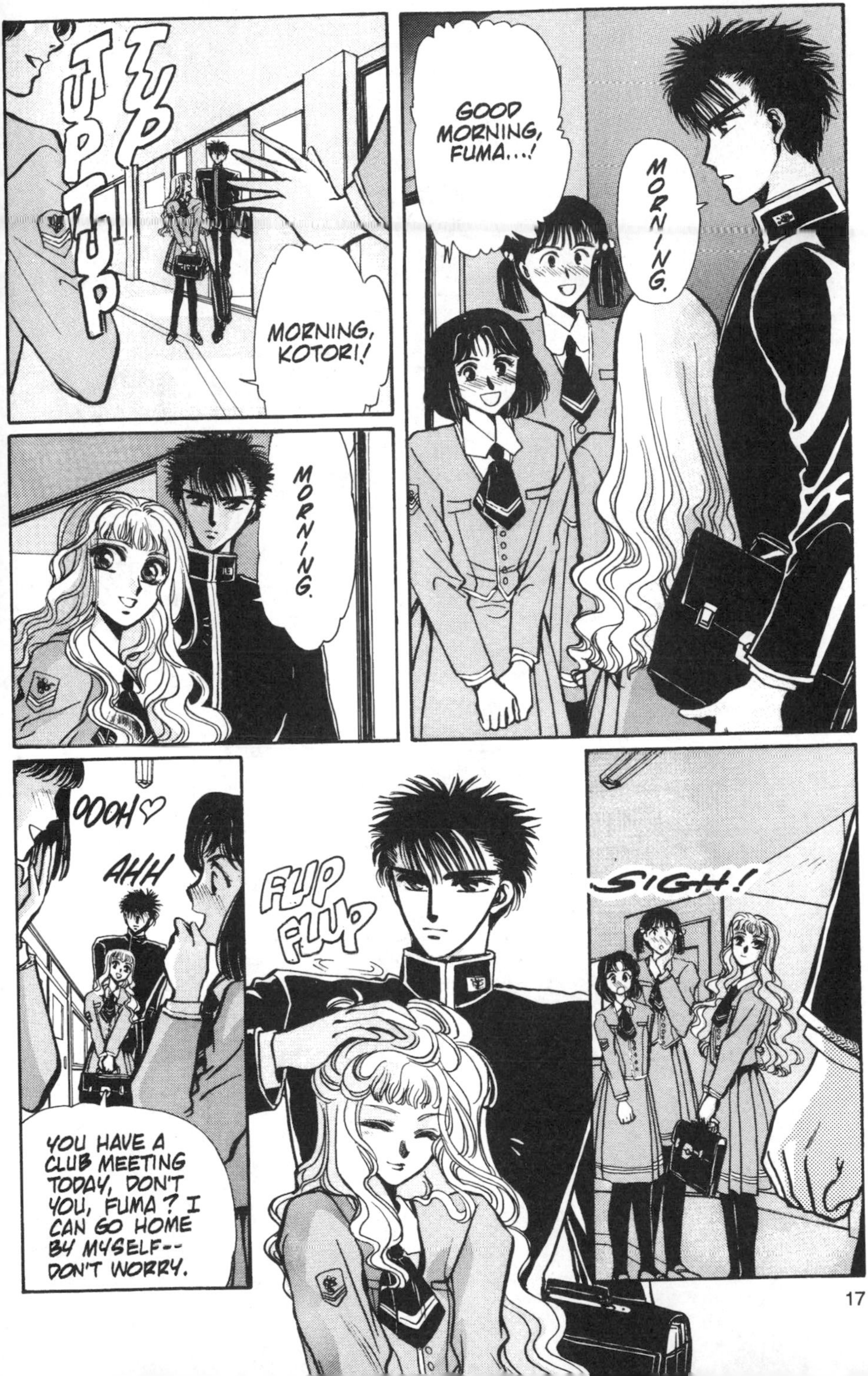
TUP TUP
TUP
MORNING, KOTORI!
MORNING.
GOOD MORNING, FUMA...!
MORNING.
OOOH♡
AHH
YOU HAVE A CLUB MEETING TODAY, DON'T YOU, FUMA? I CAN GO HOME BY MYSELF-- DON'T WORRY.
FLUP FLUP
SIGH!

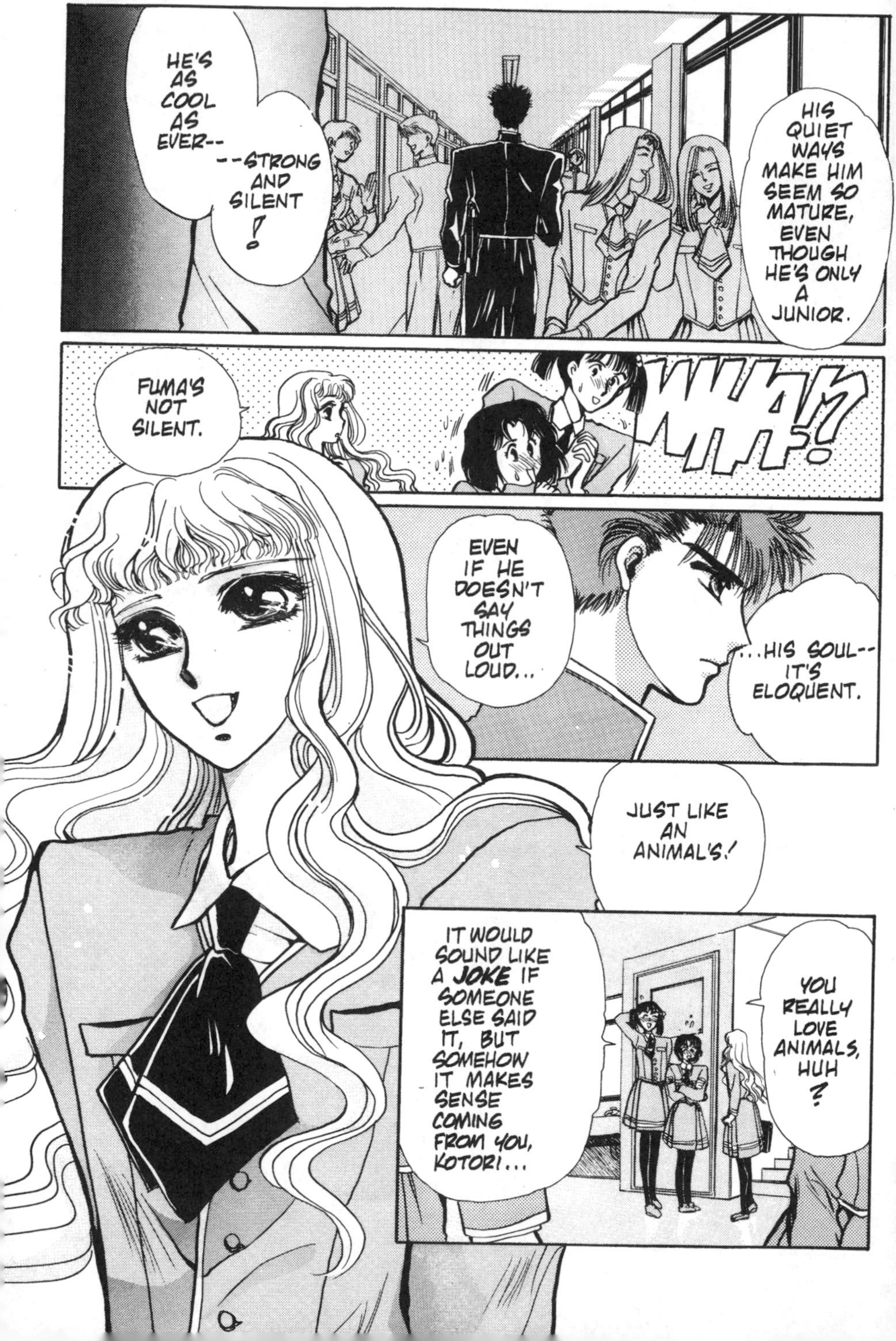
HE'S AS COOL AS EVER--
--STRONG AND SILENT!
HIS QUIET WAYS MAKE HIM SEEM SO MATURE, EVEN THOUGH HE'S ONLY A JUNIOR.
FUMA'S NOT SILENT.
WHA?!
EVEN IF HE DOESN'T SAY THINGS OUT LOUD...
...HIS SOUL--IT'S ELOQUENT.
JUST LIKE AN ANIMAL'S!
IT WOULD SOUND LIKE A **JOKE** IF SOMEONE ELSE SAID IT, BUT SOMEHOW IT MAKES SENSE COMING FROM YOU, KOTORI...
YOU REALLY LOVE ANIMALS, HUH?

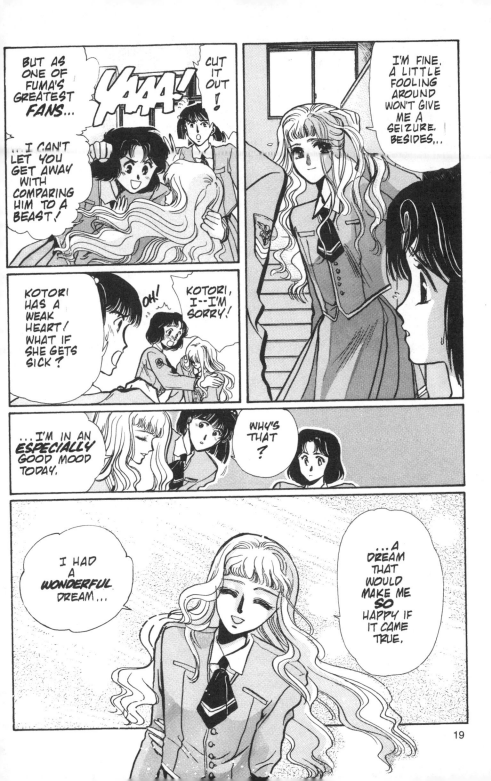

BUT AS ONE OF FUMA'S GREATEST *FANS*...

YAAA!

CUT IT OUT!

...I CAN'T LET YOU GET AWAY WITH COMPARING HIM TO A BEAST!

KOTORI HAS A WEAK HEART! WHAT IF SHE GETS SICK?

OH!

KOTORI, I--I'M SORRY!

I'M FINE, A LITTLE FOOLING AROUND WON'T GIVE ME A SEIZURE. BESIDES,...

...I'M IN AN *ESPECIALLY* GOOD MOOD TODAY.

WHY'S THAT?

I HAD A *WONDERFUL* DREAM...

...A DREAM THAT WOULD MAKE ME *SO* HAPPY IF IT CAME TRUE.

19

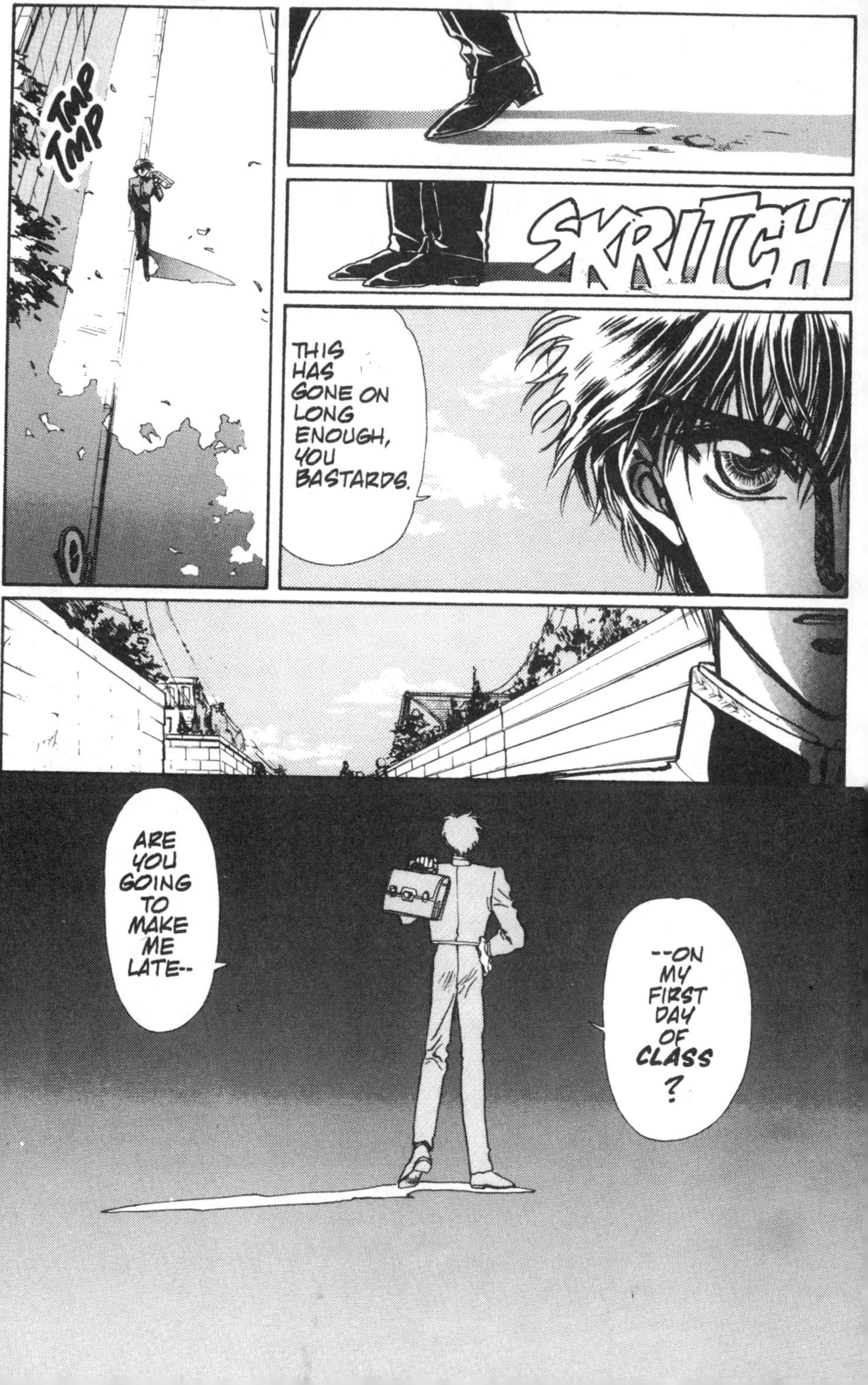
TMP TMP
SKRITCH
THIS HAS GONE ON LONG ENOUGH, YOU BASTARDS.
ARE YOU GOING TO MAKE ME LATE--
--ON MY FIRST DAY OF CLASS ?

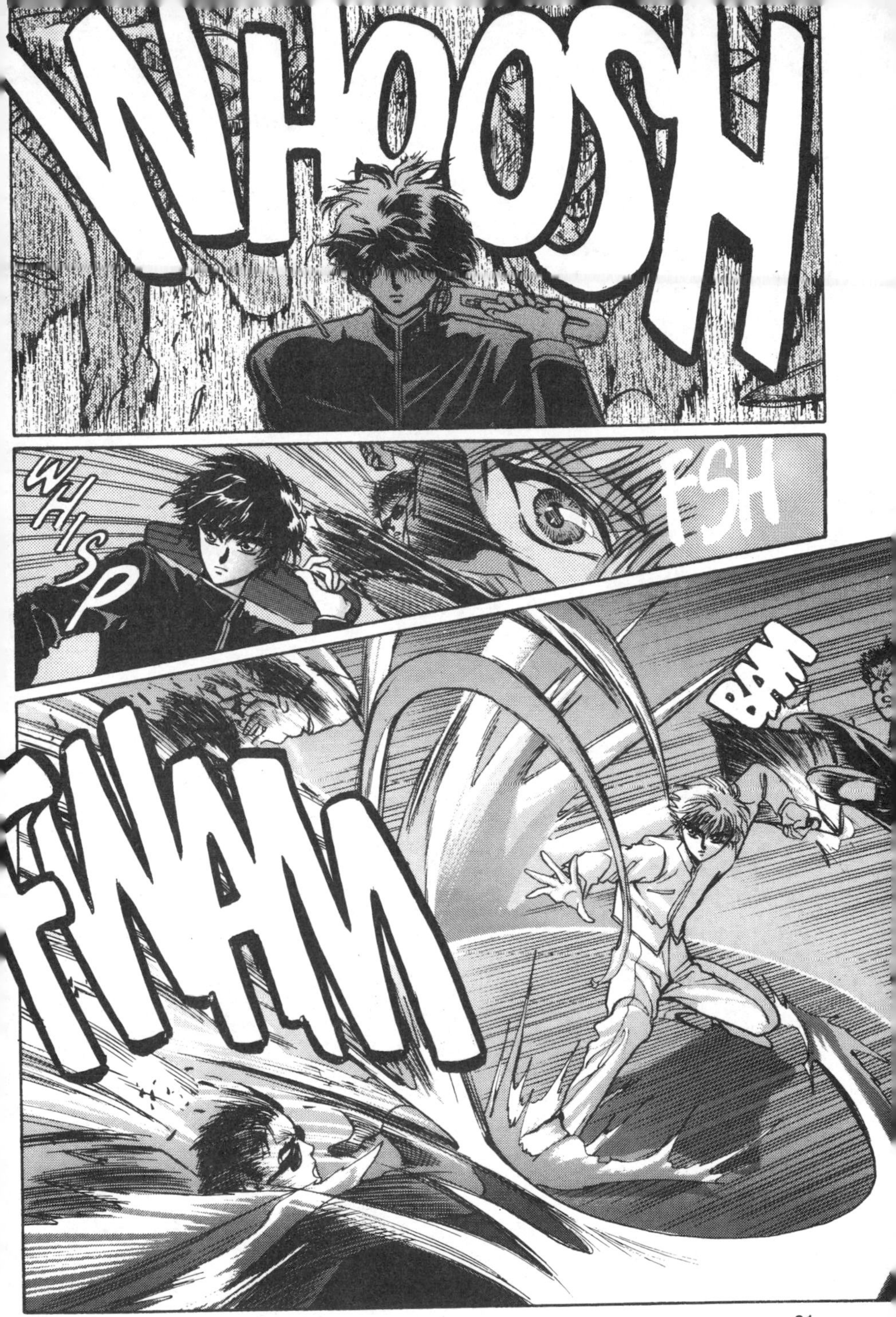
WHOOSH
WHISP
FSH
FWAM
BAM

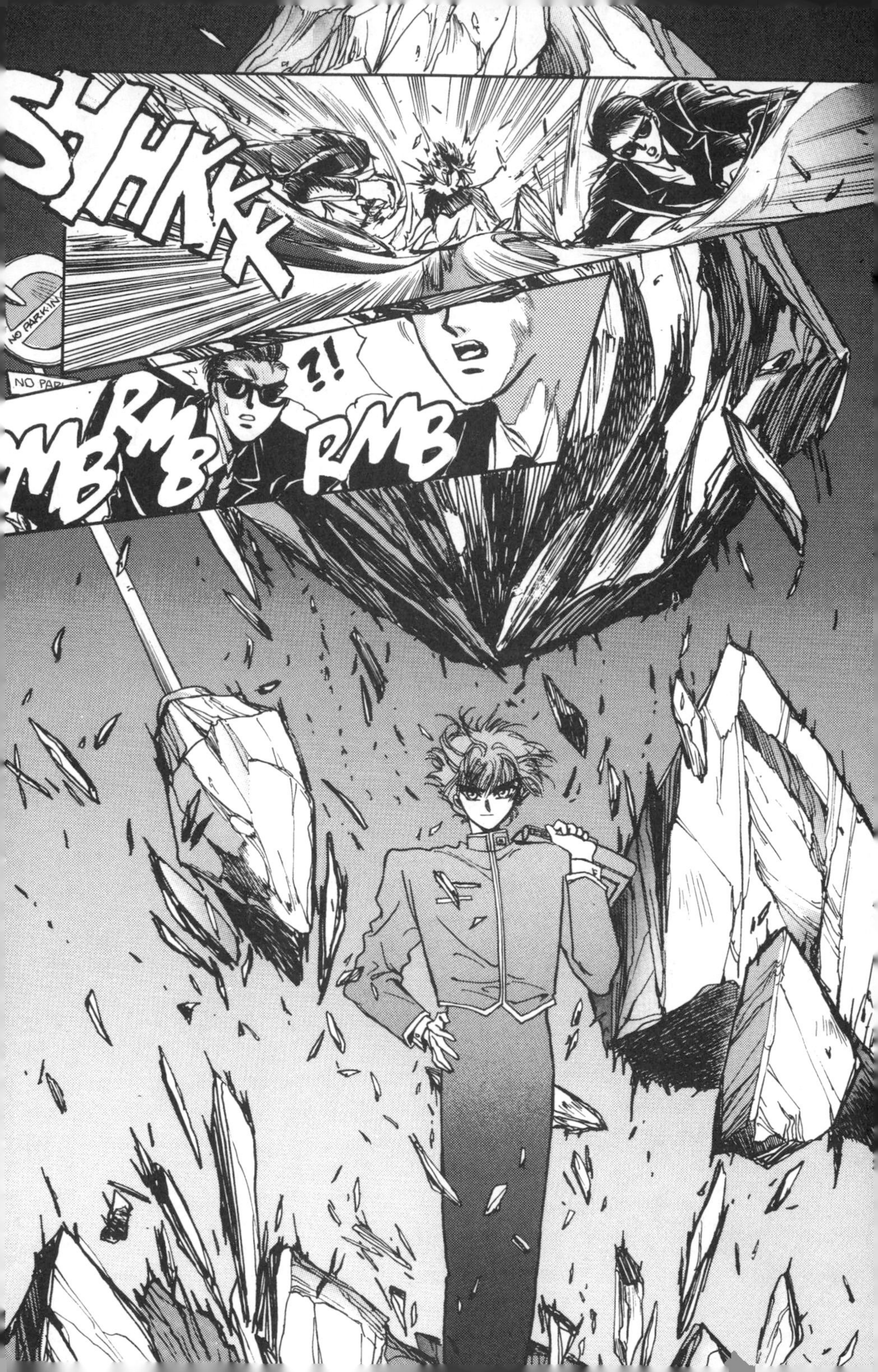
SHKK
NO PARK·IN
NO PAR
MB
RMB
?!
RMB

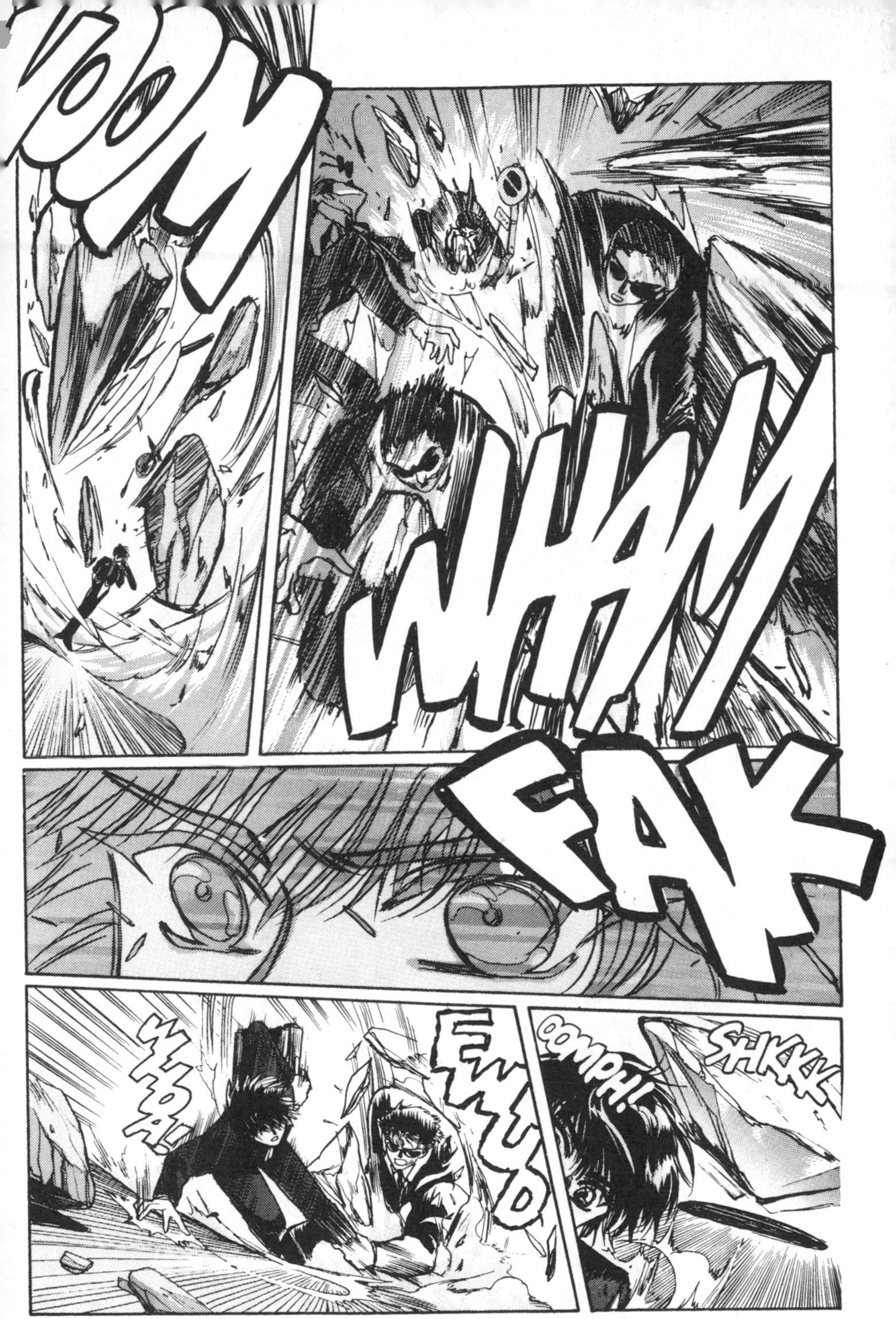
VOOOM
WHAM
FAK
WHOA!
FWUD
OOMPH!
SHKKK

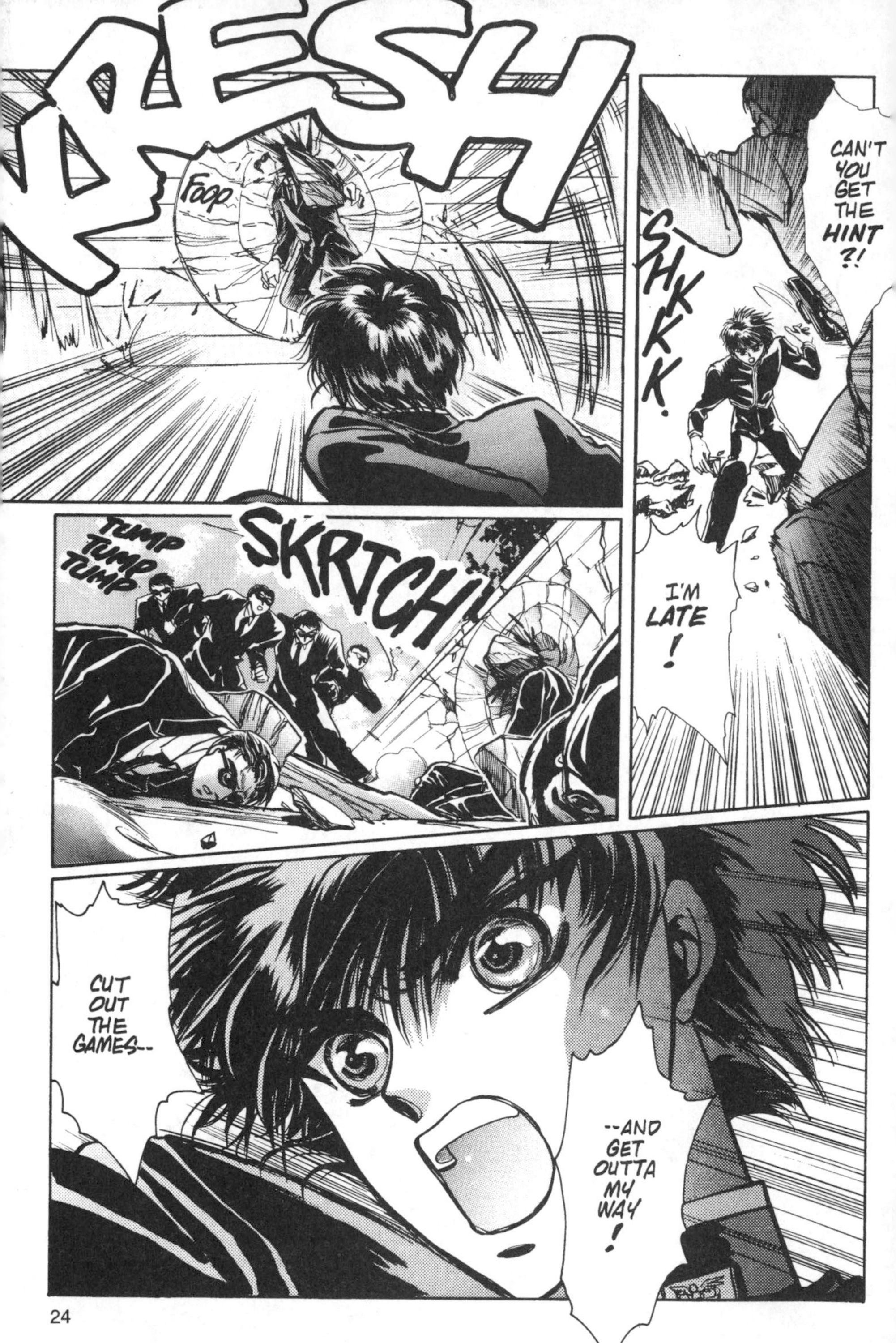
KRESH
Foop
TUMP TUMP TUMP
SKRTCH!
SHKKKK!
CAN'T YOU GET THE HINT?!
I'M LATE!
CUT OUT THE GAMES--
--AND GET OUTTA MY WAY!

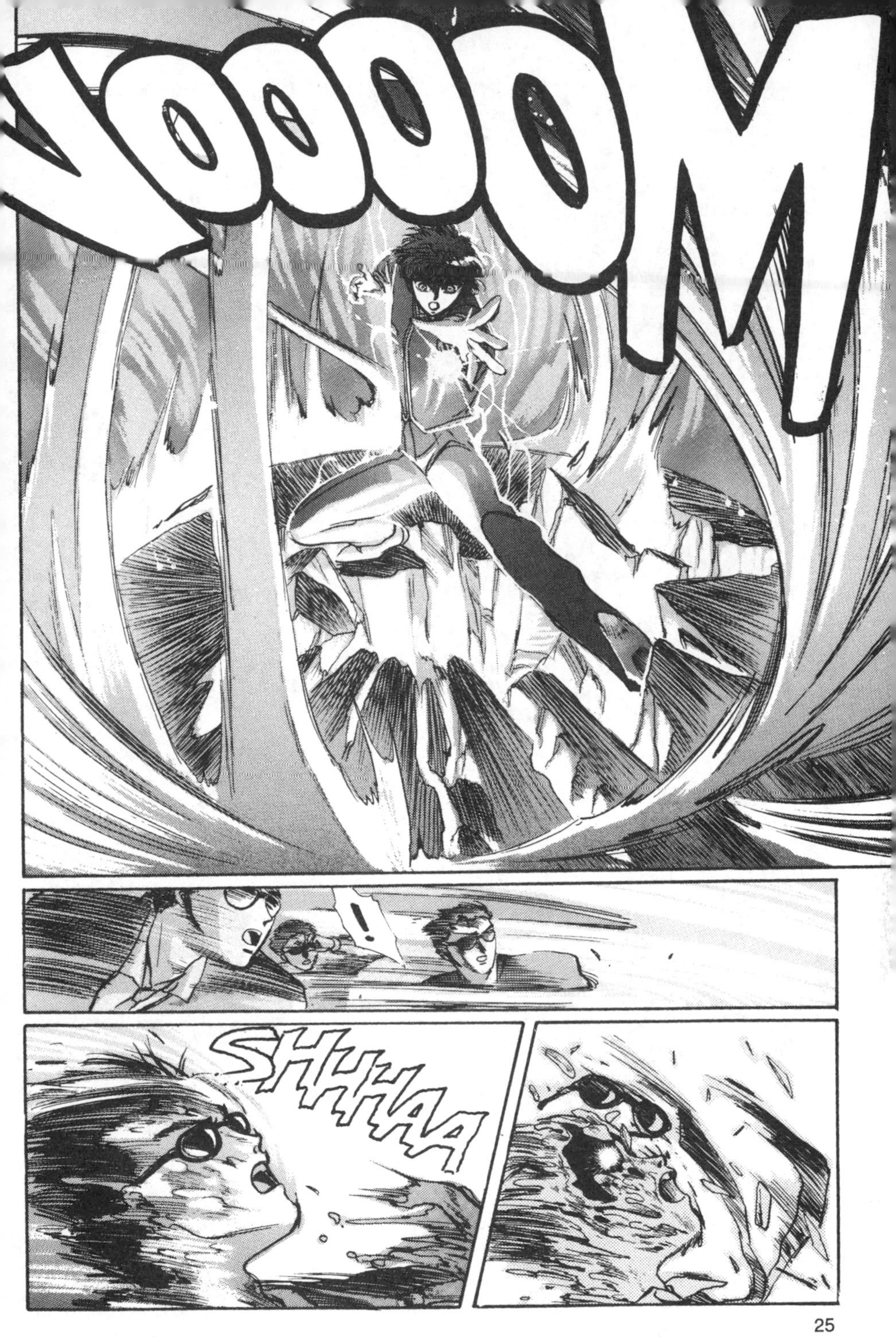
VOOOOM
!
SHUHAA

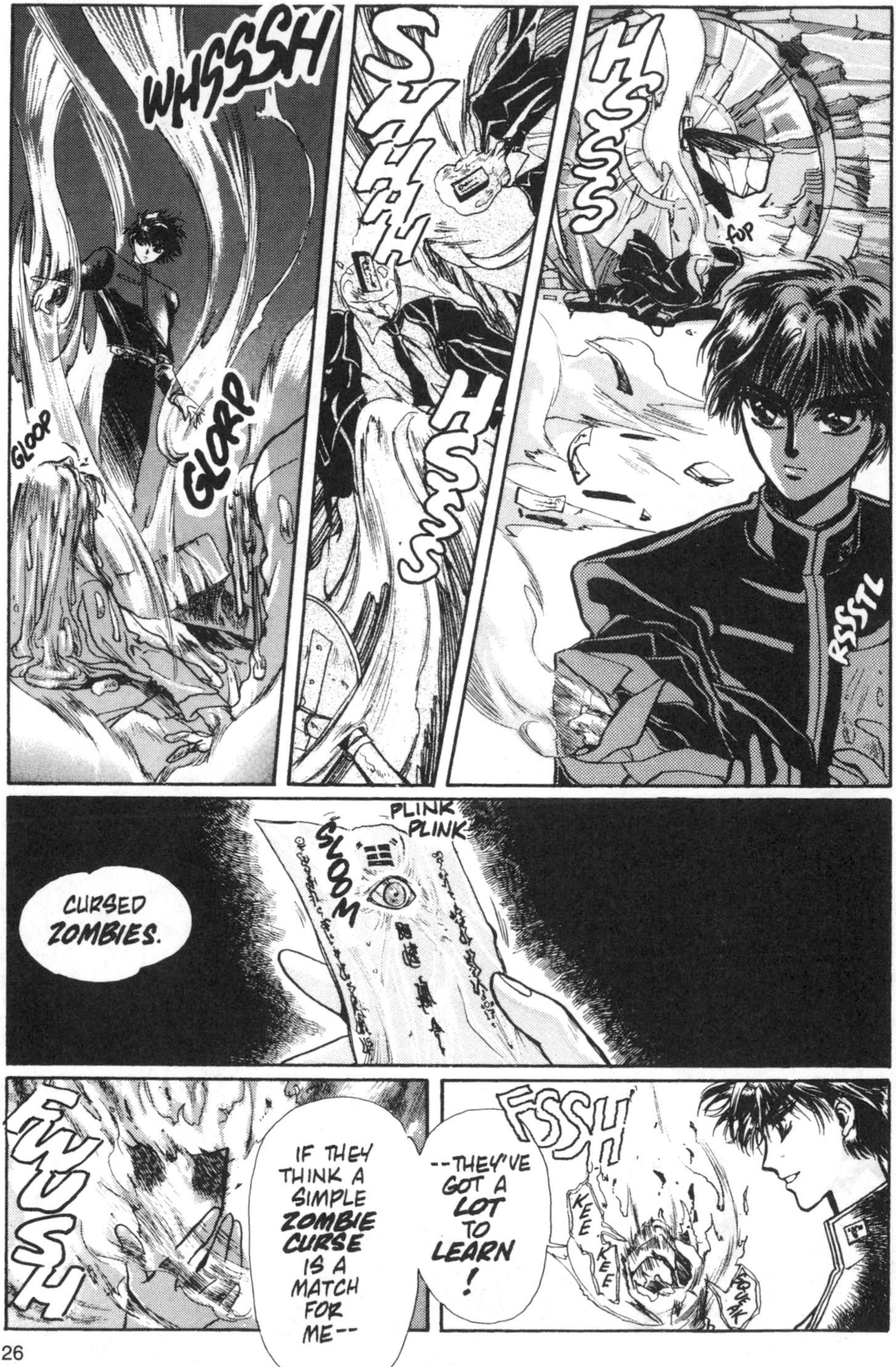
WHSSSH
GLOOP
GLORP
SHHHH
HSSSS
HSSSS
FUP
RSSSTL
PLINK
PLINK
SLOOM
CURSED ZOMBIES.
FWOOSH
IF THEY THINK A SIMPLE ZOMBIE CURSE IS A MATCH FOR ME--
--THEY'VE GOT A LOT TO LEARN!
FSSH
KEE KEE

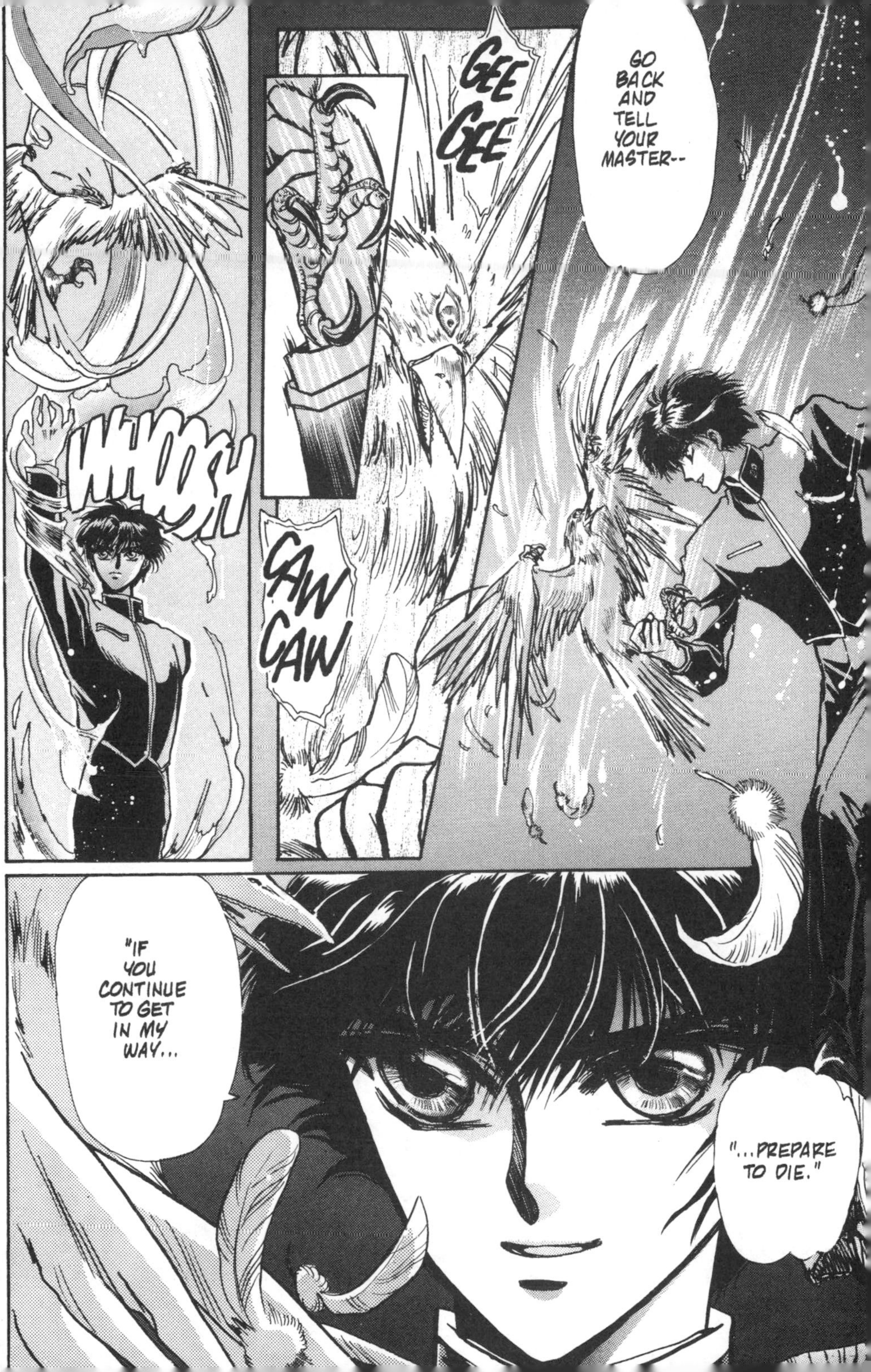
WHOOSH
GEE GEE
CAW CAW
GO BACK AND TELL YOUR MASTER--
"IF YOU CONTINUE TO GET IN MY WAY...
"...PREPARE TO DIE."

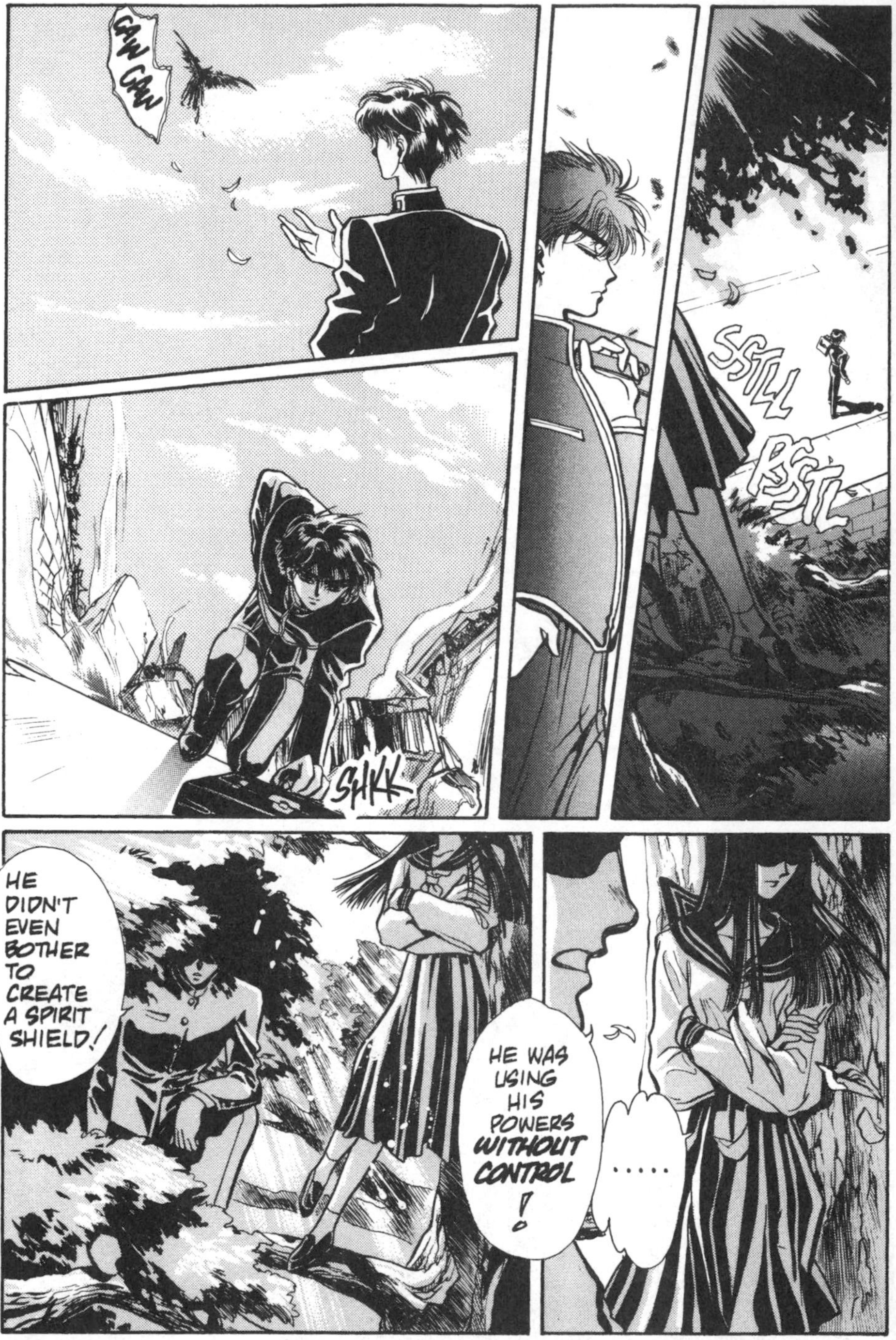
CAW CAW
SHKK
SSTLL
RSSTL
HE DIDN'T EVEN BOTHER TO CREATE A SPIRIT SHIELD!
HE WAS USING HIS POWERS WITHOUT CONTROL!
......

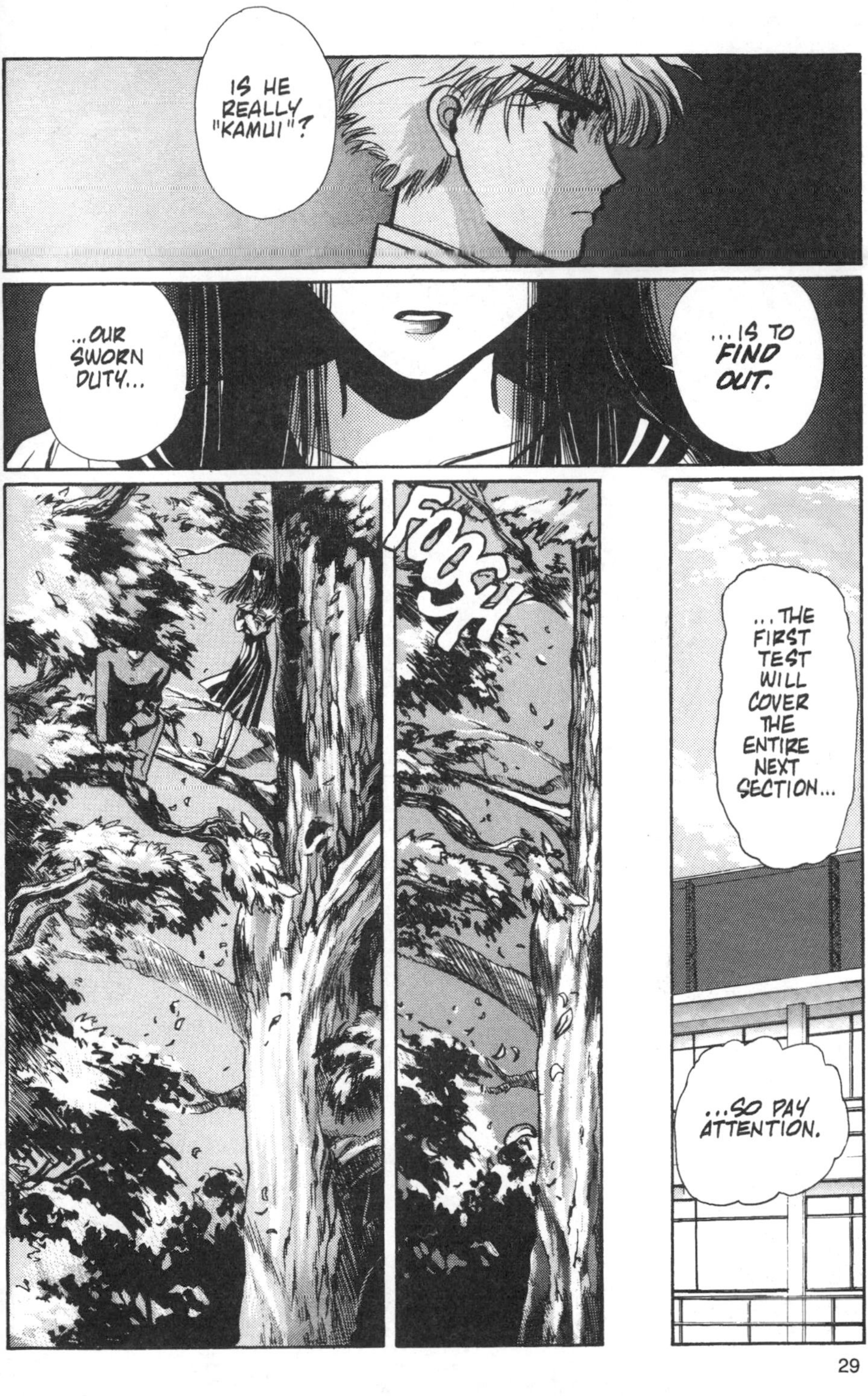
IS HE REALLY "KAMUI"?
...OUR SWORN DUTY...
...IS TO FIND OUT.
FOOSH
...THE FIRST TEST WILL COVER THE ENTIRE NEXT SECTION...
...SO PAY ATTENTION.

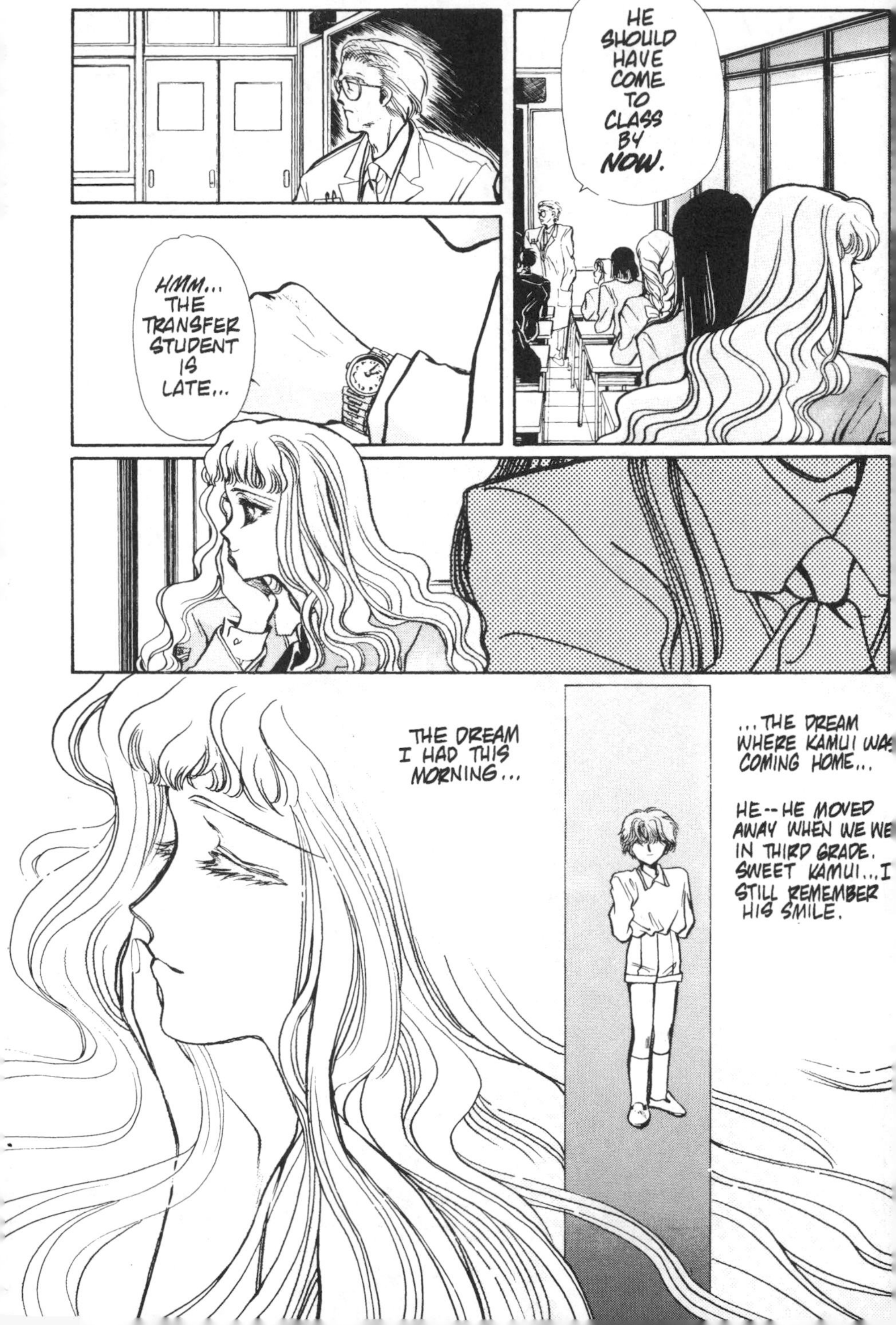
HMM... THE TRANSFER STUDENT IS LATE...
HE SHOULD HAVE COME TO CLASS BY NOW.
THE DREAM I HAD THIS MORNING...
...THE DREAM WHERE KAMUI WAS COMING HOME...
HE--HE MOVED AWAY WHEN WE WE IN THIRD GRADE. SWEET KAMUI...I STILL REMEMBER HIS SMILE.

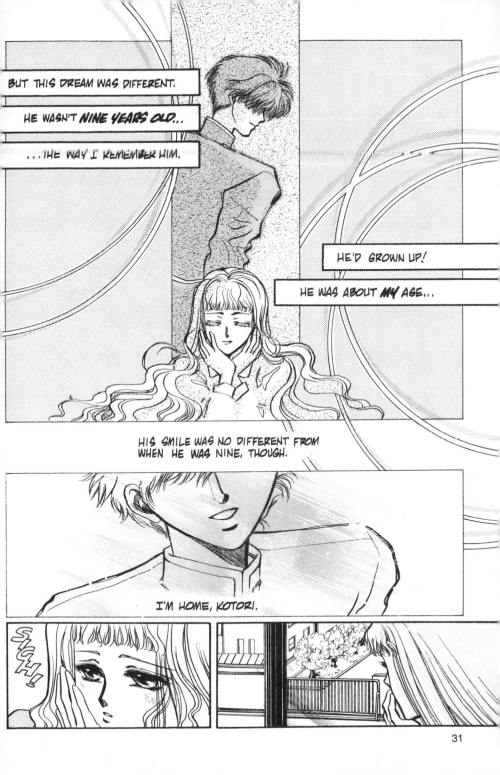

BUT THIS DREAM WAS DIFFERENT.

HE WASN'T *NINE YEARS OLD*...

...THE WAY I REMEMBER HIM.

HE'D GROWN UP!

HE WAS ABOUT *MY* AGE...

HIS SMILE WAS NO DIFFERENT FROM WHEN HE WAS NINE, THOUGH.

I'M HOME, KOTORI.

SIGH!

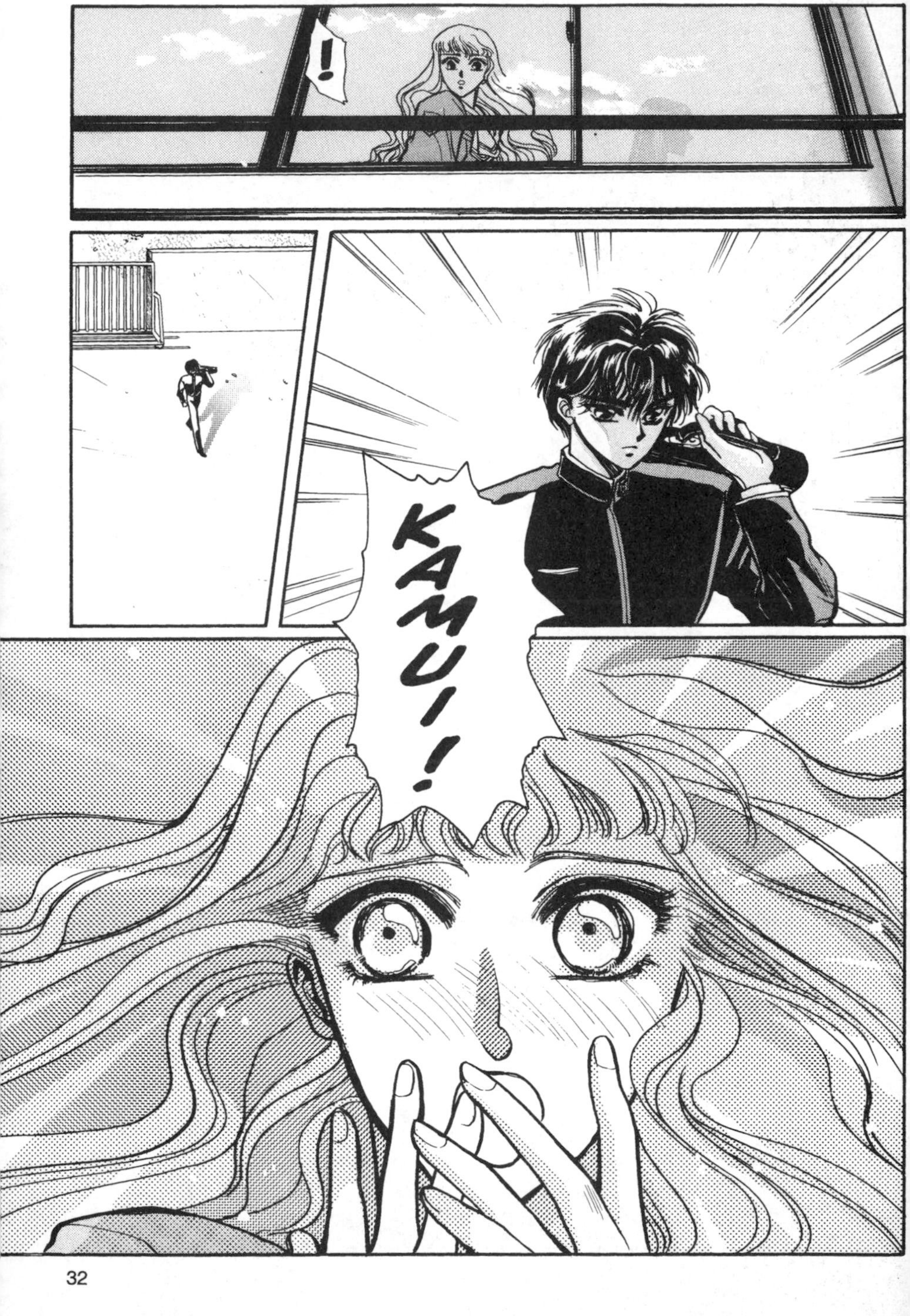
!
KAMUI!

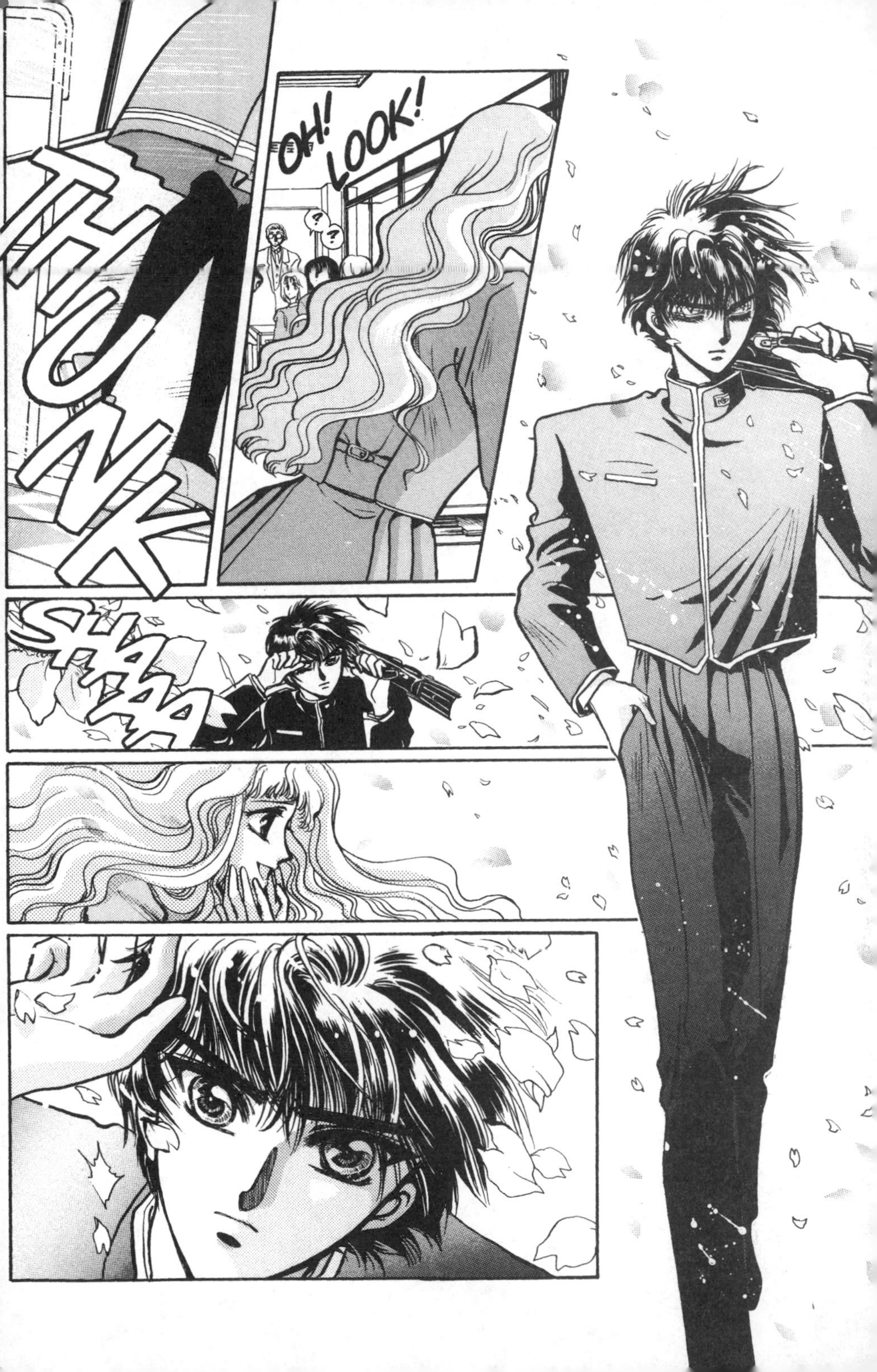
THUNK
OH! LOOK!
?
?
SHAAA

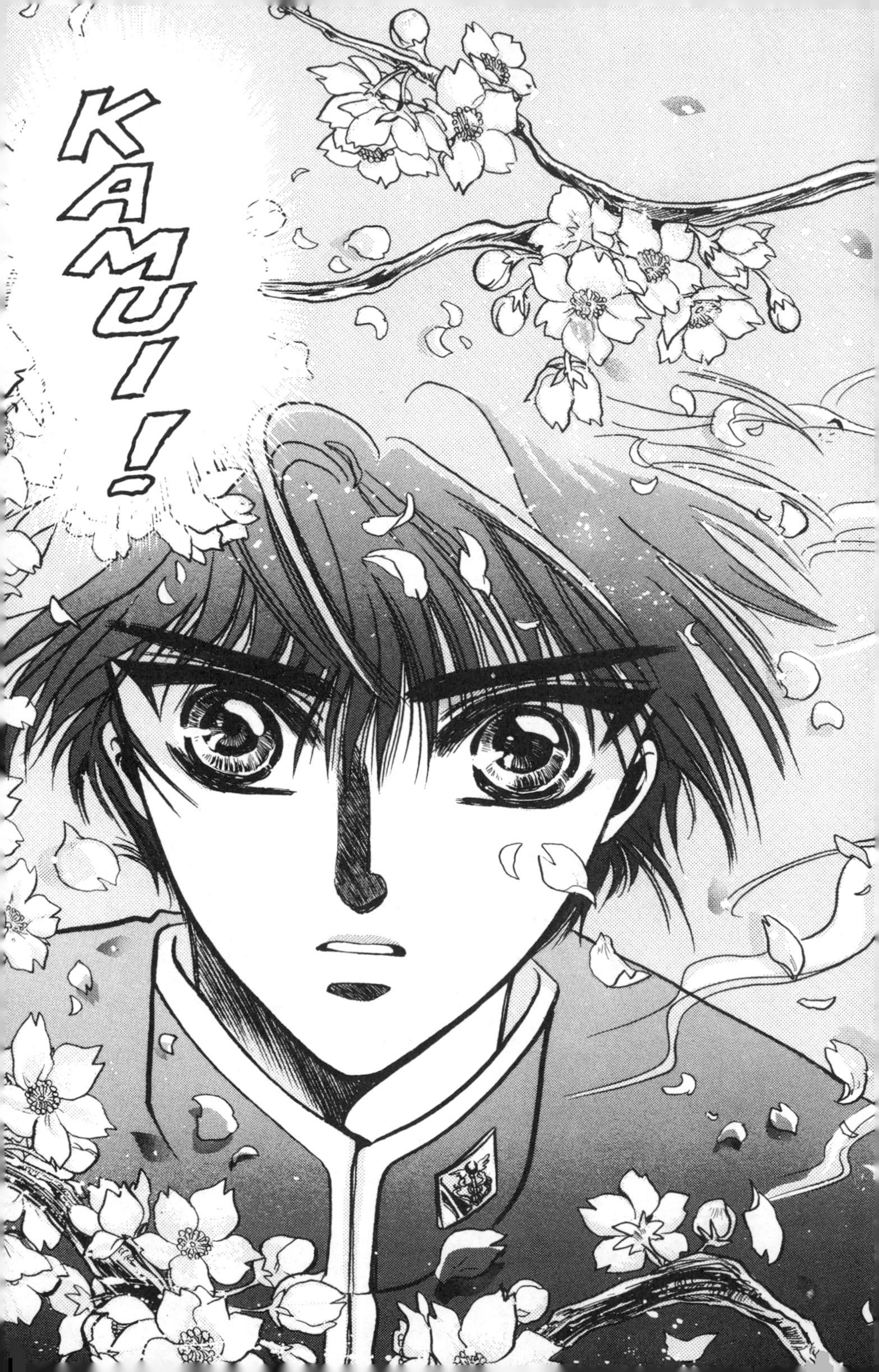
KAMUI!

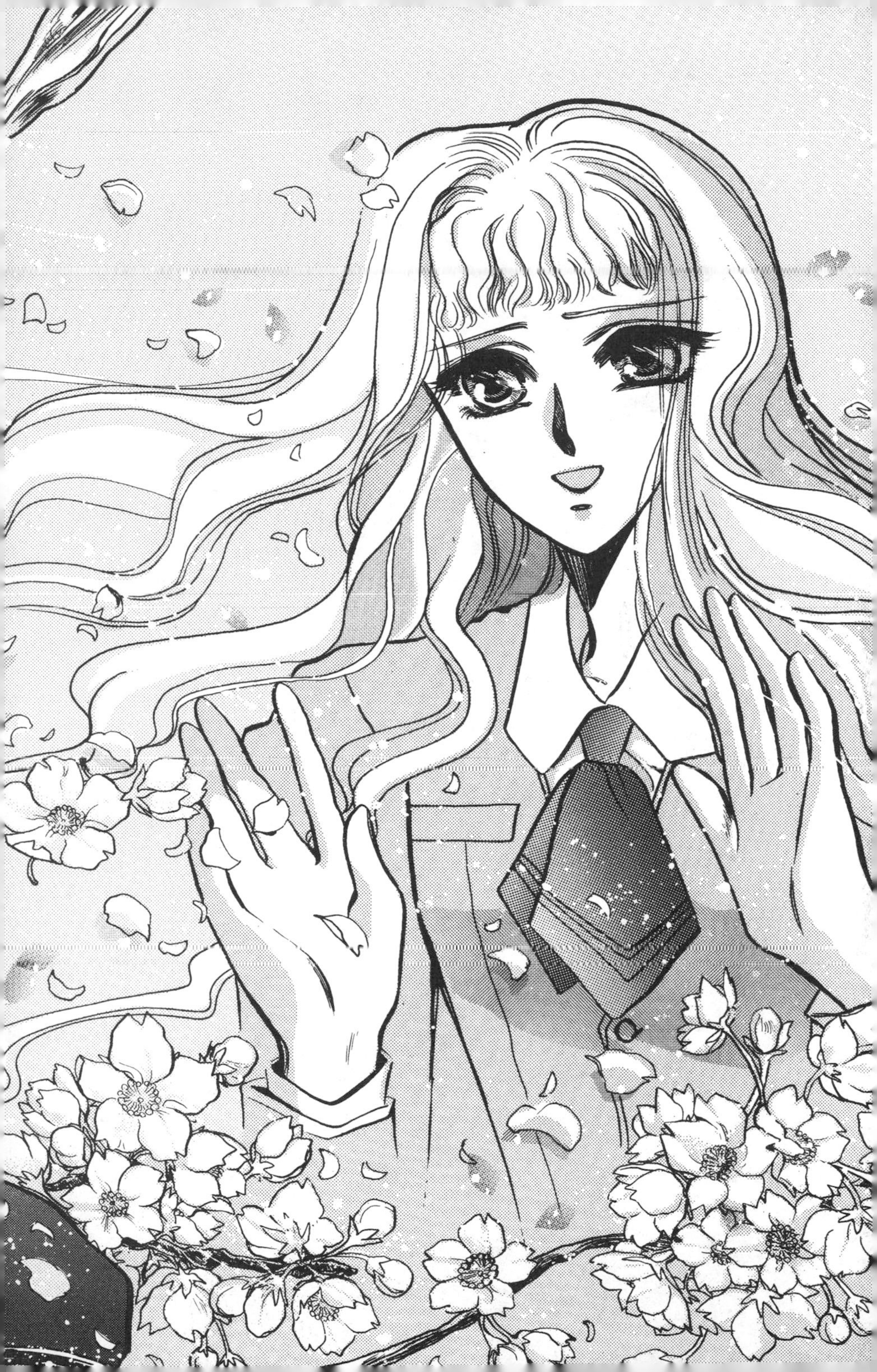

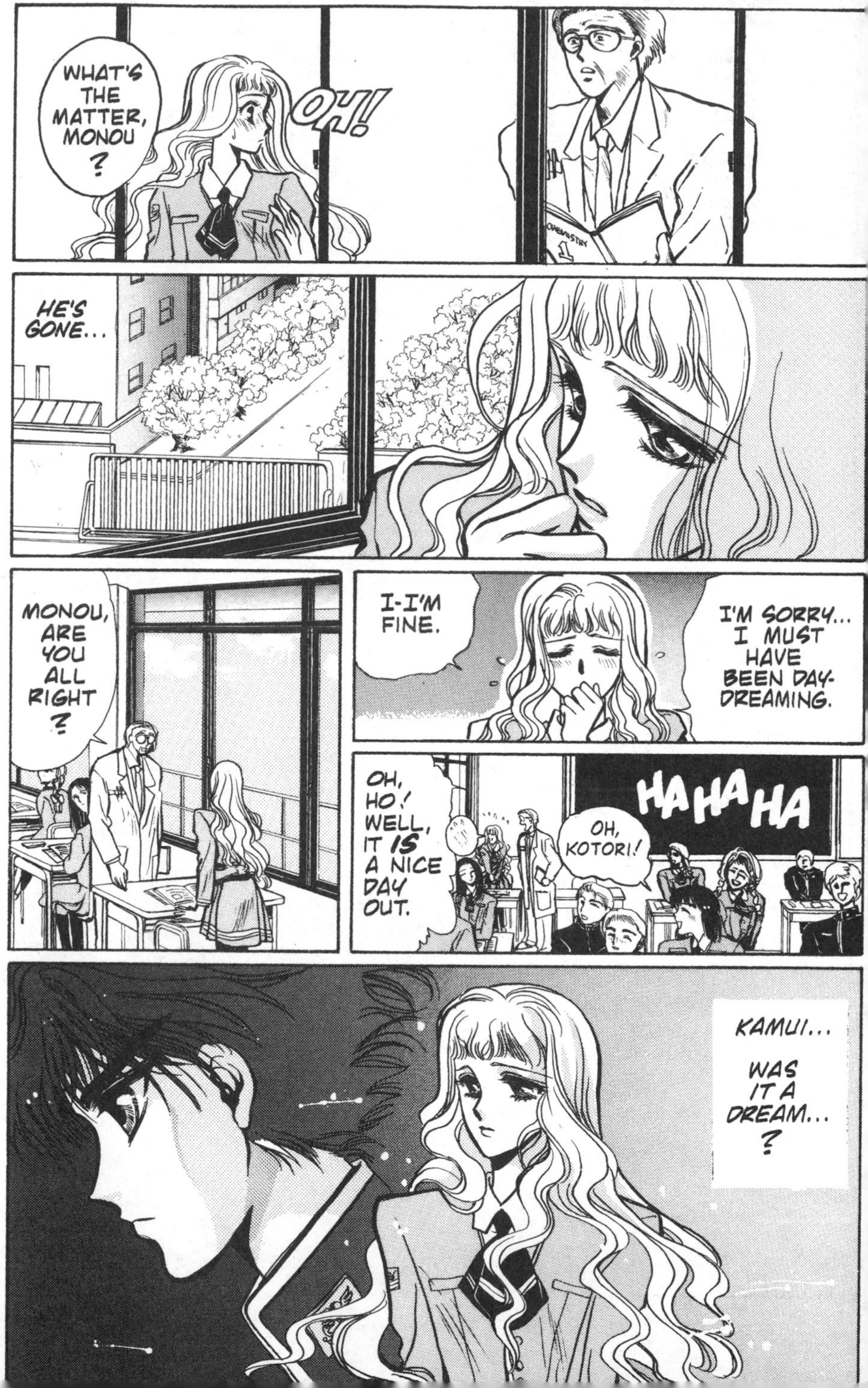
WHAT'S THE MATTER, MONOU ?
OH!
HE'S GONE...
MONOU, ARE YOU ALL RIGHT ?
I-I'M FINE.
I'M SORRY... I MUST HAVE BEEN DAY-DREAMING.
OH, HO! WELL, IT IS A NICE DAY OUT.
OH, KOTORI!
HA HA HA HA
KAMUI...
WAS IT A DREAM... ?

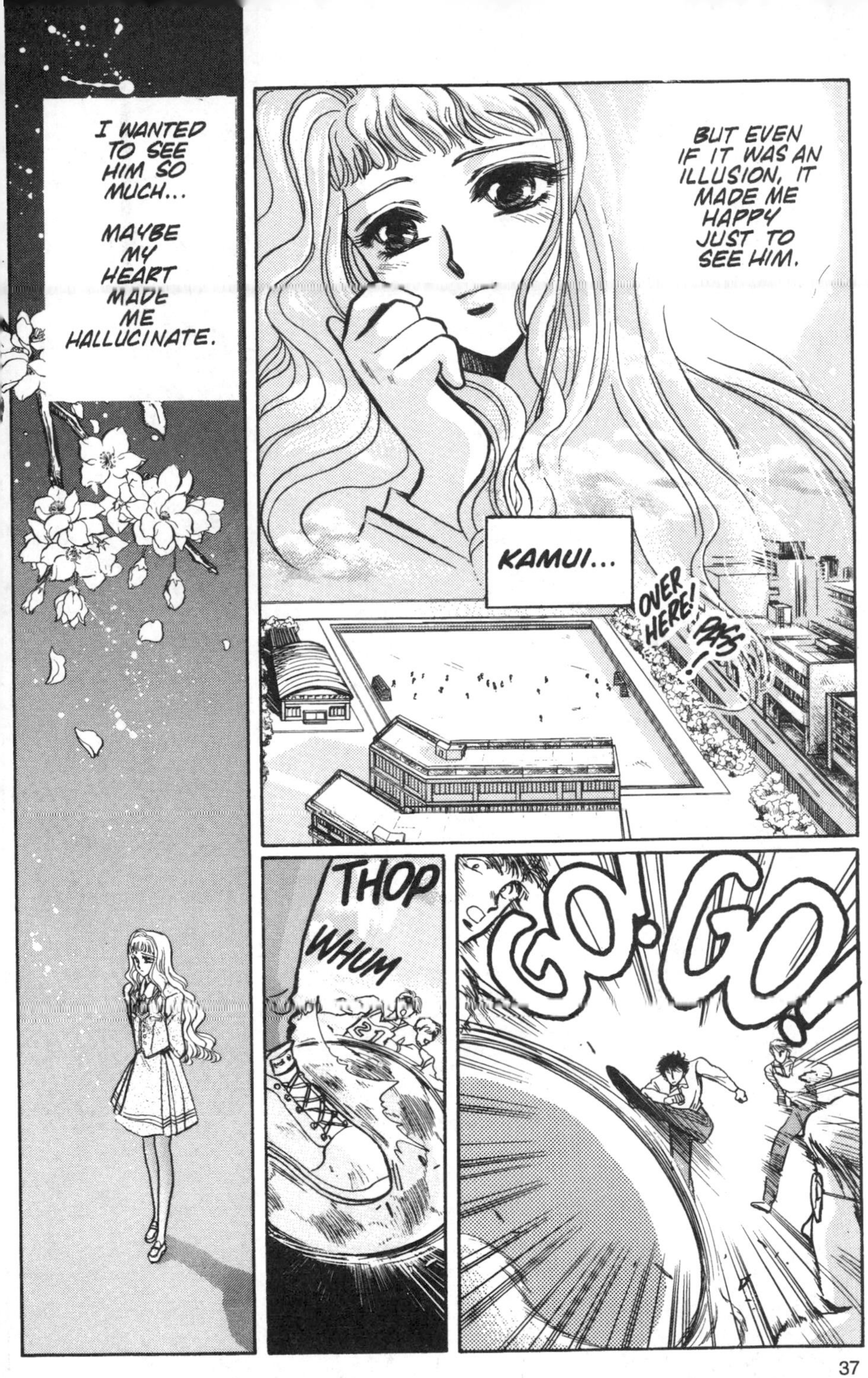
I WANTED TO SEE HIM SO MUCH...
MAYBE MY HEART MADE ME HALLUCINATE.
BUT EVEN IF IT WAS AN ILLUSION, IT MADE ME HAPPY JUST TO SEE HIM.
KAMUI...
OVER HERE!
PASS!
THOP
WHUM
GO! GO!

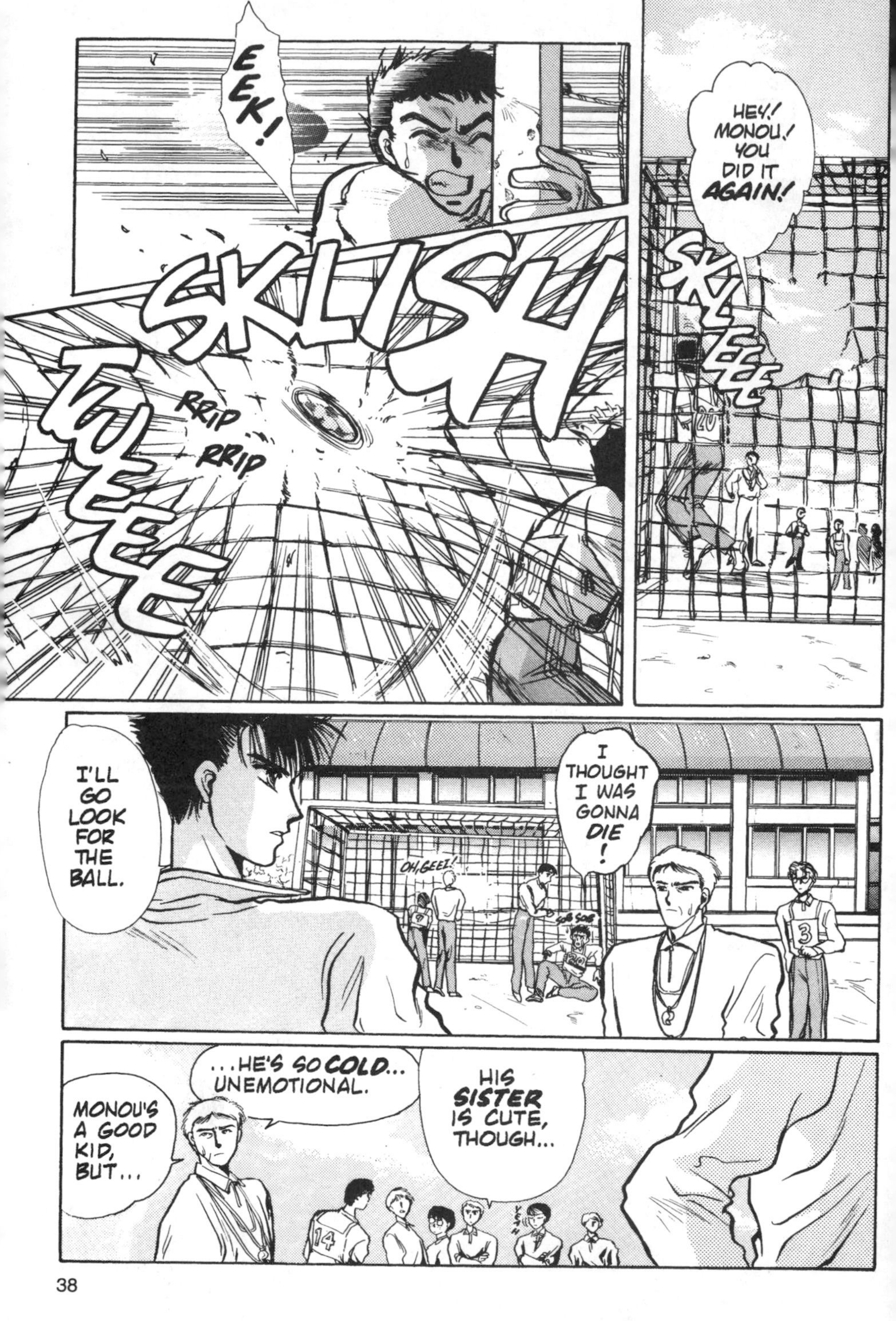
EEK!
SKLISH
TWEEEE
RRIP
RRIP
HEY! MONOU! YOU DID IT AGAIN!
SKLEEE
I'LL GO LOOK FOR THE BALL.
OH, GEEZ!
SOB SOB
I THOUGHT I WAS GONNA DIE!
MONOU'S A GOOD KID, BUT...
...HE'S SO COLD... UNEMOTIONAL.
HIS SISTER IS CUTE, THOUGH...

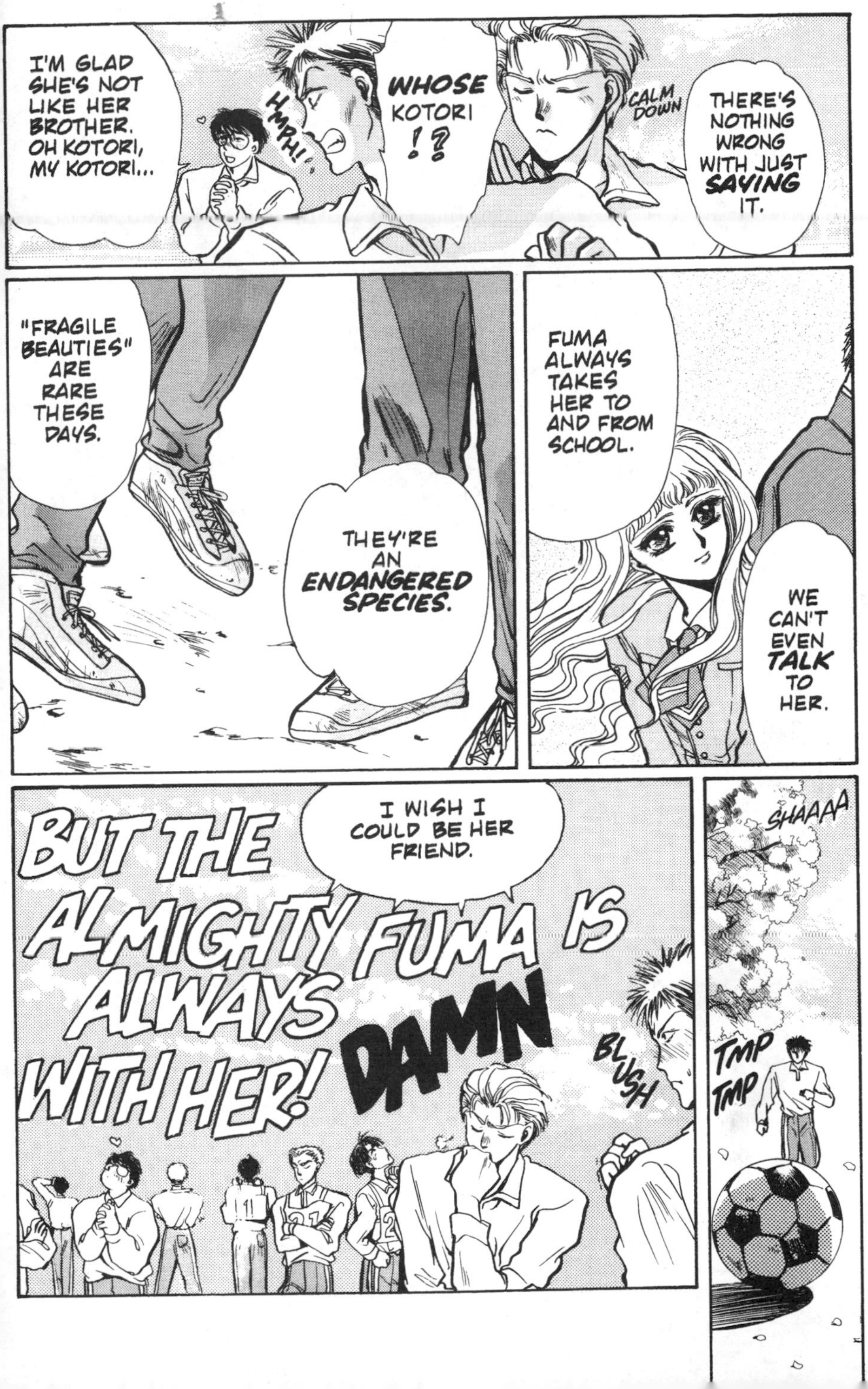
I'M GLAD SHE'S NOT LIKE HER BROTHER. OH KOTORI, MY KOTORI...
HMPH!
WHOSE KOTORI !?
CALM DOWN
THERE'S NOTHING WRONG WITH JUST SAYING IT.
"FRAGILE BEAUTIES" ARE RARE THESE DAYS.
THEY'RE AN ENDANGERED SPECIES.
FUMA ALWAYS TAKES HER TO AND FROM SCHOOL.
WE CAN'T EVEN TALK TO HER.
BUT THE ALMIGHTY FUMA IS ALWAYS WITH HER!
I WISH I COULD BE HER FRIEND.
DAMN
BLUSH
SHAAAA
TMP TMP

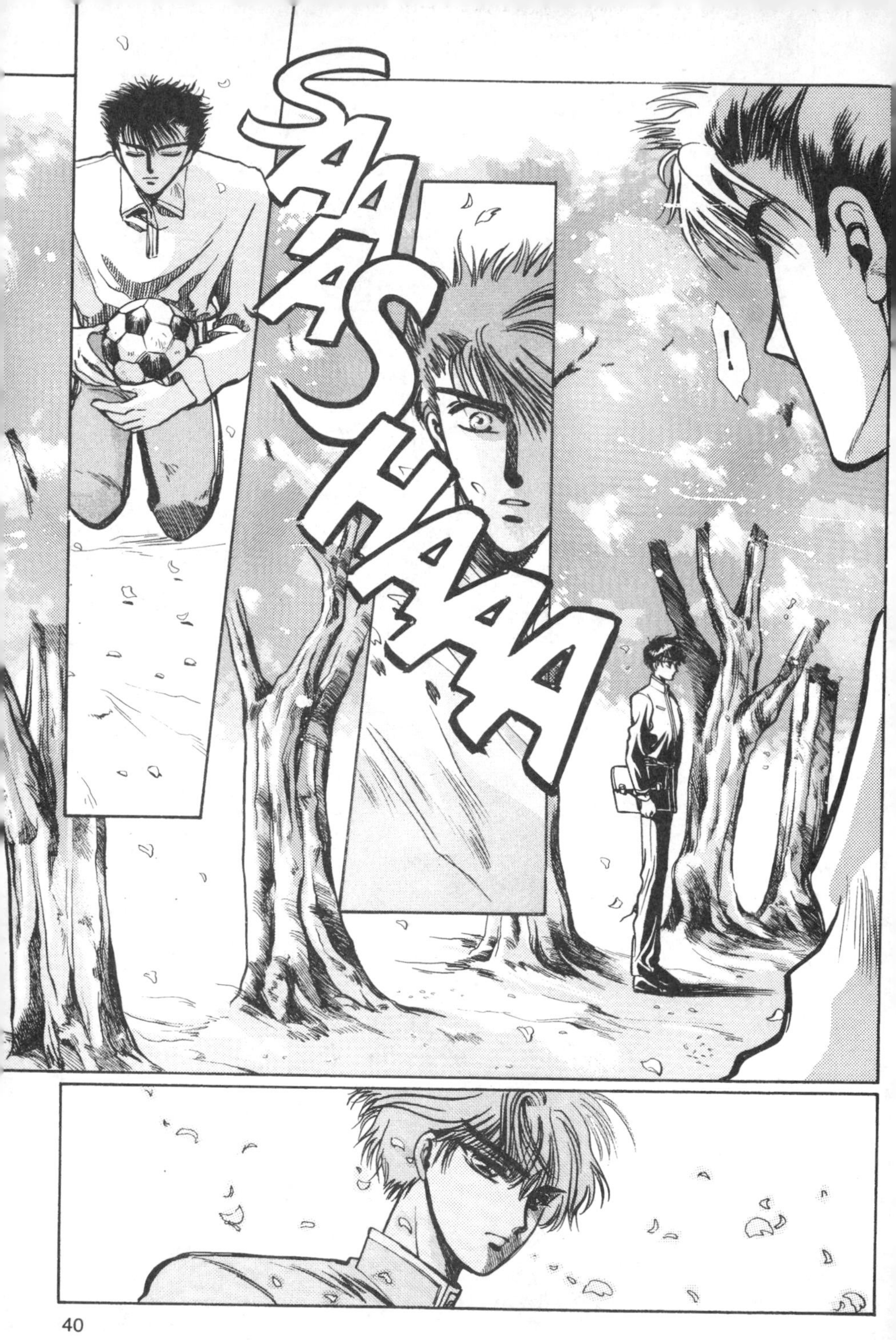
SAAASHAAA
!

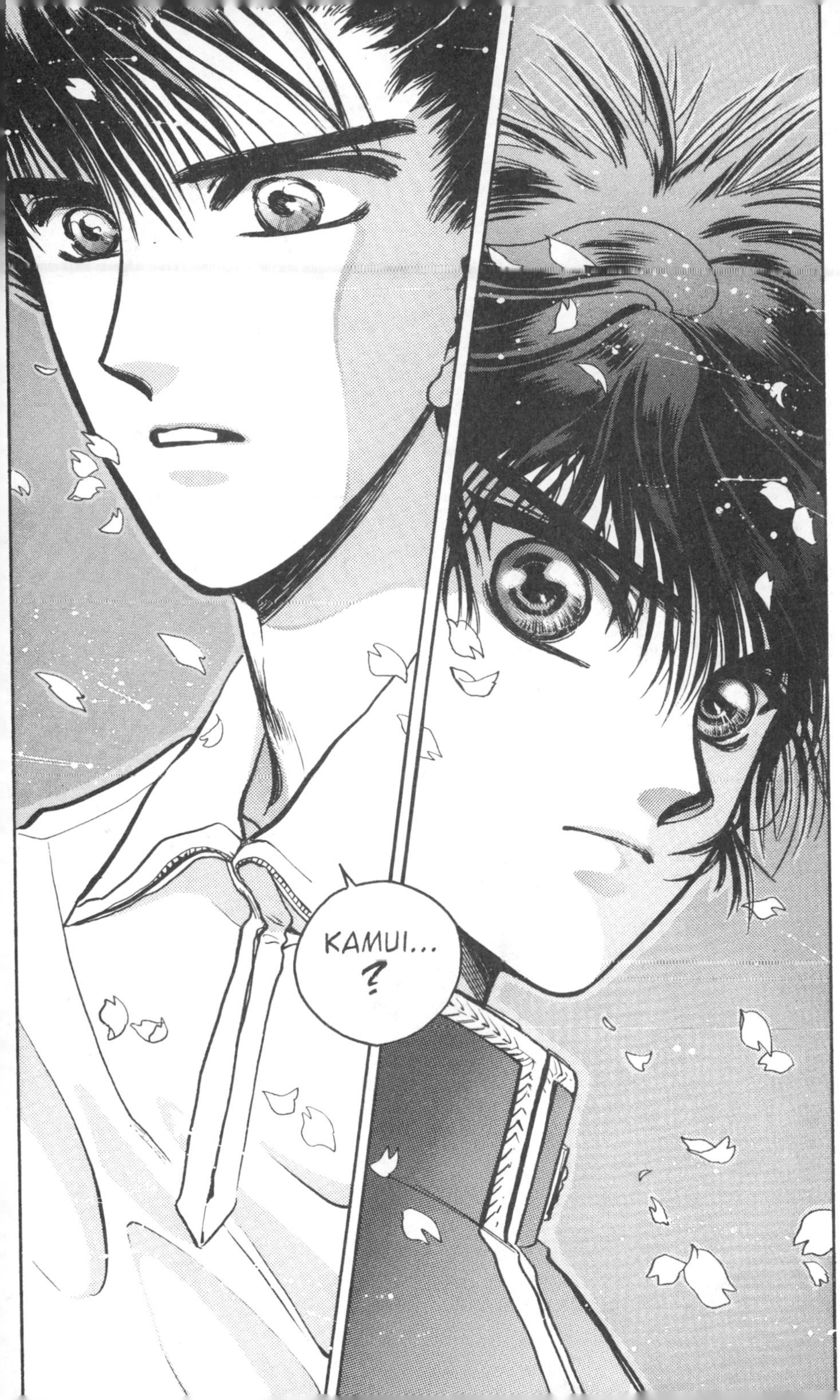
KAMUI...
?

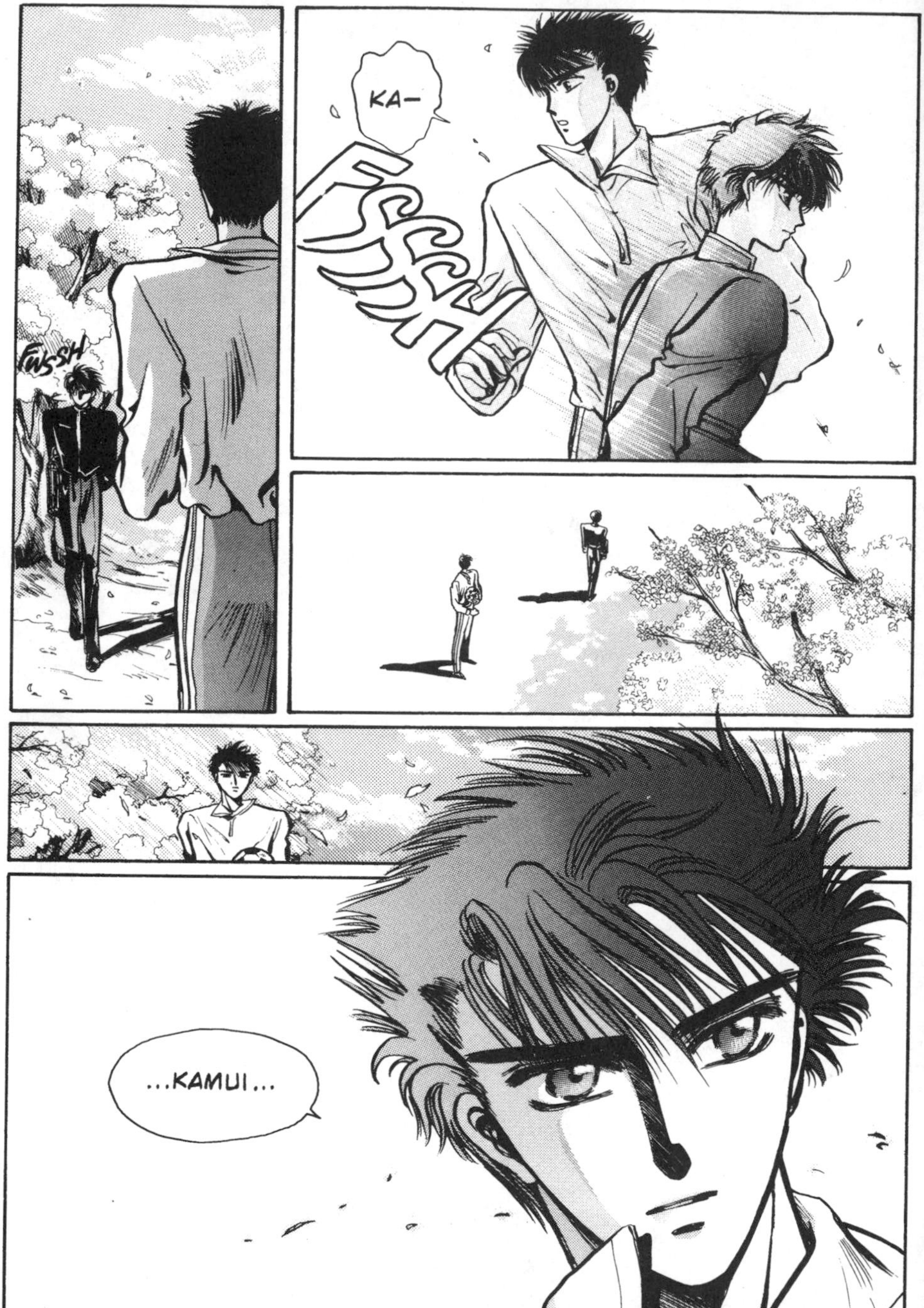
FWS-SH
KA–
FSSSH
...KAMUI...

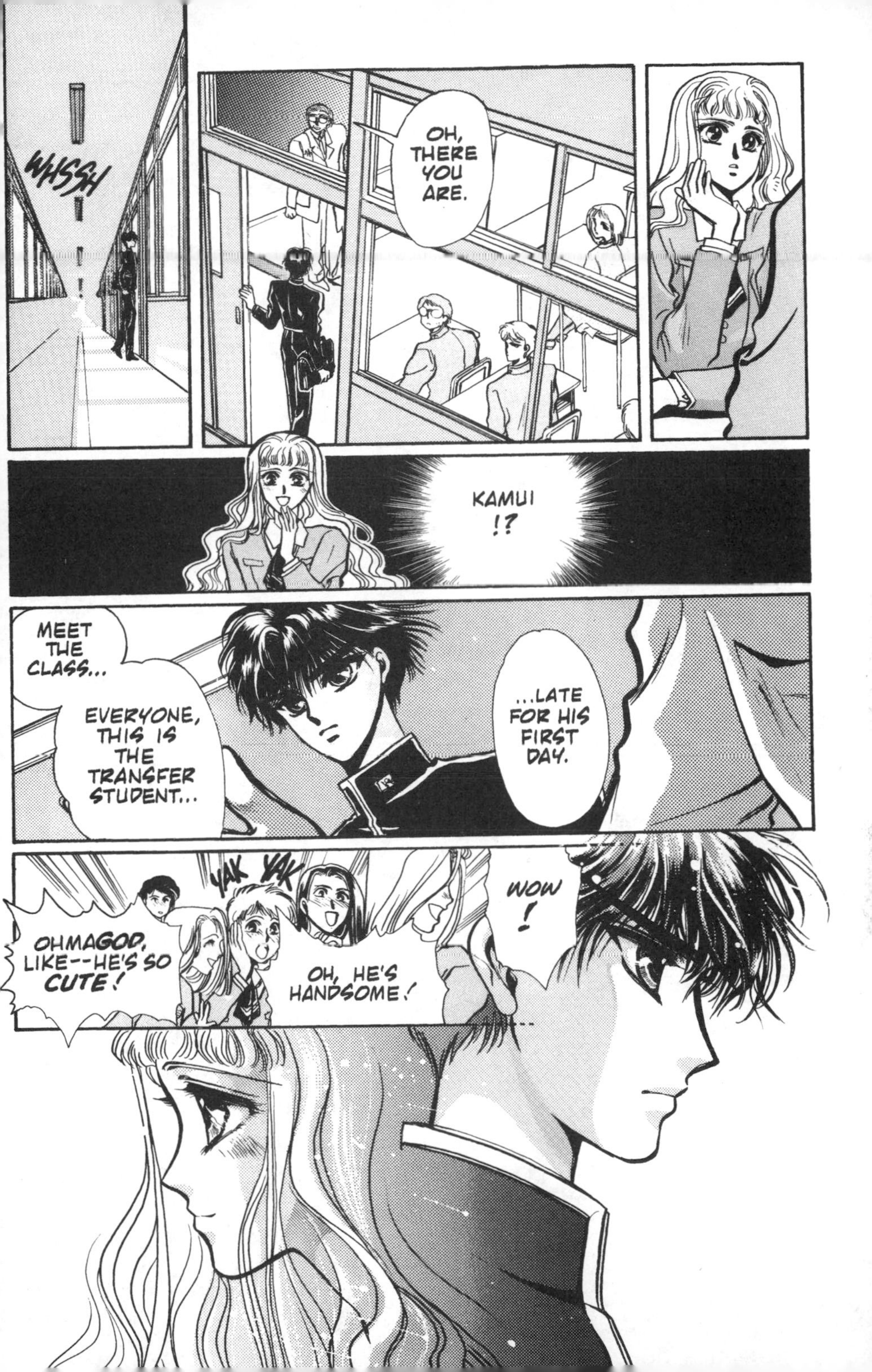
WHSSH
OH, THERE YOU ARE.
KAMUI !?
MEET THE CLASS...
EVERYONE, THIS IS THE TRANSFER STUDENT...
...LATE FOR HIS FIRST DAY.
OHMAGOD, LIKE--HE'S SO CUTE!
YAK YAK
OH, HE'S HANDSOME!
WOW!

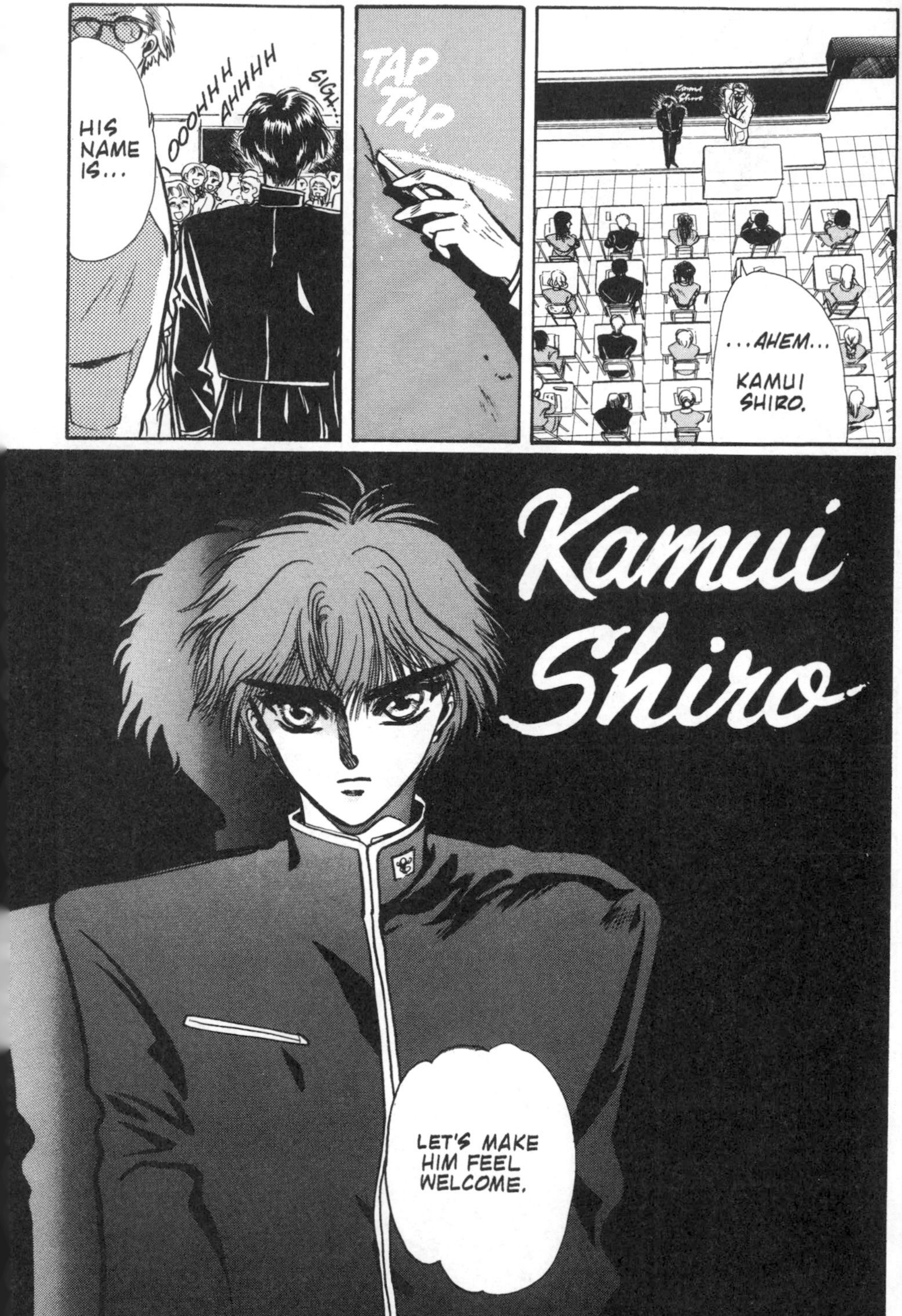
HIS NAME IS...
OOOHHH AHHHH
SIGH...
TAP TAP
...AHEM... KAMUI SHIRO.
Kamui Shiro
LET'S MAKE HIM FEEL WELCOME.

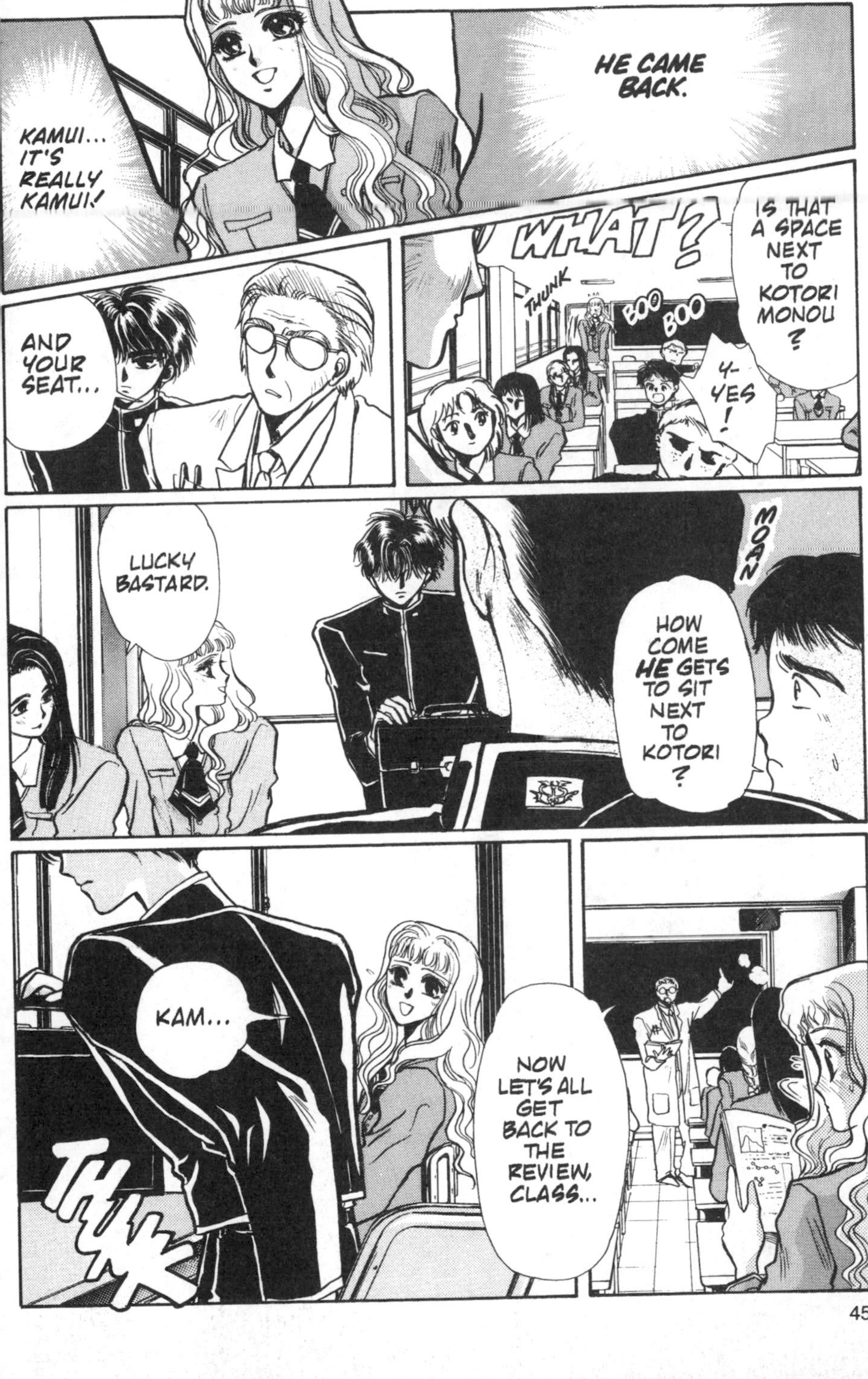
KAMUI... IT'S REALLY KAMUI!
HE CAME BACK.
AND YOUR SEAT...
WHAT?
THUNK
BOO BOO
IS THAT A SPACE NEXT TO KOTORI MONOU?
Y-YES!
LUCKY BASTARD.
MOAN
HOW COME HE GETS TO SIT NEXT TO KOTORI?
KAM...
THUNK
NOW LET'S ALL GET BACK TO THE REVIEW, CLASS...

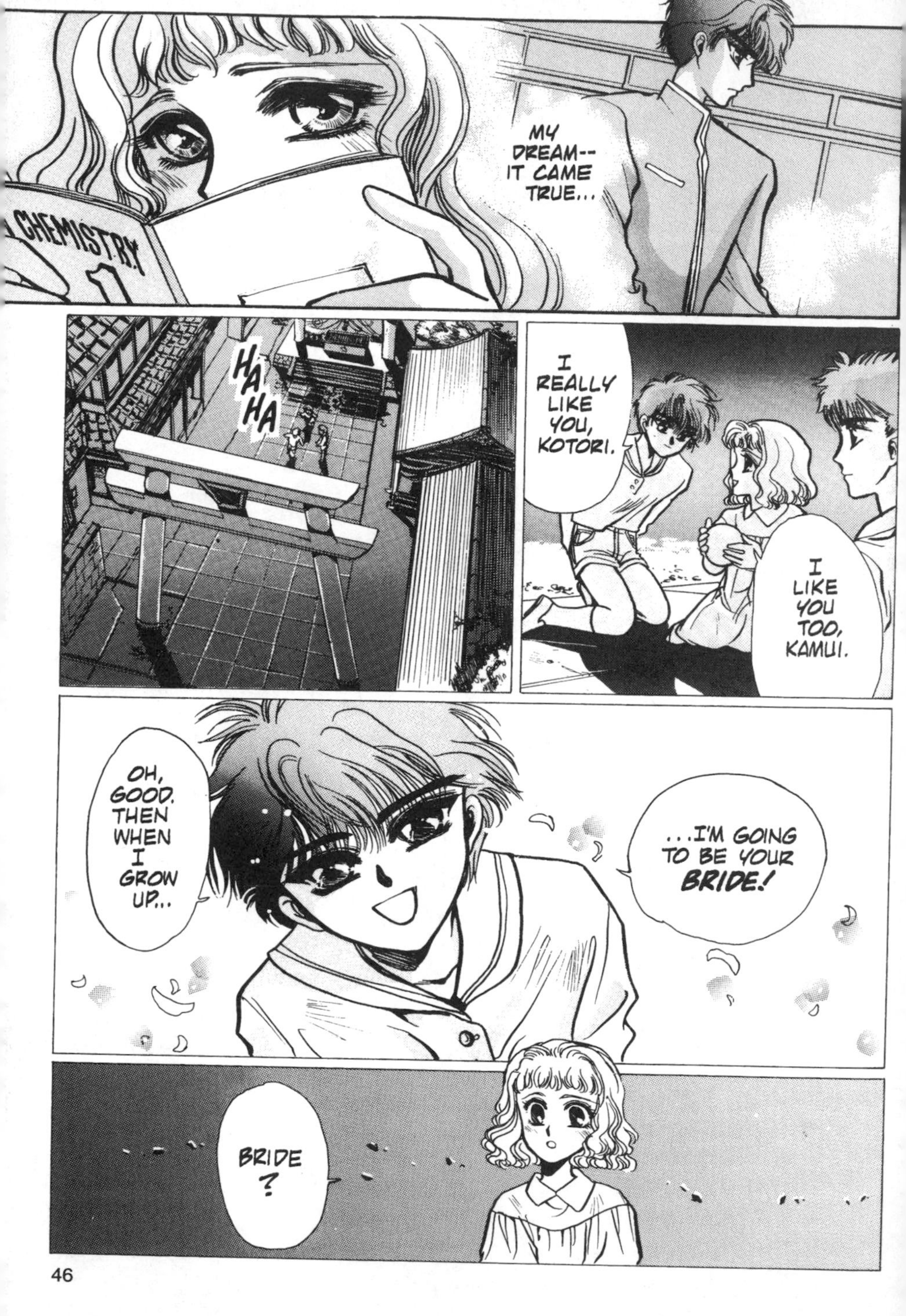
CHEMISTRY
MY DREAM-- IT CAME TRUE...
HA HA HA
I REALLY LIKE YOU, KOTORI.
I LIKE YOU TOO, KAMUI.
OH, GOOD. THEN WHEN I GROW UP...
...I'M GOING TO BE YOUR BRIDE!
BRIDE?

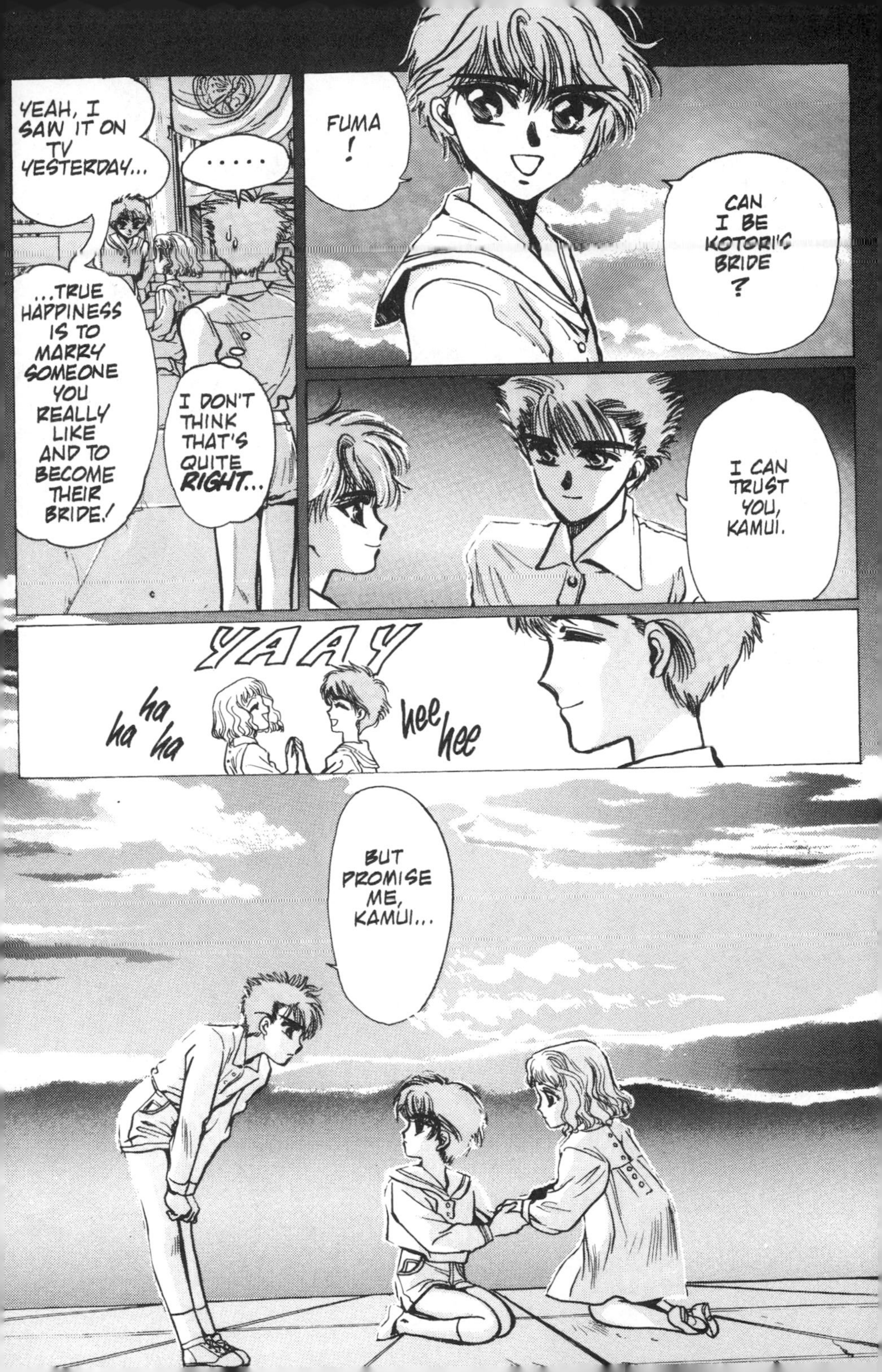

YEAH, I SAW IT ON TV YESTERDAY...
......
...TRUE HAPPINESS IS TO MARRY SOMEONE YOU REALLY LIKE AND TO BECOME THEIR BRIDE!
I DON'T THINK THAT'S QUITE RIGHT...
FUMA!
CAN I BE KOTORI'S BRIDE?
I CAN TRUST YOU, KAMUI.
YAAY
ha ha ha
hee hee
BUT PROMISE ME, KAMUI...

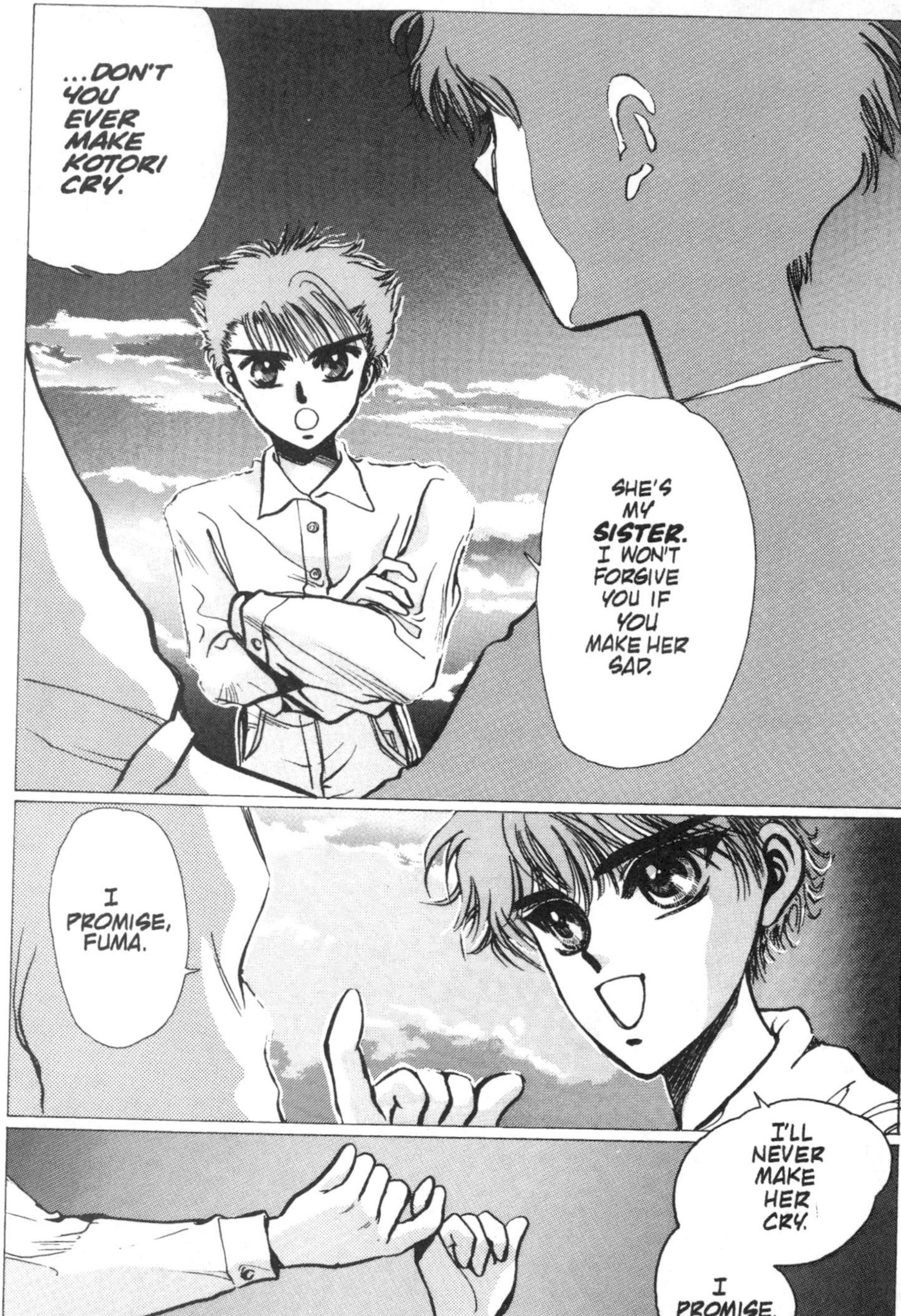
...DON'T YOU EVER MAKE KOTORI CRY.
SHE'S MY SISTER. I WON'T FORGIVE YOU IF YOU MAKE HER SAD.
I PROMISE, FUMA.
I'LL NEVER MAKE HER CRY.
I PROMISE.

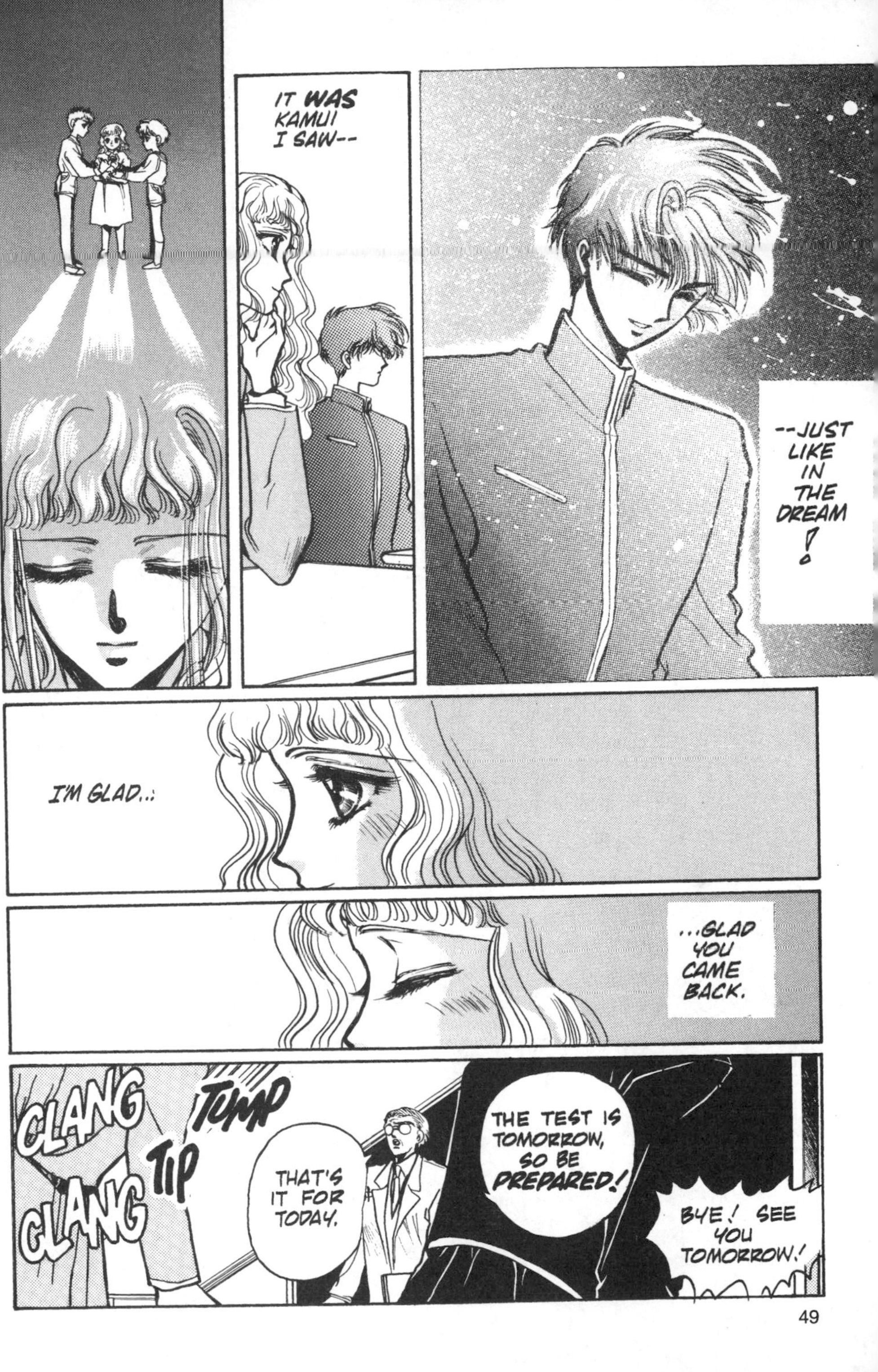
IT WAS KAMUI I SAW--
--JUST LIKE IN THE DREAM!
I'M GLAD...
...GLAD YOU CAME BACK.
CLANG
TUMP
TIP
CLANG
THAT'S IT FOR TODAY.
THE TEST IS TOMORROW, SO BE PREPARED!
BYE! SEE YOU TOMORROW!

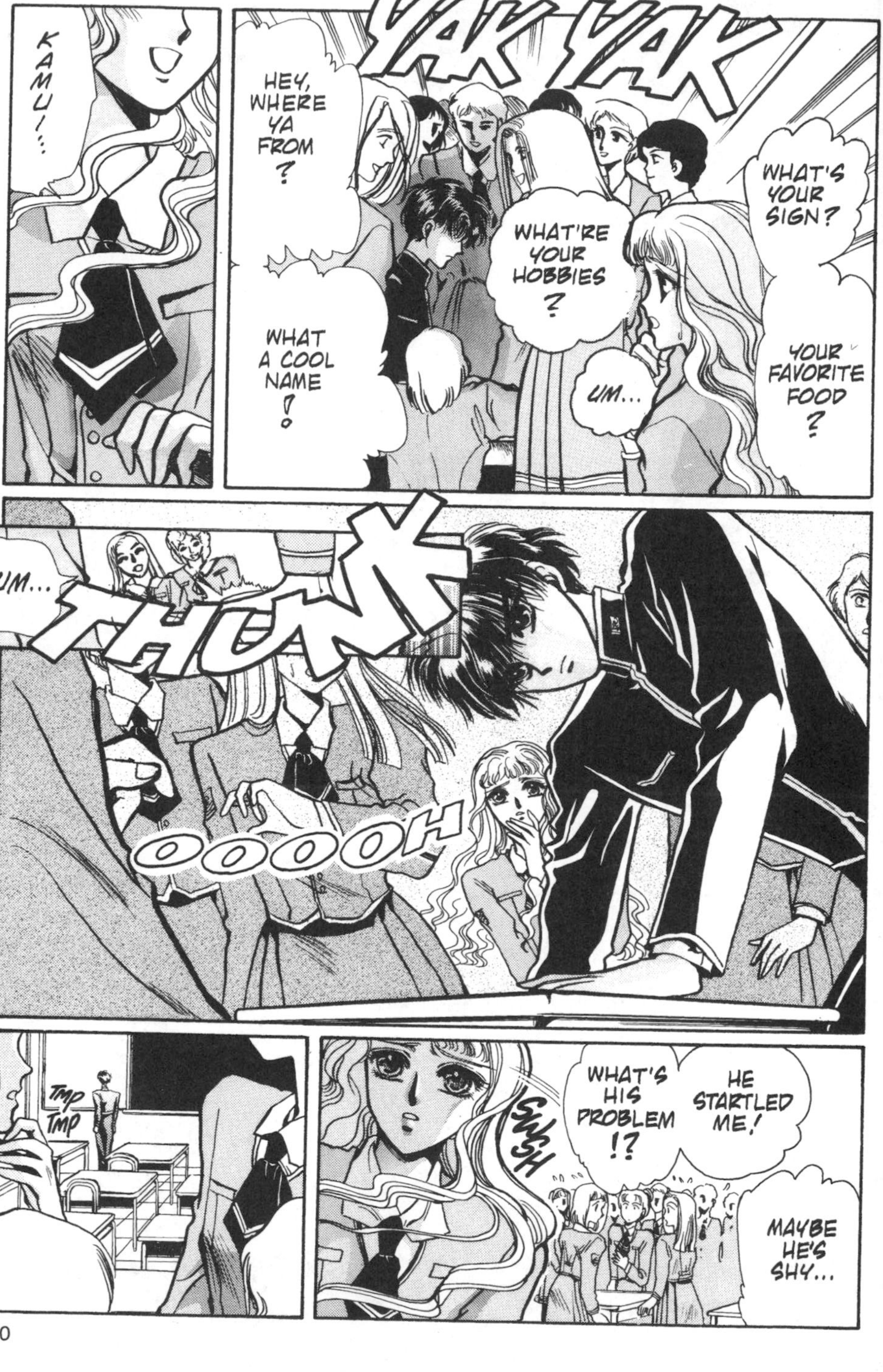
KAMUI!...
YAK YAK
HEY, WHERE YA FROM?
WHAT'S YOUR SIGN?
WHAT'RE YOUR HOBBIES?
WHAT A COOL NAME!
UM...
YOUR FAVORITE FOOD?
UM...
THUNK
OOOOH
TMP TMP
SWISH
WHAT'S HIS PROBLEM!?
HE STARTLED ME!
MAYBE HE'S SHY...

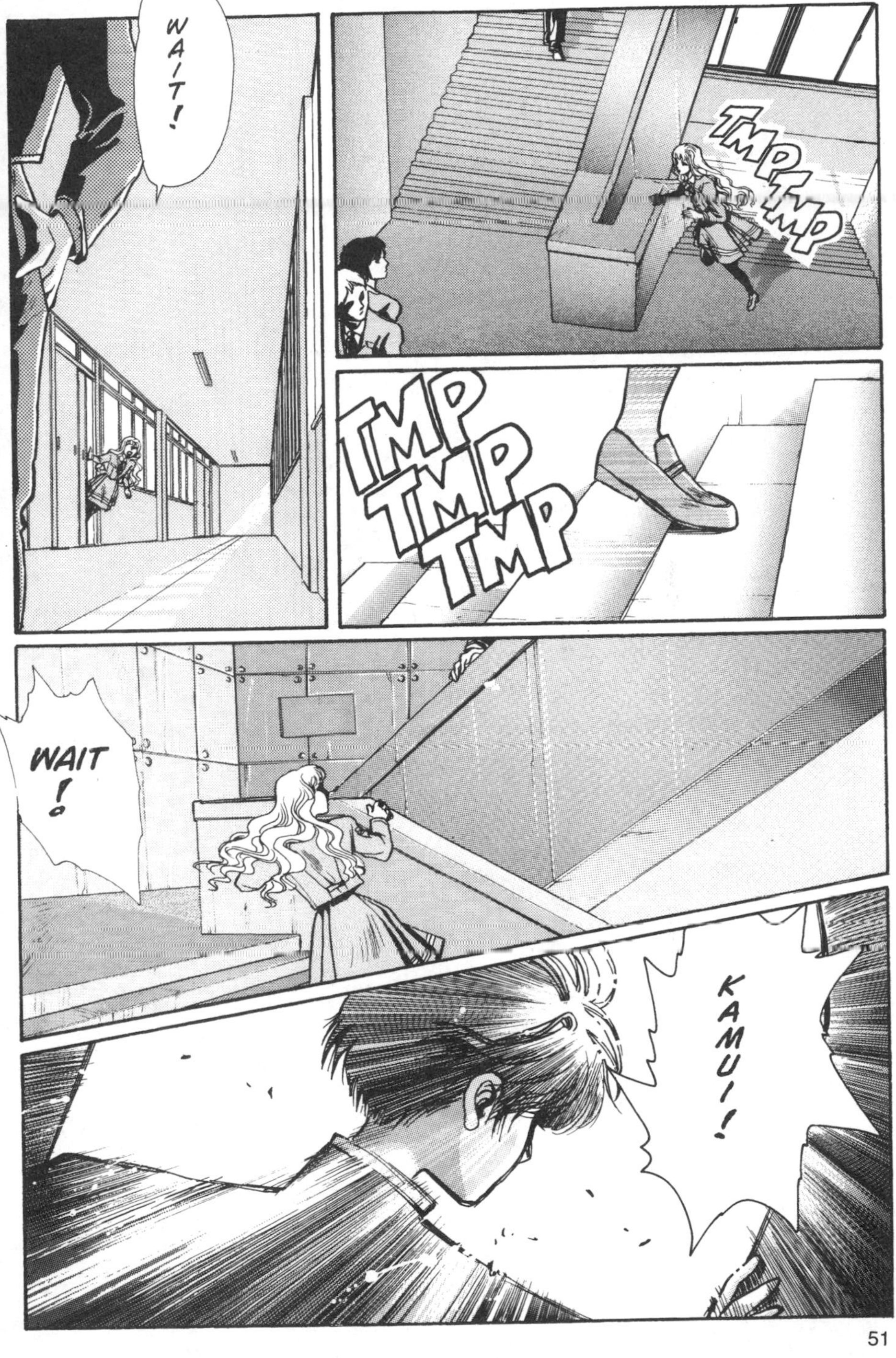
WAIT!
TMP TMP TMP
TMP TMP TMP
WAIT!
KAMUI!

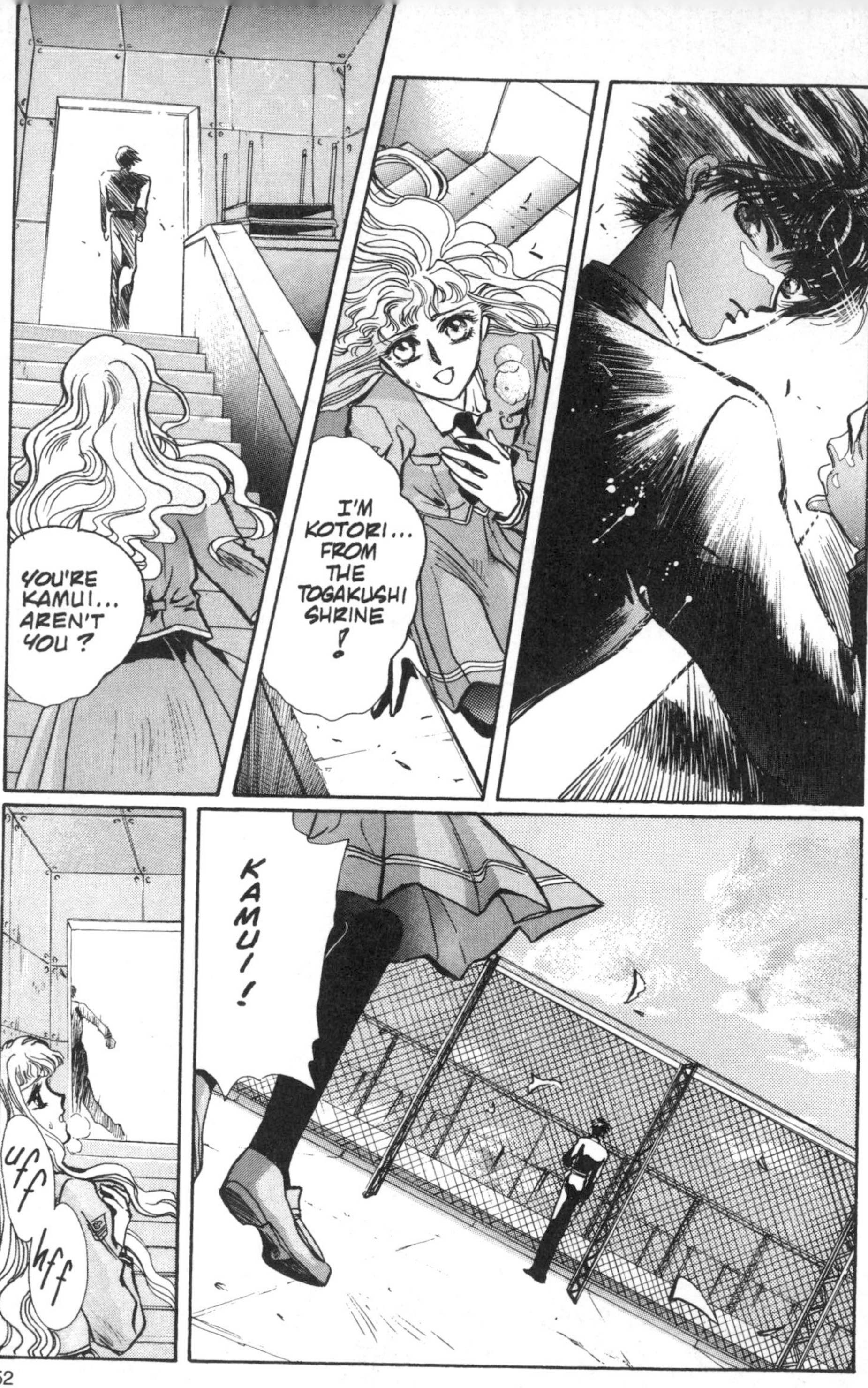
YOU'RE KAMUI... AREN'T YOU?
I'M KOTORI... FROM THE TOGAKUSHI SHRINE!
uff hff
KAMUI!

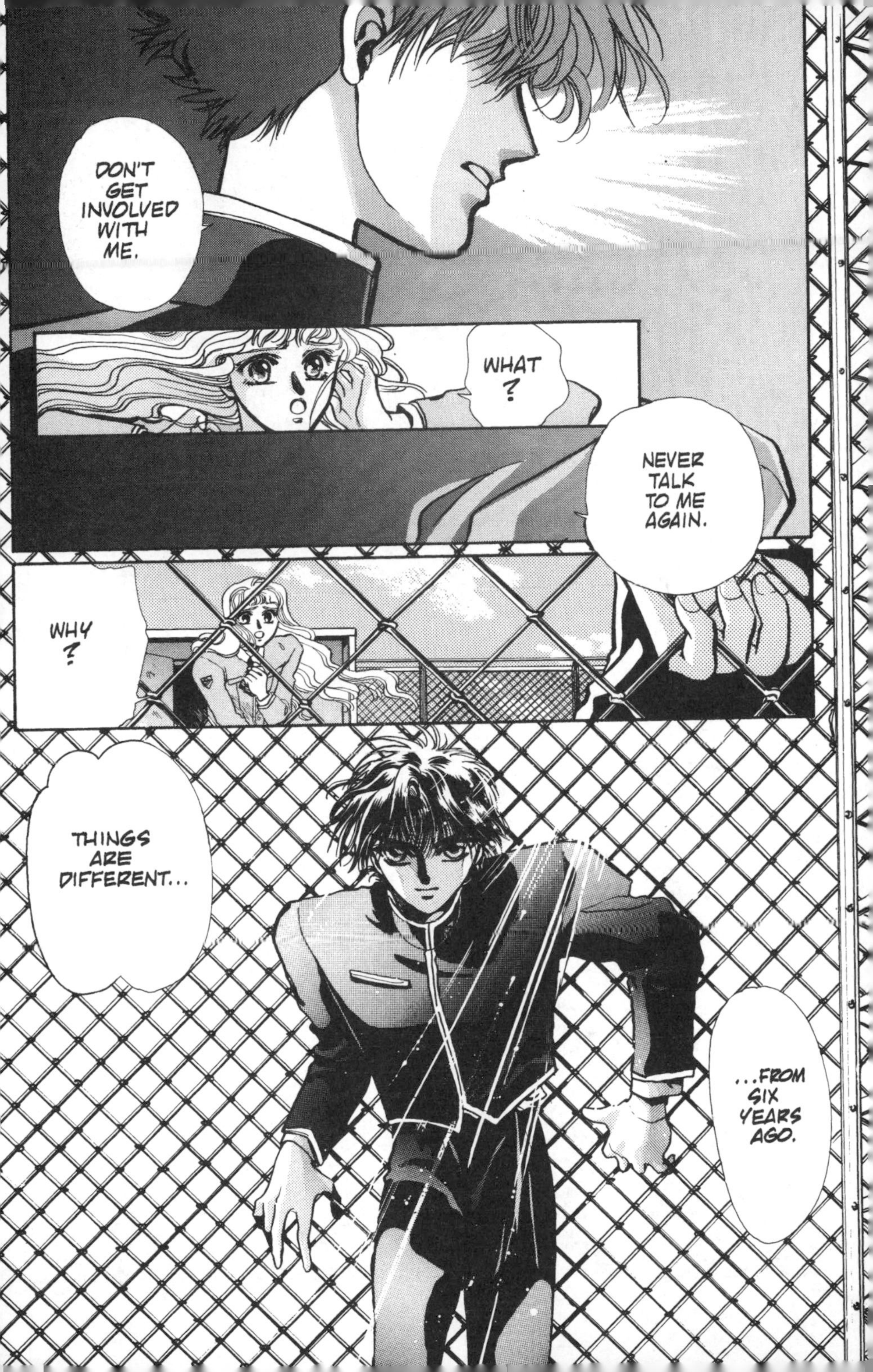
DON'T GET INVOLVED WITH ME.
WHAT ?
NEVER TALK TO ME AGAIN.
WHY ?
THINGS ARE DIFFERENT...
...FROM SIX YEARS AGO.

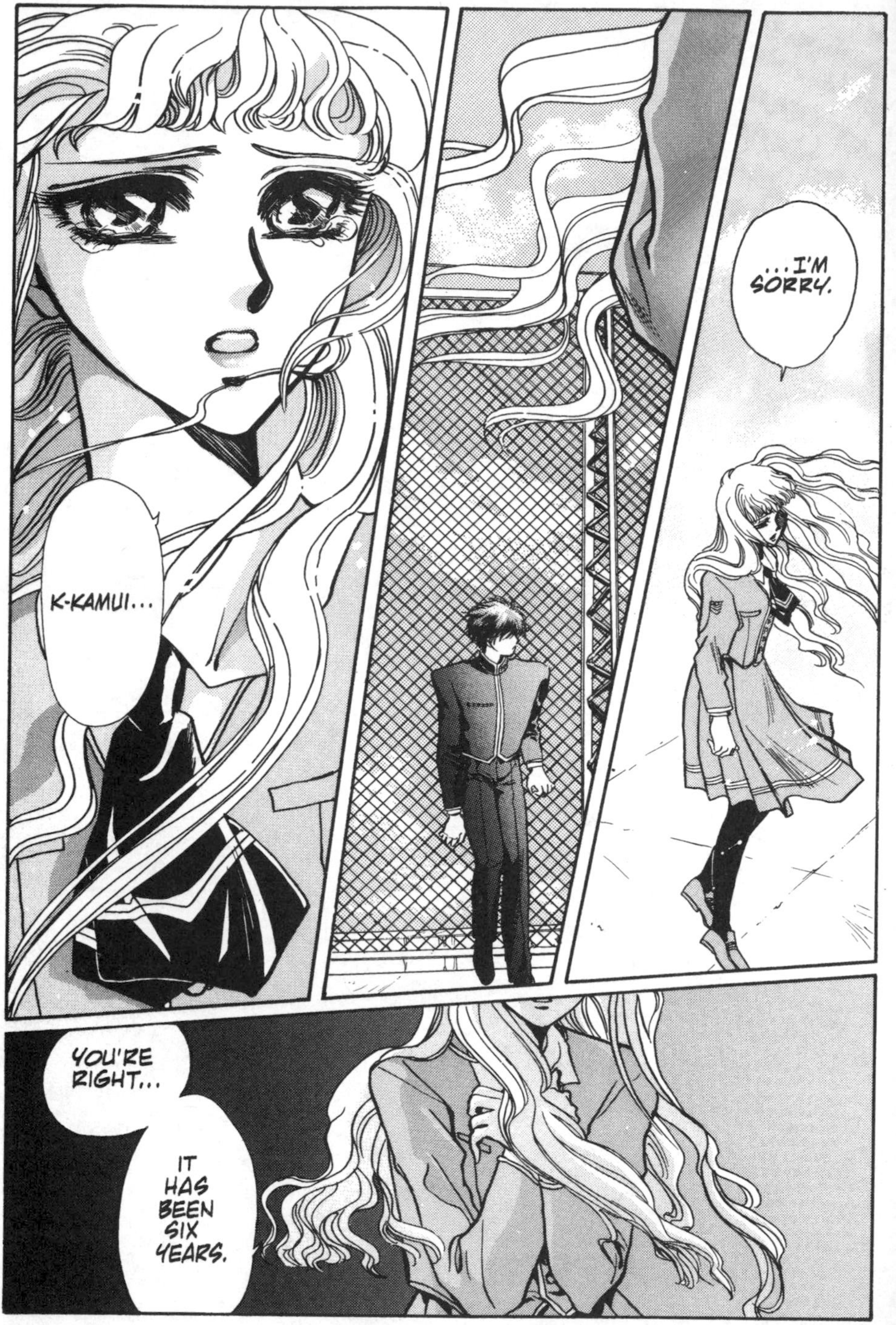
K-KAMUI...
...I'M SORRY.
YOU'RE RIGHT...
IT HAS BEEN SIX YEARS.

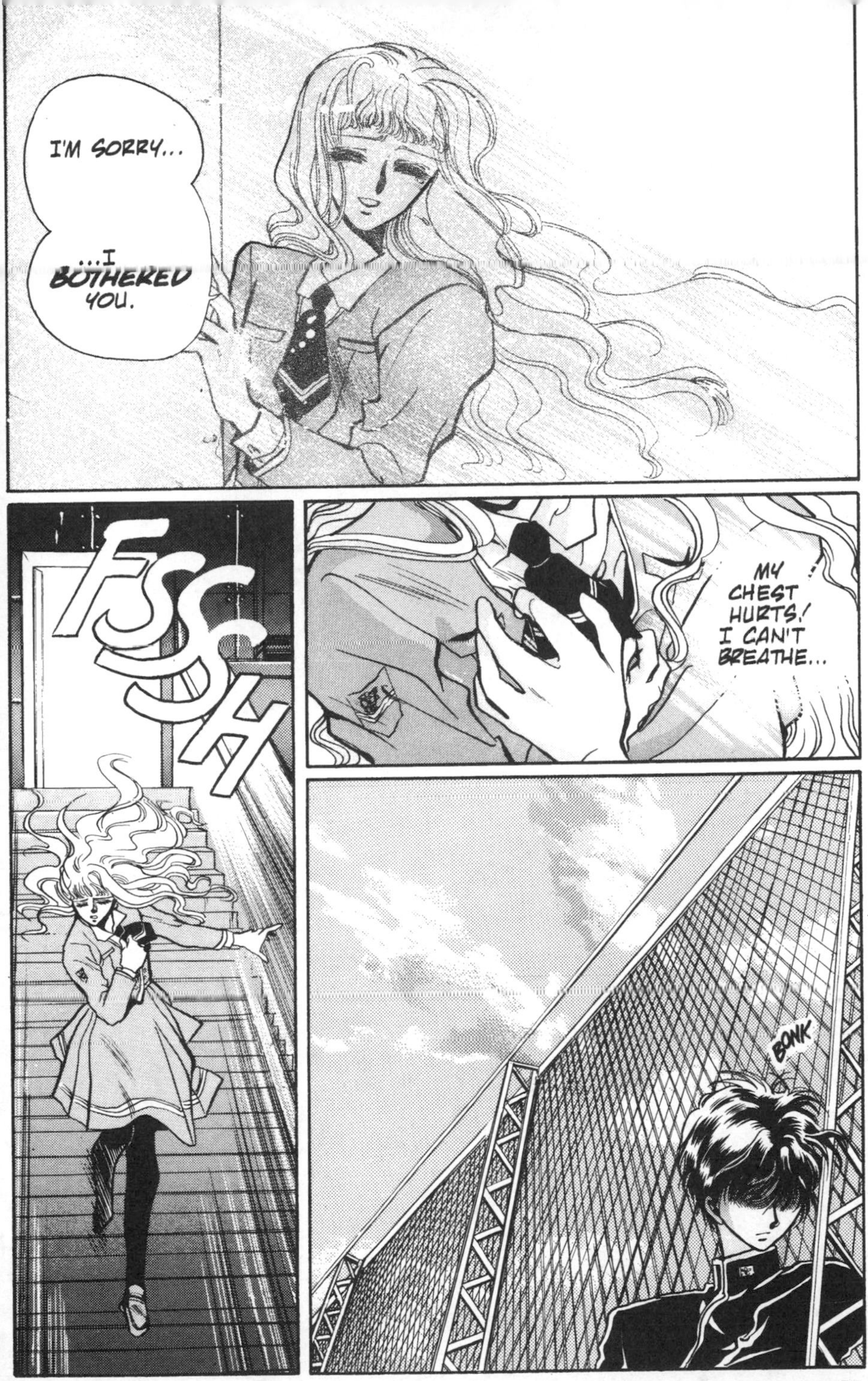
I'M SORRY...
...I BOTHERED YOU.
FSSH
MY CHEST HURTS! I CAN'T BREATHE...
BONK

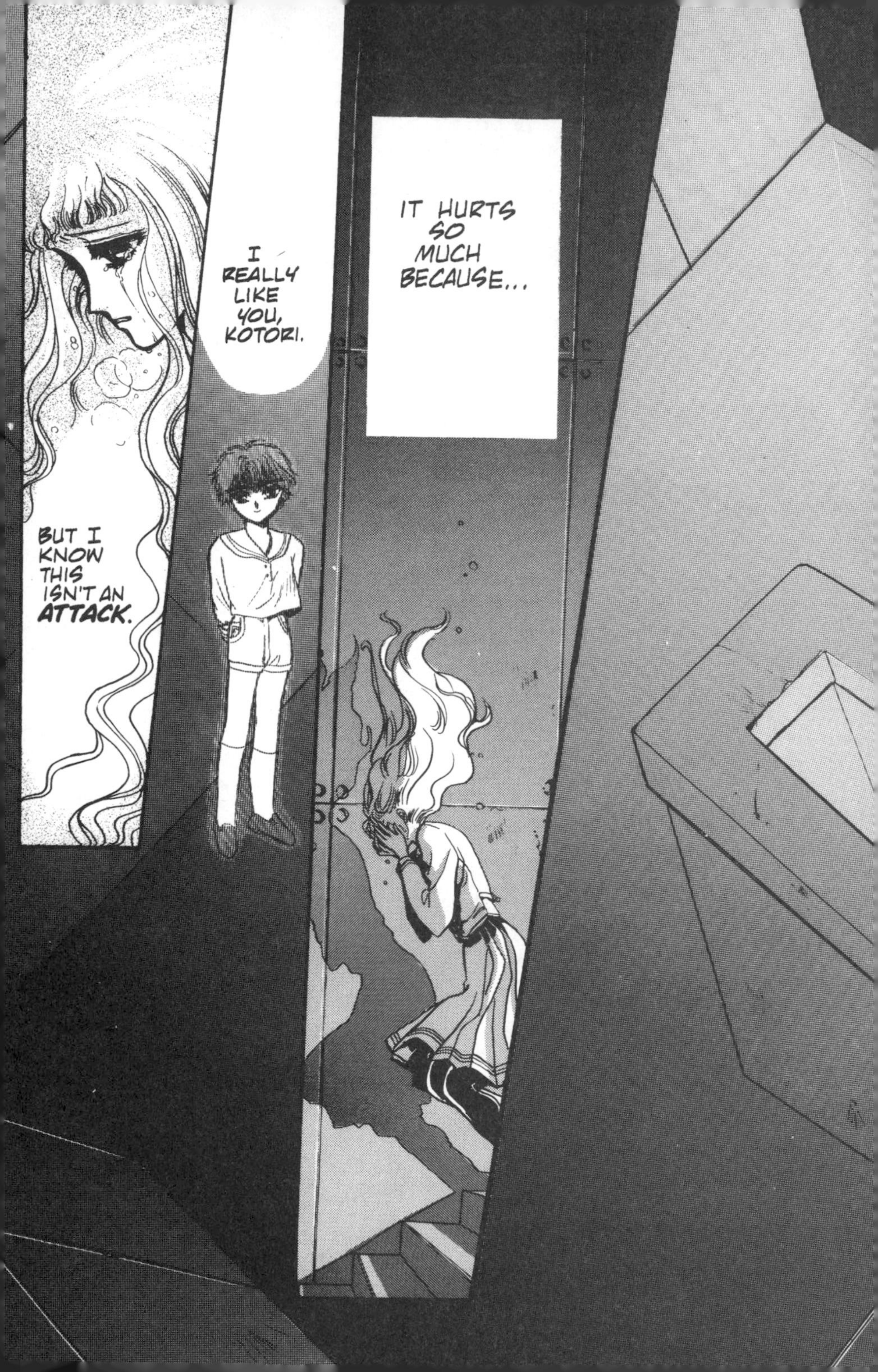
BUT I KNOW THIS ISN'T AN **ATTACK**.
I REALLY LIKE YOU, KOTORI.
IT HURTS SO MUCH BECAUSE...

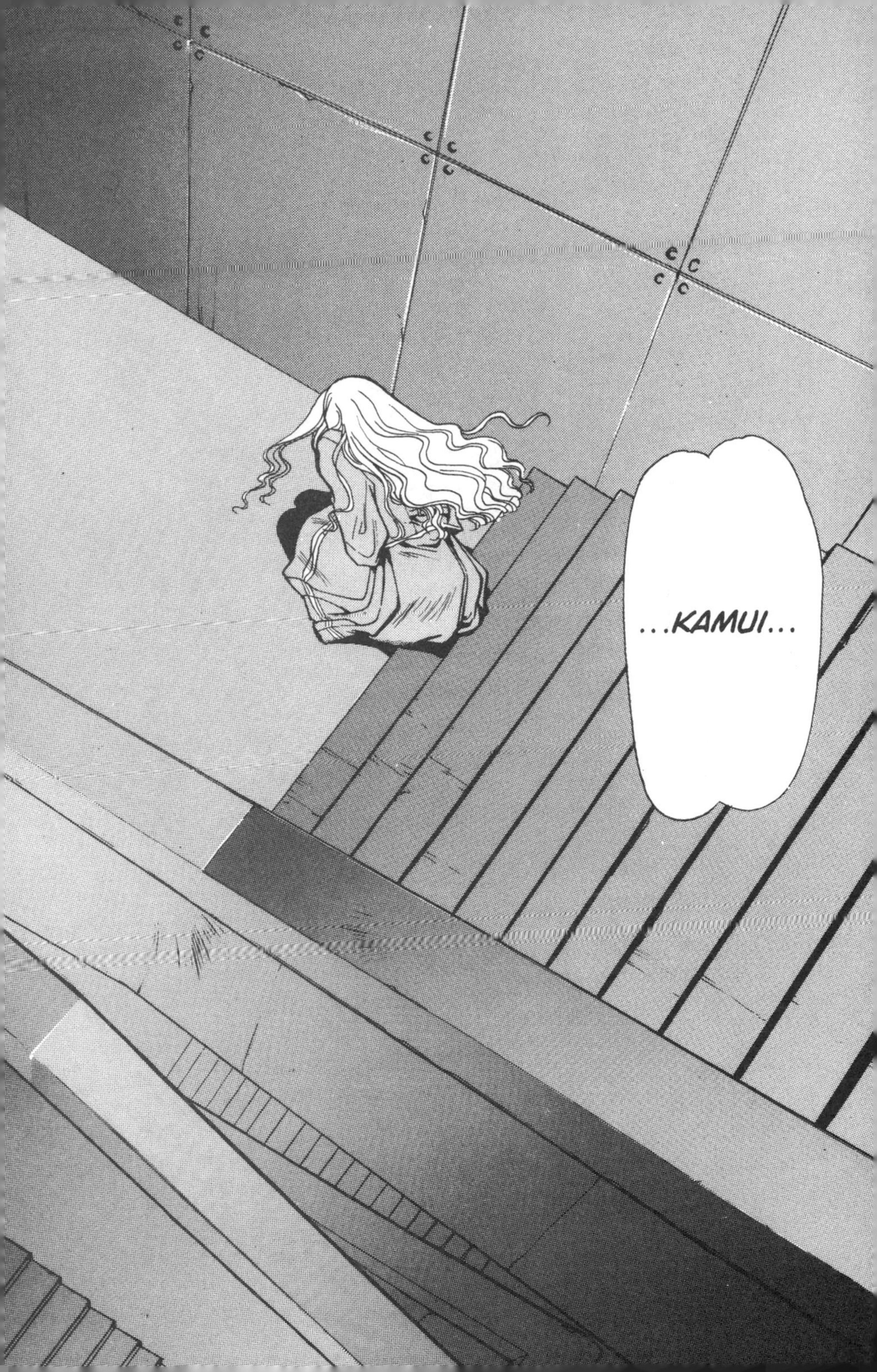
...KAMUI...

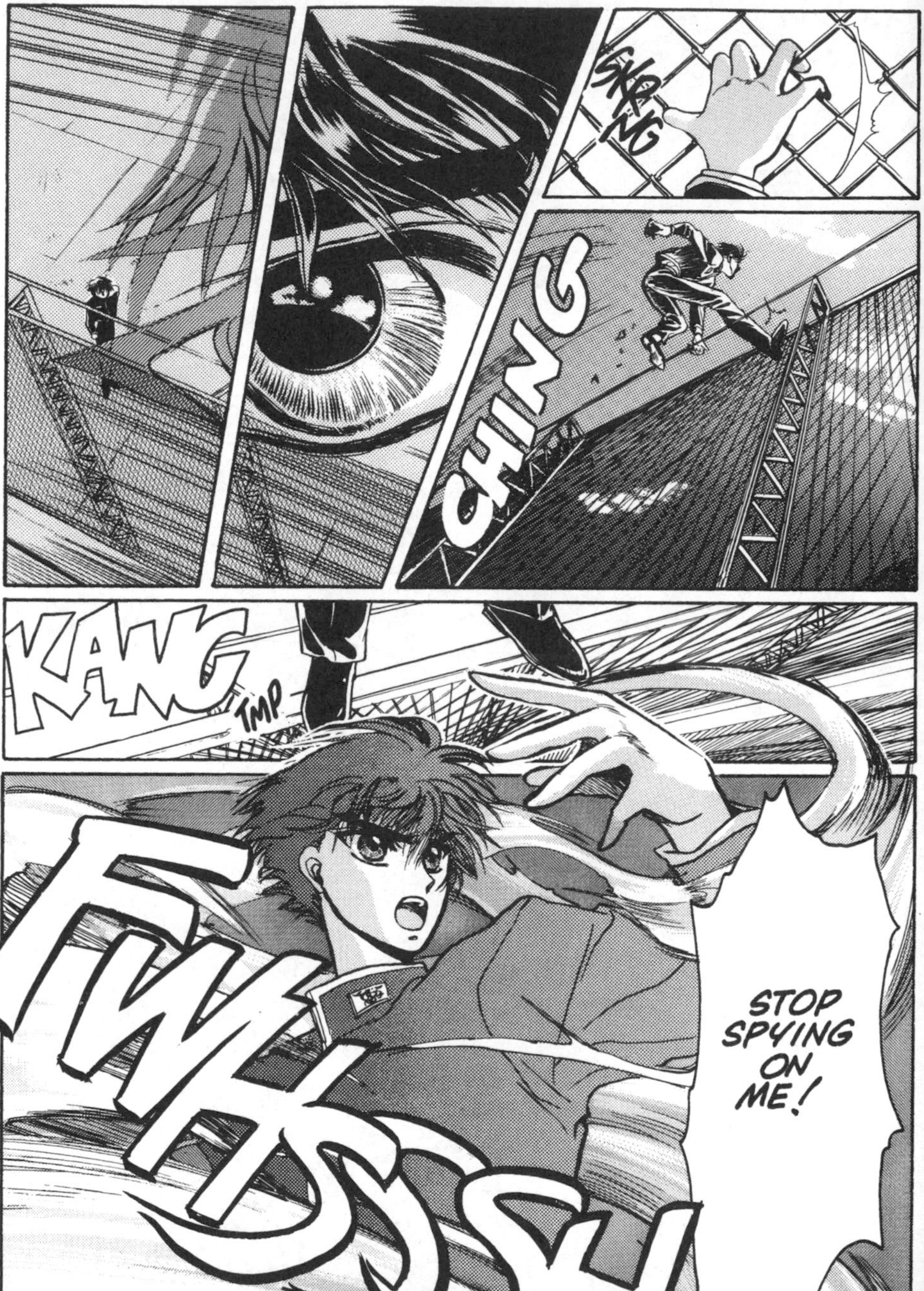
SKRING
CHING
KANG
TMP
FWHSSH
STOP SPYING ON ME!

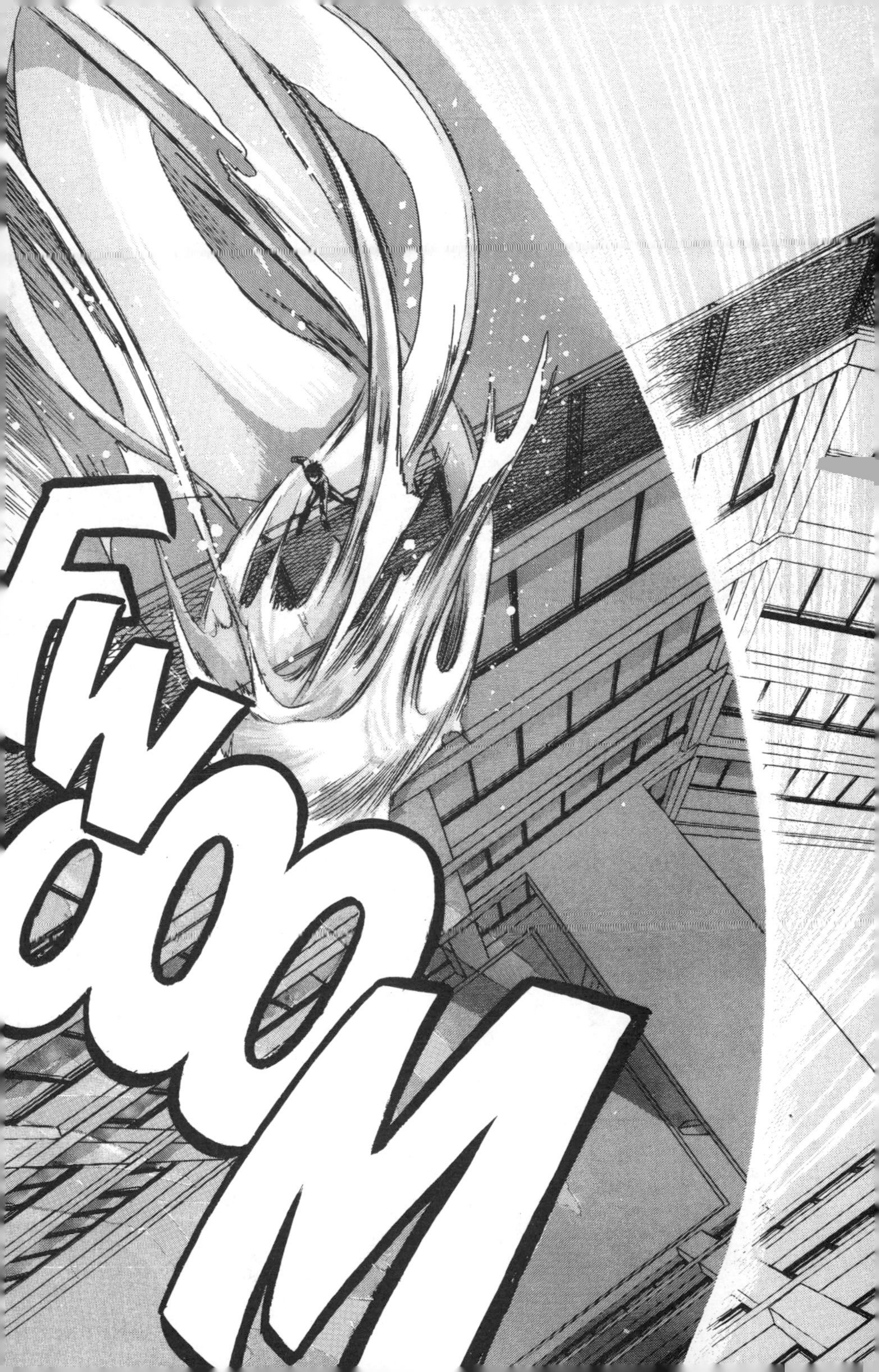
FWOOM

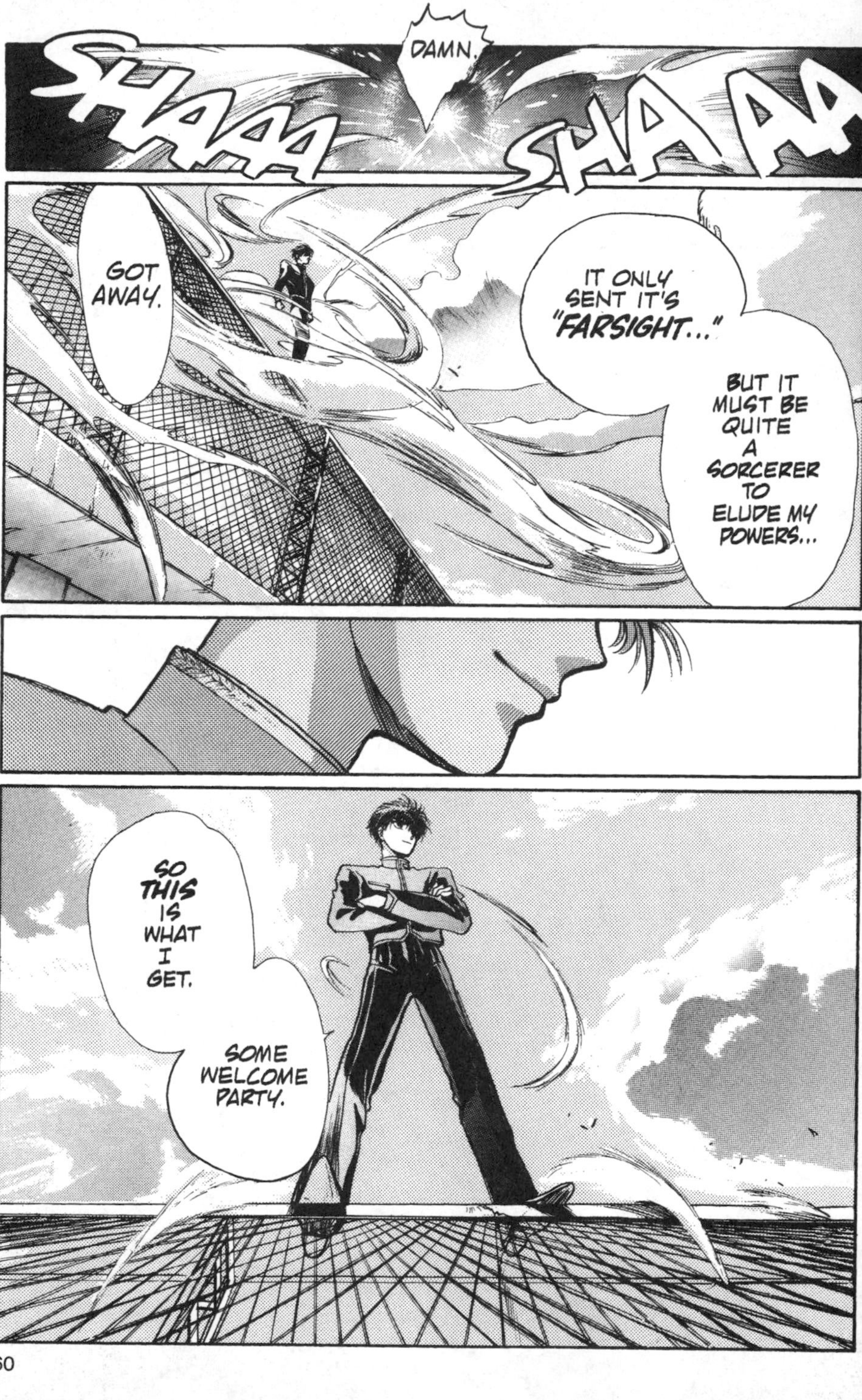
SHAAA
DAMN.
SHAAA
GOT AWAY.
IT ONLY SENT IT'S "FARSIGHT..."
BUT IT MUST BE QUITE A SORCERER TO ELUDE MY POWERS...
SO THIS IS WHAT I GET.
SOME WELCOME PARTY.

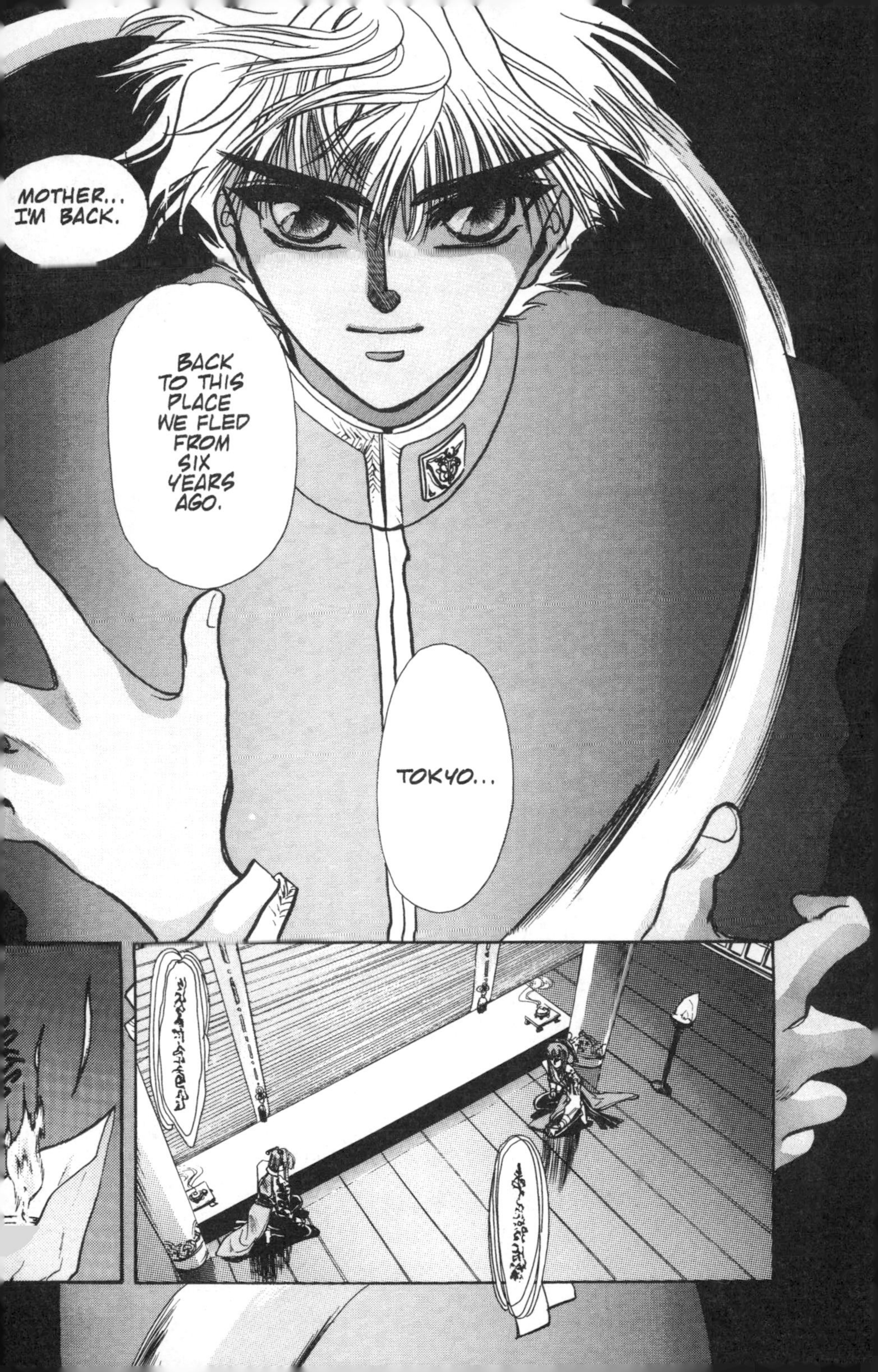
MOTHER... I'M BACK.
BACK TO THIS PLACE WE FLED FROM SIX YEARS AGO.
TOKYO...

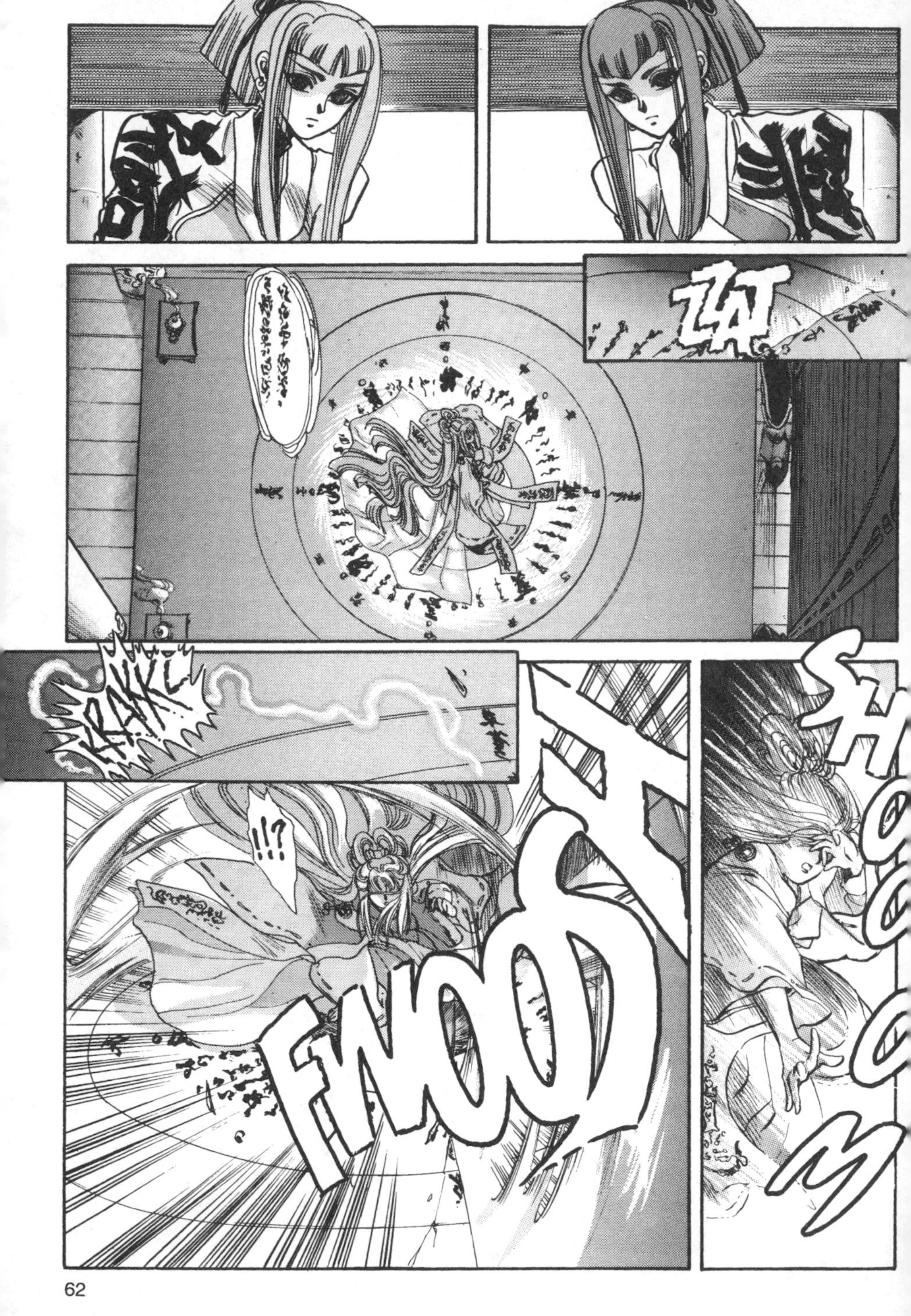
ZAT
KRAKL
!!?
FWOOSH
SHOOOOM

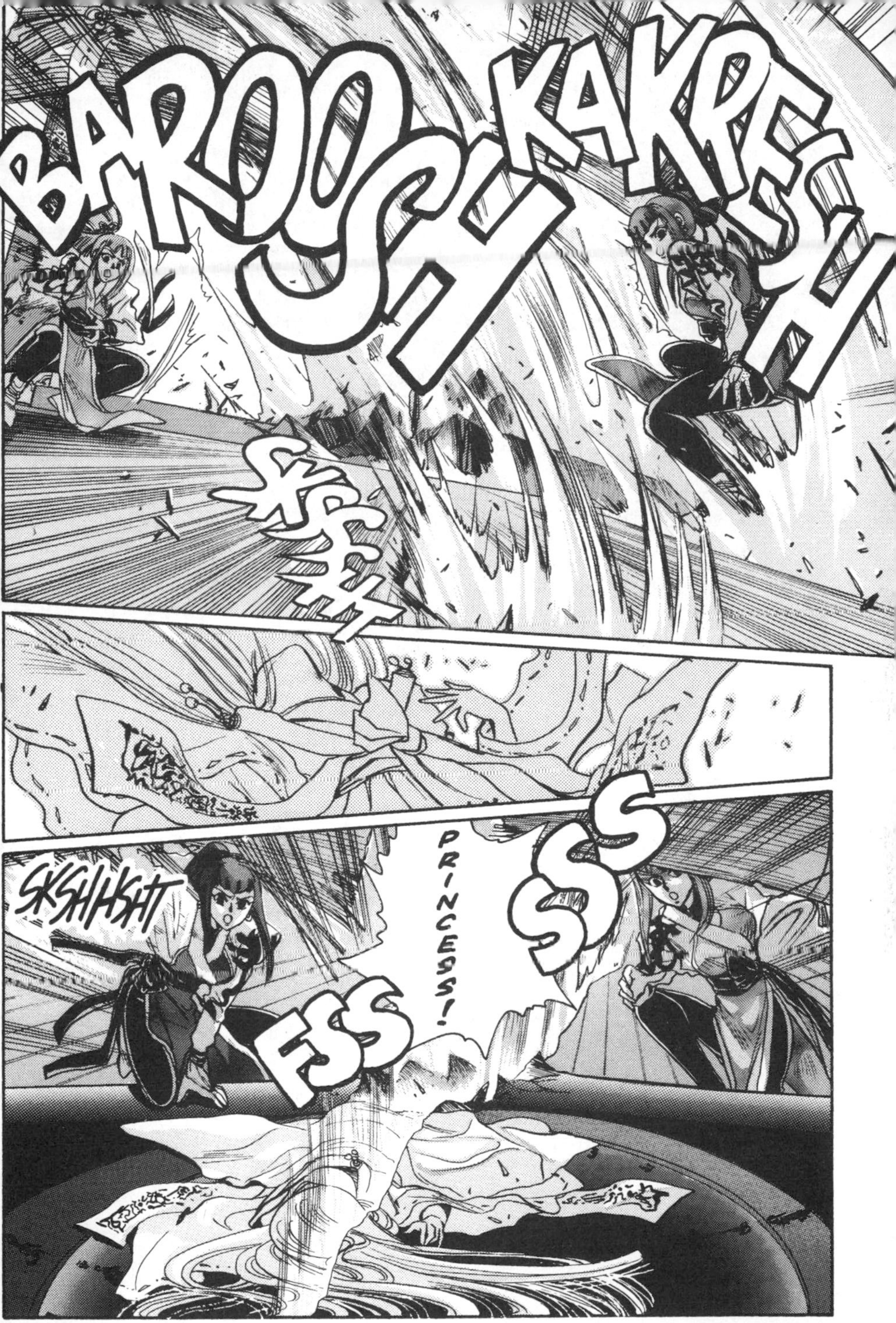
BAROOSH-KAKREESH
SKSHHSHT
PRINCESS!
FSSSSS

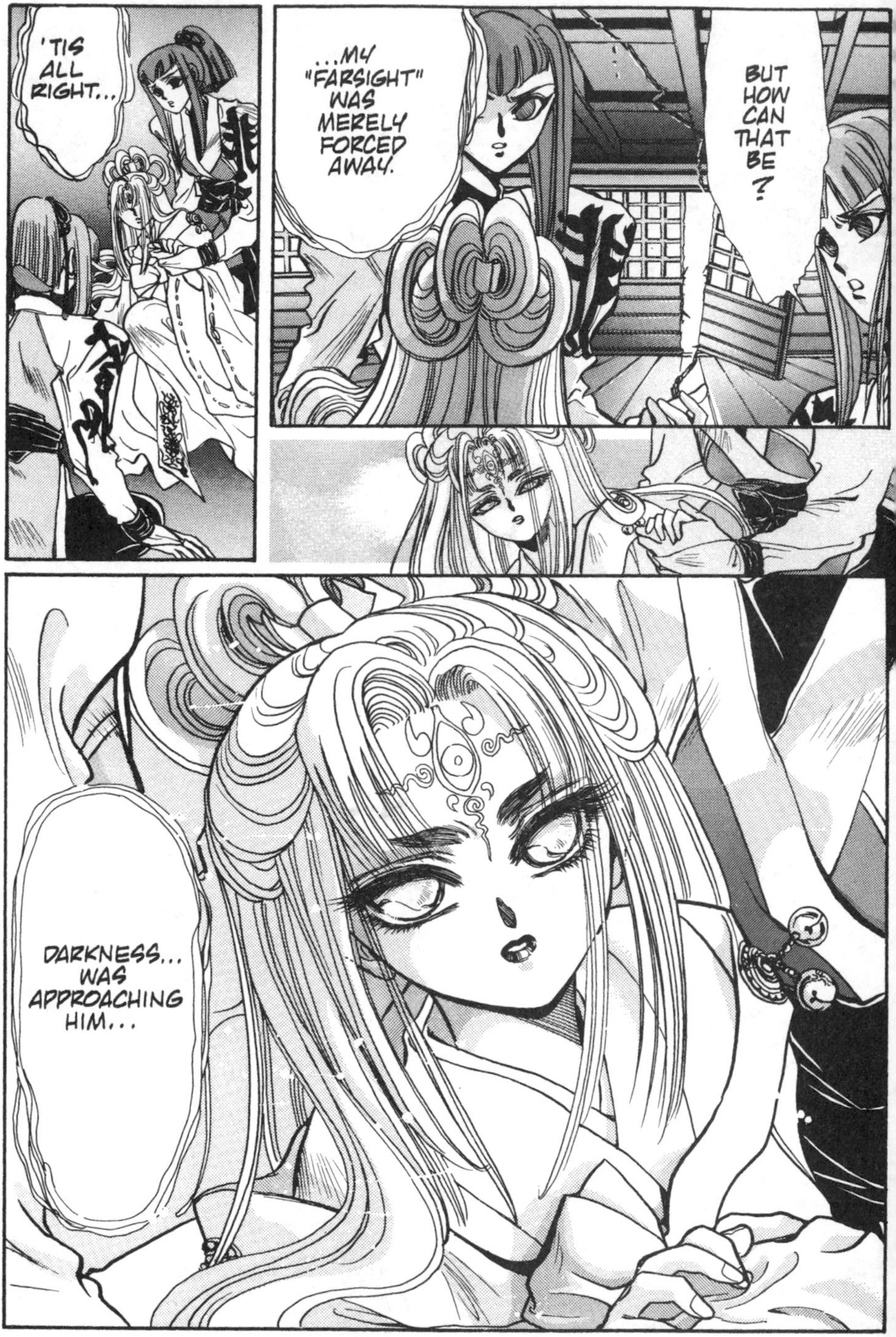
'TIS ALL RIGHT...
...MY "FARSIGHT" WAS MERELY FORCED AWAY.
BUT HOW CAN THAT BE?
DARKNESS... WAS APPROACHING HIM...

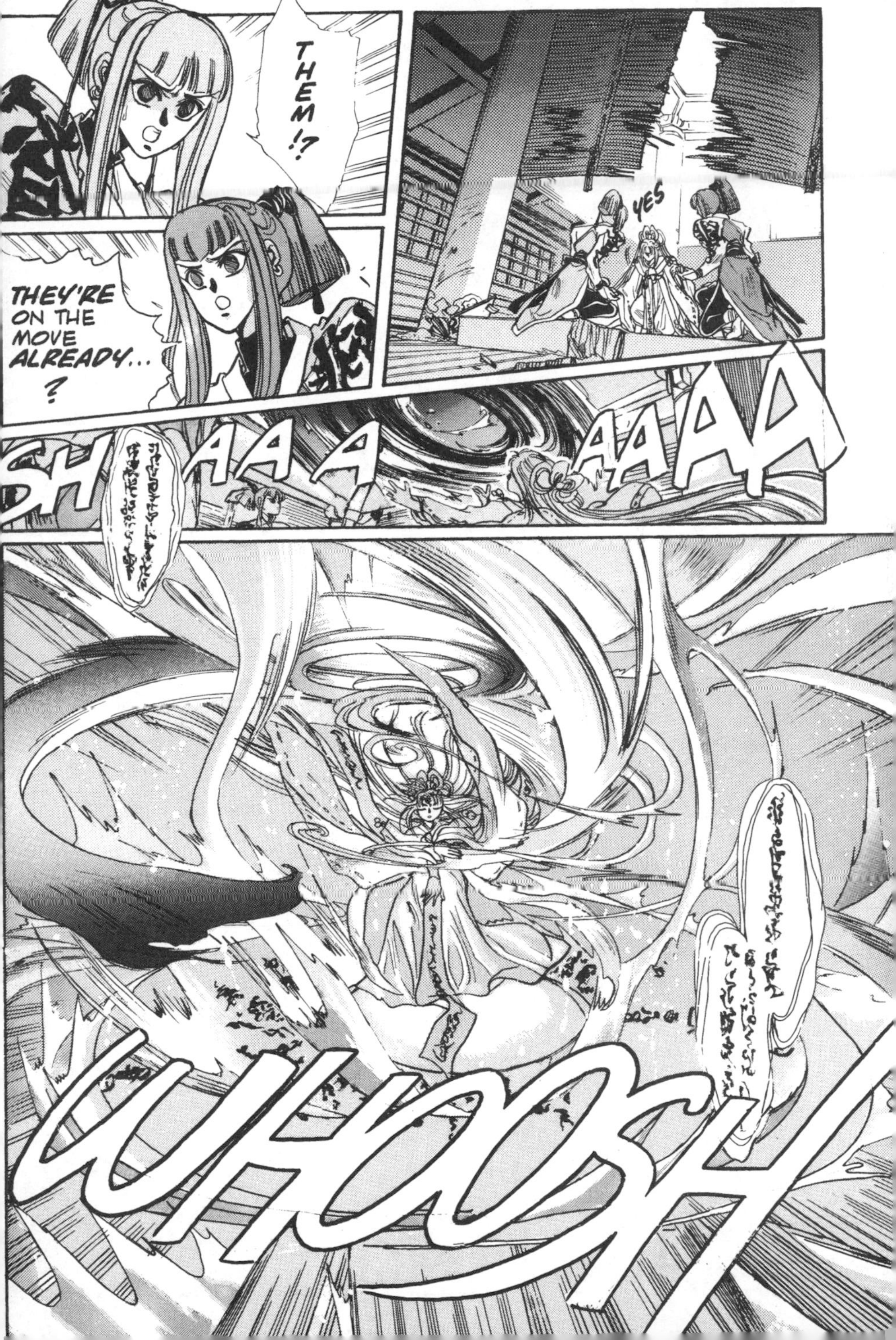

THEM!?
THEY'RE ON THE MOVE ALREADY...?
YES
SHAAAAAAAAA
WHUSH

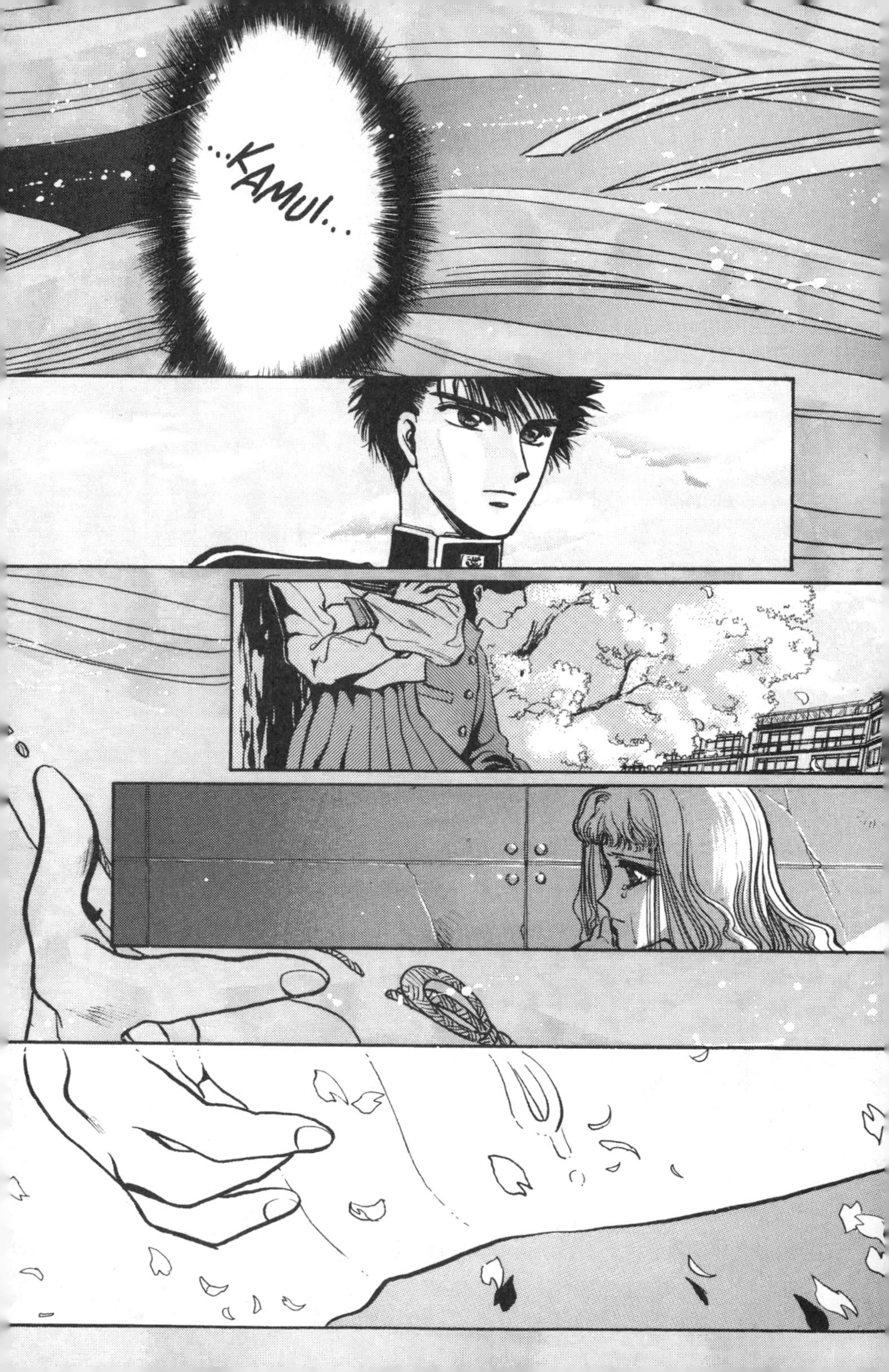
...KAMUI...

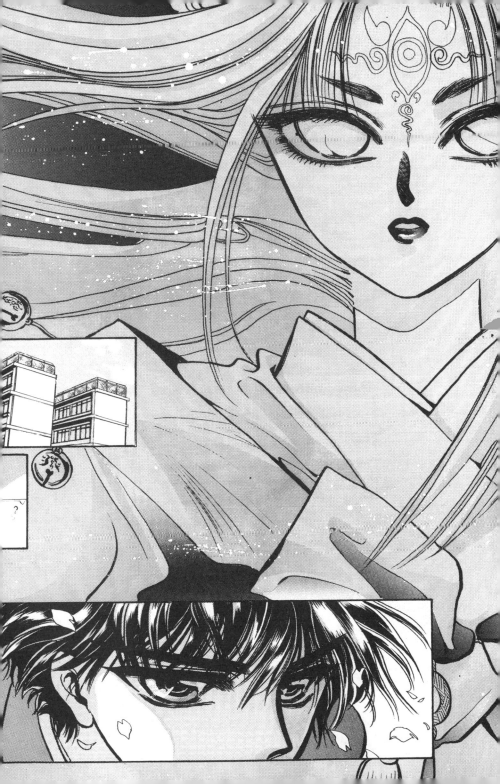

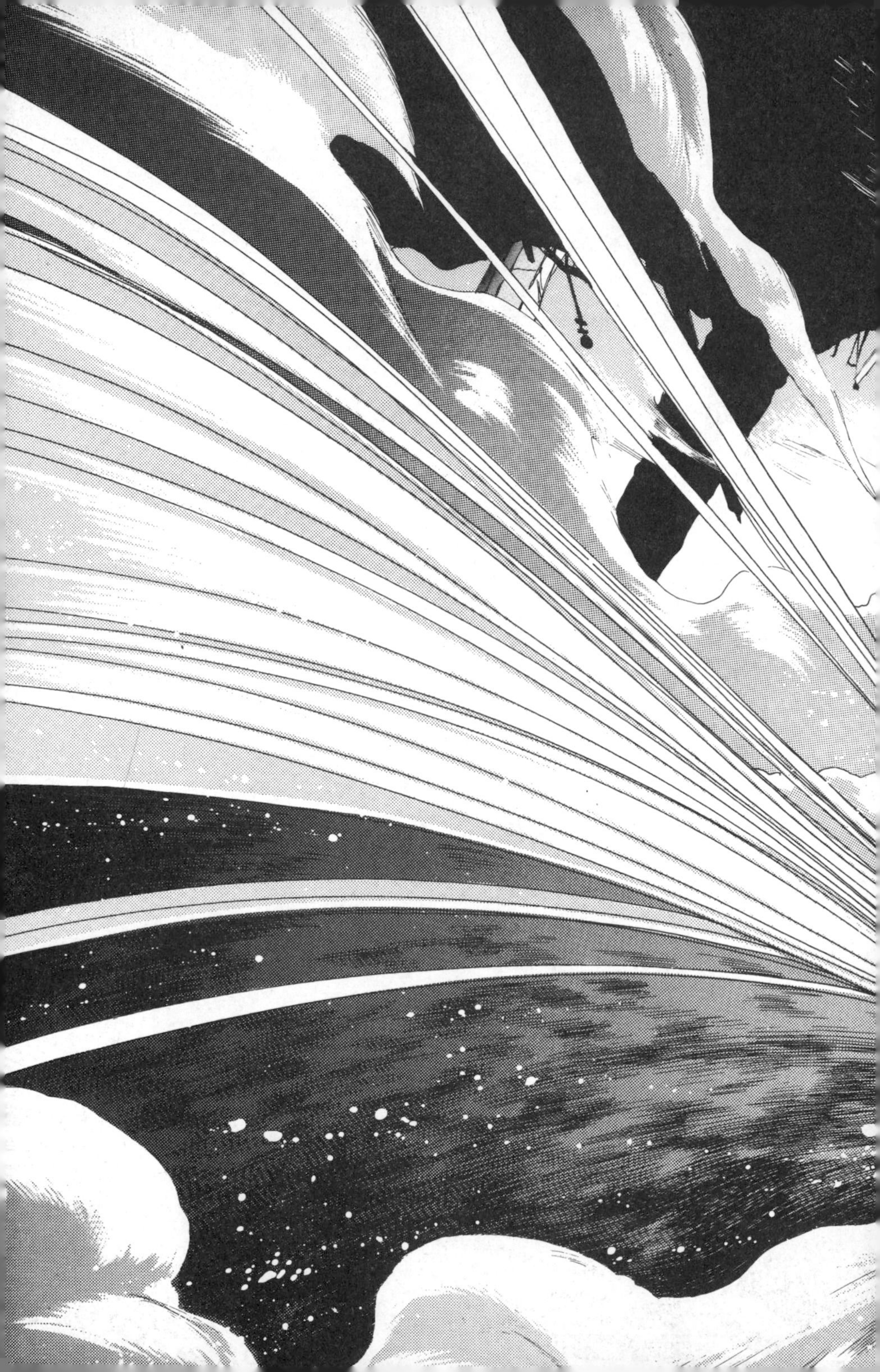

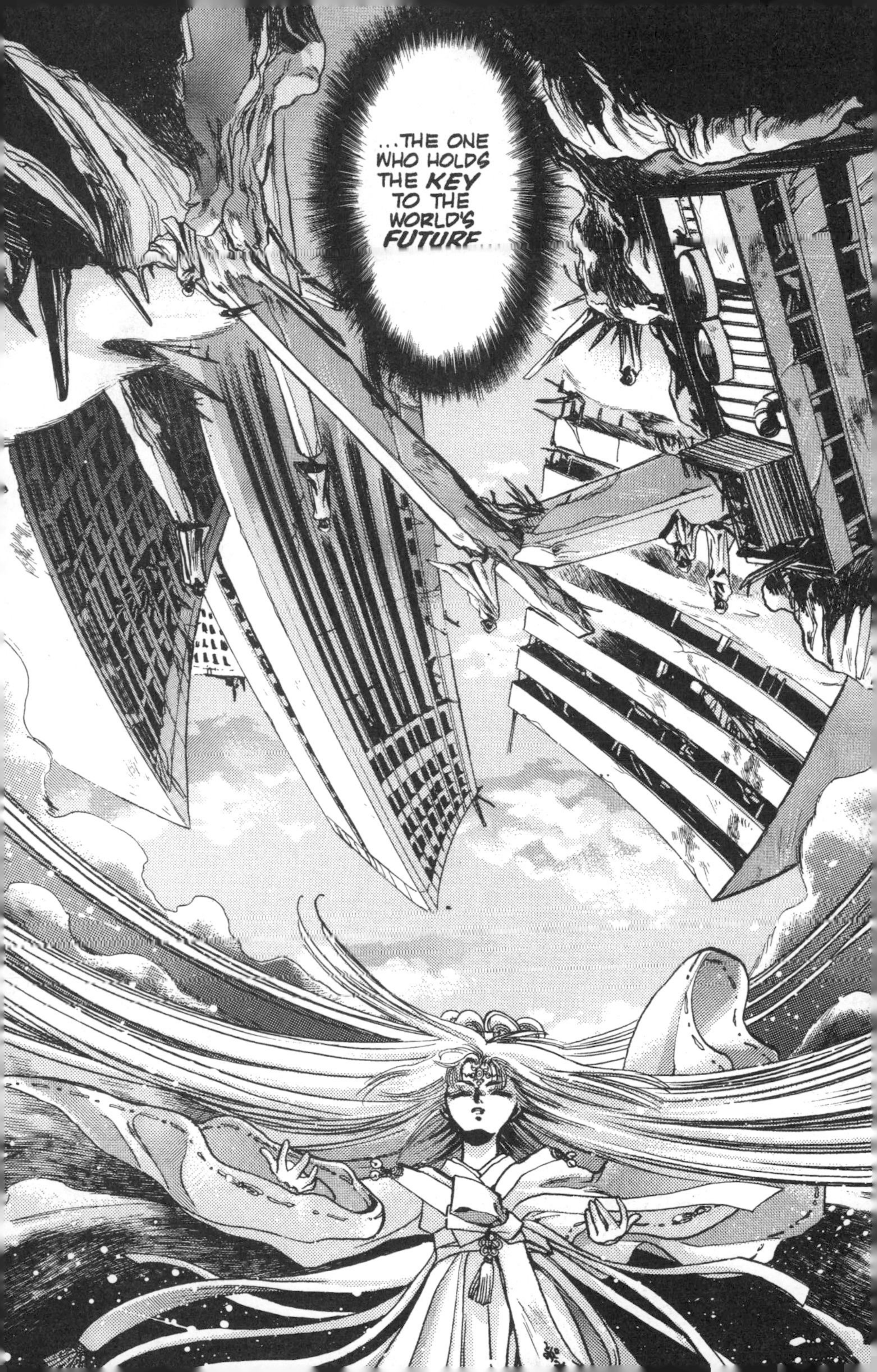
...THE ONE WHO HOLDS THE KEY TO THE WORLD'S FUTURE...

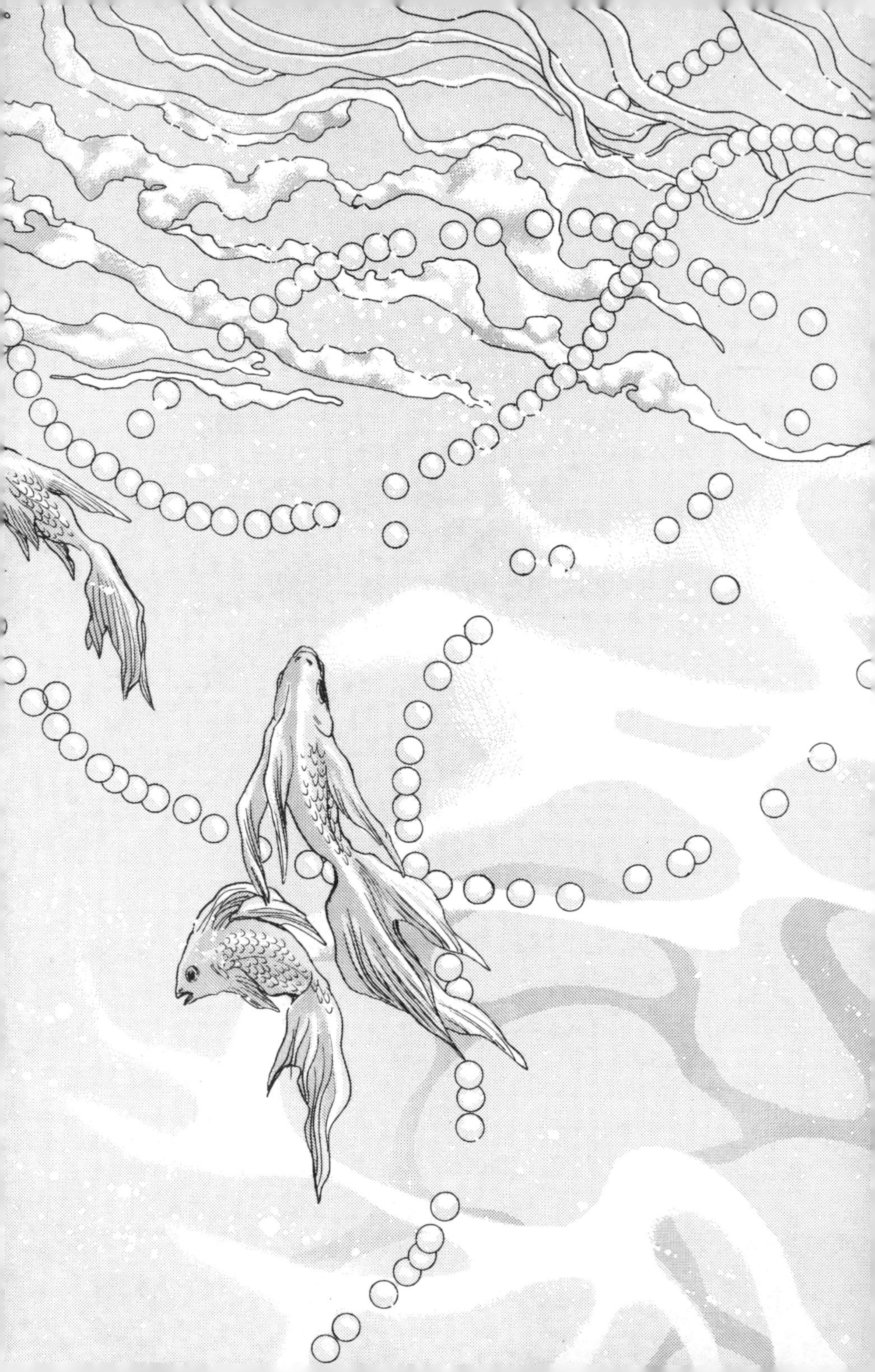

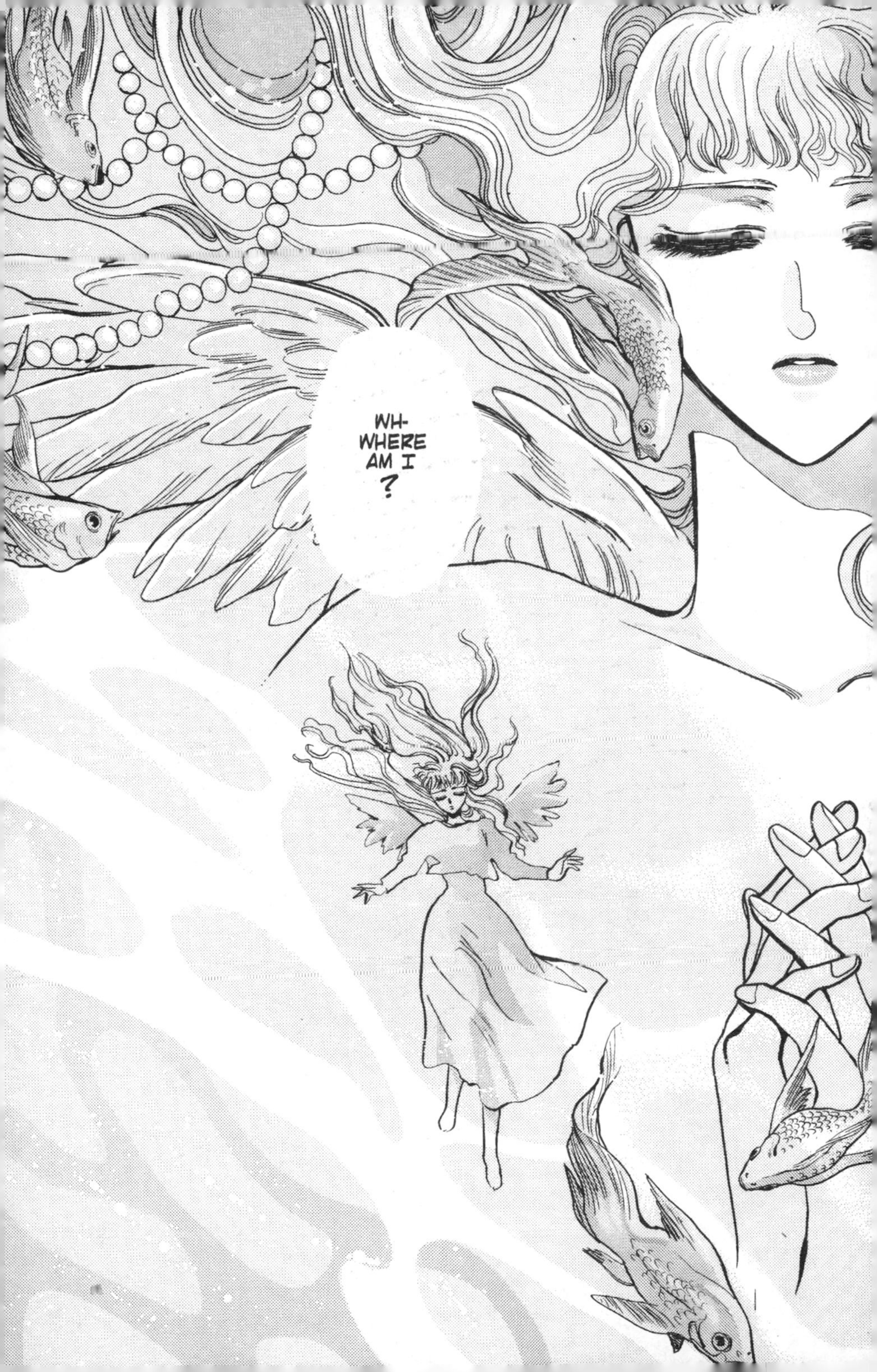
WH-WHERE AM I?

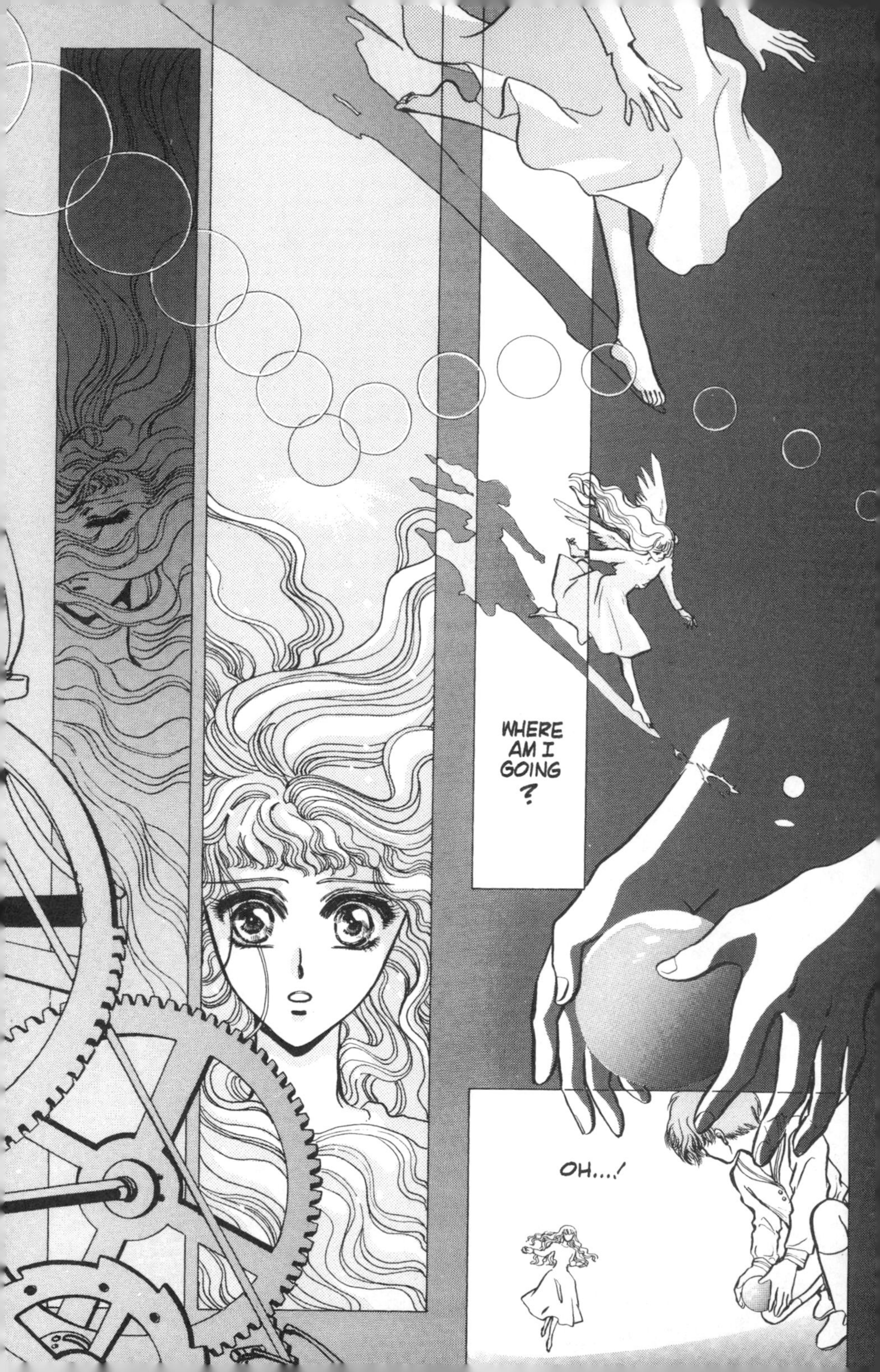
WHERE AM I GOING?
OH...!

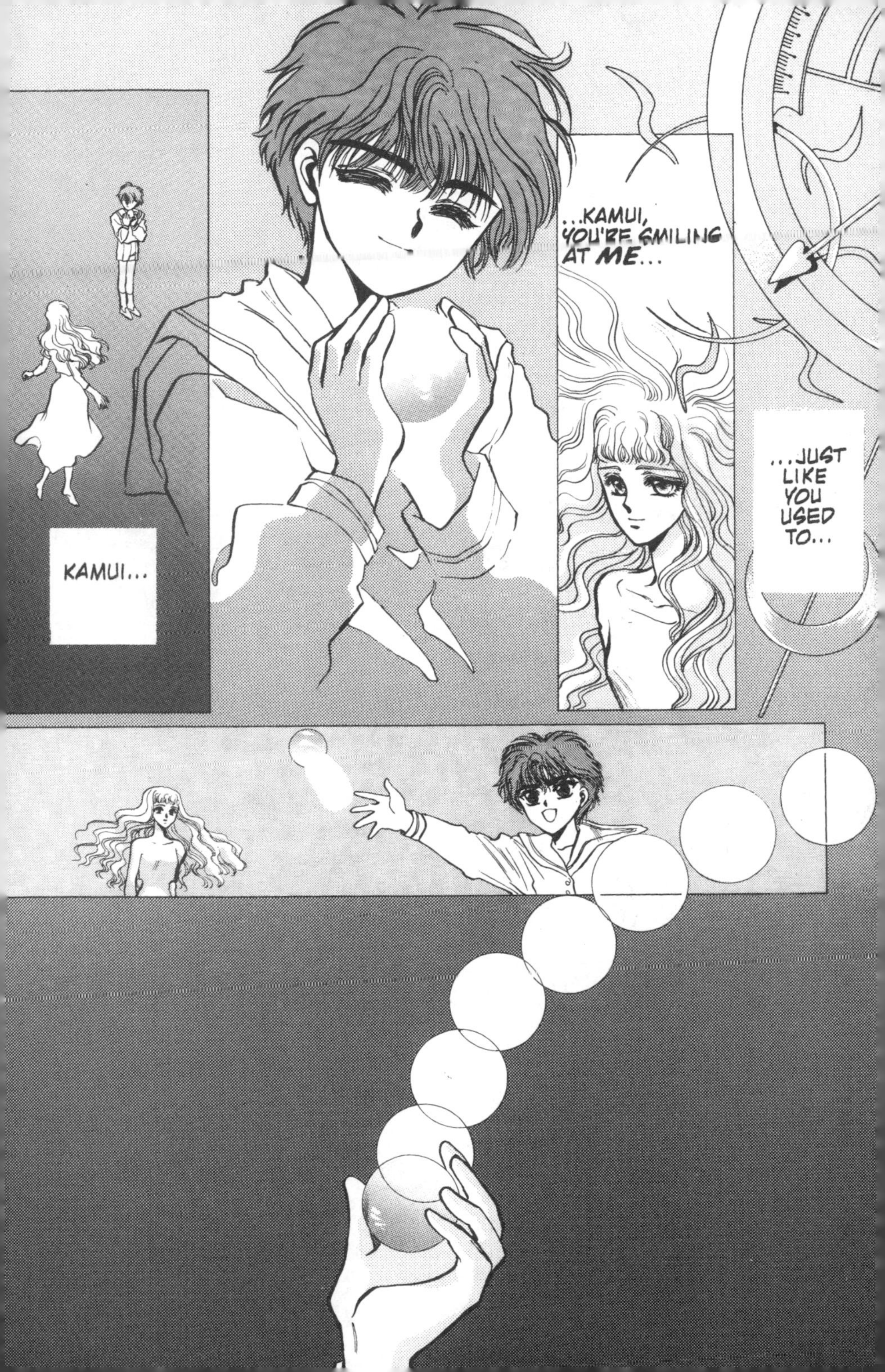
KAMUI...
...KAMUI, YOU'RE SMILING AT ME...
...JUST LIKE YOU USED TO...

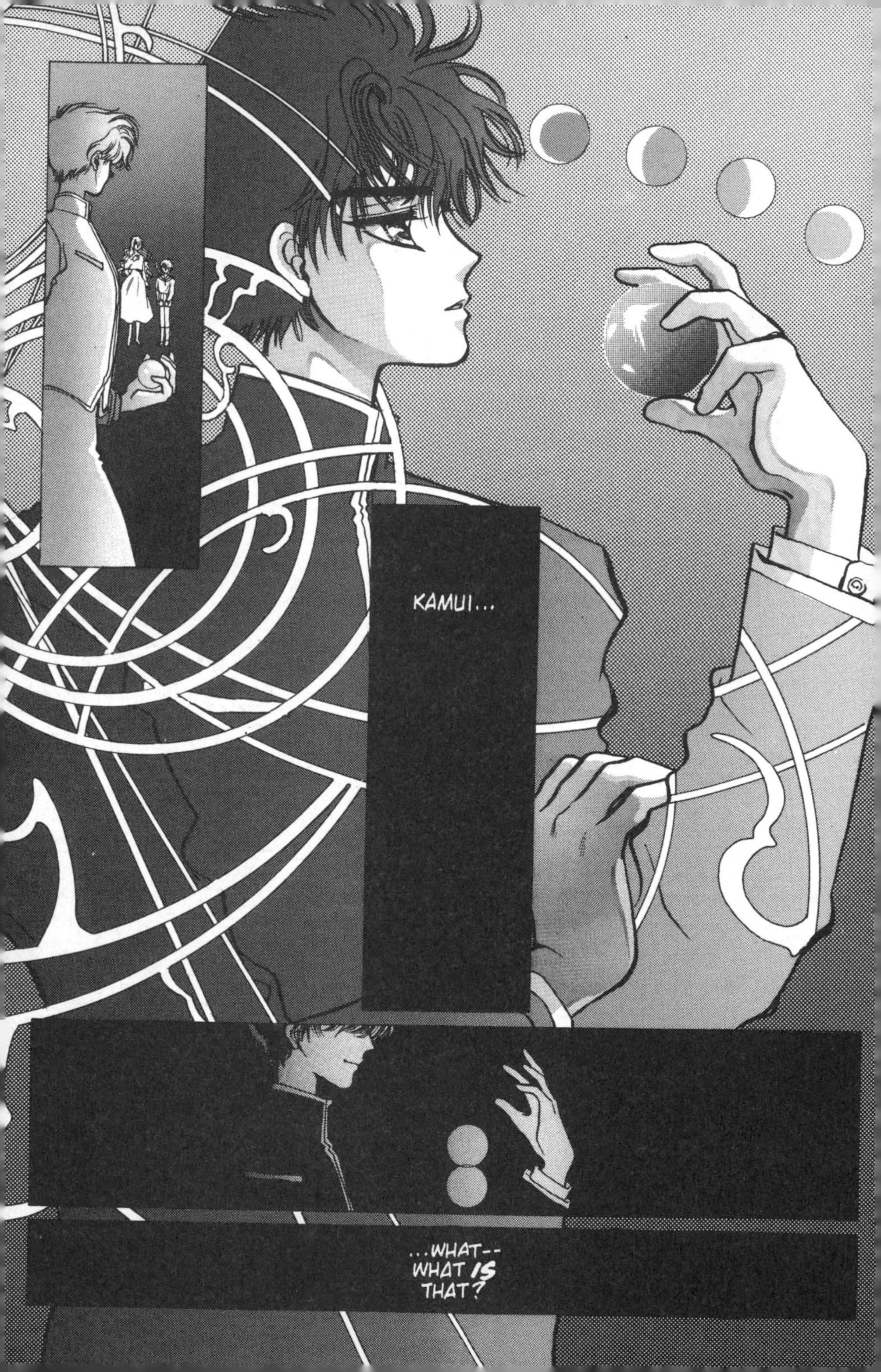
KAMUI...
...WHAT--
WHAT IS
THAT?

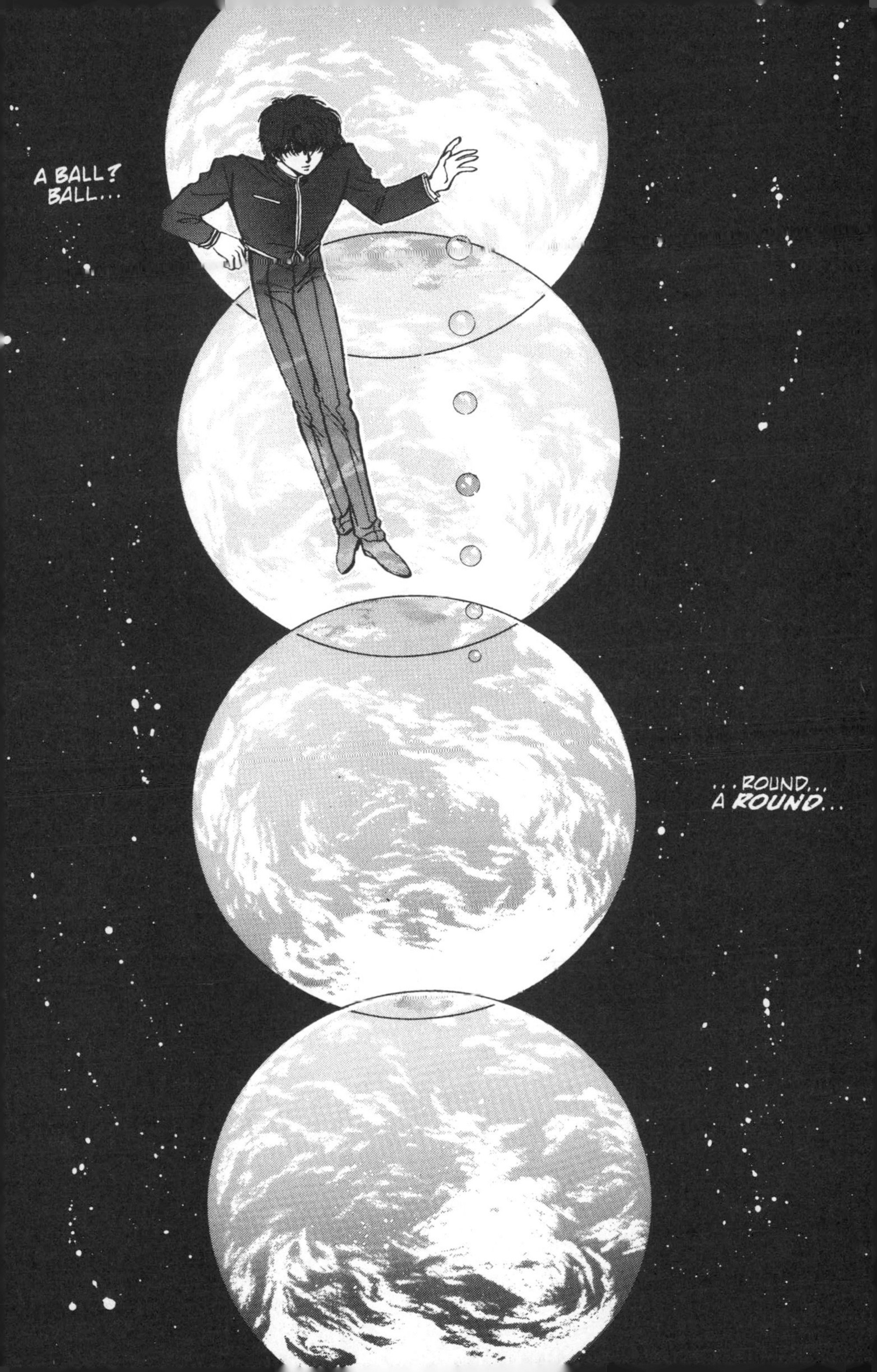
A BALL? BALL...
...ROUND... A ROUND...

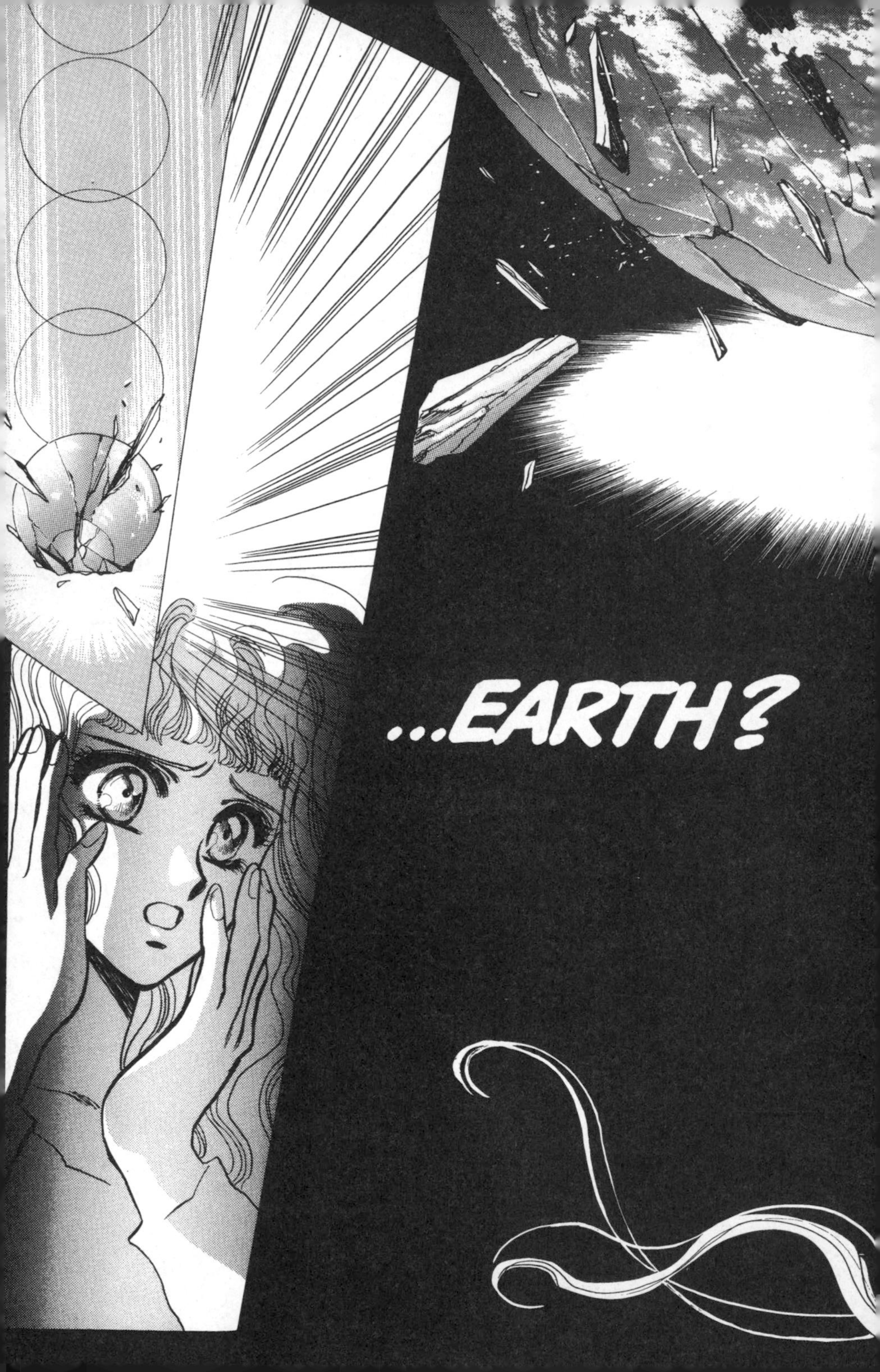
...EARTH?

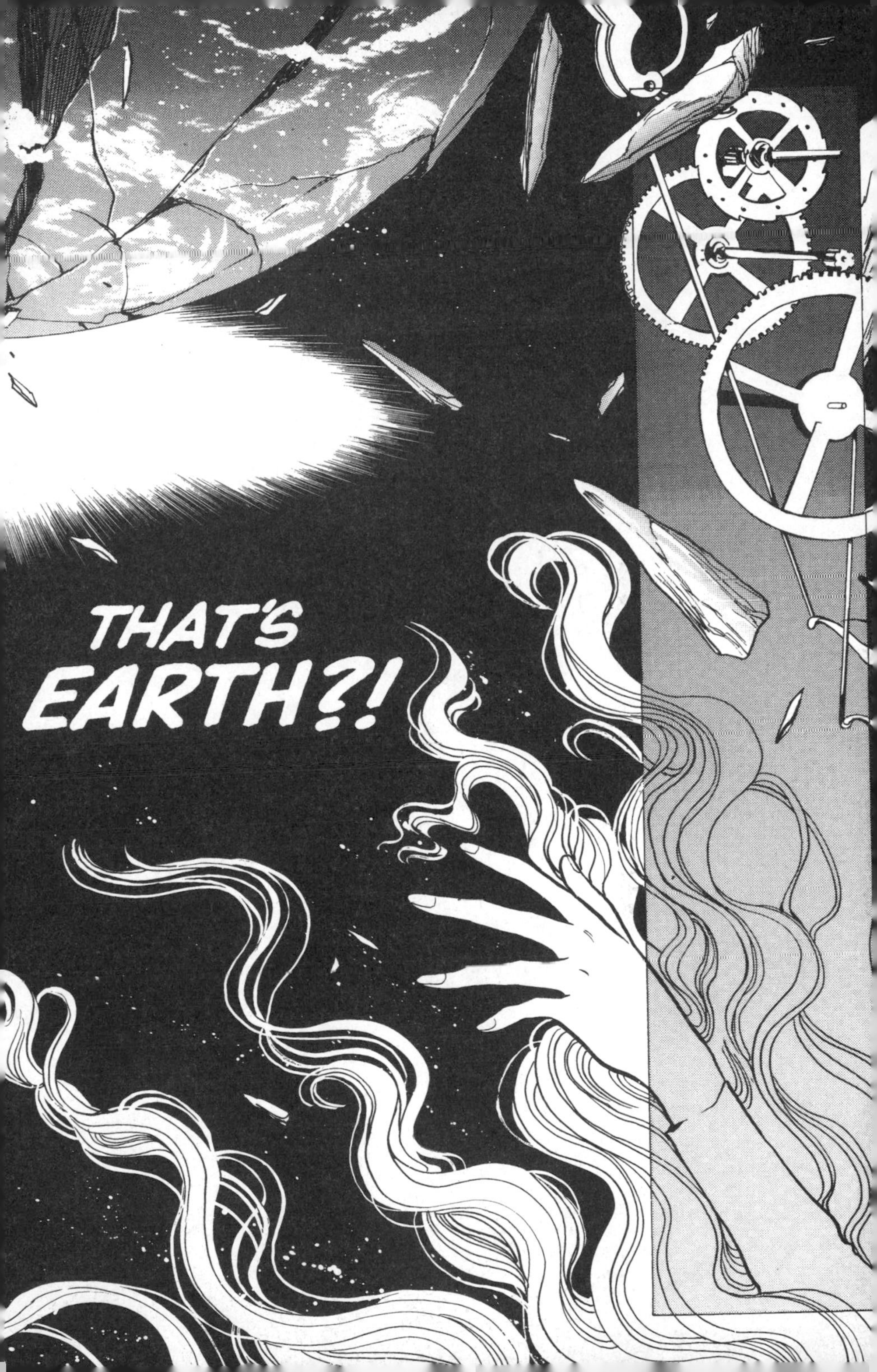
THAT'S EARTH?!

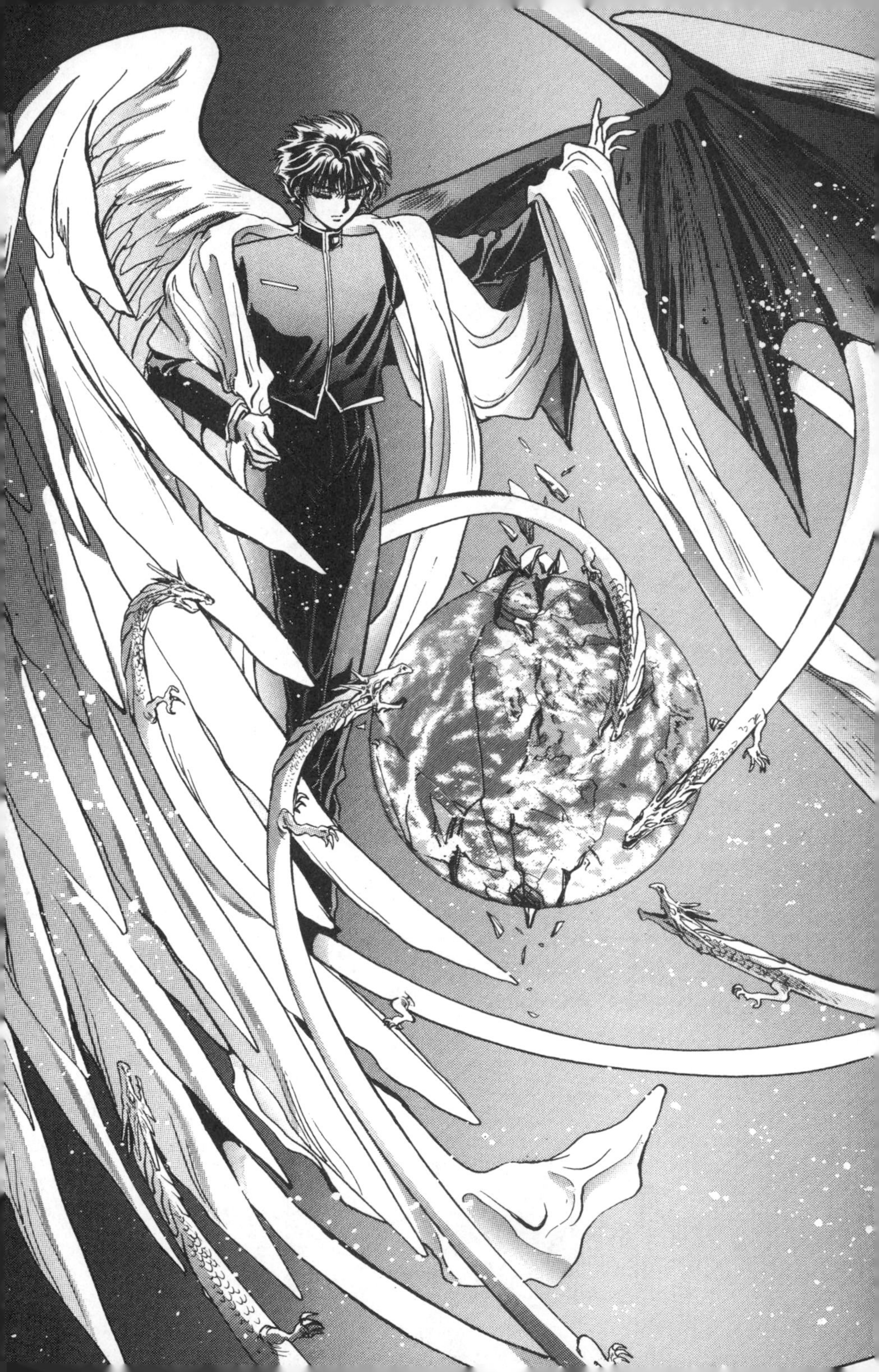

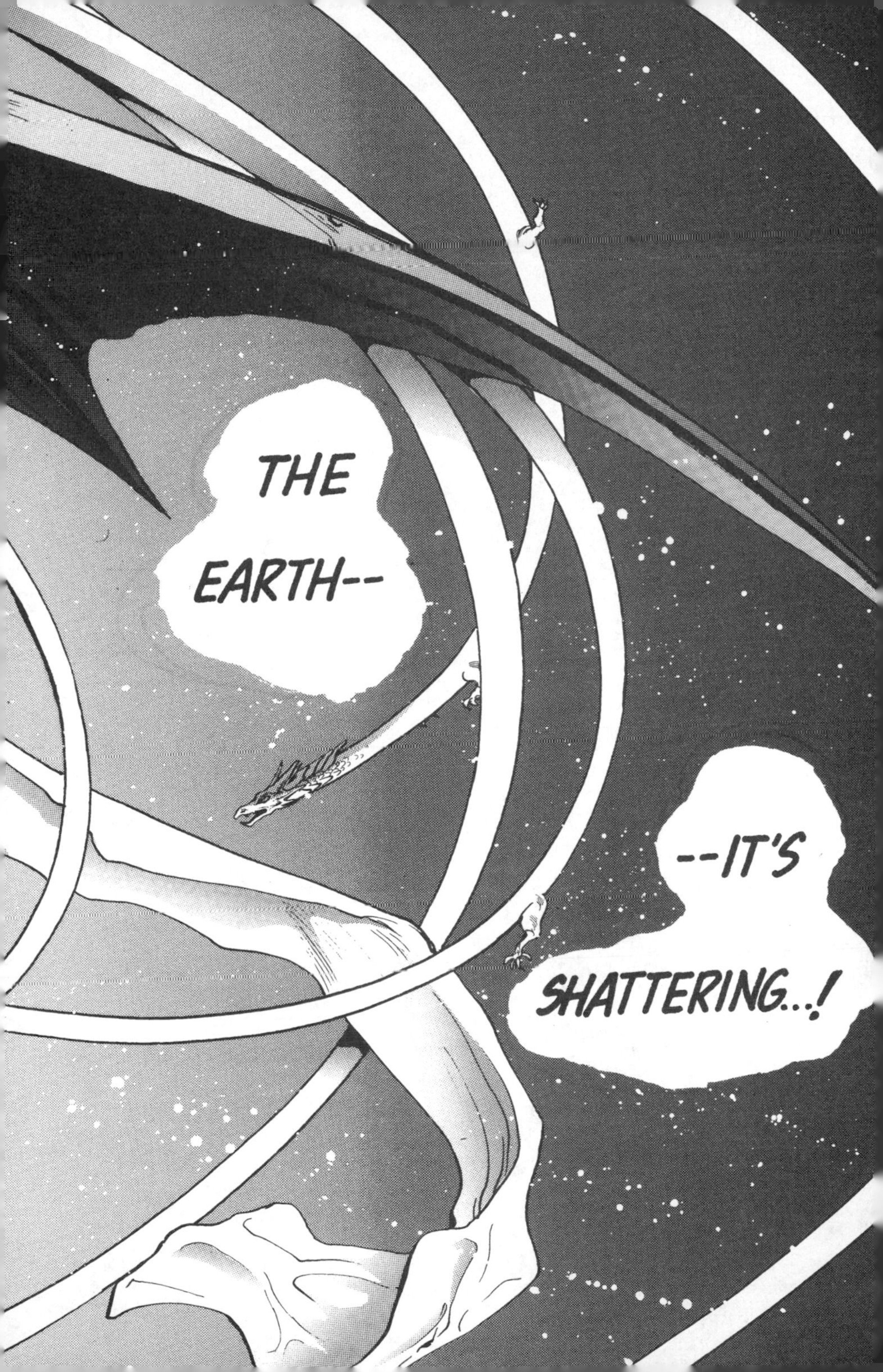
THE EARTH--
--IT'S SHATTERING..!

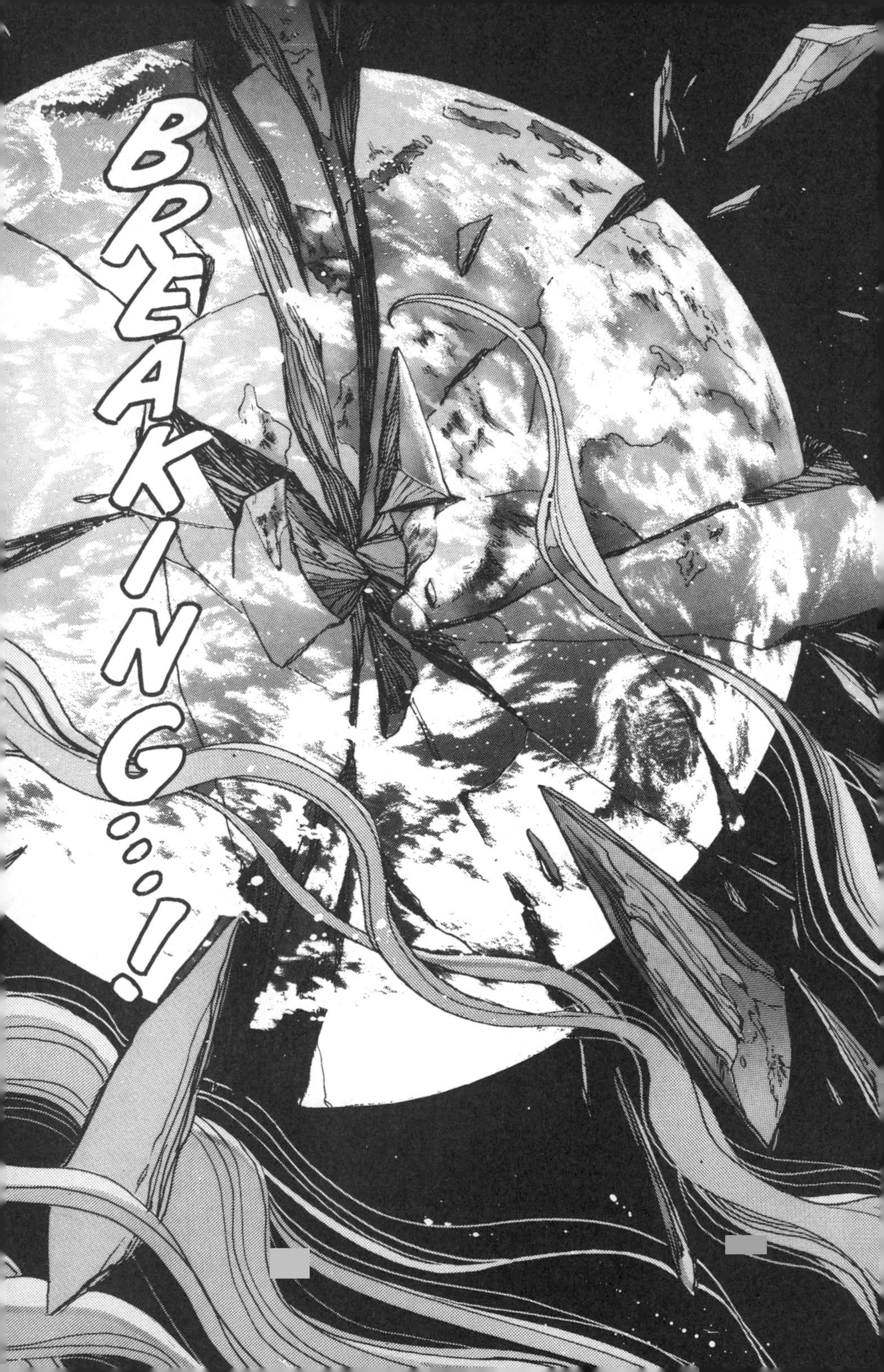
BREAKING...!

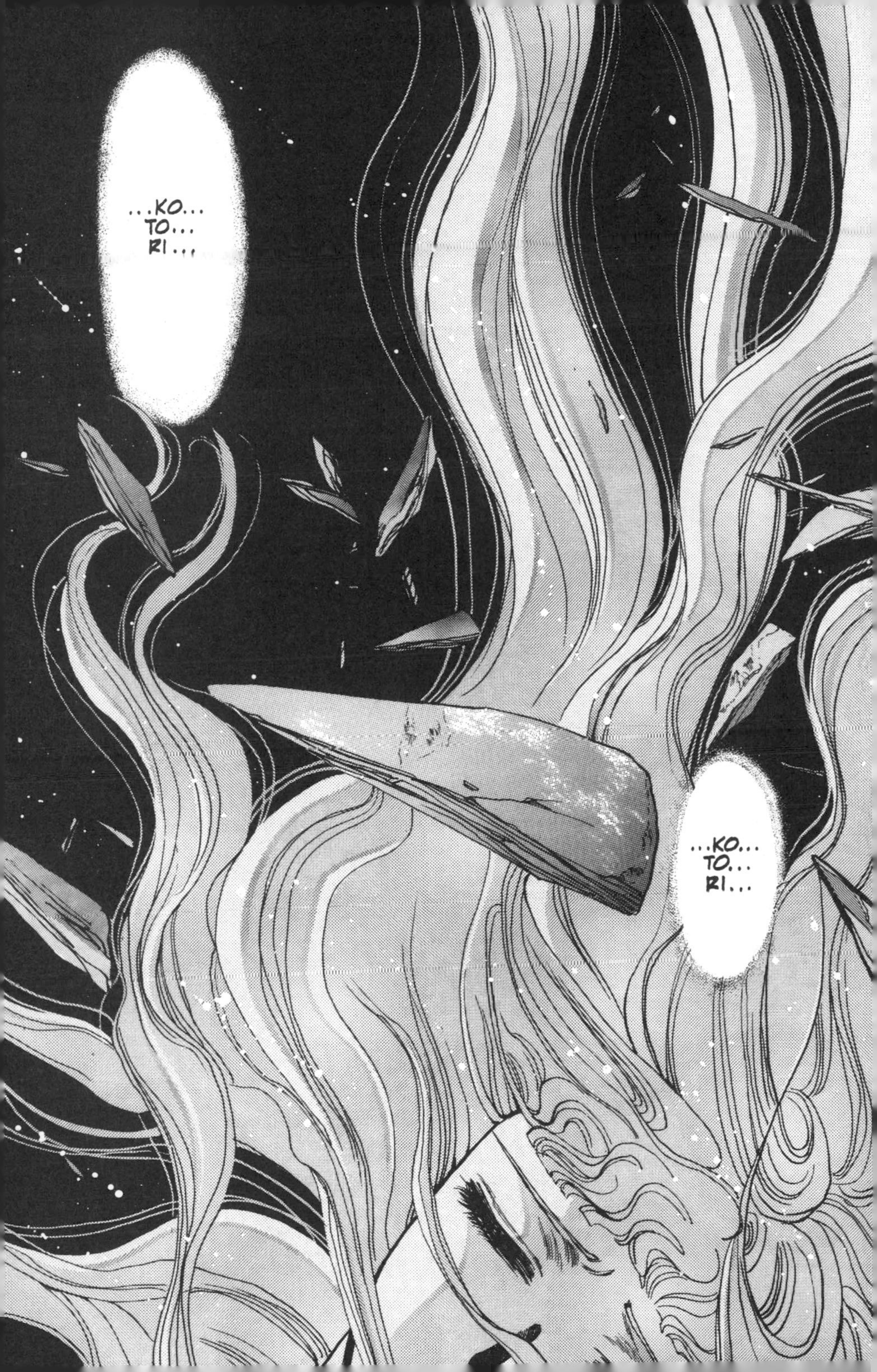
...KO... TO... RI...
...KO... TO... RI...

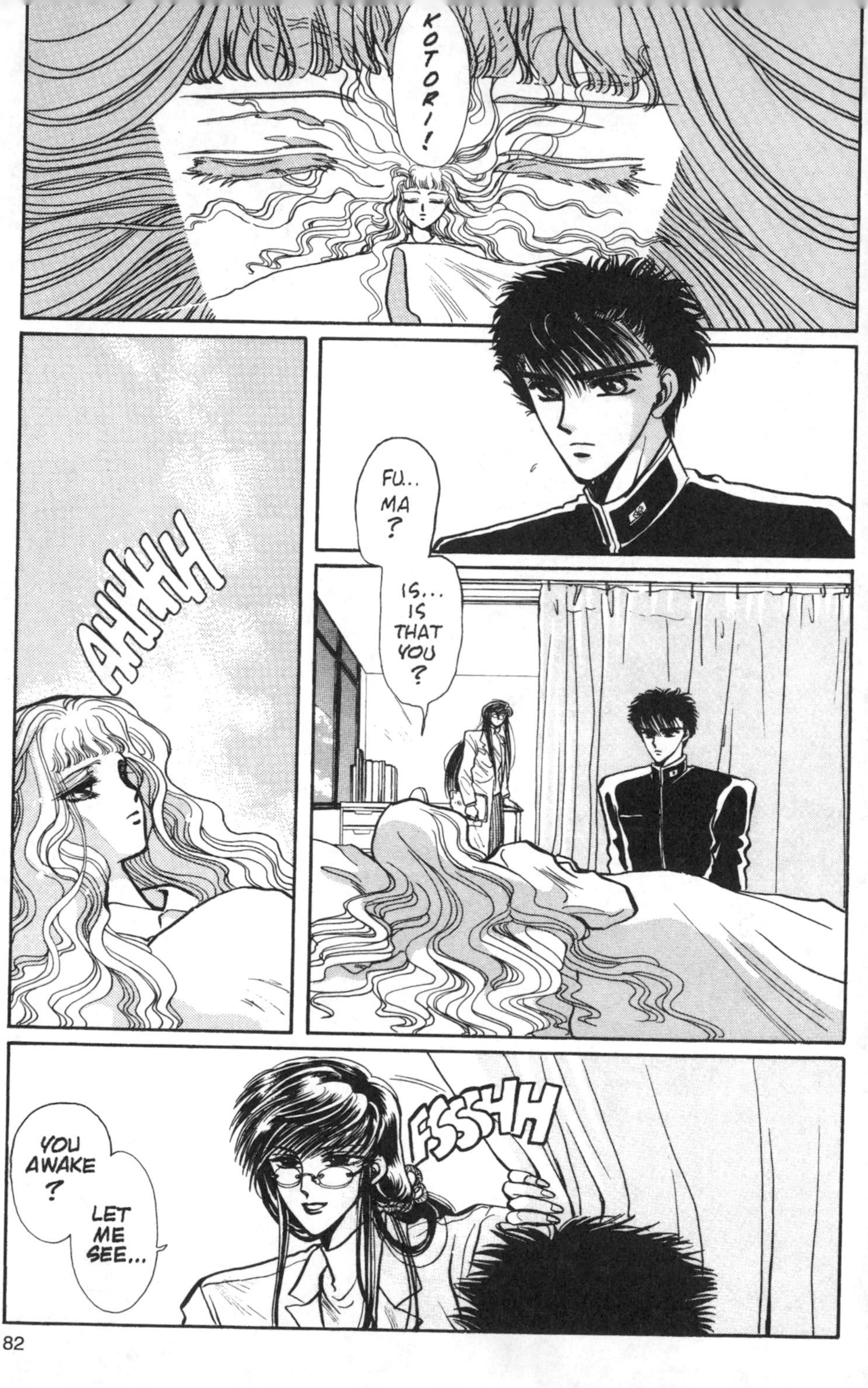
KOTORI!!
AHHHH
FU... MA?
IS... IS THAT YOU?
YOU AWAKE?
LET ME SEE...
FSSSHH

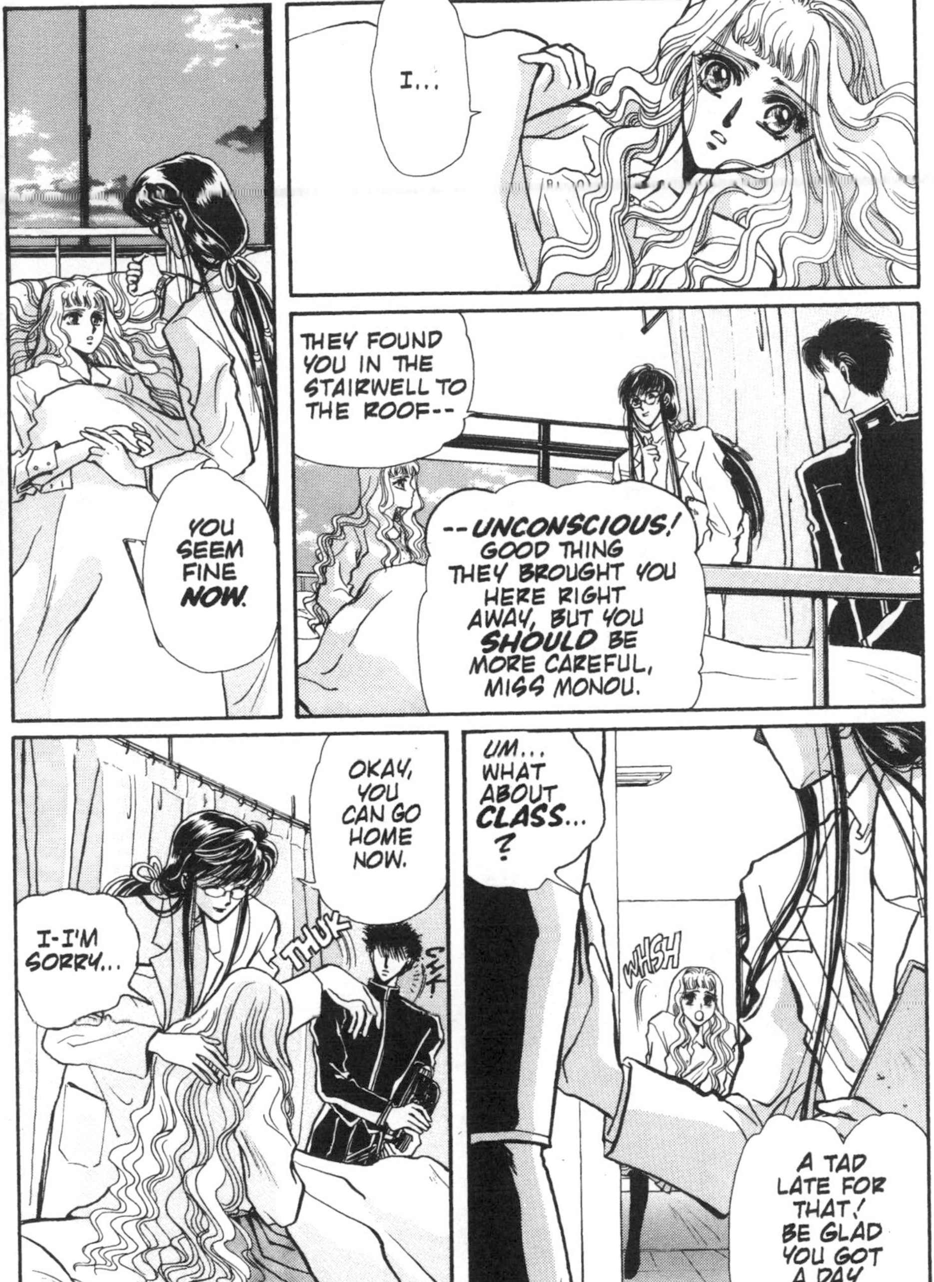
YOU SEEM FINE NOW.
I...
THEY FOUND YOU IN THE STAIRWELL TO THE ROOF--
--UNCONSCIOUS! GOOD THING THEY BROUGHT YOU HERE RIGHT AWAY, BUT YOU SHOULD BE MORE CAREFUL, MISS MONOU.
OKAY, YOU CAN GO HOME NOW.
I-I'M SORRY...
THUK
CLIK
UM... WHAT ABOUT CLASS...?
WHSH
A TAD LATE FOR THAT! BE GLAD YOU GOT A DAY OFF.

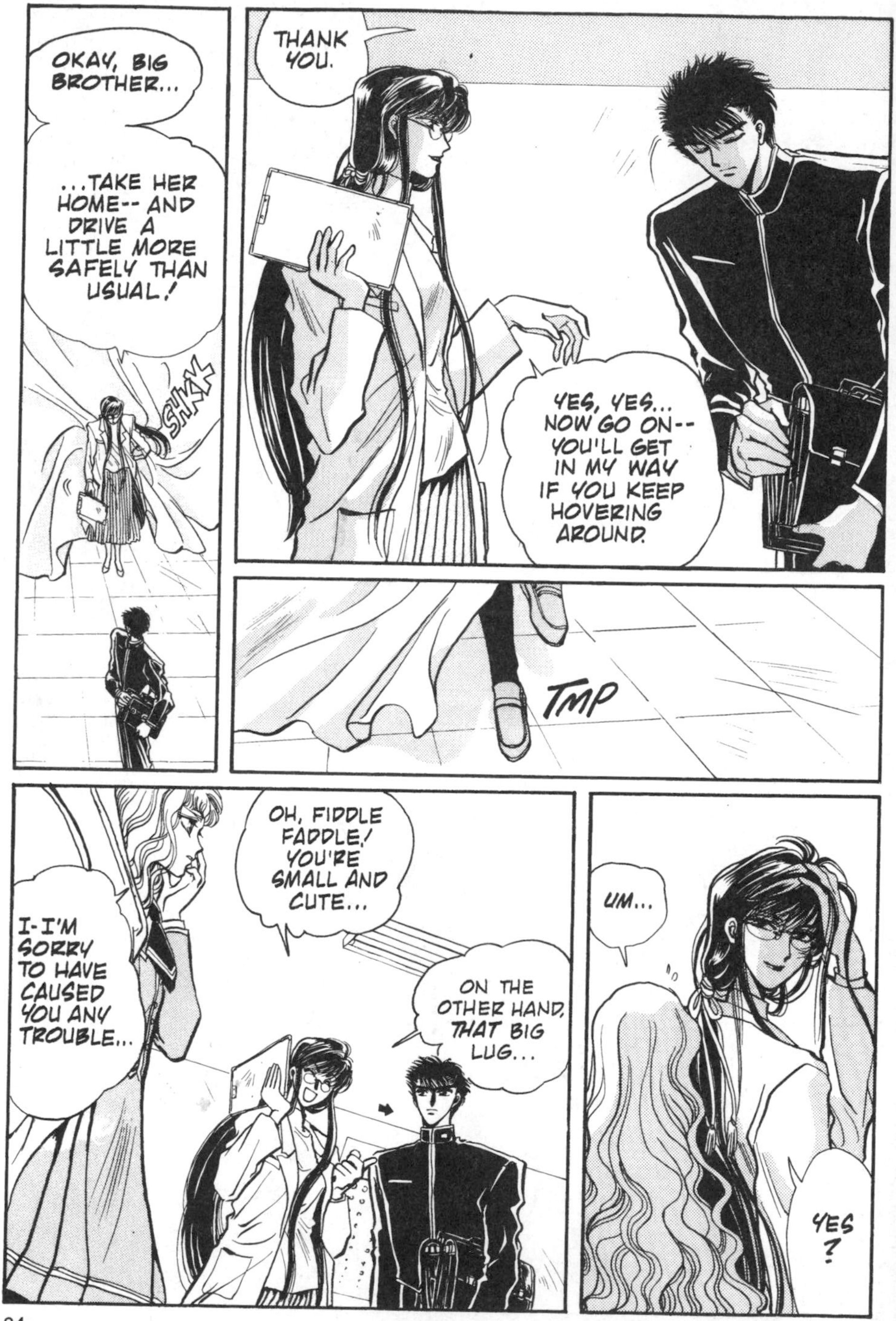

OKAY, BIG BROTHER...
...TAKE HER HOME-- AND DRIVE A LITTLE MORE SAFELY THAN USUAL!
SHAK
THANK YOU.
YES, YES... NOW GO ON-- YOU'LL GET IN MY WAY IF YOU KEEP HOVERING AROUND.
TMP
I-I'M SORRY TO HAVE CAUSED YOU ANY TROUBLE...
OH, FIDDLE FADDLE! YOU'RE SMALL AND CUTE...
ON THE OTHER HAND, THAT BIG LUG...
UM...
YES?

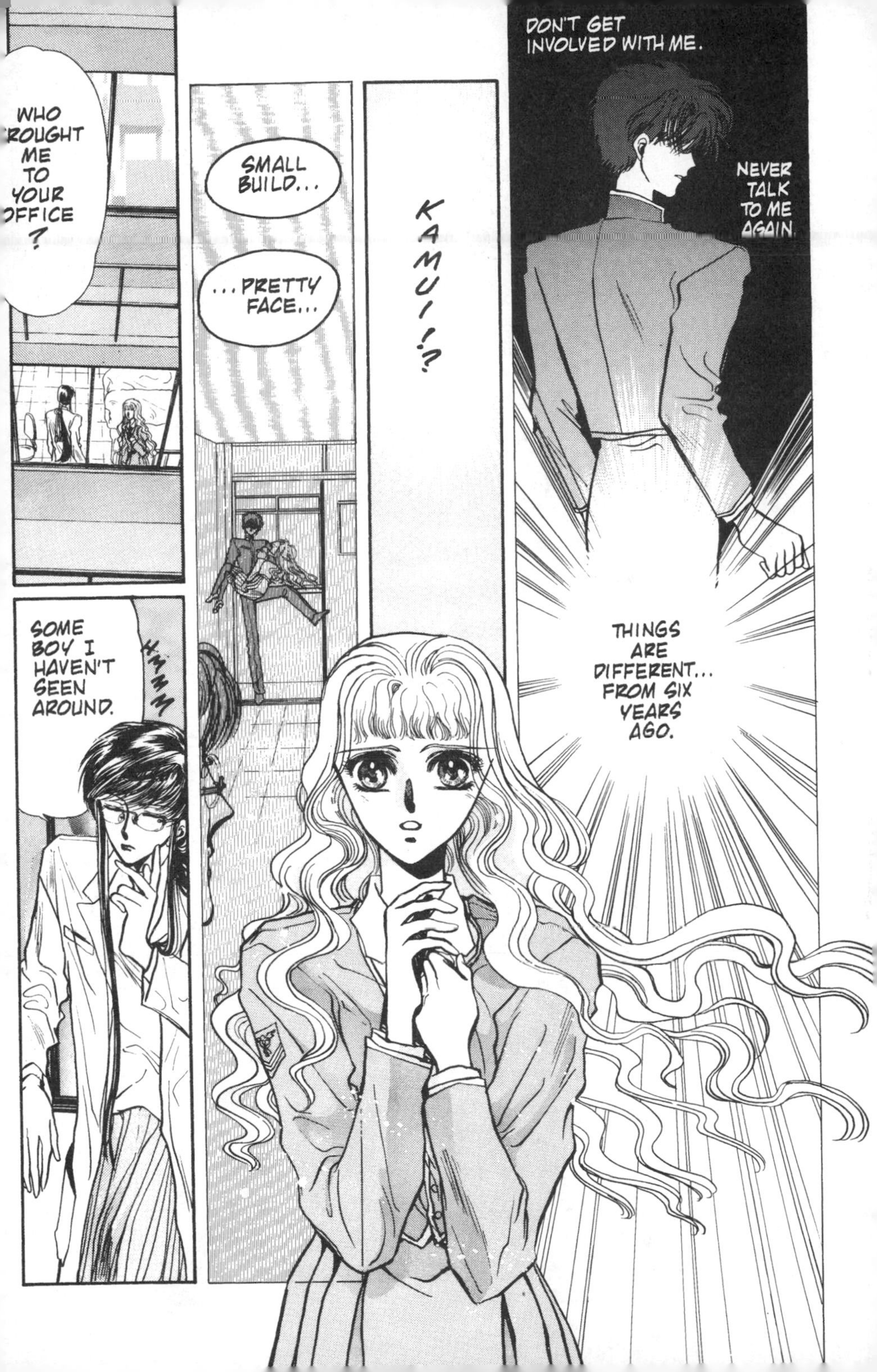
WHO BROUGHT ME TO YOUR OFFICE?
SOME BOY I HAVEN'T SEEN AROUND.
HMMMM
SMALL BUILD...
...PRETTY FACE...
KAMUI!?
DON'T GET INVOLVED WITH ME.
NEVER TALK TO ME AGAIN.
THINGS ARE DIFFERENT... FROM SIX YEARS AGO.

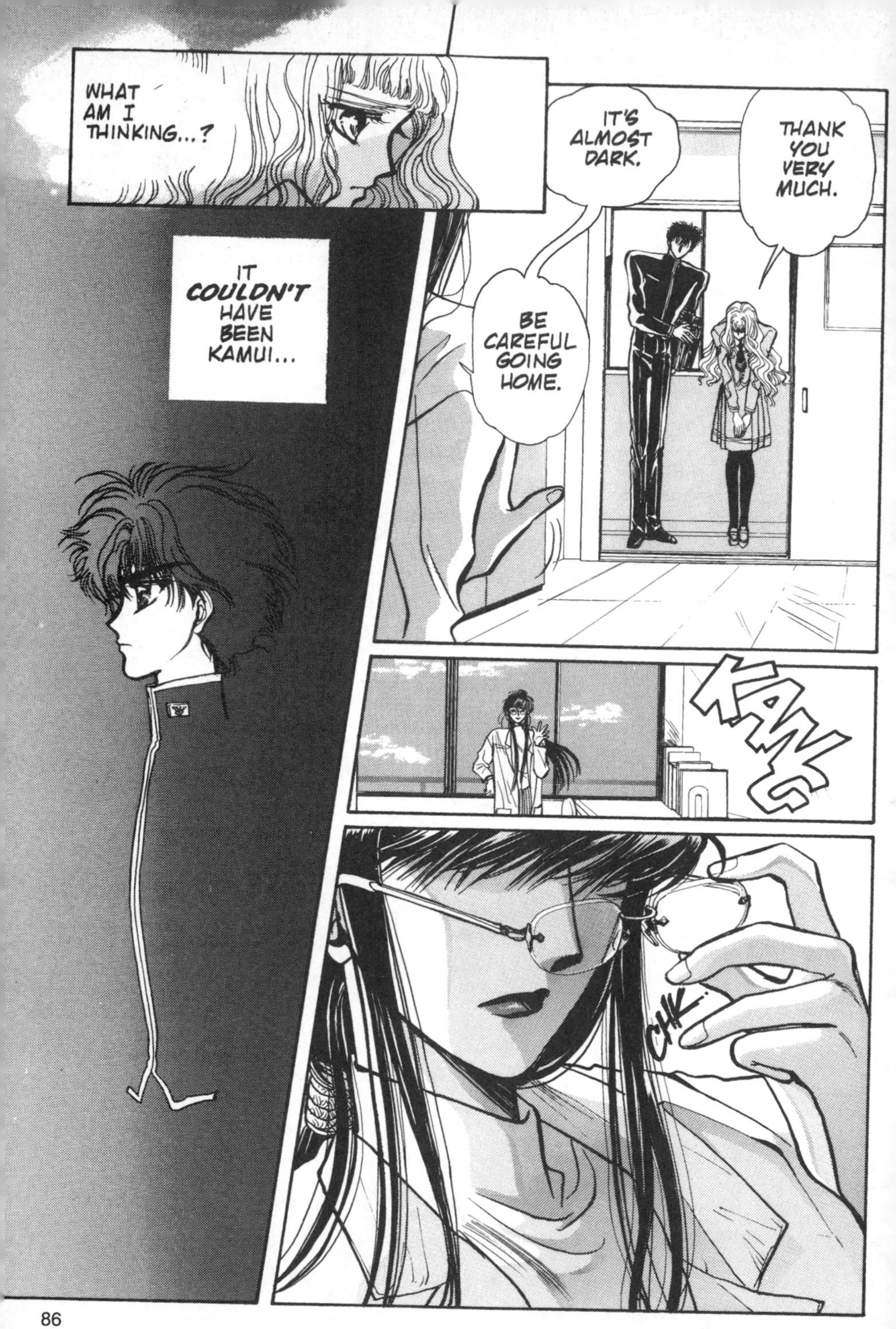
WHAT AM I THINKING...?
IT *COULDN'T* HAVE BEEN KAMUI...
IT'S ALMOST DARK.
BE CAREFUL GOING HOME.
THANK YOU VERY MUCH.
KANG
CHK

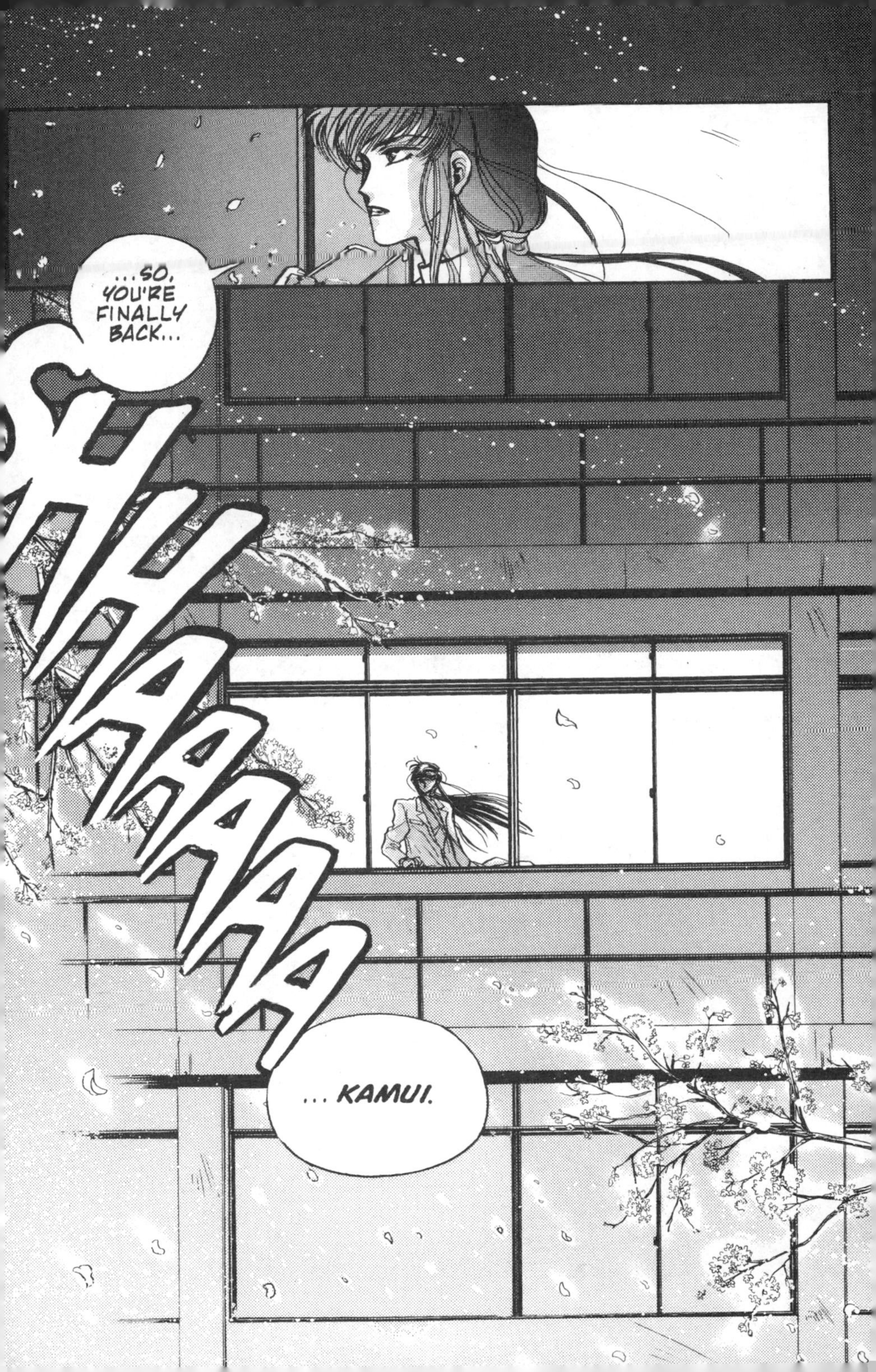
...SO, YOU'RE FINALLY BACK...
HHAAAAAA
... KAMUI.

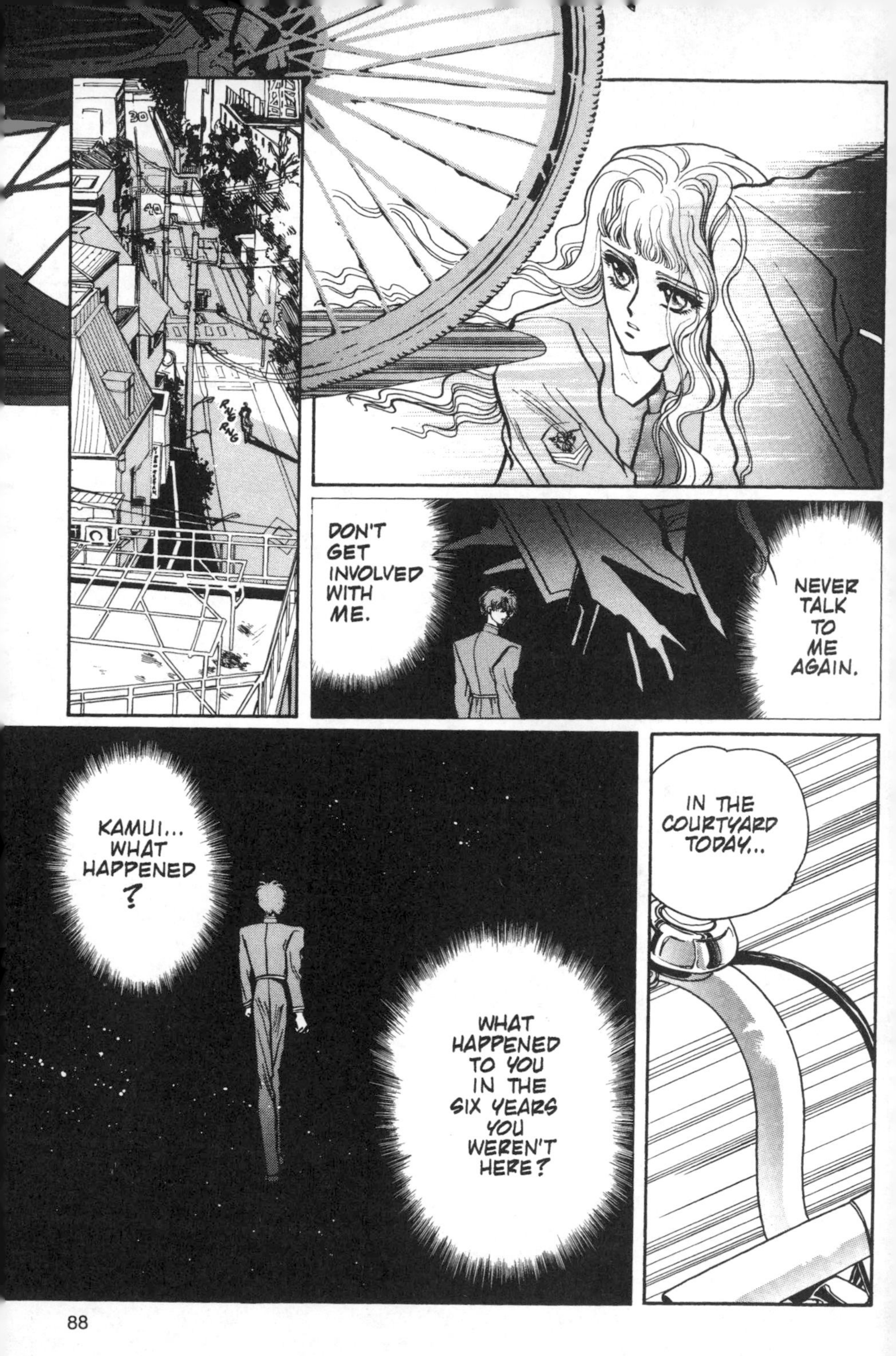
RNG RNG
DON'T GET INVOLVED WITH ME.
NEVER TALK TO ME AGAIN.
KAMUI... WHAT HAPPENED?
WHAT HAPPENED TO YOU IN THE SIX YEARS YOU WEREN'T HERE?
IN THE COURTYARD TODAY...

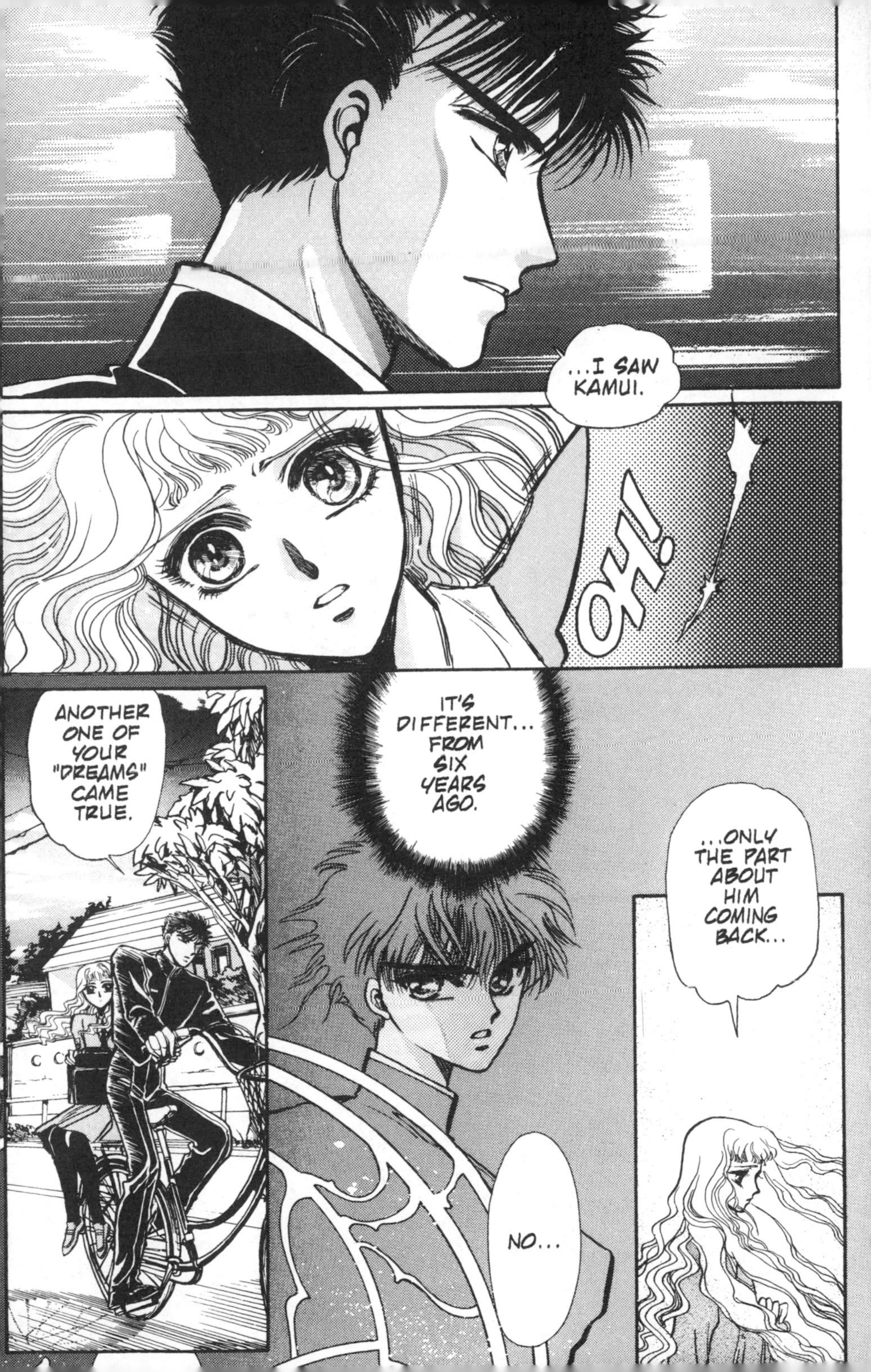
...I SAW KAMUI.
OH!!
ANOTHER ONE OF YOUR "DREAMS" CAME TRUE.
IT'S DIFFERENT... FROM SIX YEARS AGO.
NO...
...ONLY THE PART ABOUT HIM COMING BACK...

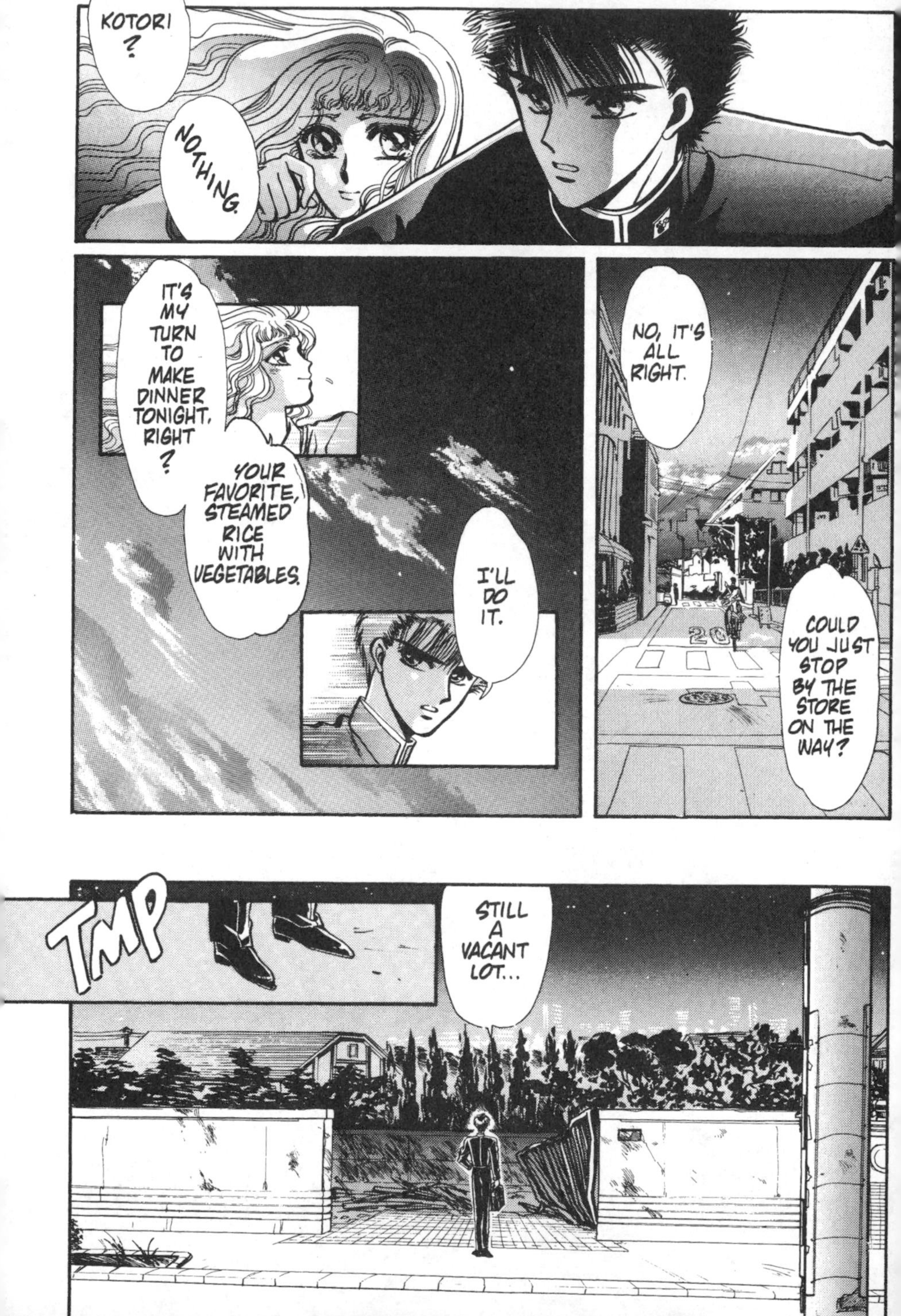

KOTORI?
NOTHING.
IT'S MY TURN TO MAKE DINNER TONIGHT, RIGHT?
YOUR FAVORITE, STEAMED RICE WITH VEGETABLES.
I'LL DO IT.
NO, IT'S ALL RIGHT.
COULD YOU JUST STOP BY THE STORE ON THE WAY?
TMP
STILL A VACANT LOT...

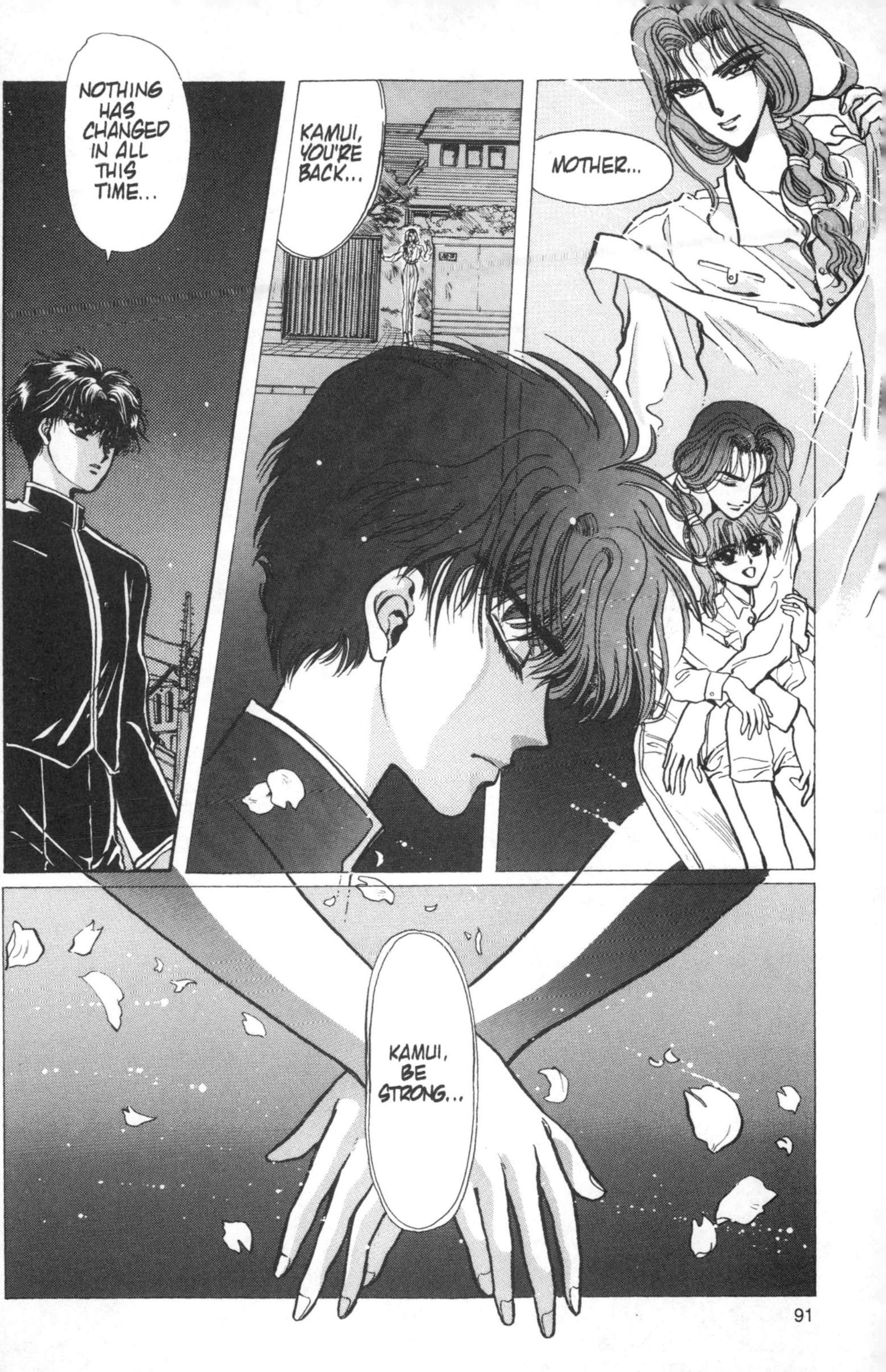
NOTHING HAS CHANGED IN ALL THIS TIME...
KAMUI, YOU'RE BACK...
MOTHER...
KAMUI, BE STRONG...

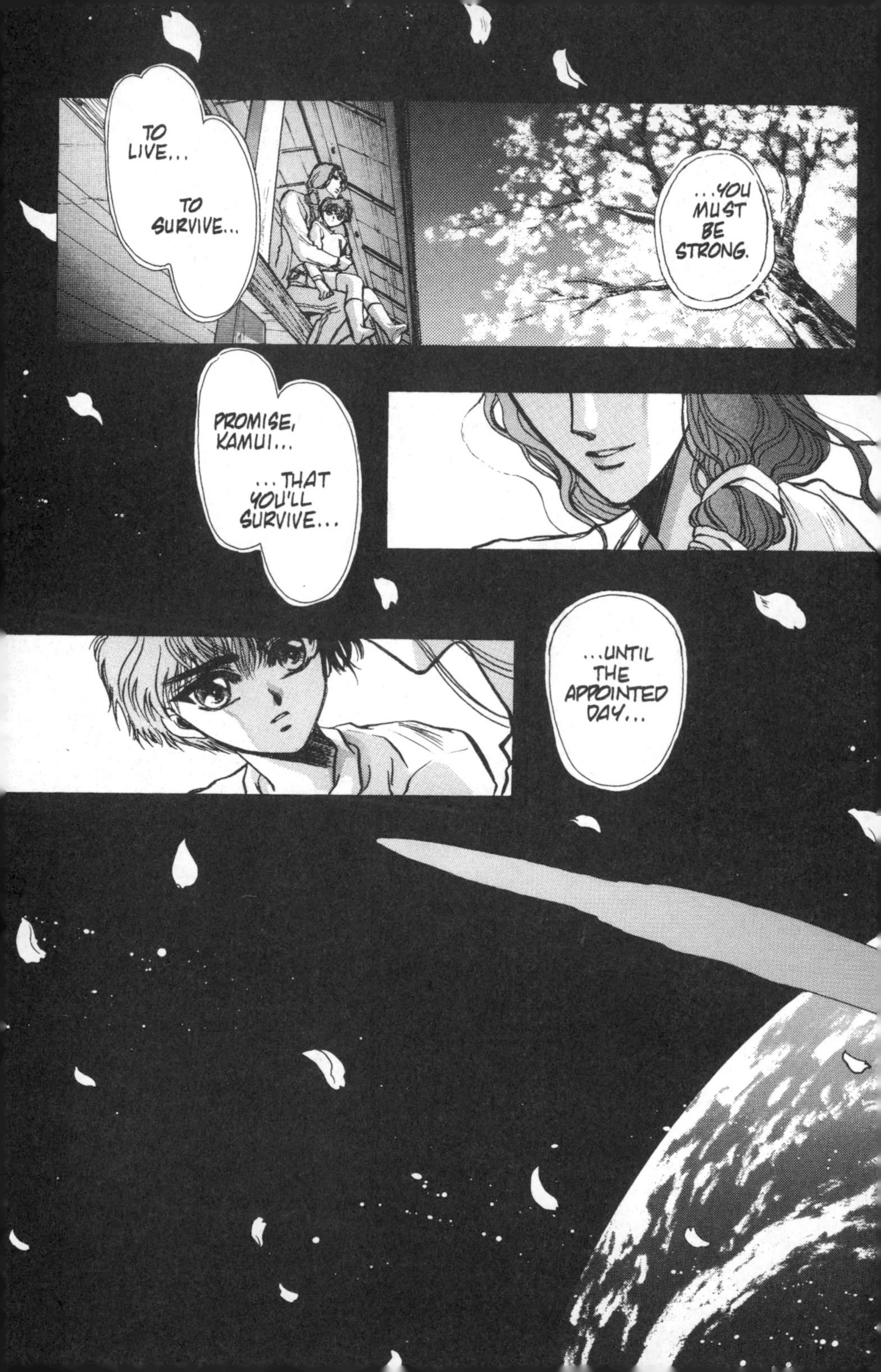
TO LIVE... TO SURVIVE...
...YOU MUST BE STRONG.
PROMISE, KAMUI... ...THAT YOU'LL SURVIVE...
...UNTIL THE APPOINTED DAY...

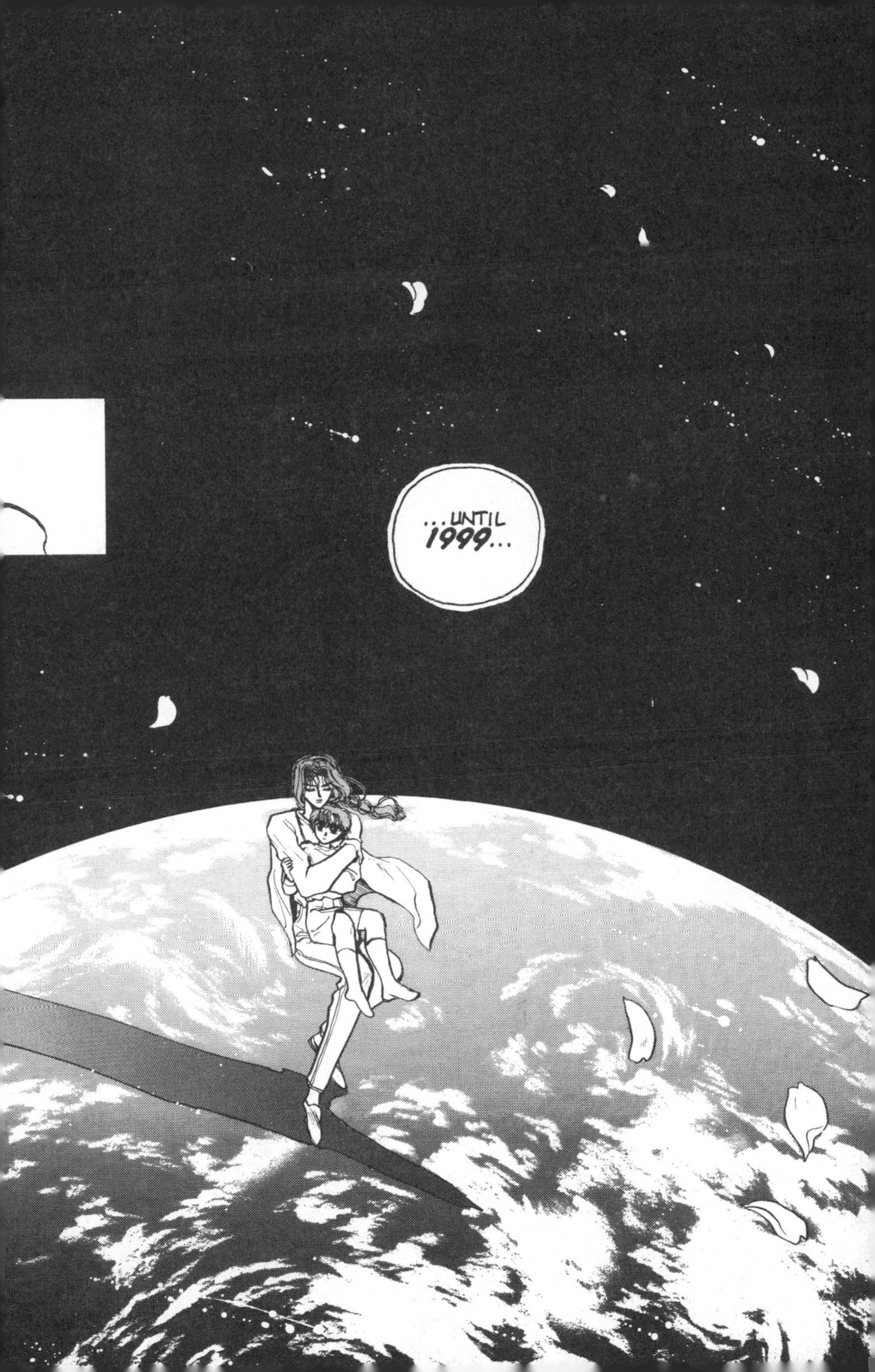
...UNTIL 1999...

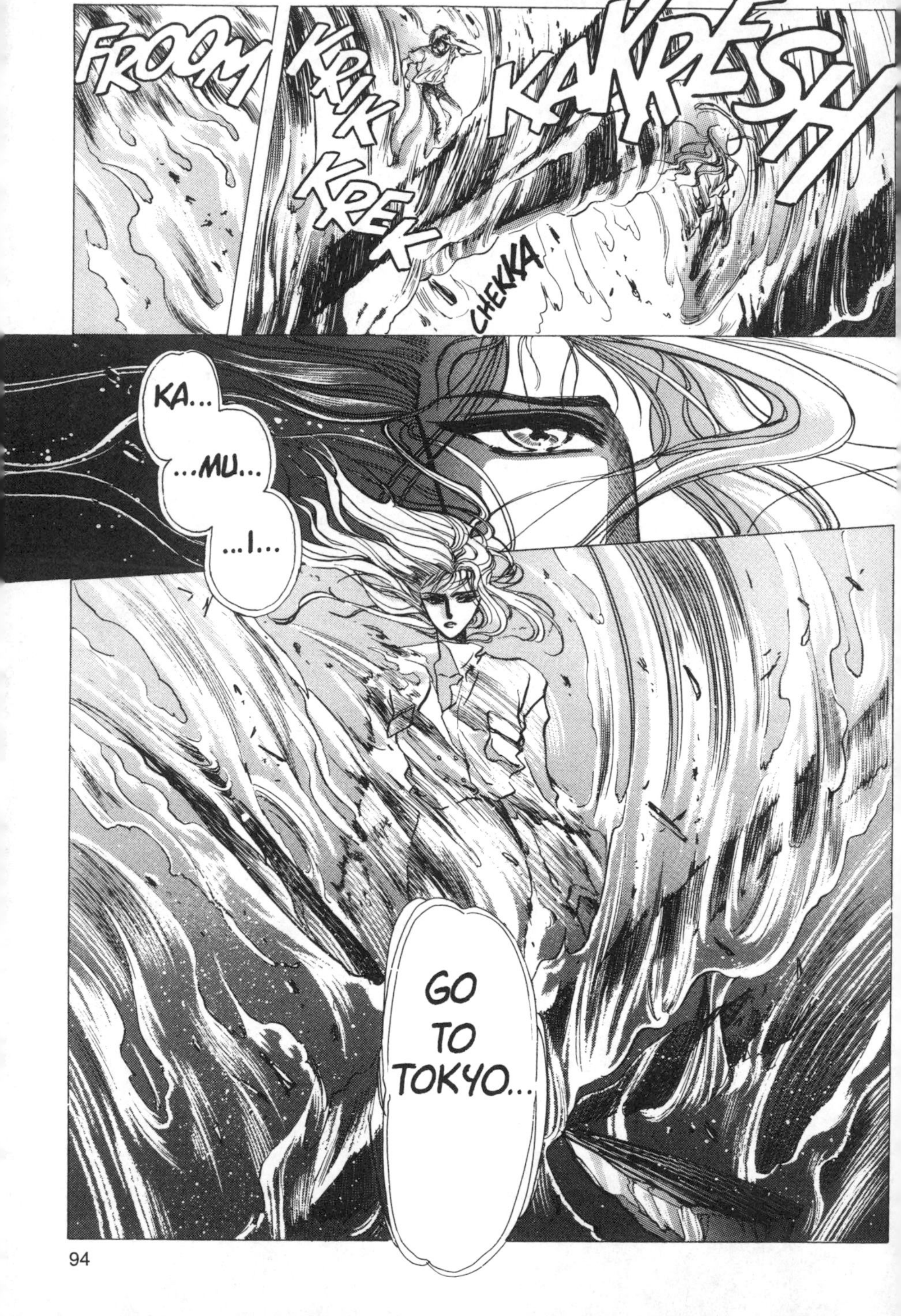
FROOM
KRIK KRIK
KREK
KAKRESH
CHEKKA
KA...
...MU...
...I...
GO TO TOKYO...

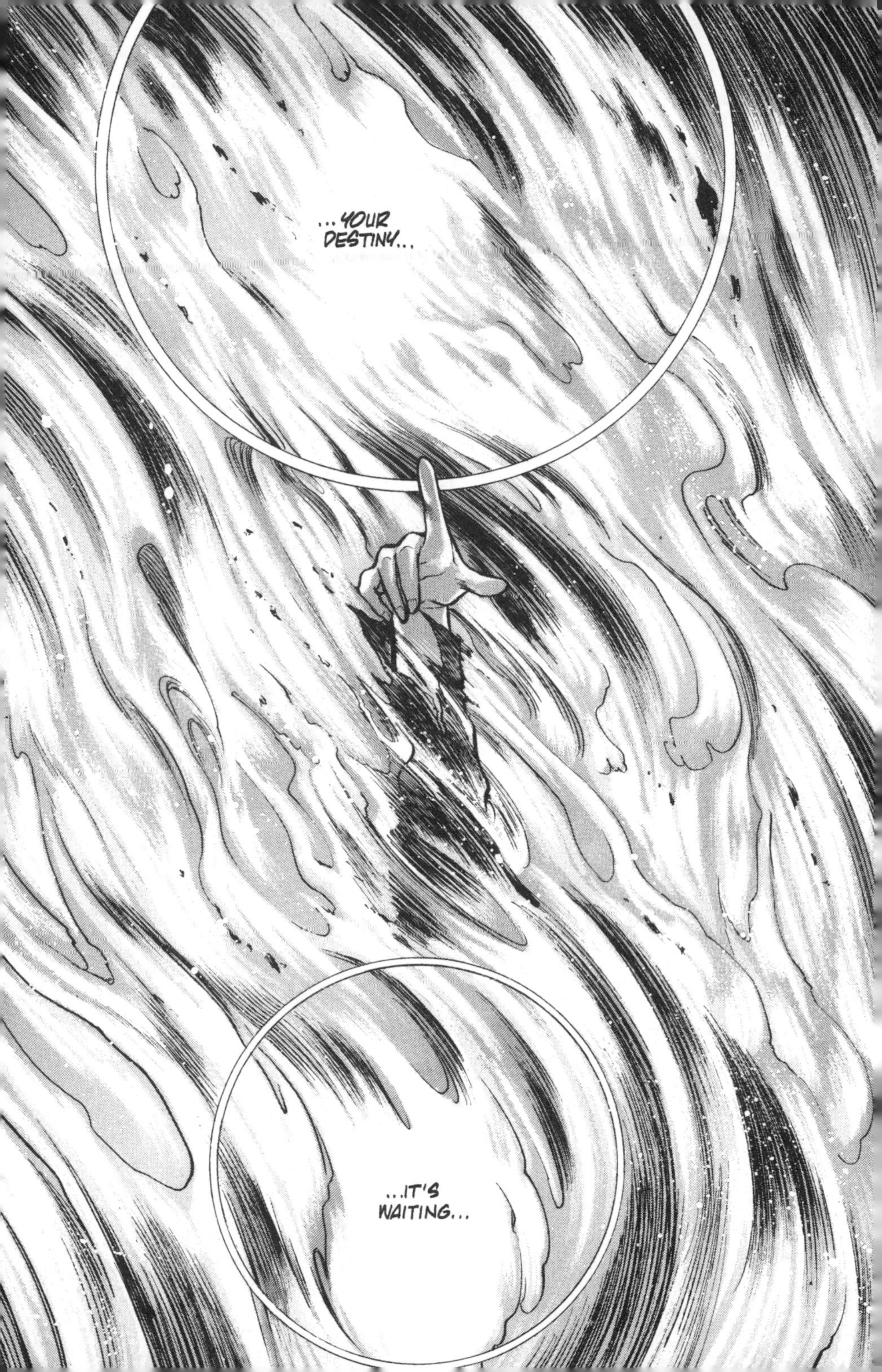
...YOUR DESTINY...
...IT'S WAITING...

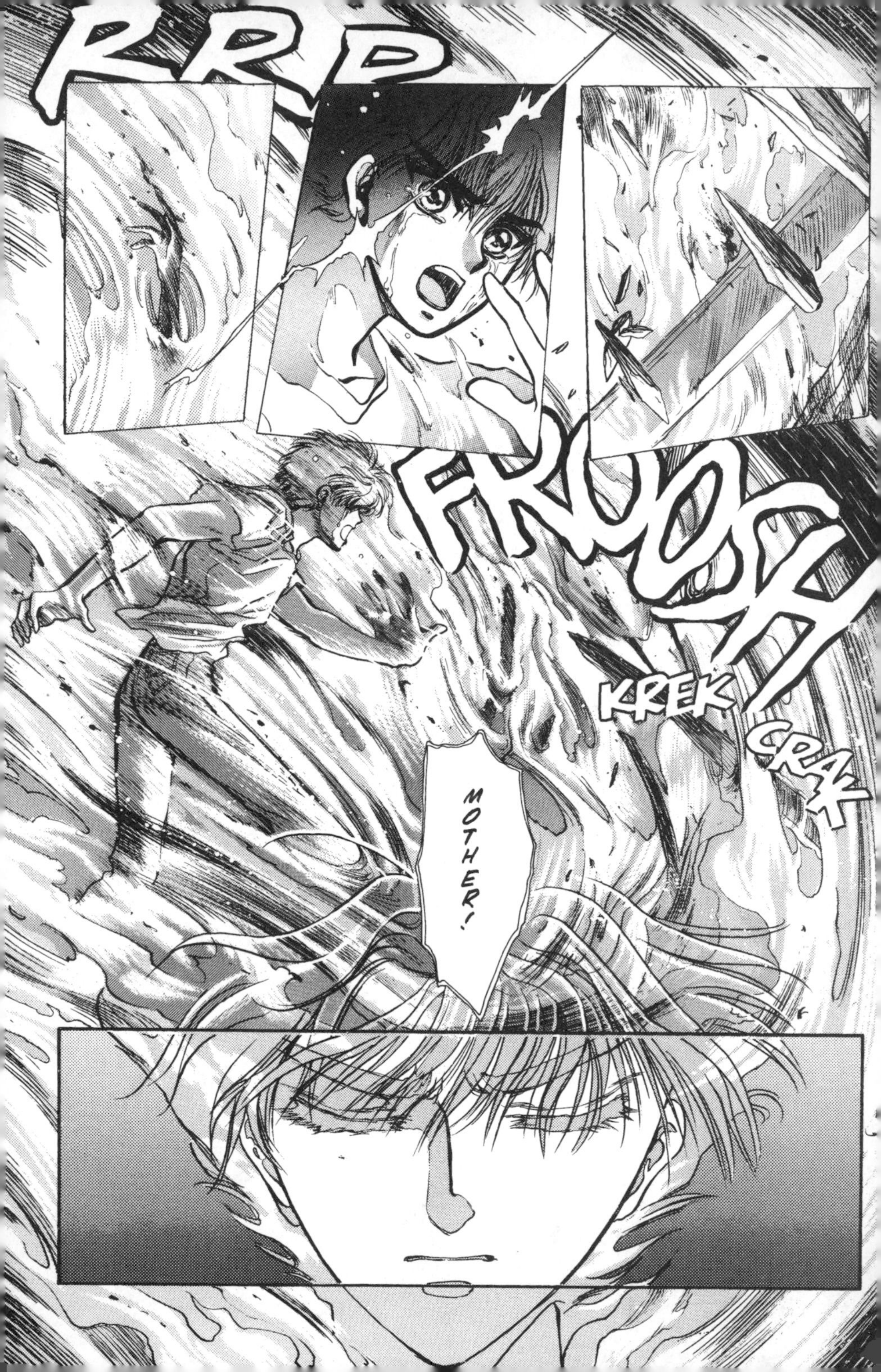
RRP
FROOSH
KREK
CRAK
MOTHER!

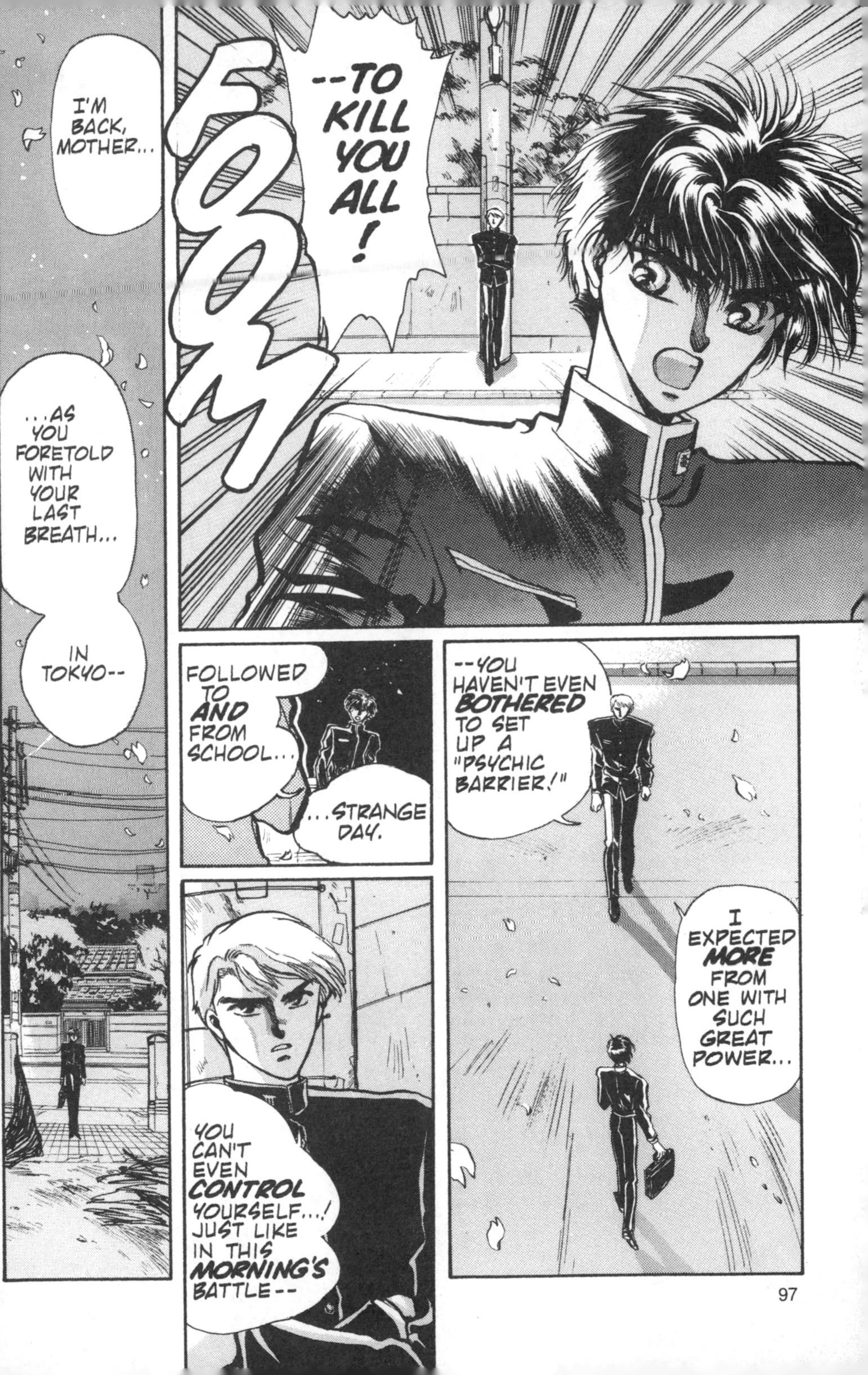
I'M BACK, MOTHER...
...AS YOU FORETOLD WITH YOUR LAST BREATH...
IN TOKYO--
--TO KILL YOU ALL!
FOOM
FOLLOWED TO AND FROM SCHOOL...
...STRANGE DAY.
YOU CAN'T EVEN CONTROL YOURSELF...! JUST LIKE IN THIS MORNING'S BATTLE--
--YOU HAVEN'T EVEN BOTHERED TO SET UP A "PSYCHIC BARRIER!"
I EXPECTED MORE FROM ONE WITH SUCH GREAT POWER...

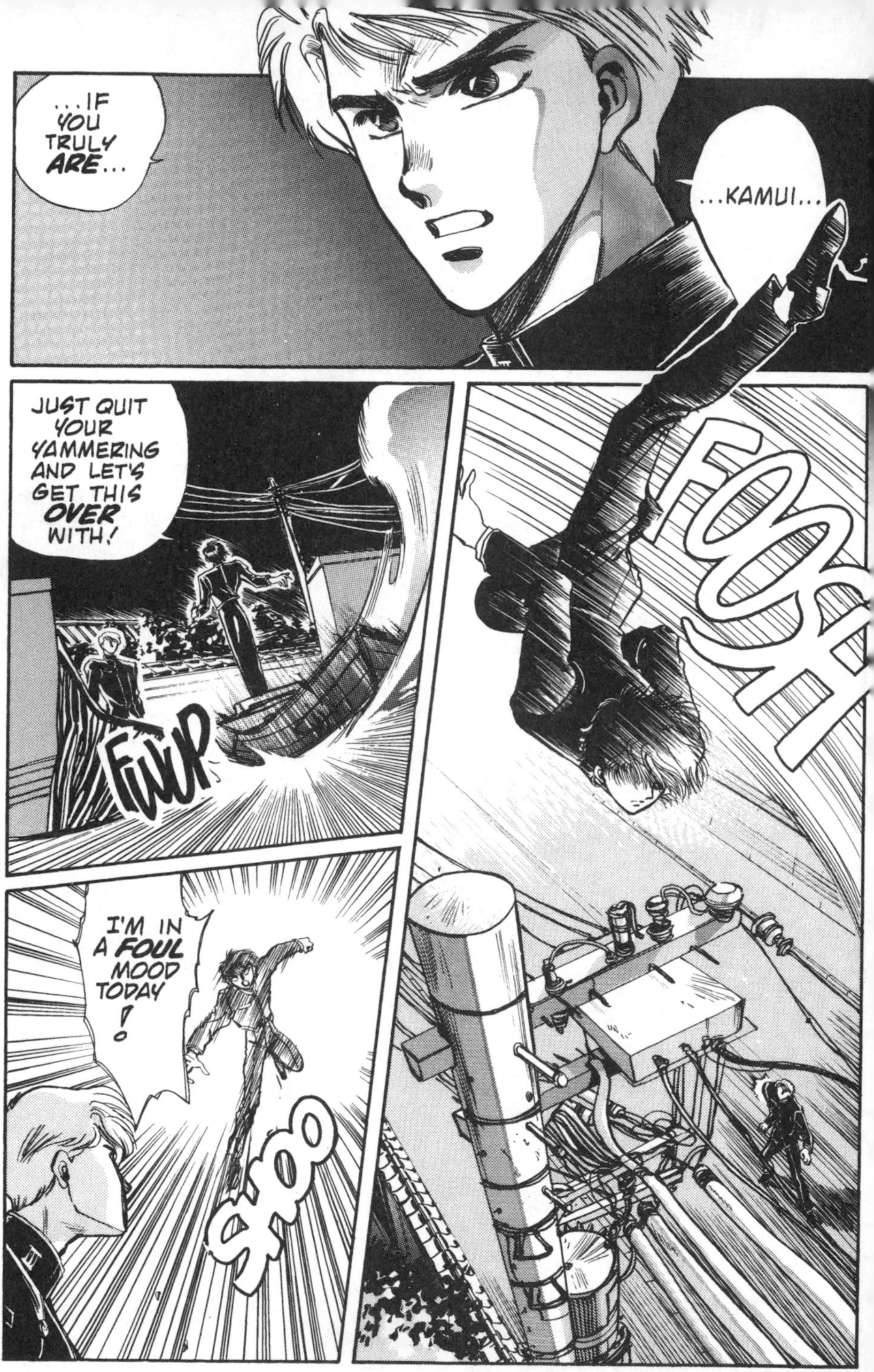
...IF YOU TRULY ARE...
...KAMUI...
JUST QUIT YOUR YAMMERING AND LET'S GET THIS OVER WITH!
FWUP
FOOSH
I'M IN A FOUL MOOD TODAY!
SHOO

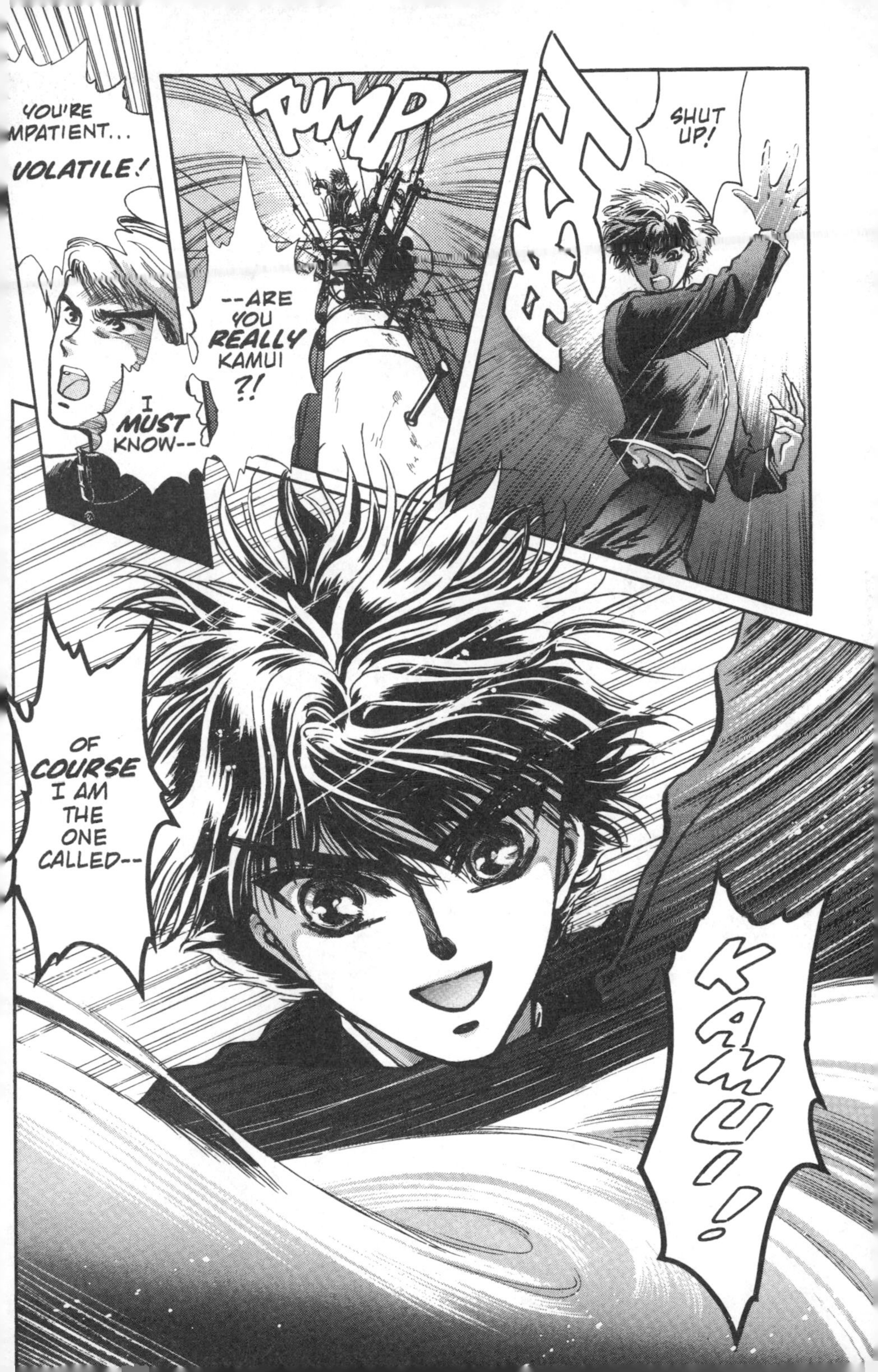
YOU'RE MPATIENT... VOLATILE!
I MUST KNOW--
--ARE YOU REALLY KAMUI?!
TUMP
FSH
SHUT UP!
OF COURSE I AM THE ONE CALLED--
KAMUI!

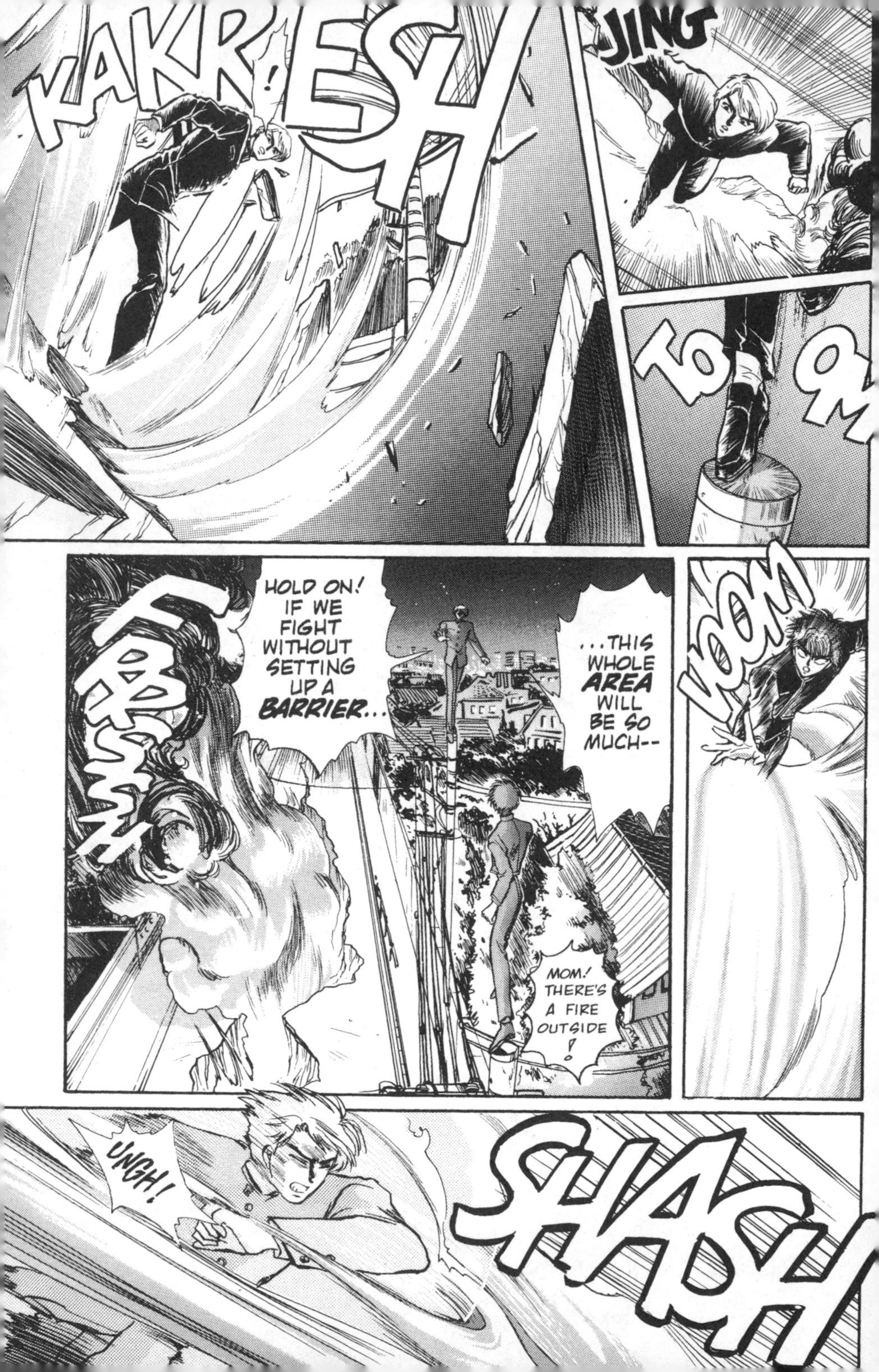
KAKR!ESH
JING
TOOM
HOLD ON! IF WE FIGHT WITHOUT SETTING UP A BARRIER...
FWASHH
...THIS WHOLE AREA WILL BE SO MUCH--
MOM! THERE'S A FIRE OUTSIDE!
VOOM
UNGH!
SHASHH

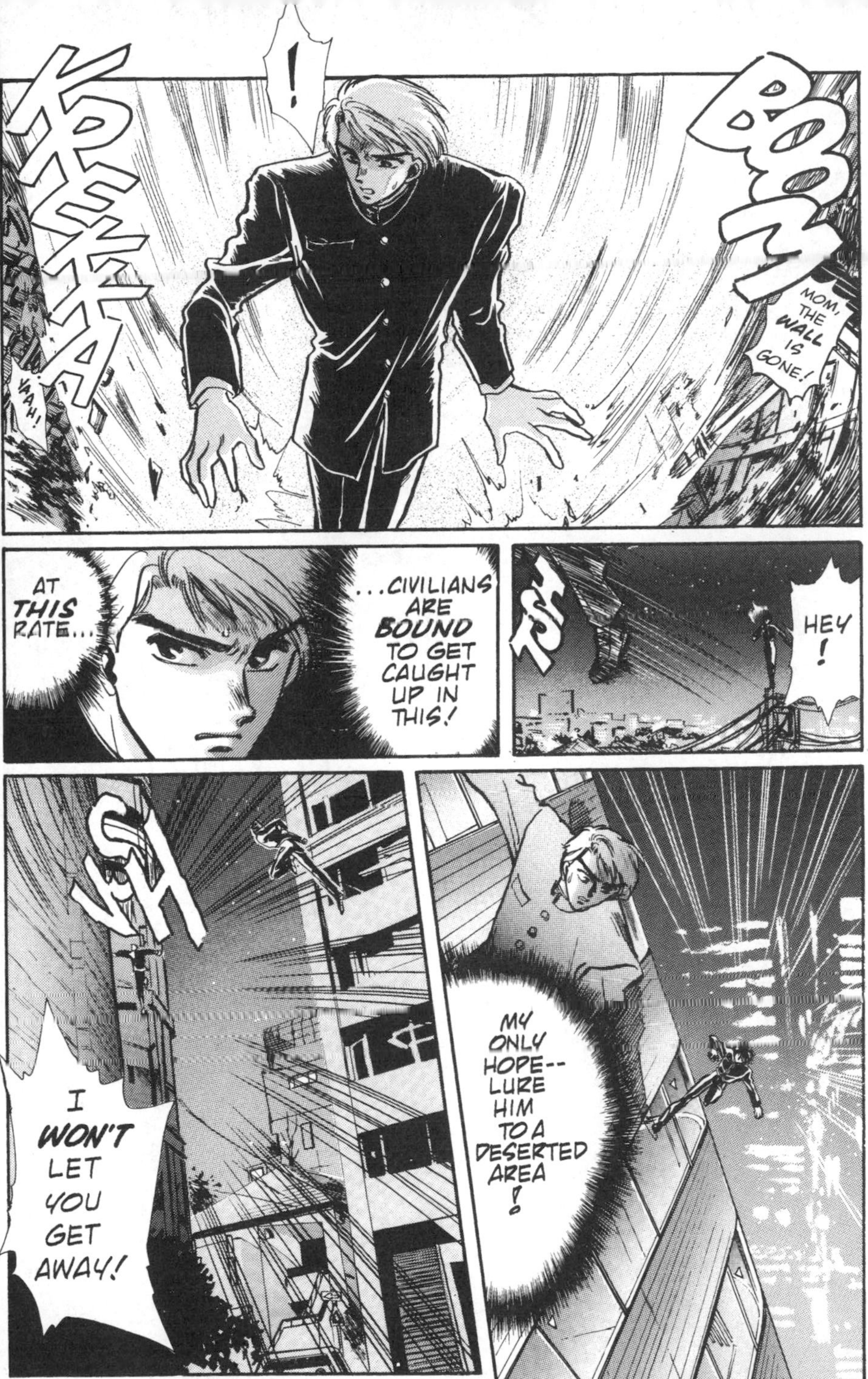
!
YAAH!
BOOM
MOM, THE WALL IS GONE!
AT THIS RATE...
...CIVILIANS ARE BOUND TO GET CAUGHT UP IN THIS!
HEY!
I WON'T LET YOU GET AWAY!
MY ONLY HOPE--LURE HIM TO A DESERTED AREA!

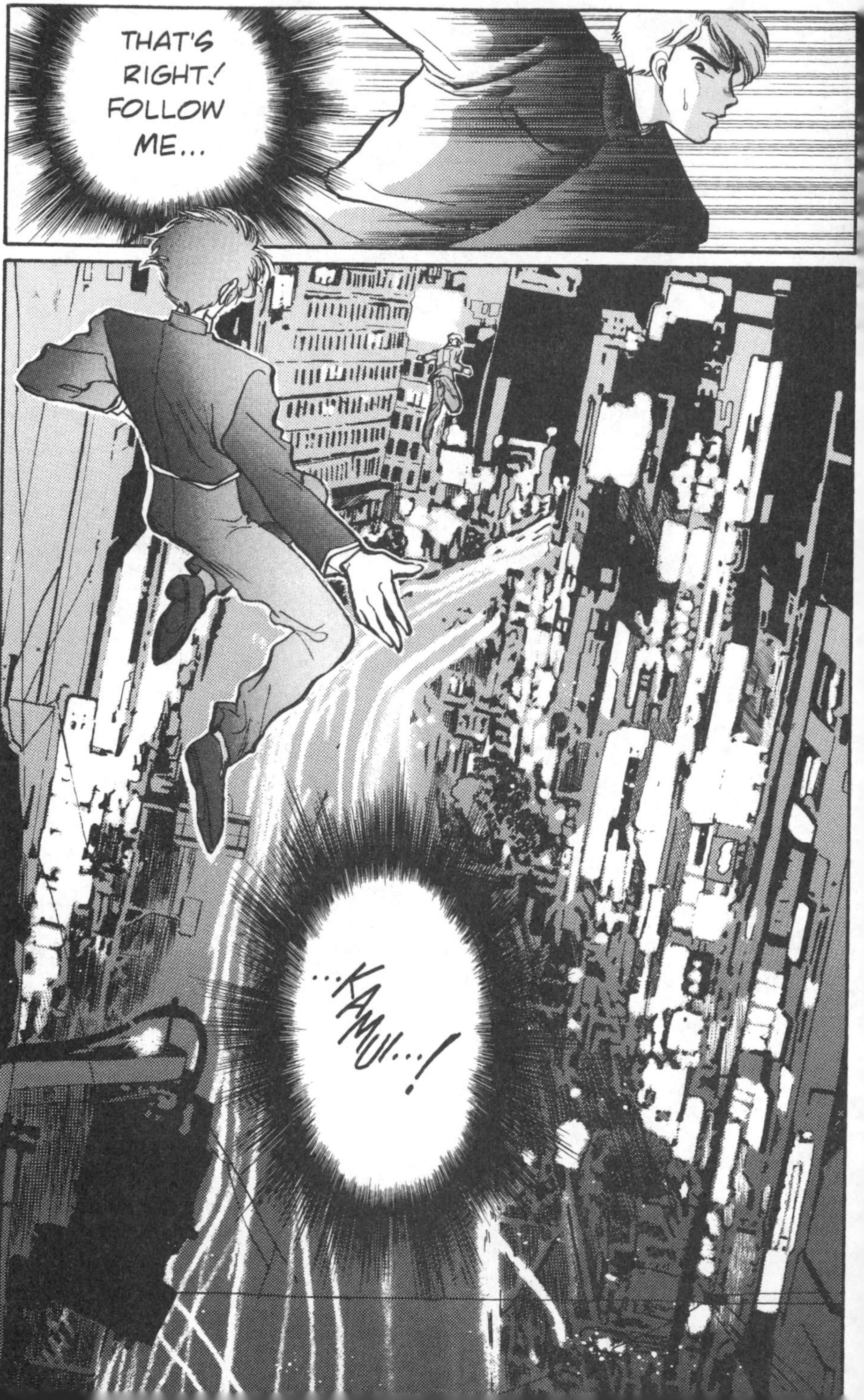
THAT'S RIGHT! FOLLOW ME...
...KAMUI...!

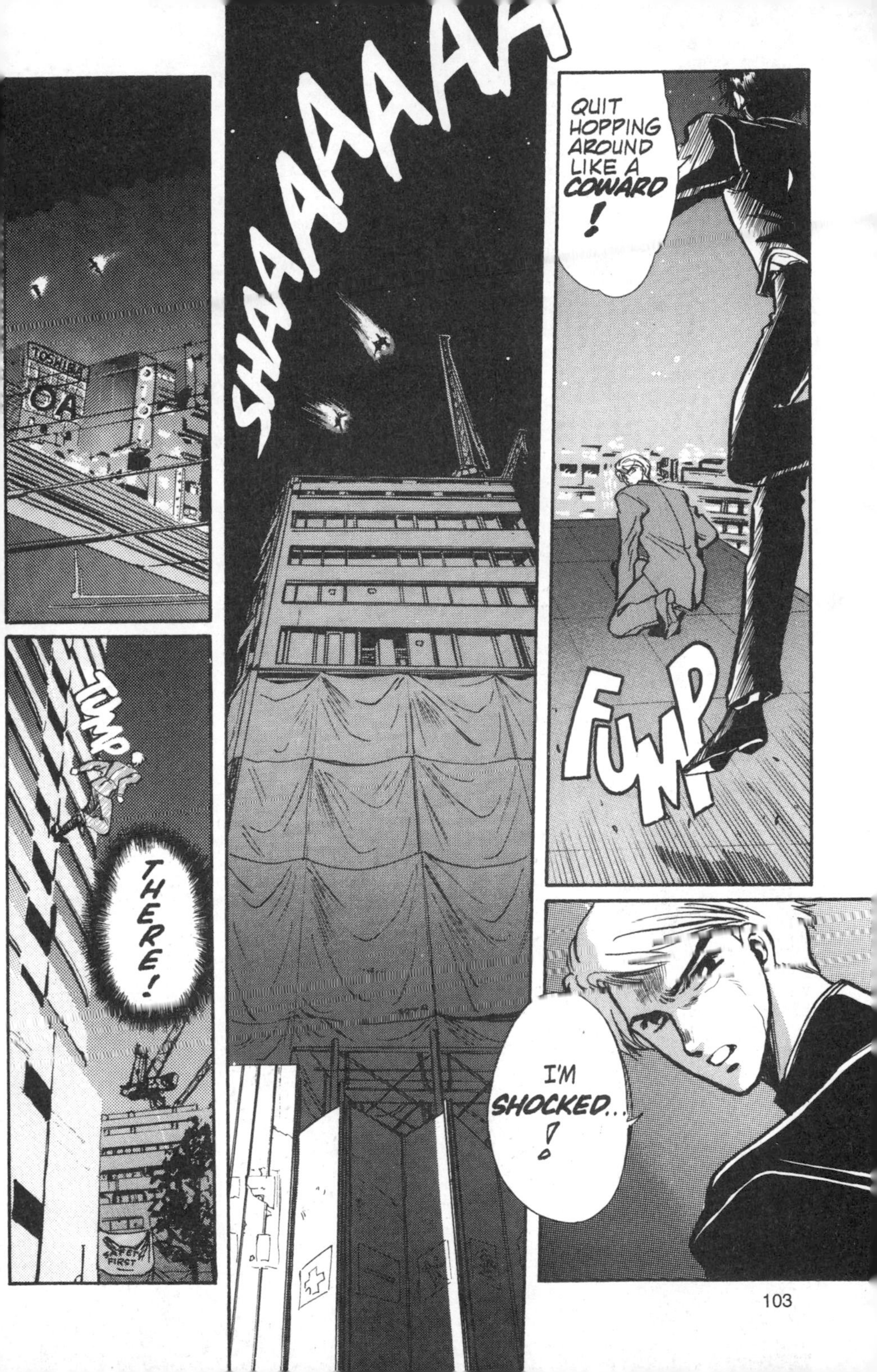
TUMP
THERE!
SHAAAAAAA
QUIT HOPPING AROUND LIKE A COWARD!
FUMP!
I'M SHOCKED...!

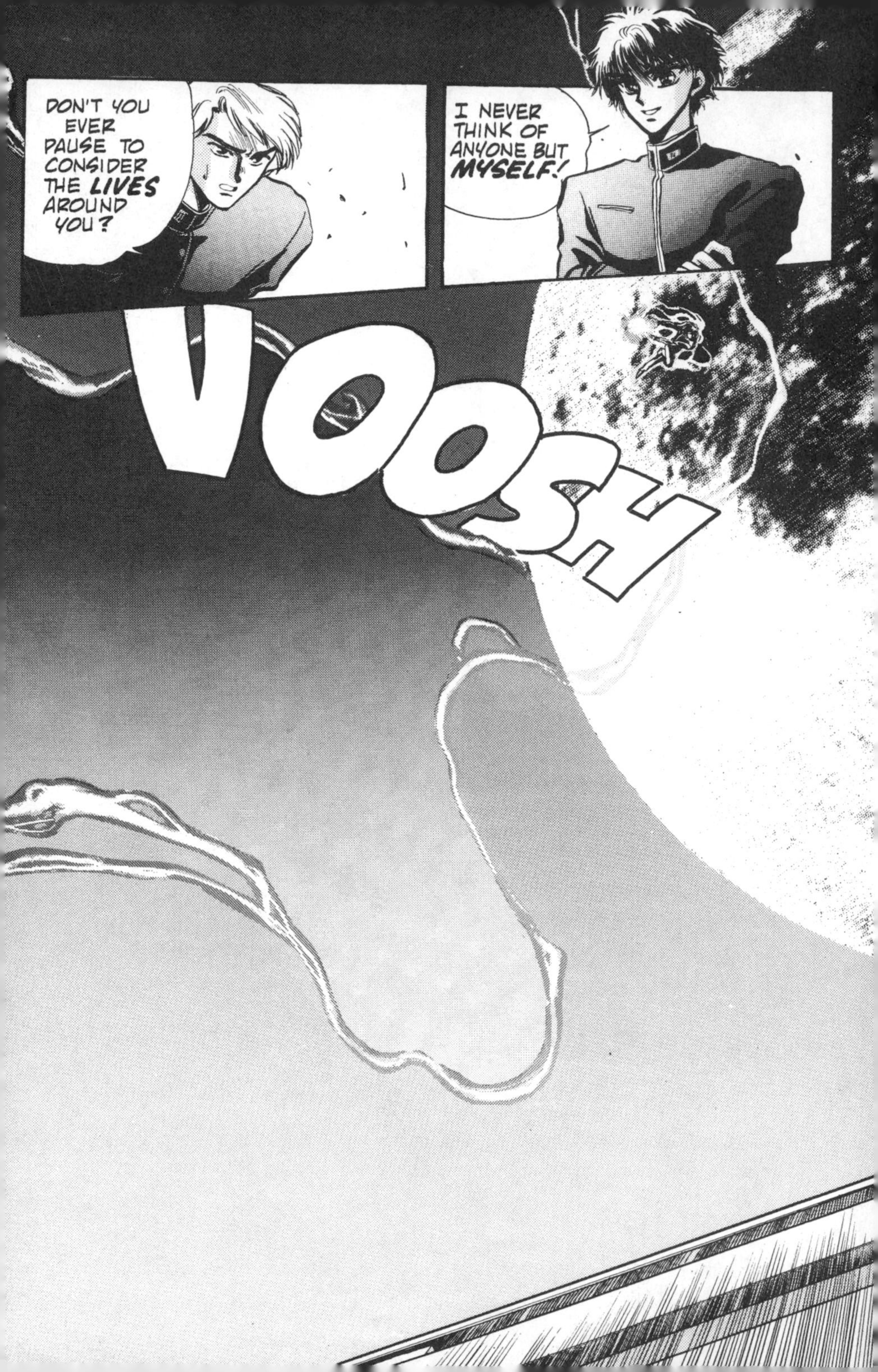
DON'T YOU EVER PAUSE TO CONSIDER THE **LIVES** AROUND YOU?
I NEVER THINK OF ANYONE BUT **MYSELF**!
VOOSH

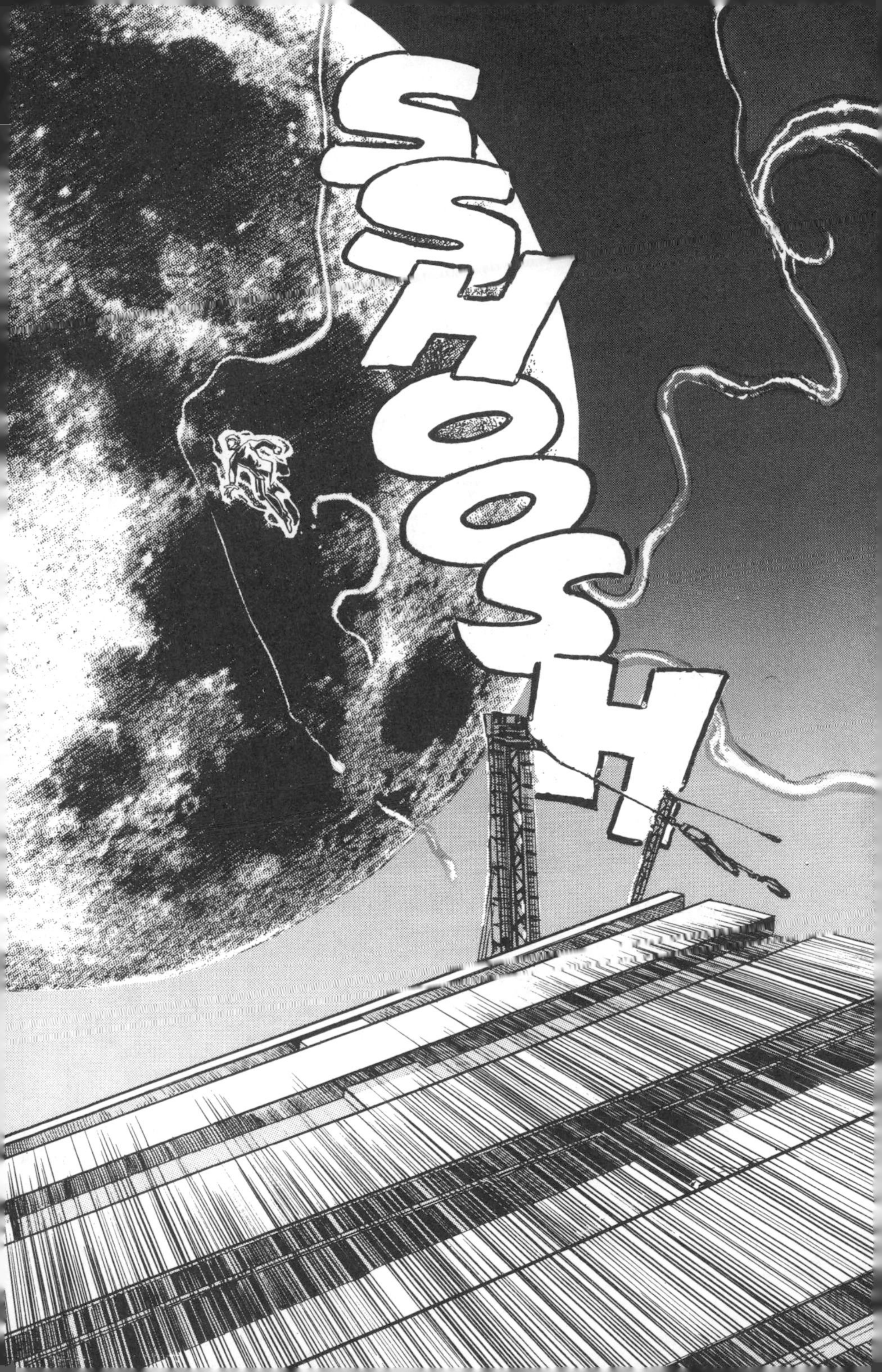
SSHOOSH

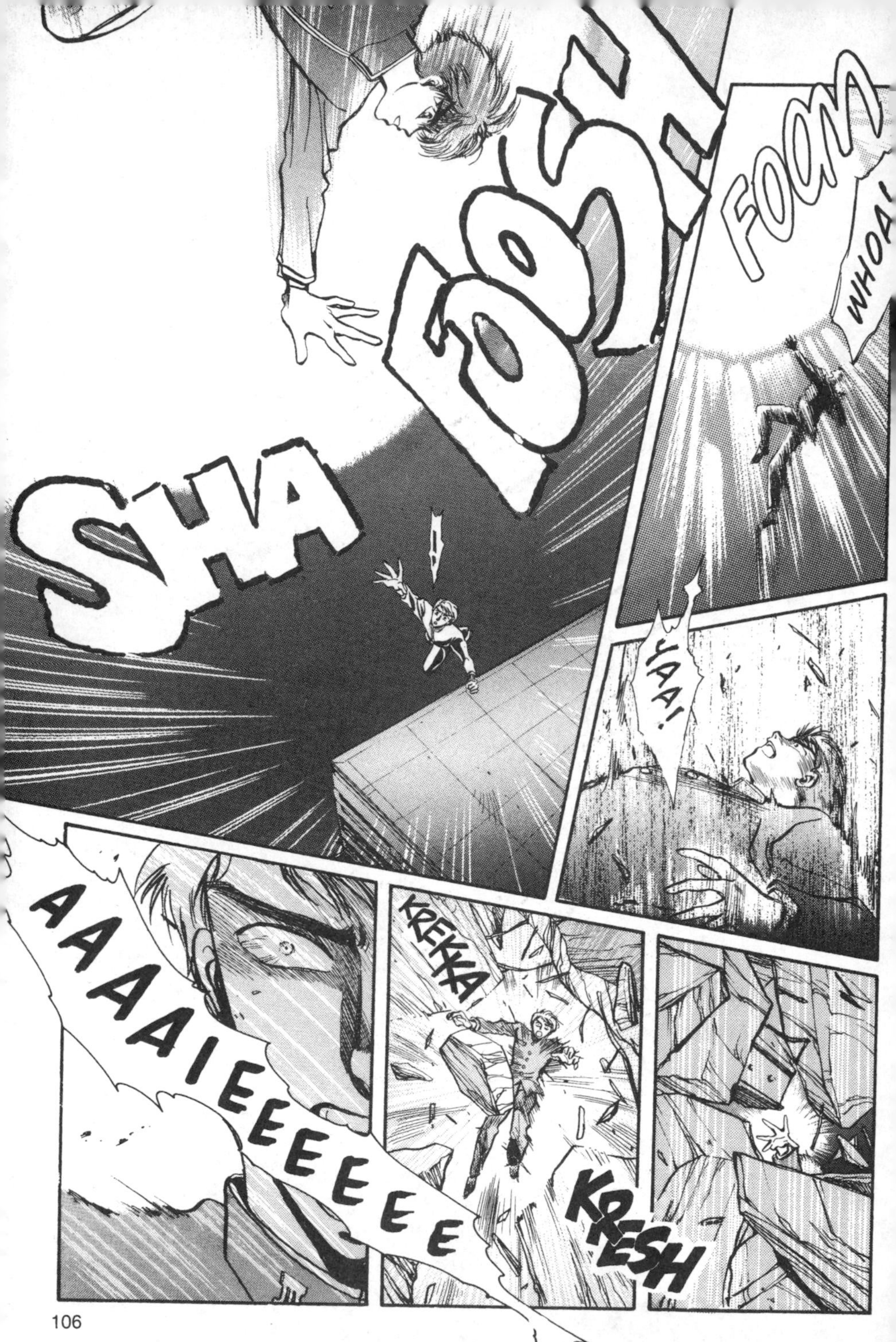
SHA
DOO!
!
FOOM
WHOA!
YAA!
AAAAIEEEEEEE
KREKKA
KRESH

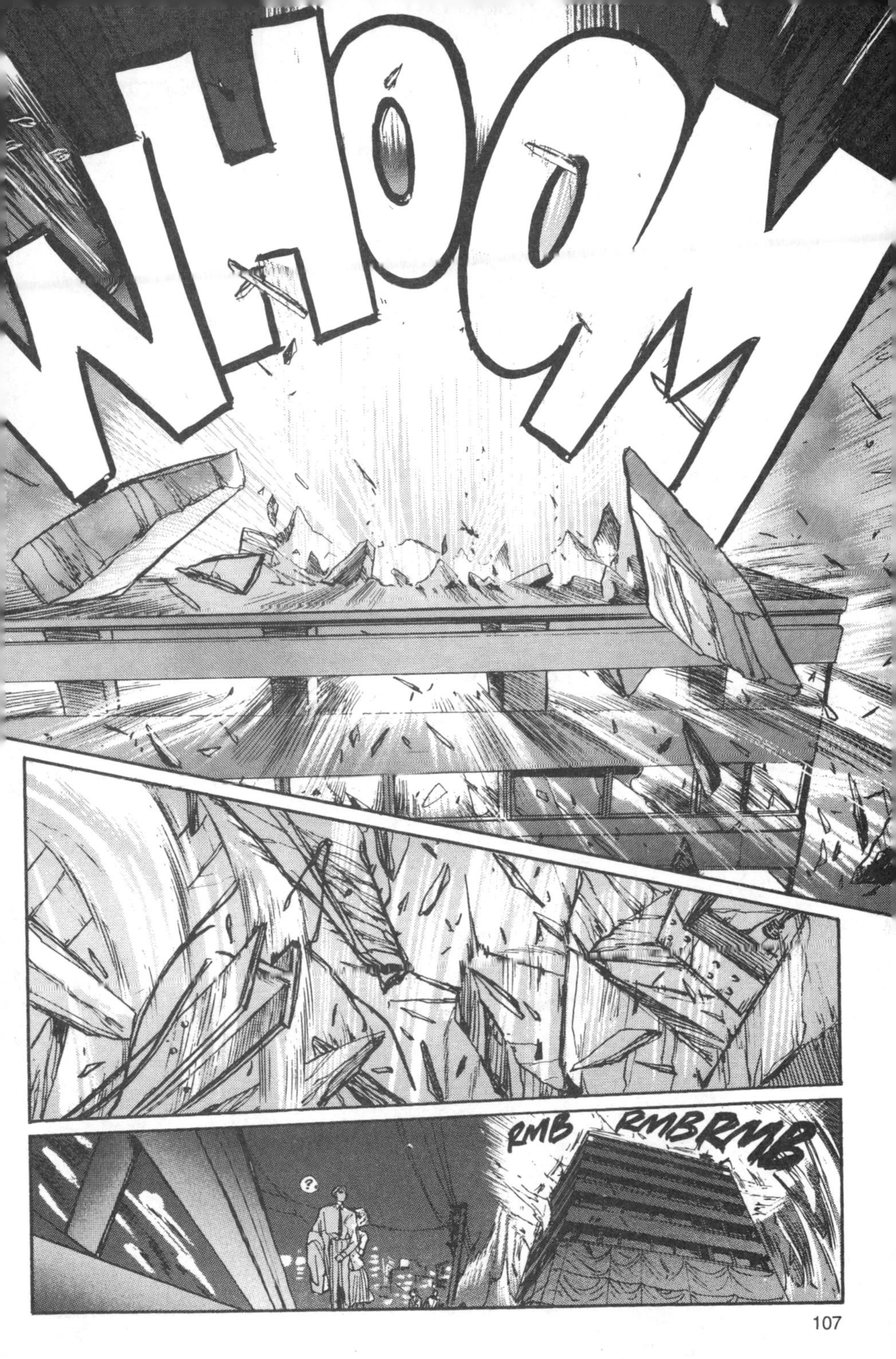
WHOOM
?
RMB
RMBRMB

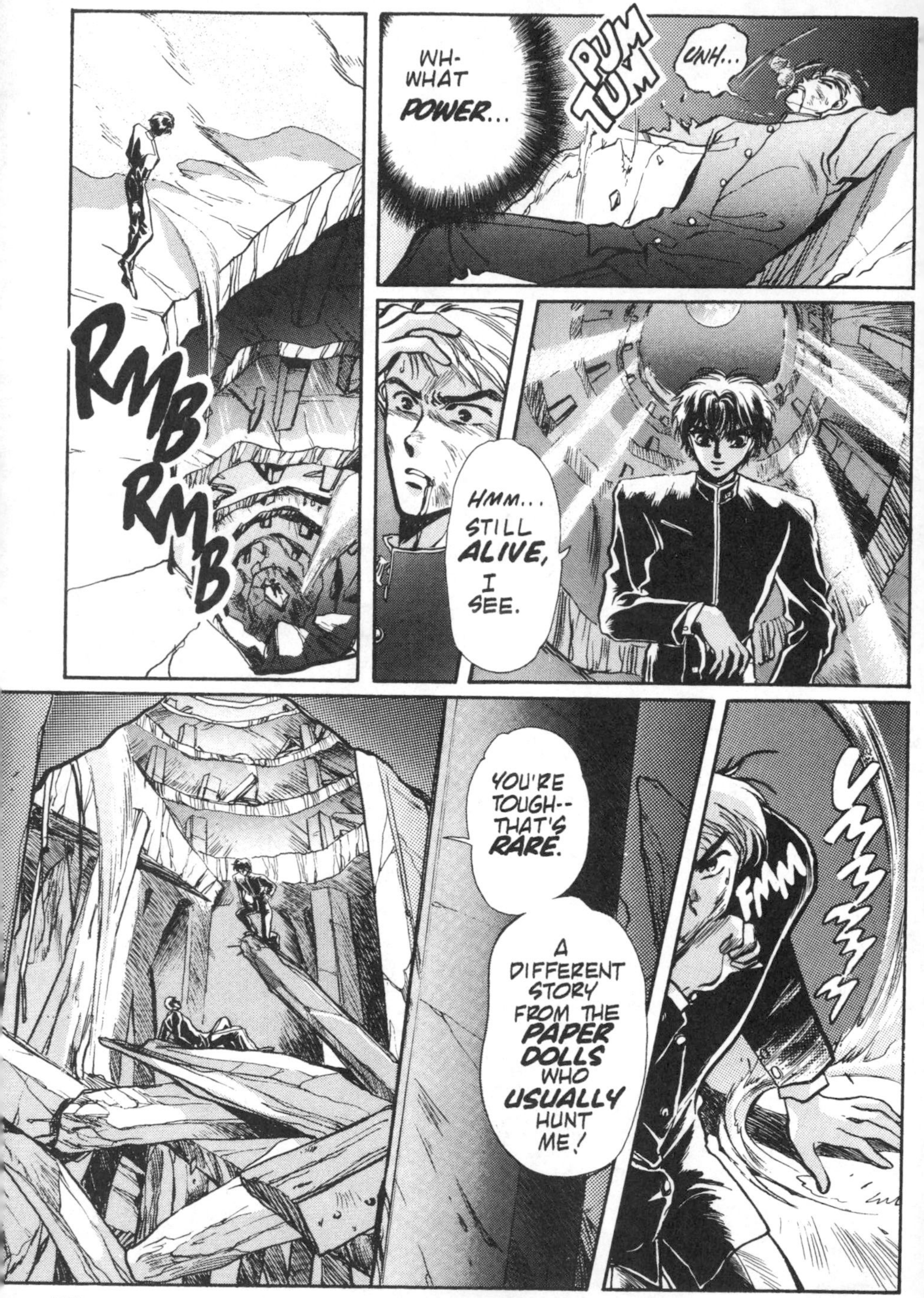
RMB RMB
WH- WHAT POWER...
PUM TUM
UNH...
HMM... STILL ALIVE, I SEE.
YOU'RE TOUGH-- THAT'S RARE.
A DIFFERENT STORY FROM THE PAPER DOLLS WHO USUALLY HUNT ME!
FMM
UMMMMMM

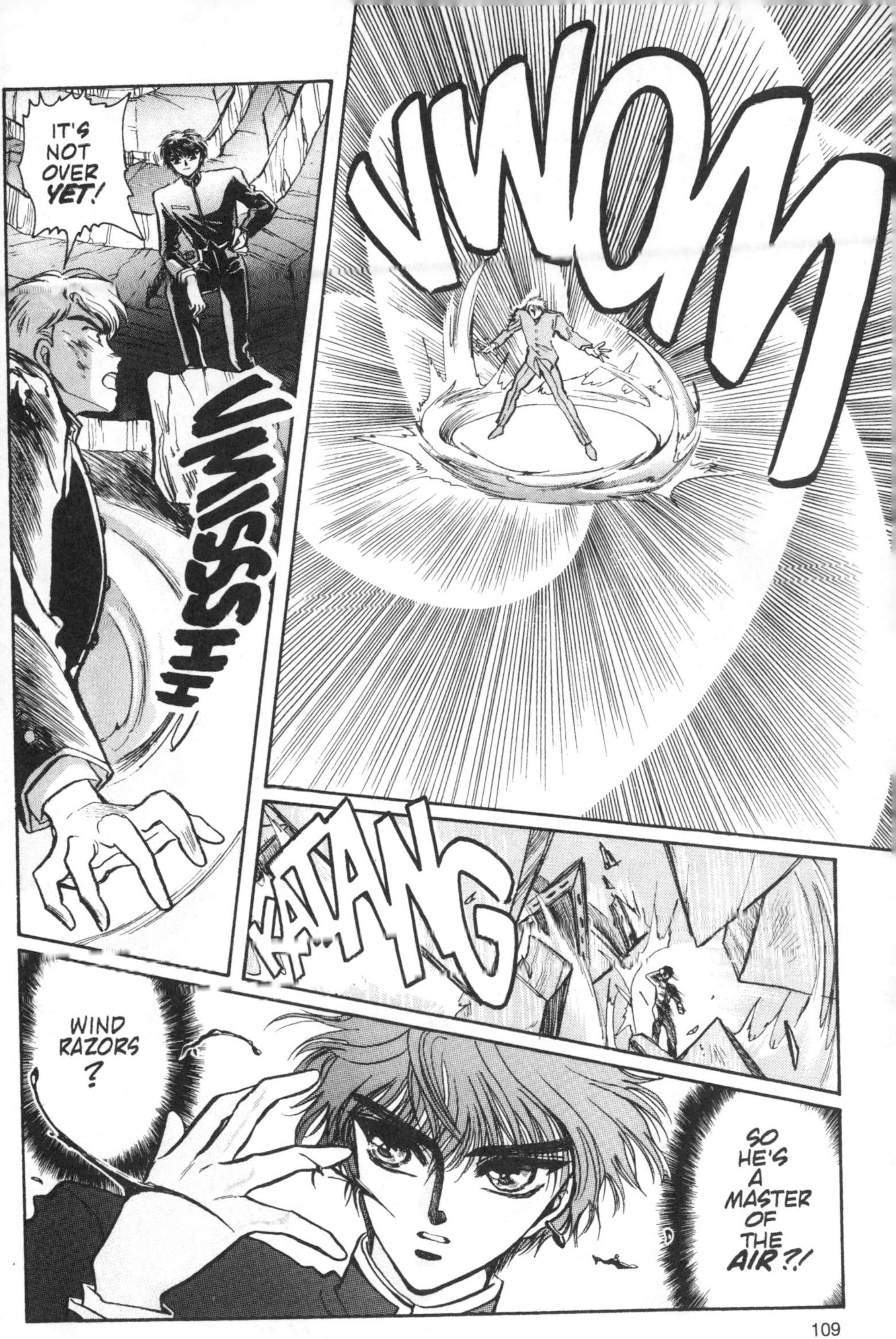
IT'S NOT OVER YET!
WHISSSHHH
VWOM
KATANG
WIND RAZORS?
SO HE'S A MASTER OF THE AIR?!

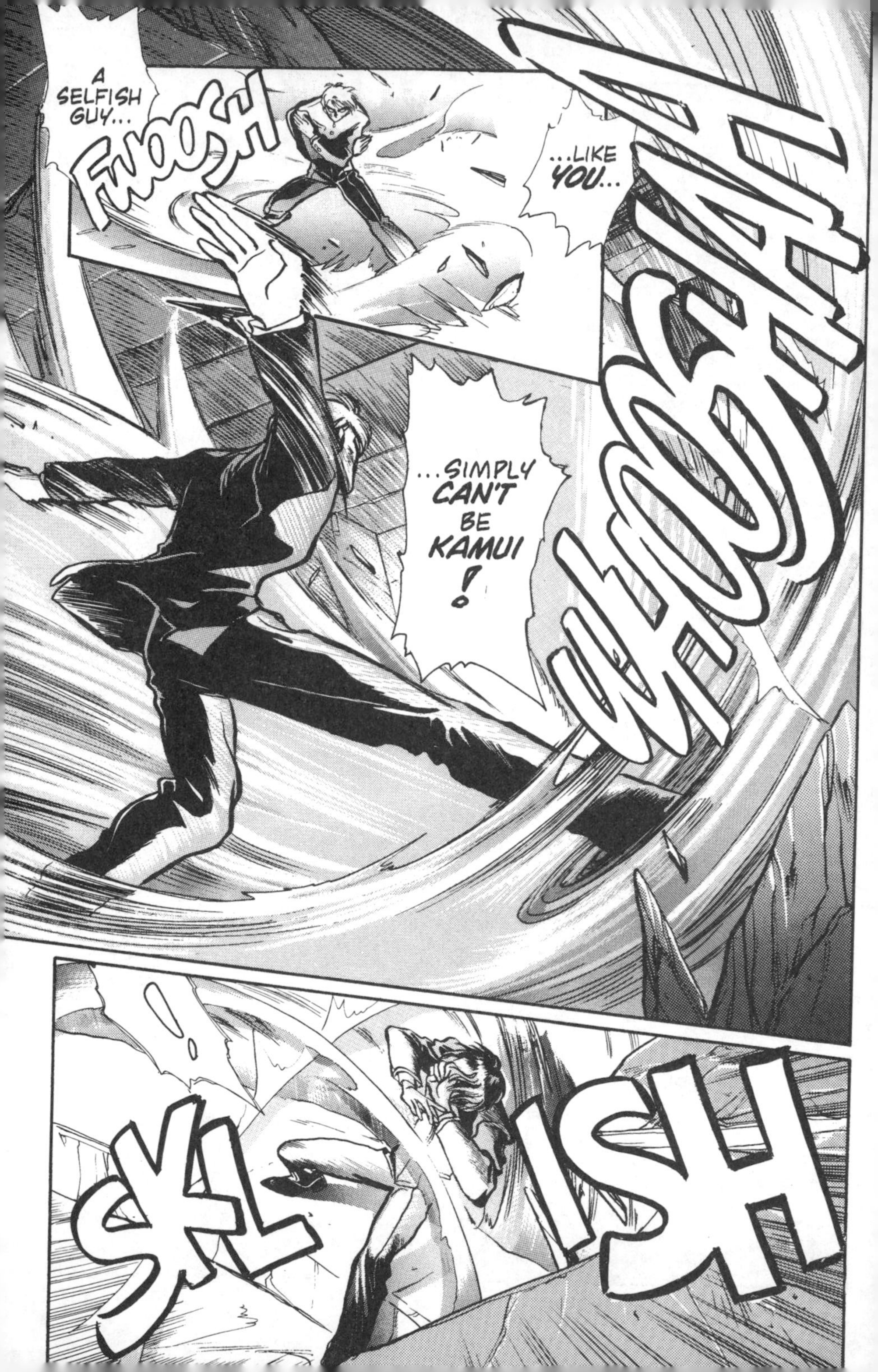
A SELFISH GUY...
FWOOSH
...LIKE YOU...
...SIMPLY CAN'T BE KAMUI!
SHOOOM
!
SKLISH

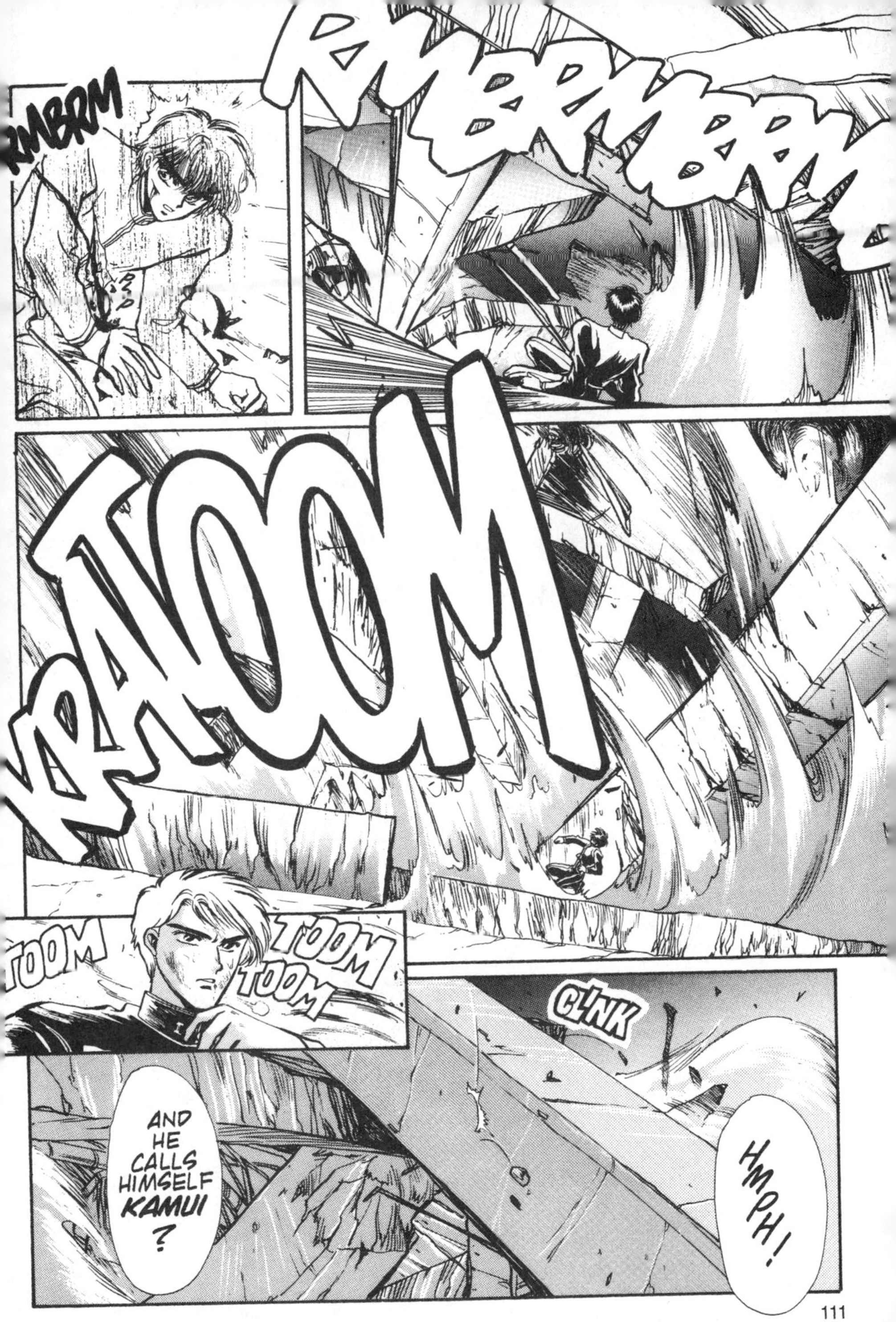
RMBRM
RMBRMBRM
KRAOOOM
TOOM
TOOM TOOM
CLINK
AND HE CALLS HIMSELF *KAMUI*?
HMPH!

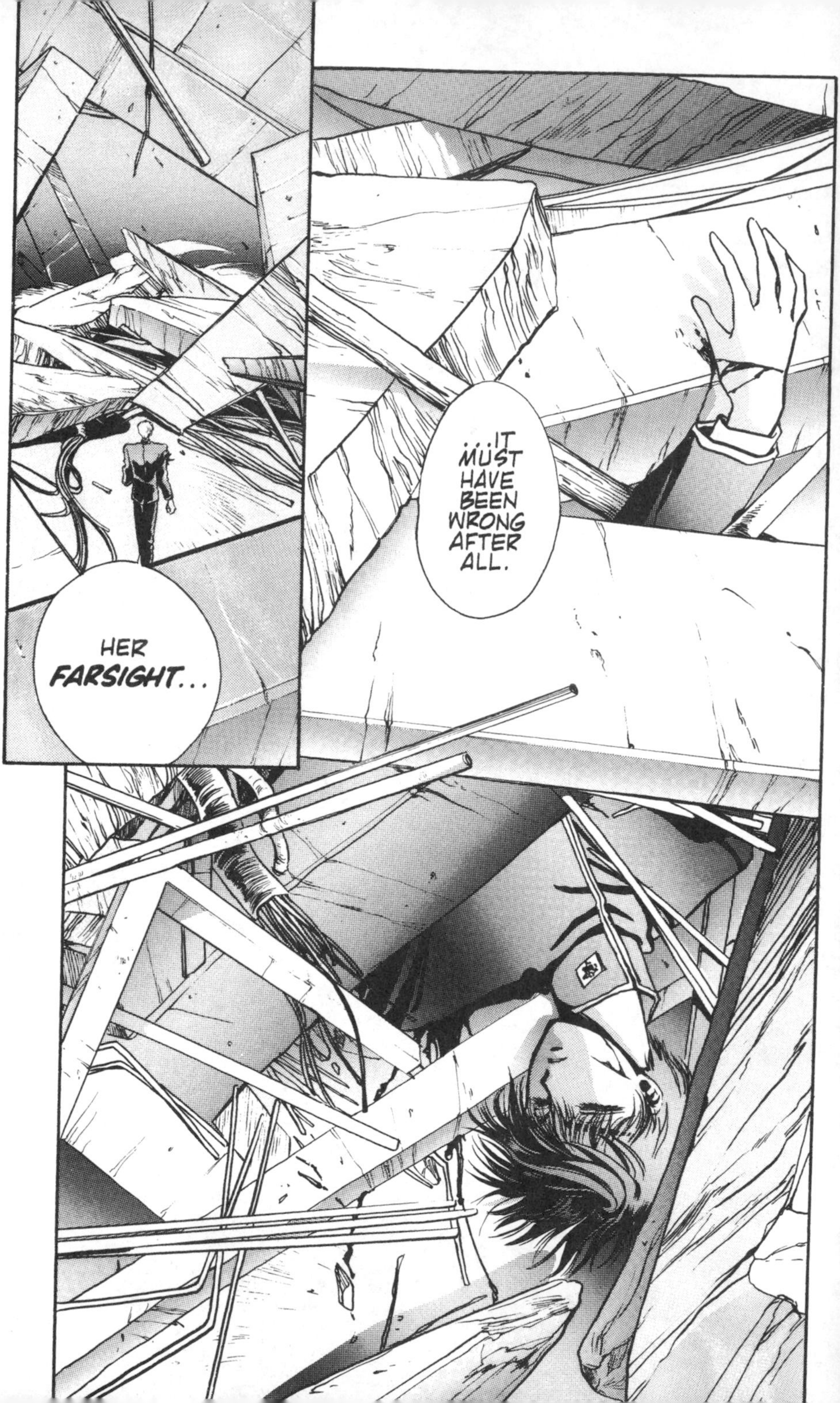
HER FARSIGHT...
...IT MUST HAVE BEEN WRONG AFTER ALL.

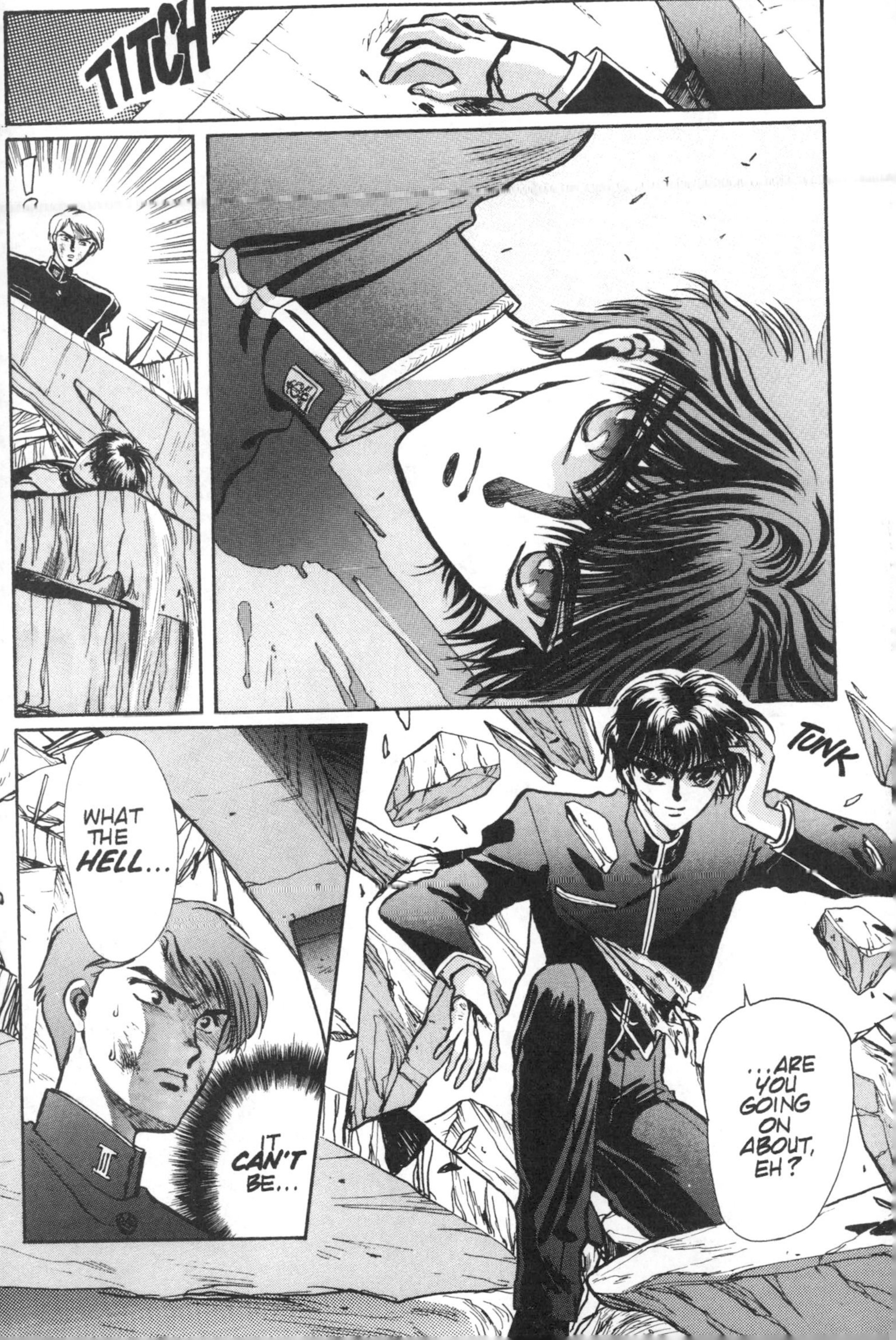
TITCH
!
WHAT THE HELL...
IT CAN'T BE...
TUNK
...ARE YOU GOING ON ABOUT, EH?

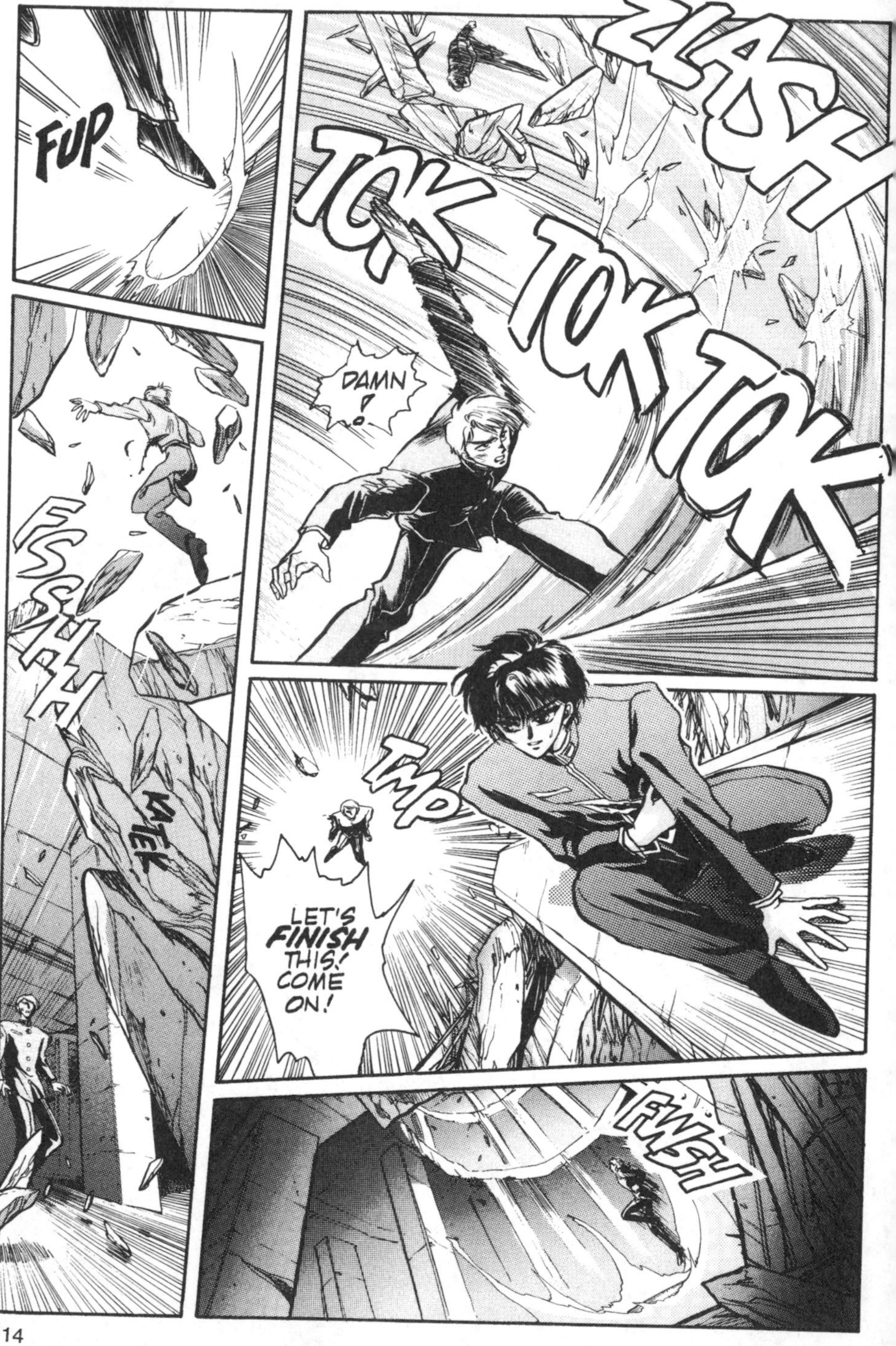
FUP
ZLASH
TOK
TOK
TOK
DAMN!
FSSHH
KATEK
TMP
LET'S **FINISH** THIS! COME ON!
FWSH

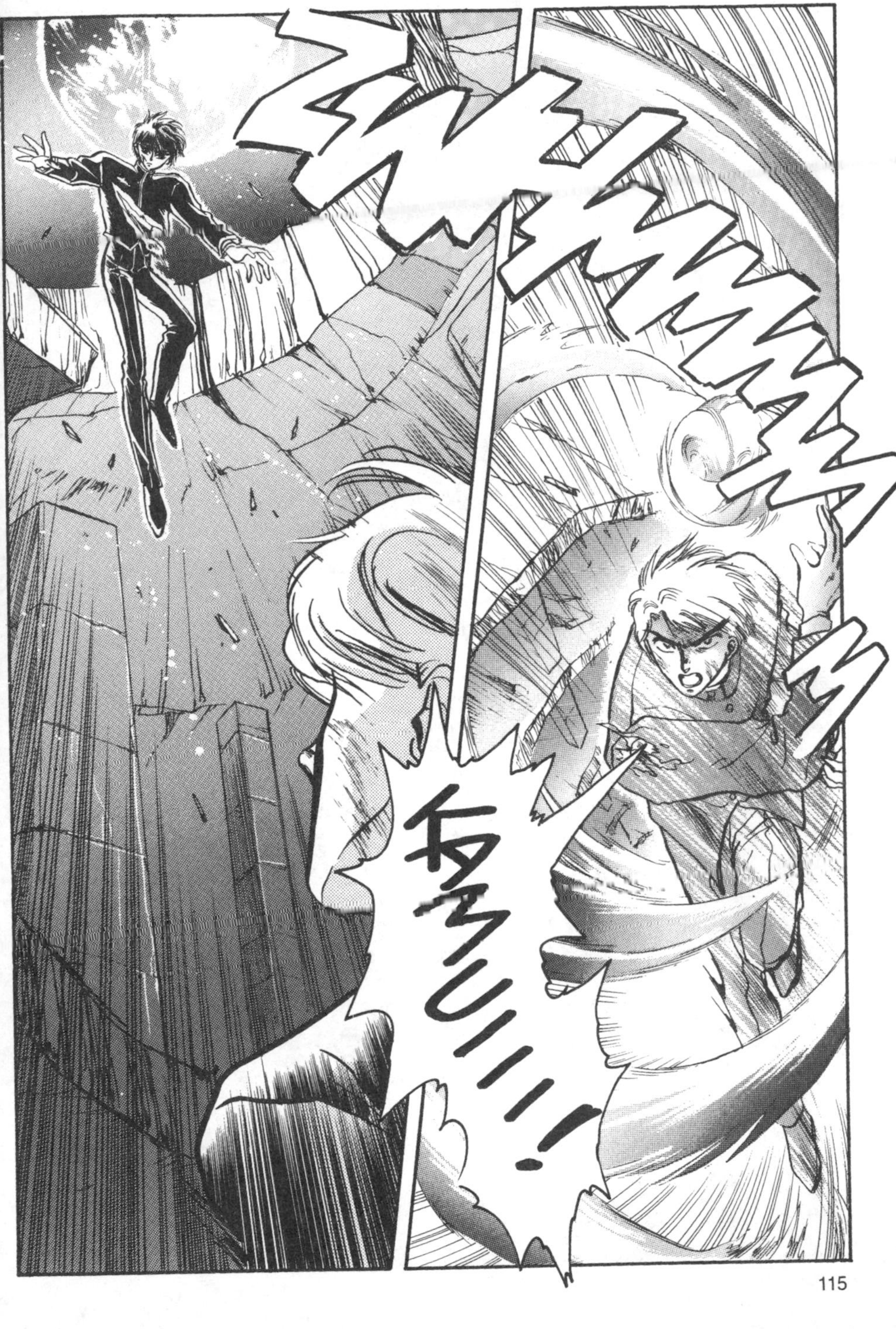

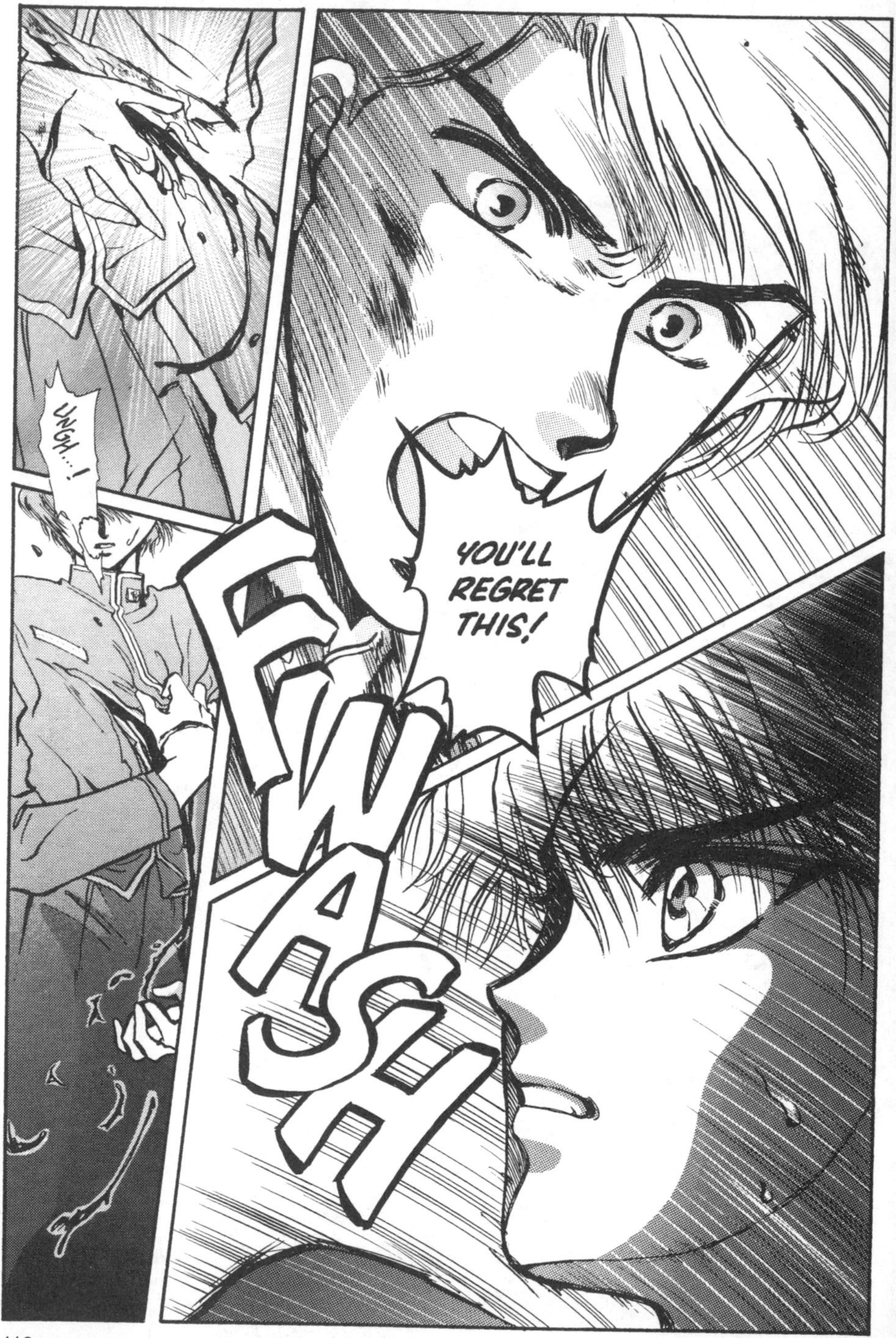
UNGH...!
YOU'LL REGRET THIS!
FWASH

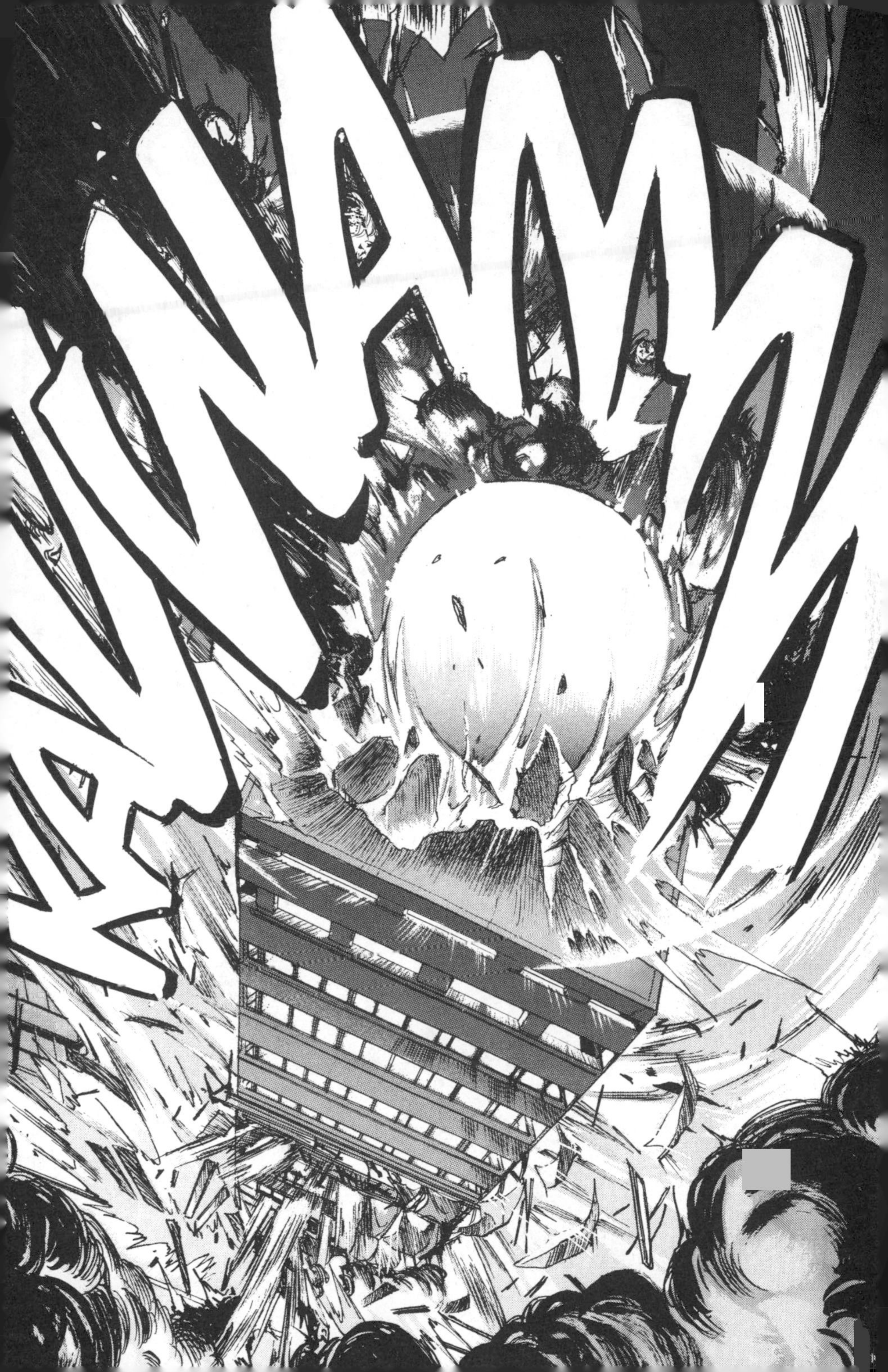

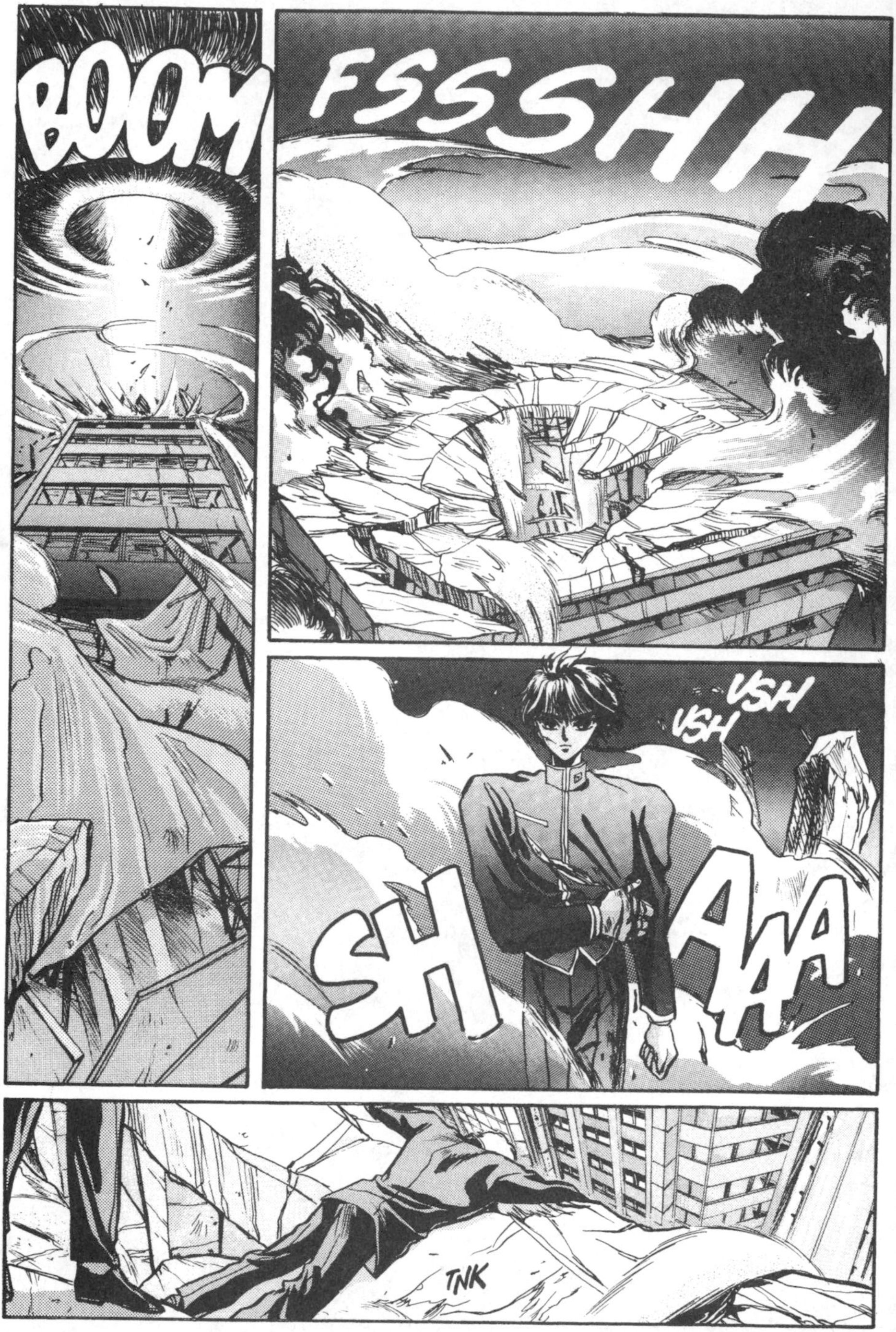
BOOM
FSSSHH
VSH
VSH
SHAAA
TNK

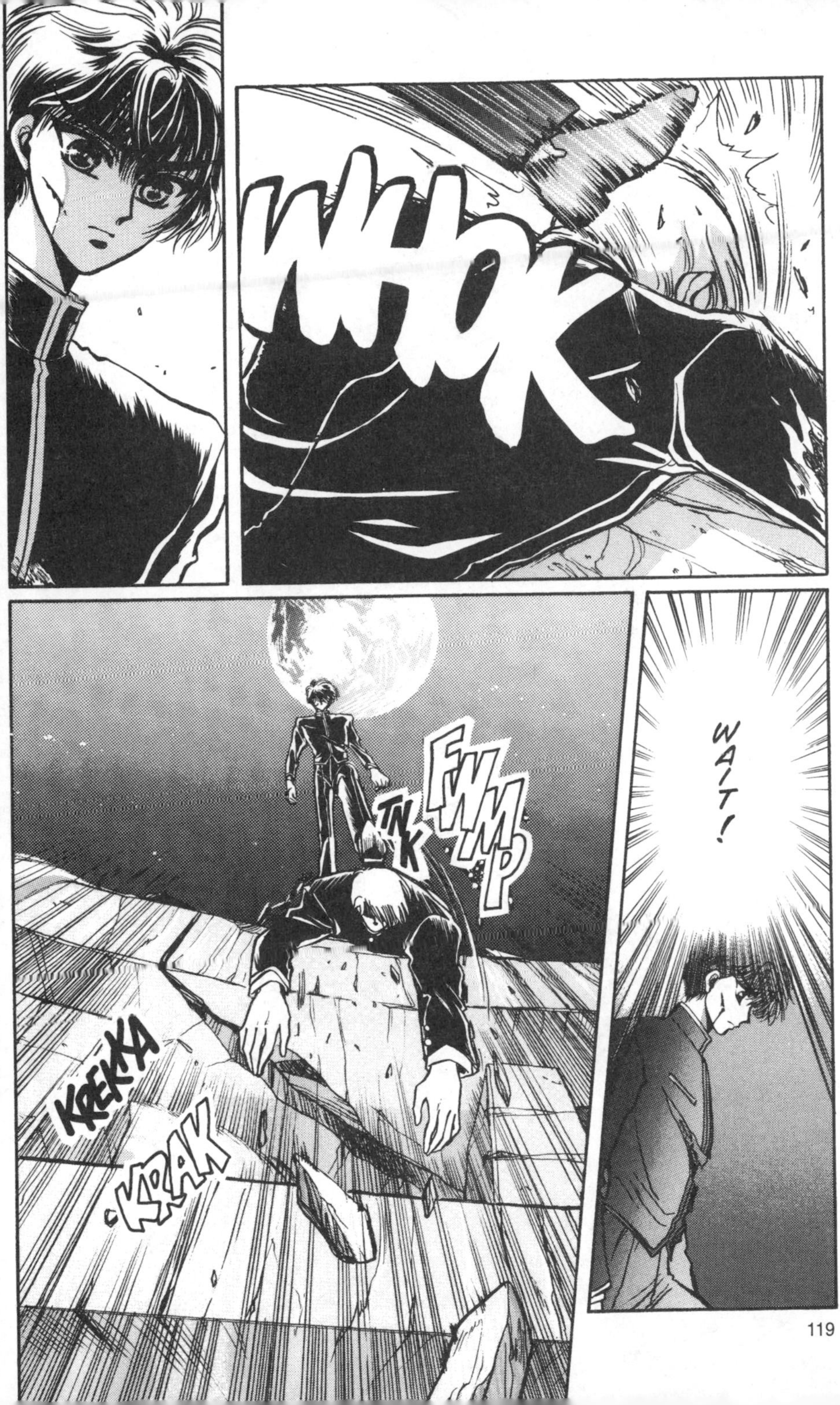
WHOK
FWMP
TNK
KREKKA
KRAK
WAIT!

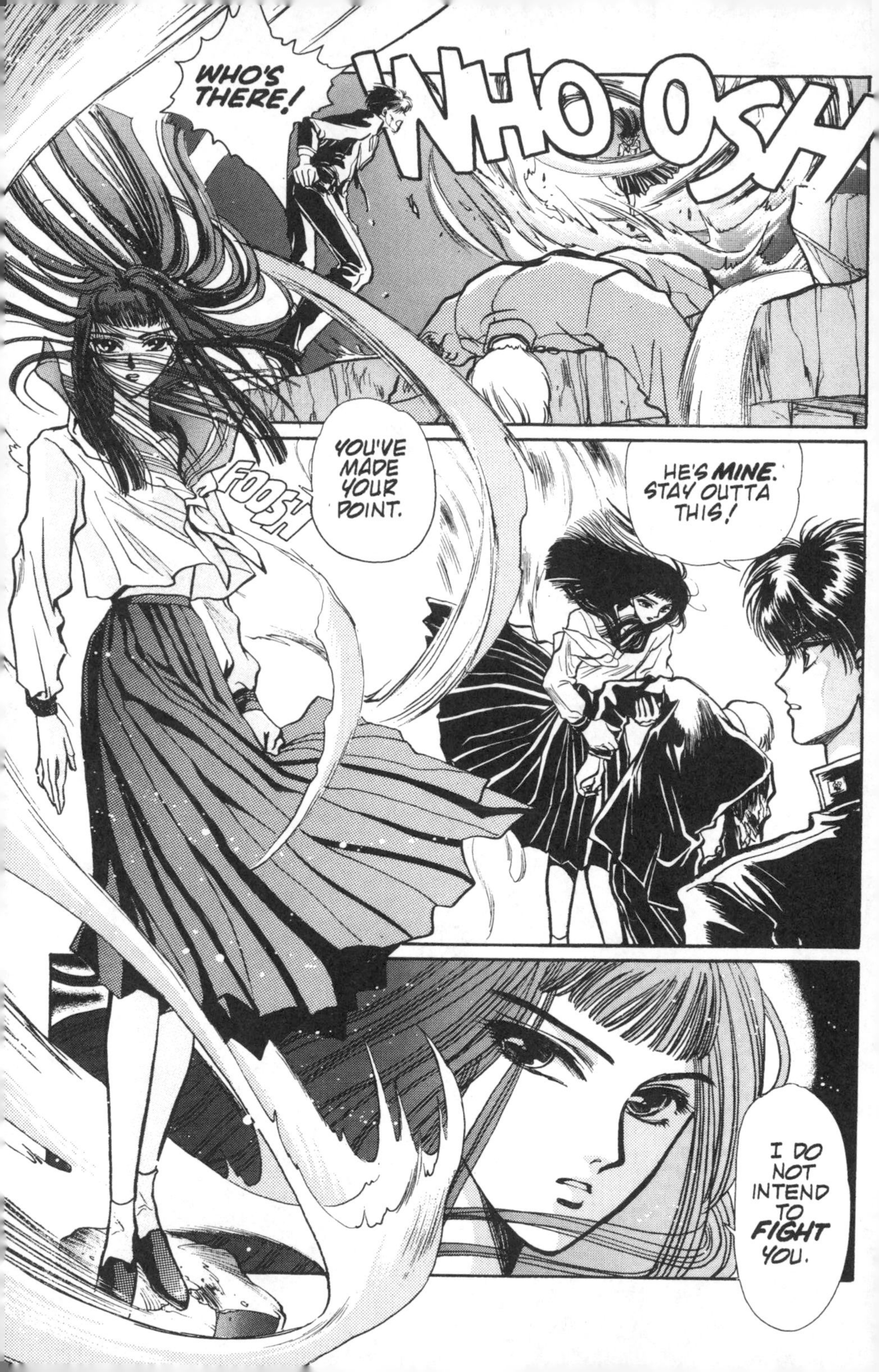
WHO'S THERE!
WHOOSH
FOOSH
YOU'VE MADE YOUR POINT.
HE'S MINE. STAY OUTTA THIS!
I DO NOT INTEND TO FIGHT YOU.

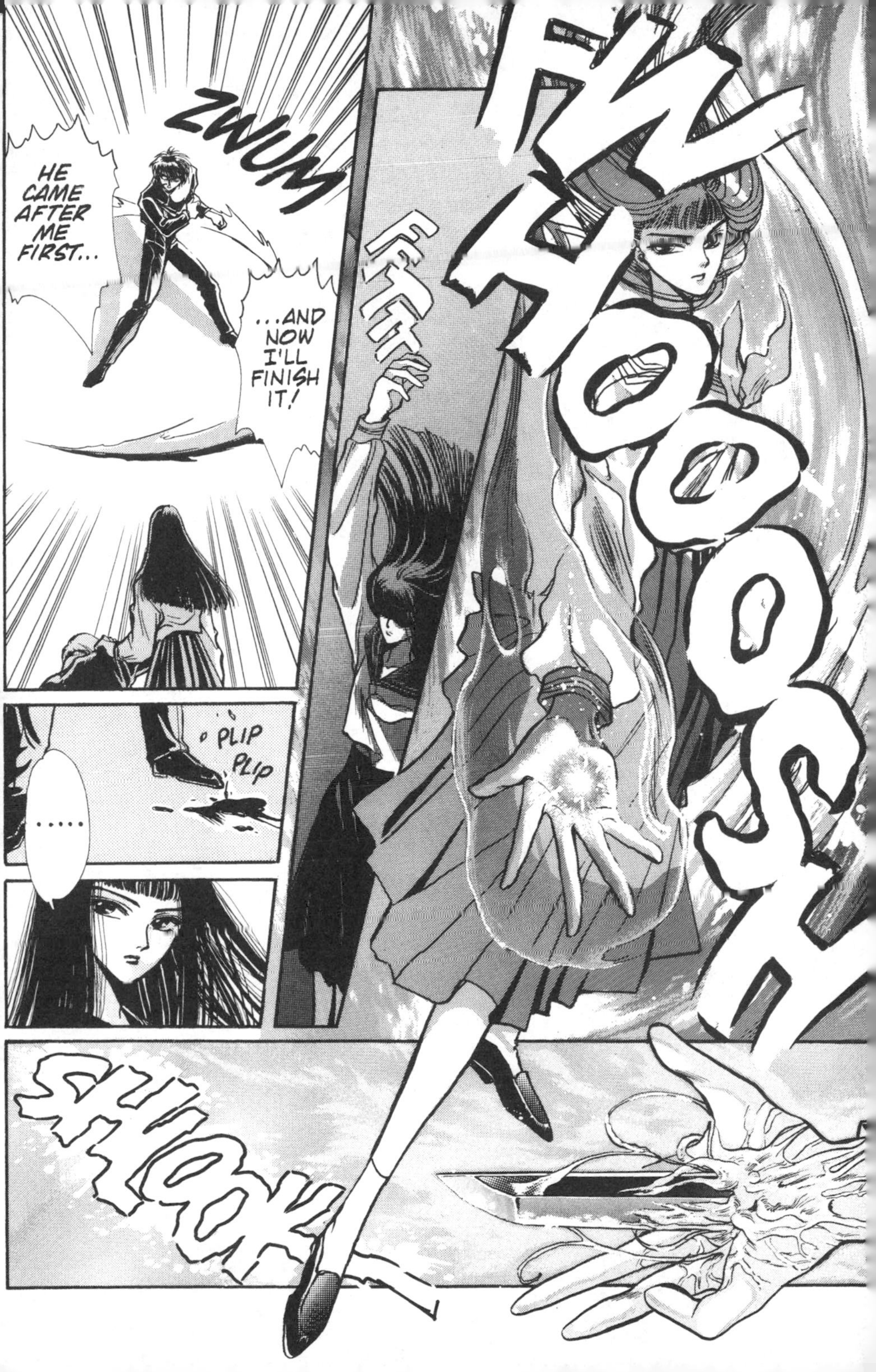
ZWUUM
HE CAME AFTER ME FIRST...
...AND NOW I'LL FINISH IT!
PLIP PLIP
.....
FFTT
FWOOOSH
SHACK

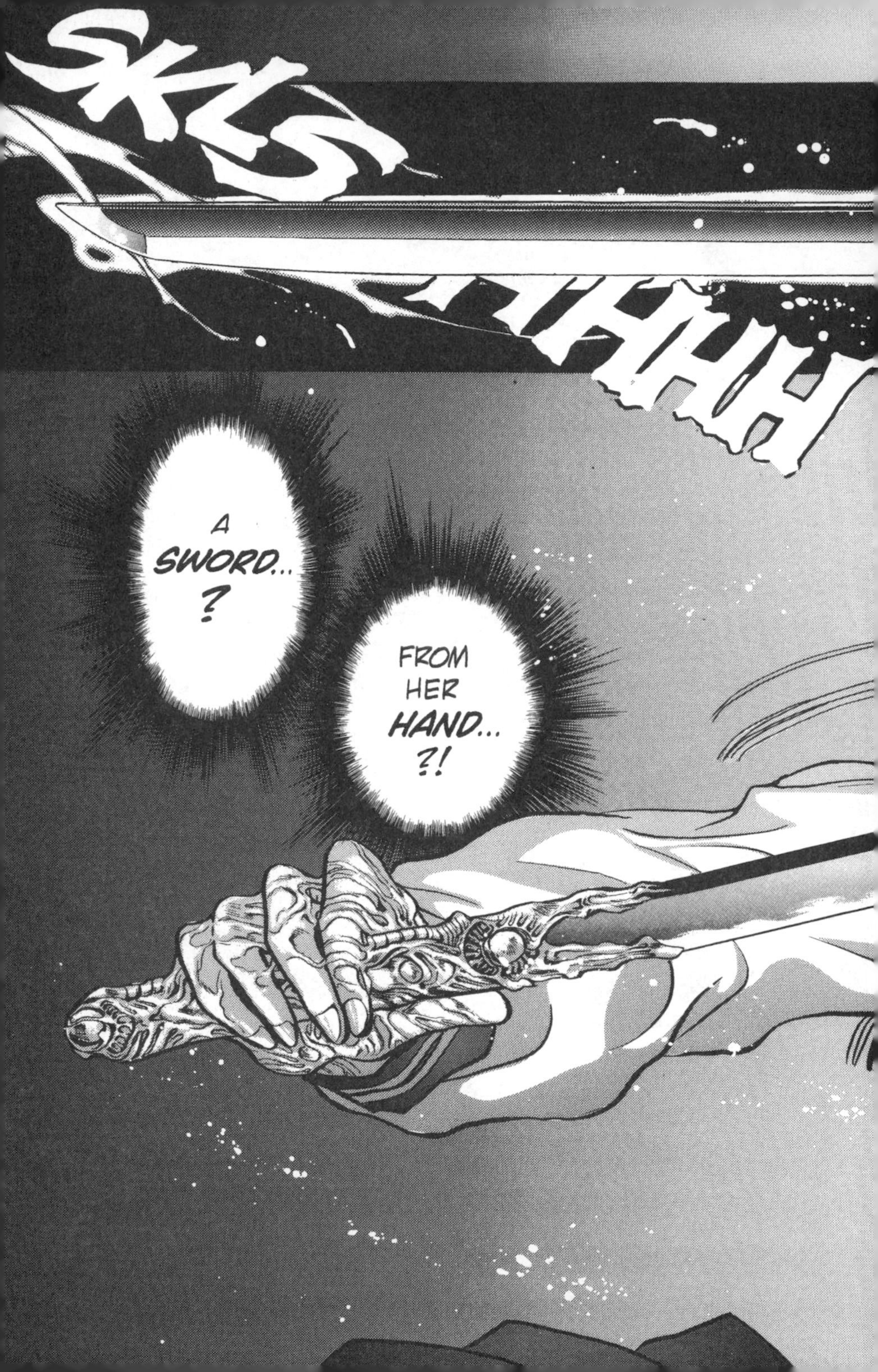
SKLSHHHH
A SWORD...?
FROM HER HAND...?!

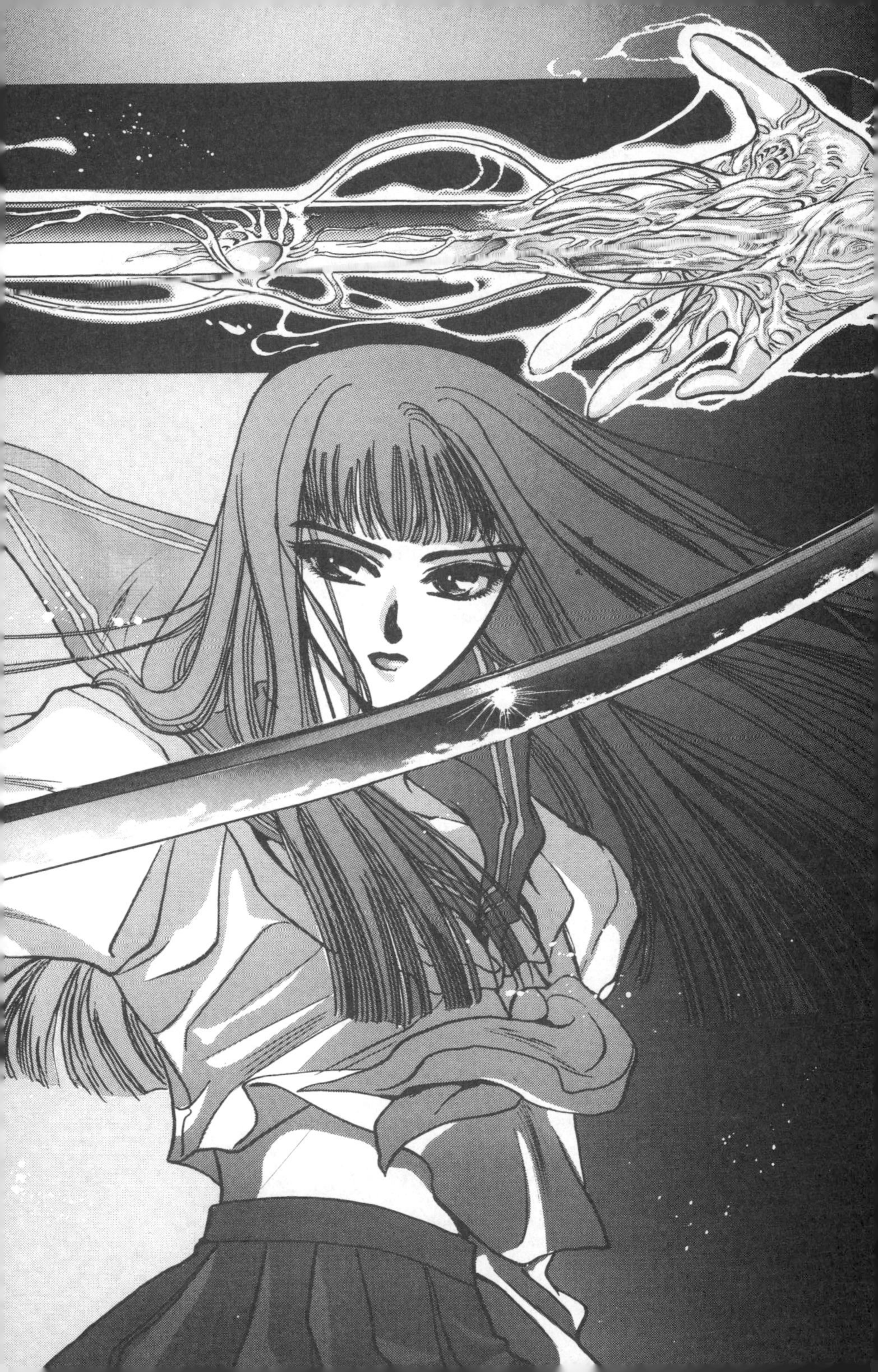

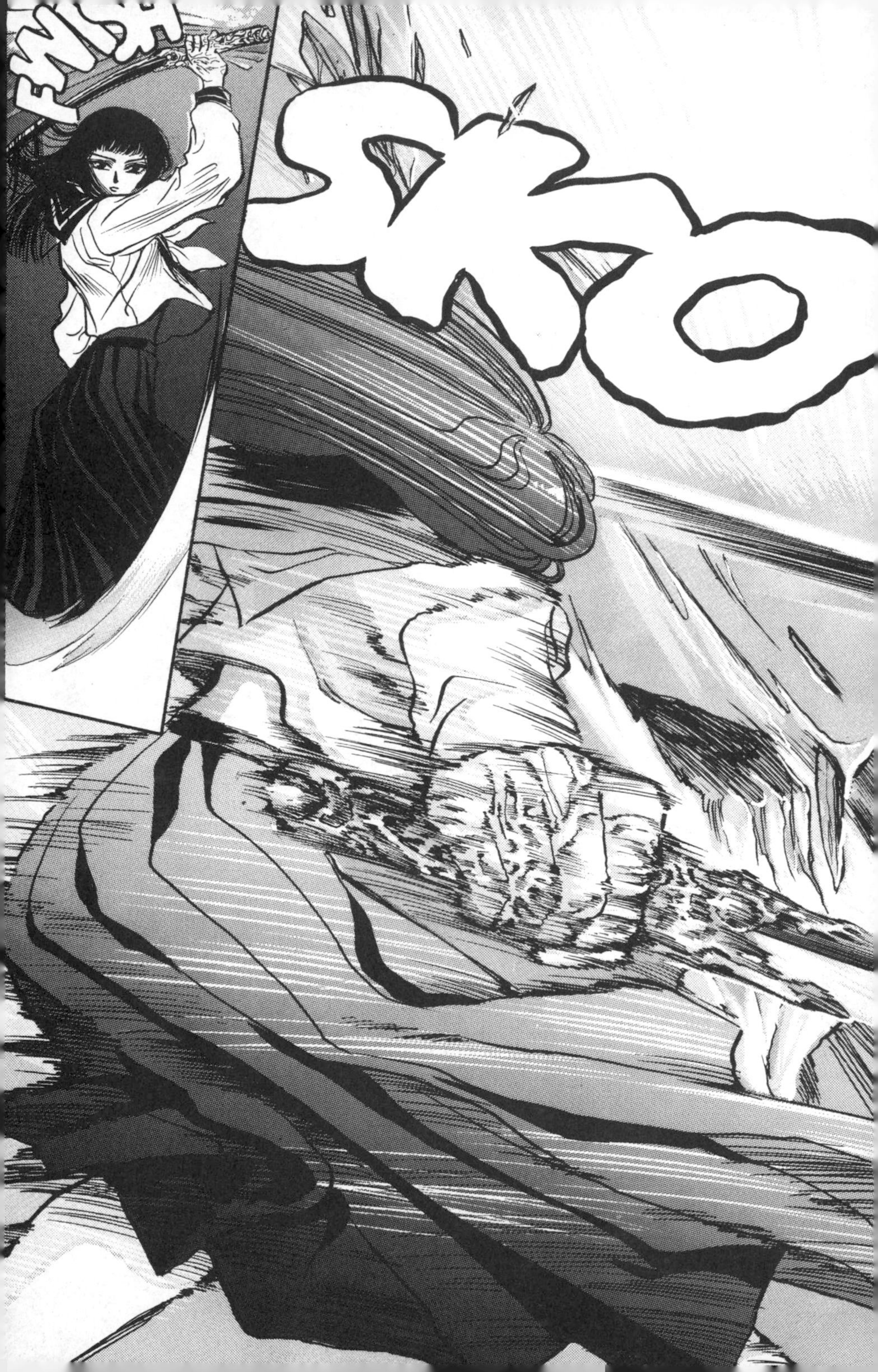
FWISH

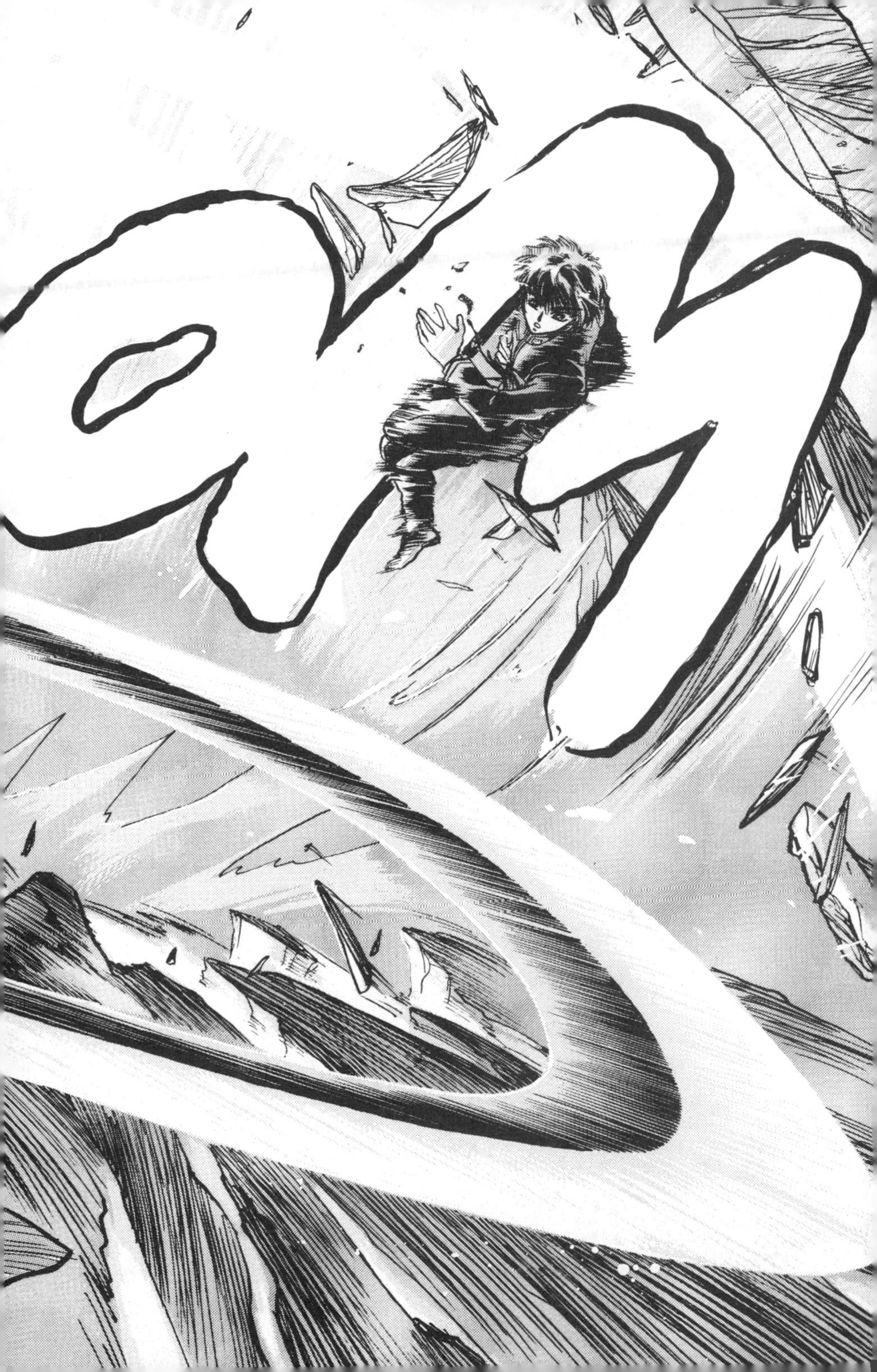

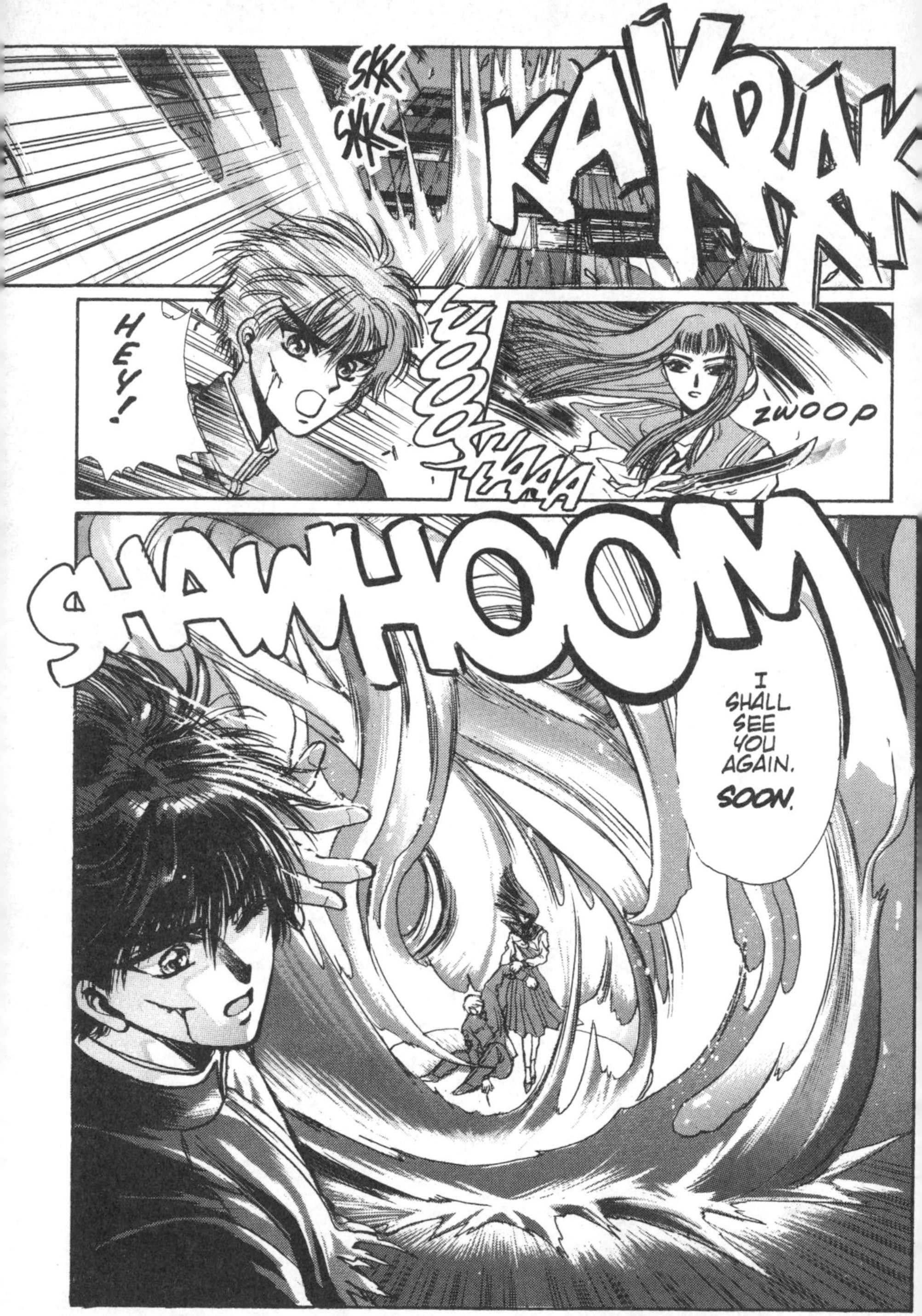
SKK
SKK
KAKRAK
HEY!
WOOOSHAAA
ZWOOP
SHAWHOOM
I SHALL SEE YOU AGAIN. SOON.

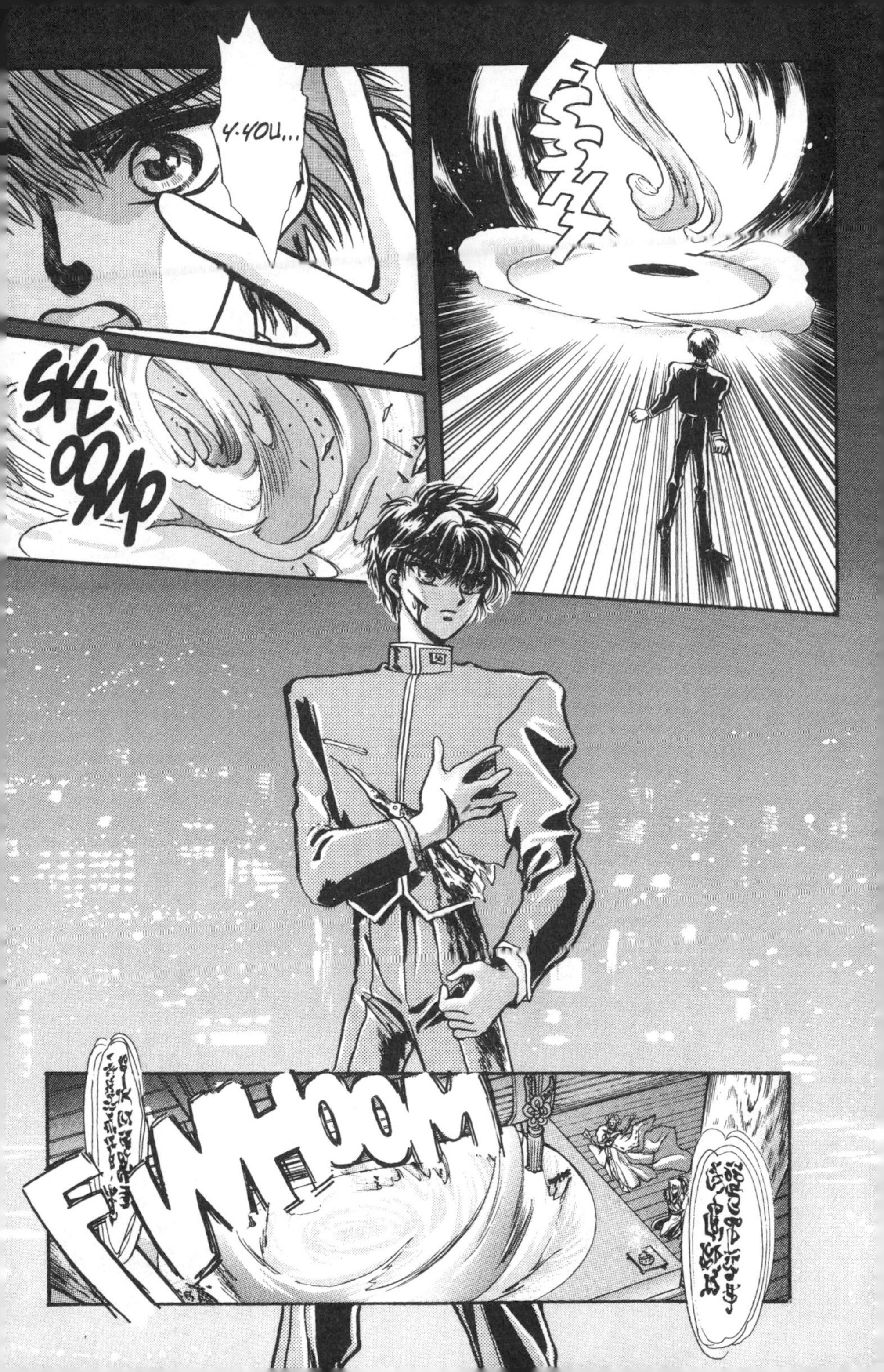
Y-YOU...
FWHOOM

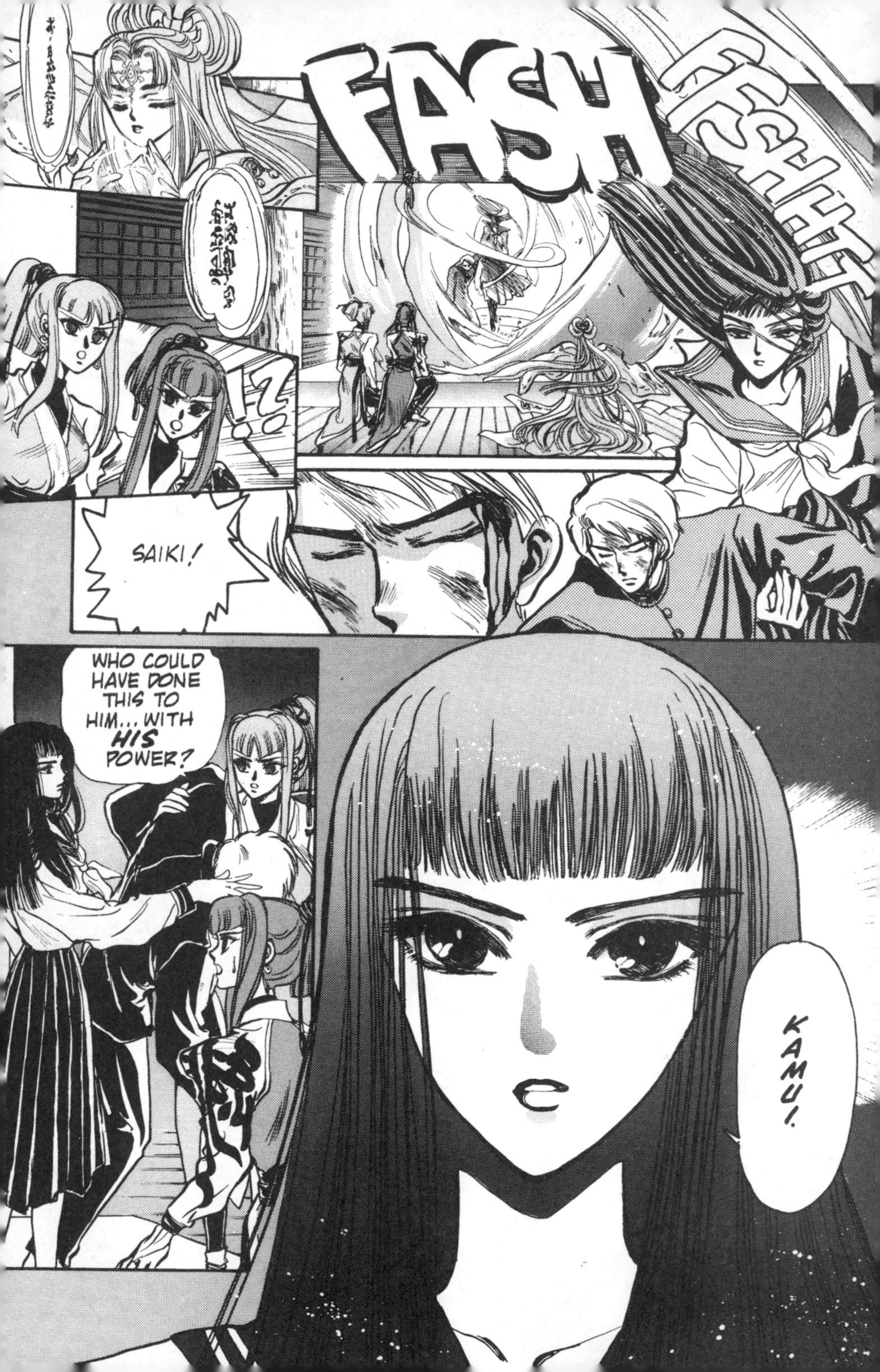
FASH
FSSHHT
!?
SAIKI!
WHO COULD HAVE DONE THIS TO HIM... WITH HIS POWER?
KAMUI.

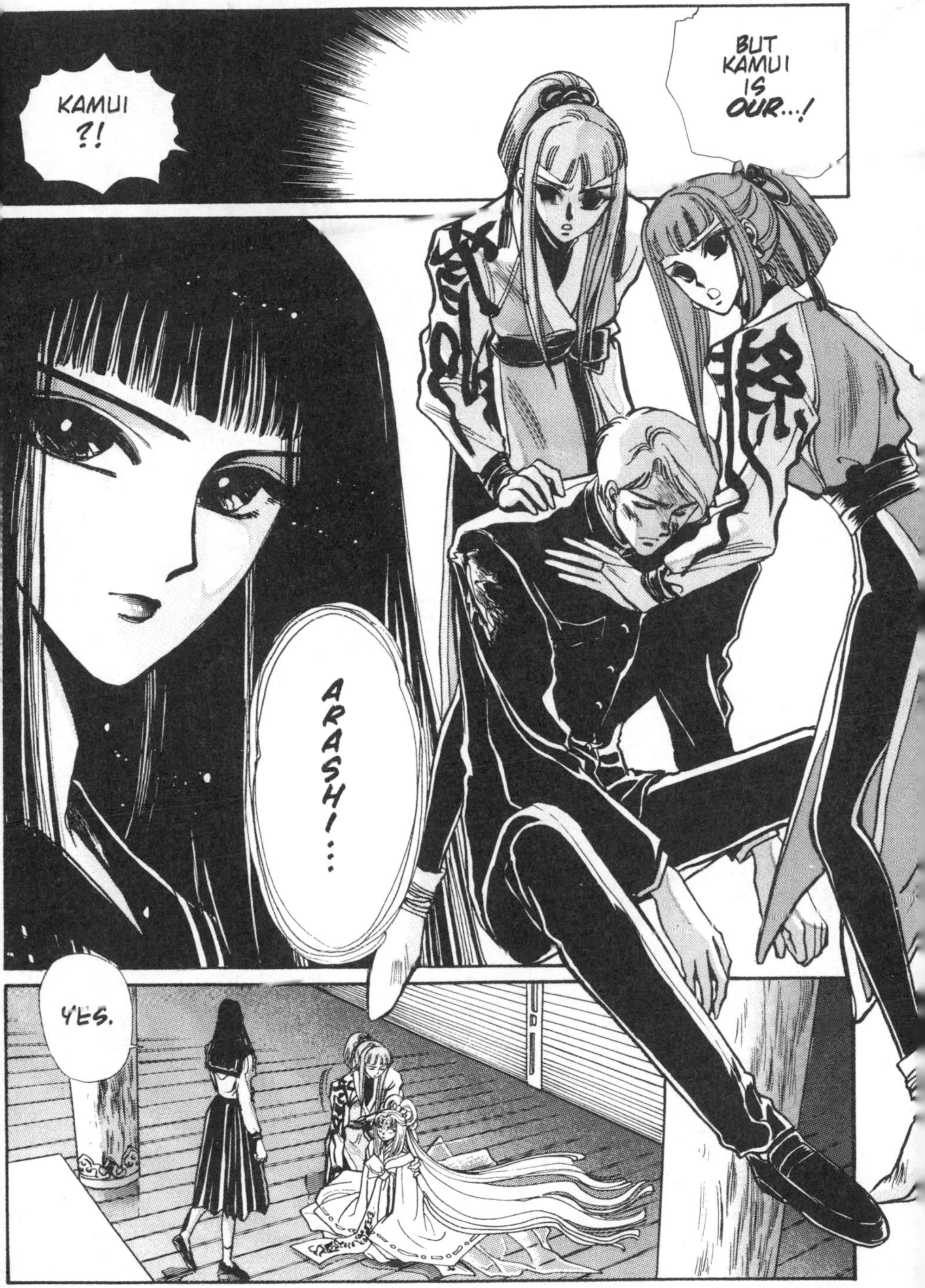
KAMUI ?!
BUT KAMUI IS OUR...!
ARASHI...
YES.

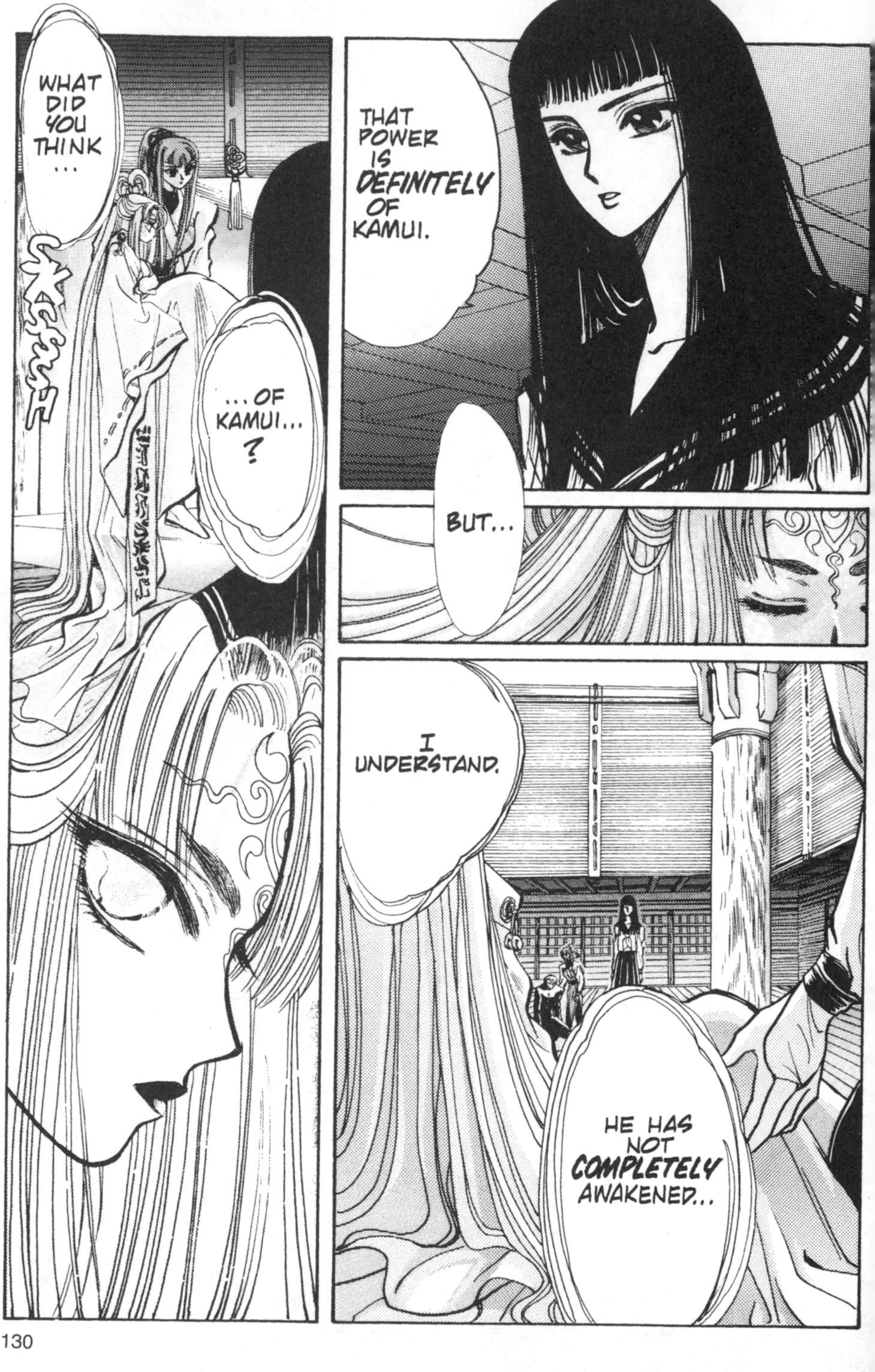
WHAT DID YOU THINK...
...OF KAMUI...?
THAT POWER IS DEFINITELY OF KAMUI.
BUT...
I UNDERSTAND.
HE HAS NOT COMPLETELY AWAKENED...

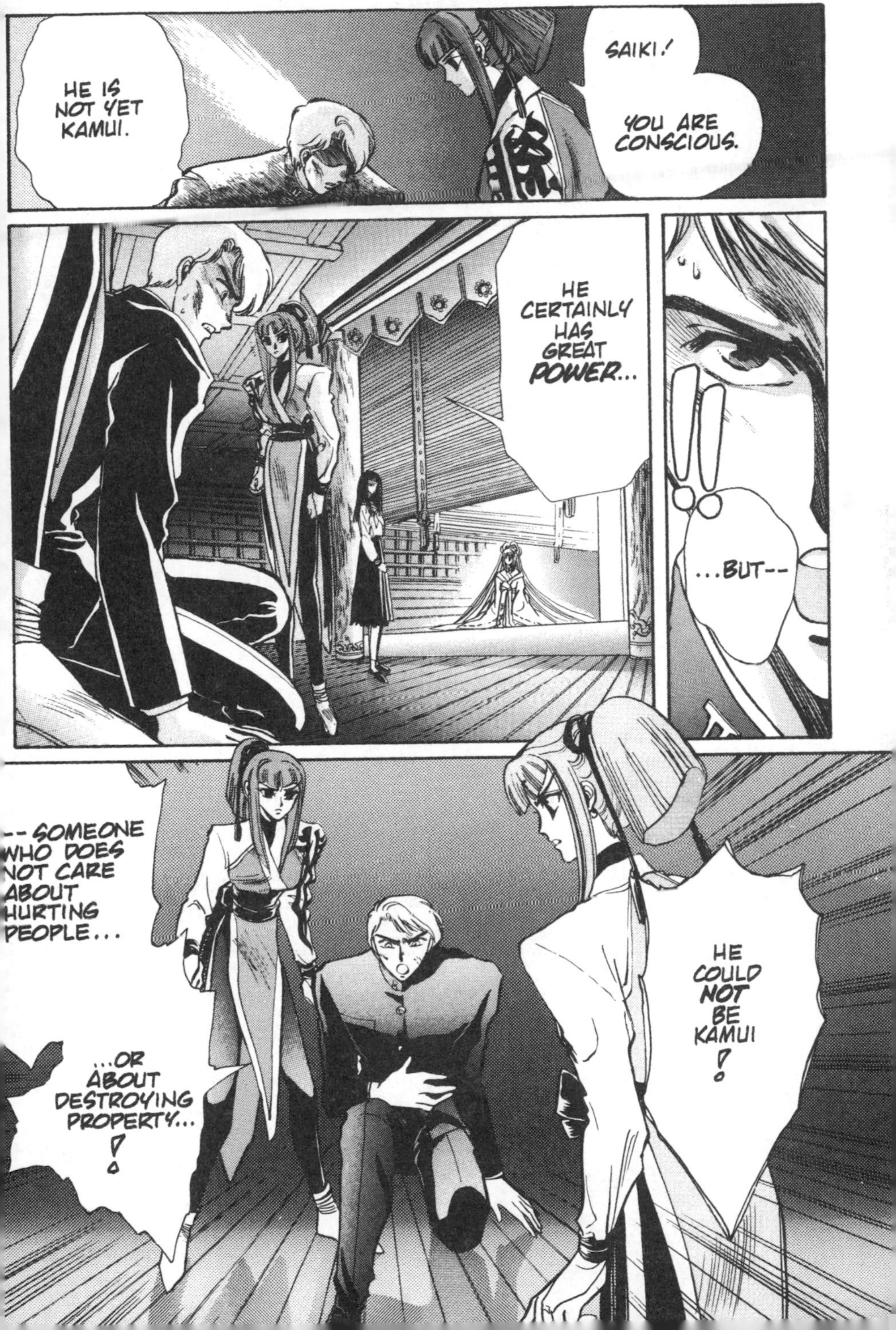
HE IS NOT YET KAMUI.
SAIKI!
YOU ARE CONSCIOUS.
HE CERTAINLY HAS GREAT POWER...
!!
...BUT--
--SOMEONE WHO DOES NOT CARE ABOUT HURTING PEOPLE...
...OR ABOUT DESTROYING PROPERTY...!
HE COULD NOT BE KAMUI!

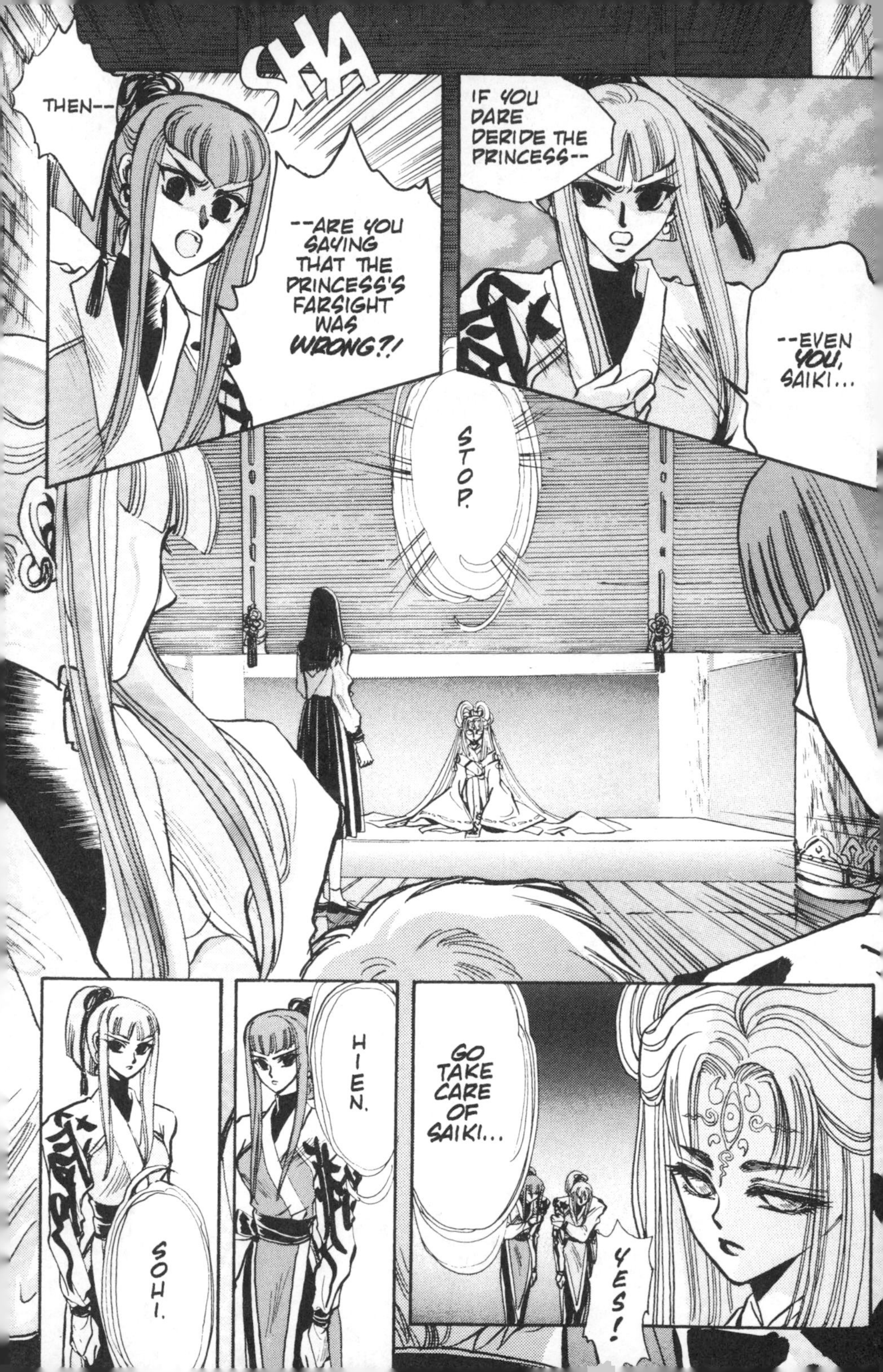
THEN--
SHA
--ARE YOU SAYING THAT THE PRINCESS'S FARSIGHT WAS WRONG?!
IF YOU DARE DERIDE THE PRINCESS--
--EVEN YOU, SAIKI...
STOP.
SOHI.
HIEN.
GO TAKE CARE OF SAIKI...
YES!

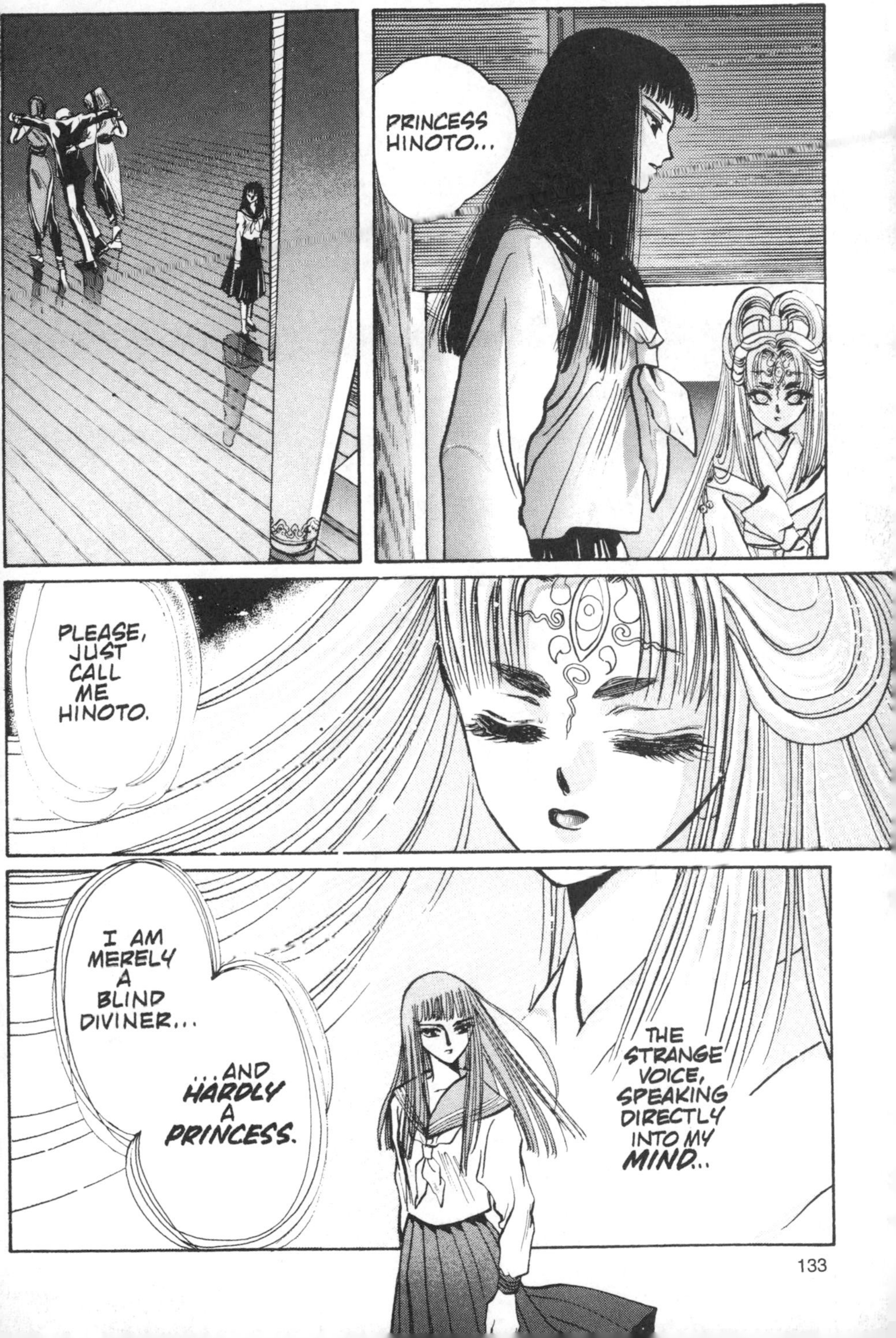
PRINCESS HINOTO...
PLEASE, JUST CALL ME HINOTO.
I AM MERELY A BLIND DIVINER...
...AND HARDLY A PRINCESS.
THE STRANGE VOICE, SPEAKING DIRECTLY INTO MY MIND...

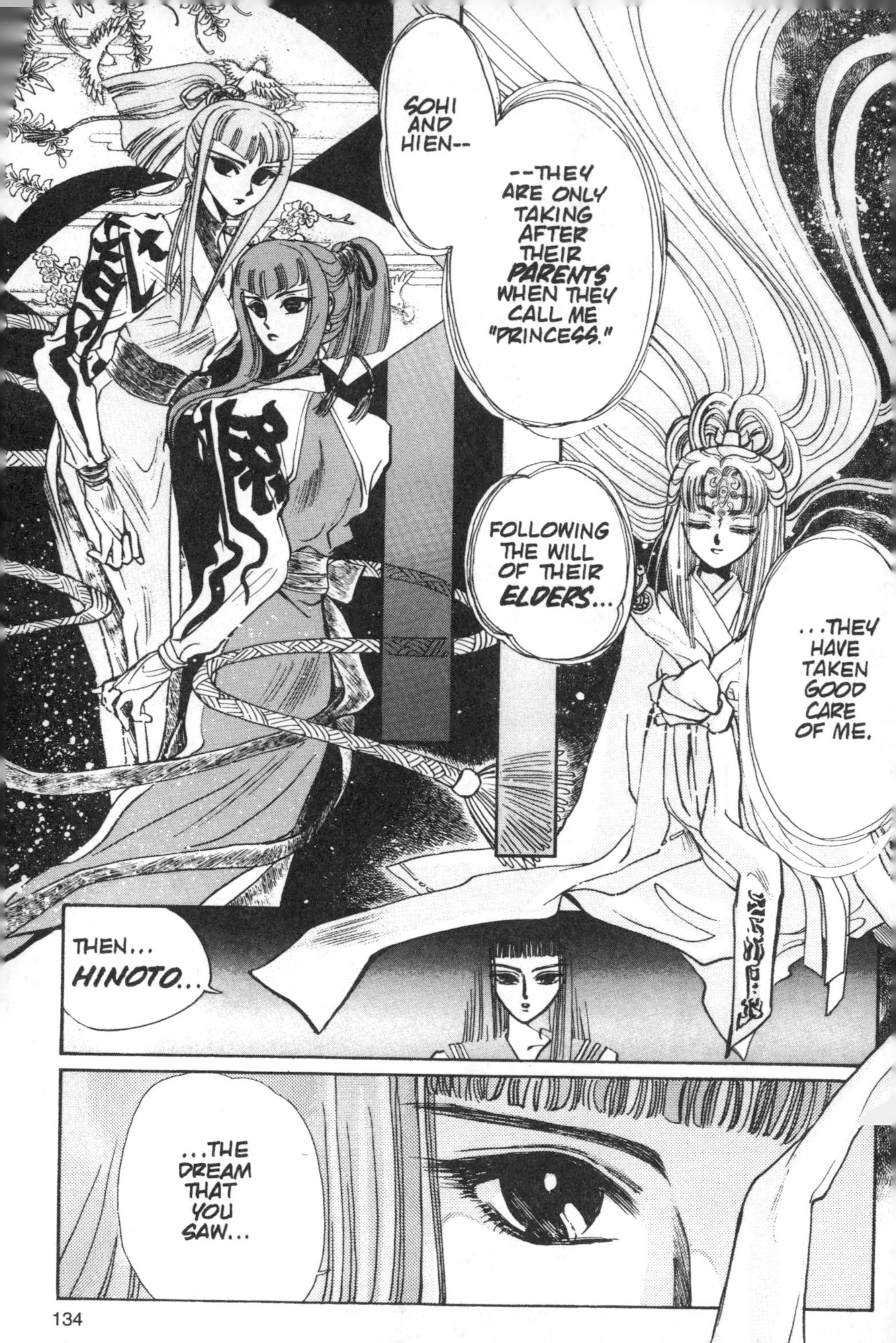
SOHI AND HIEN--
--THEY ARE ONLY TAKING AFTER THEIR PARENTS WHEN THEY CALL ME "PRINCESS."
FOLLOWING THE WILL OF THEIR ELDERS...
...THEY HAVE TAKEN GOOD CARE OF ME.
THEN... HINOTO...
...THE DREAM THAT YOU SAW...

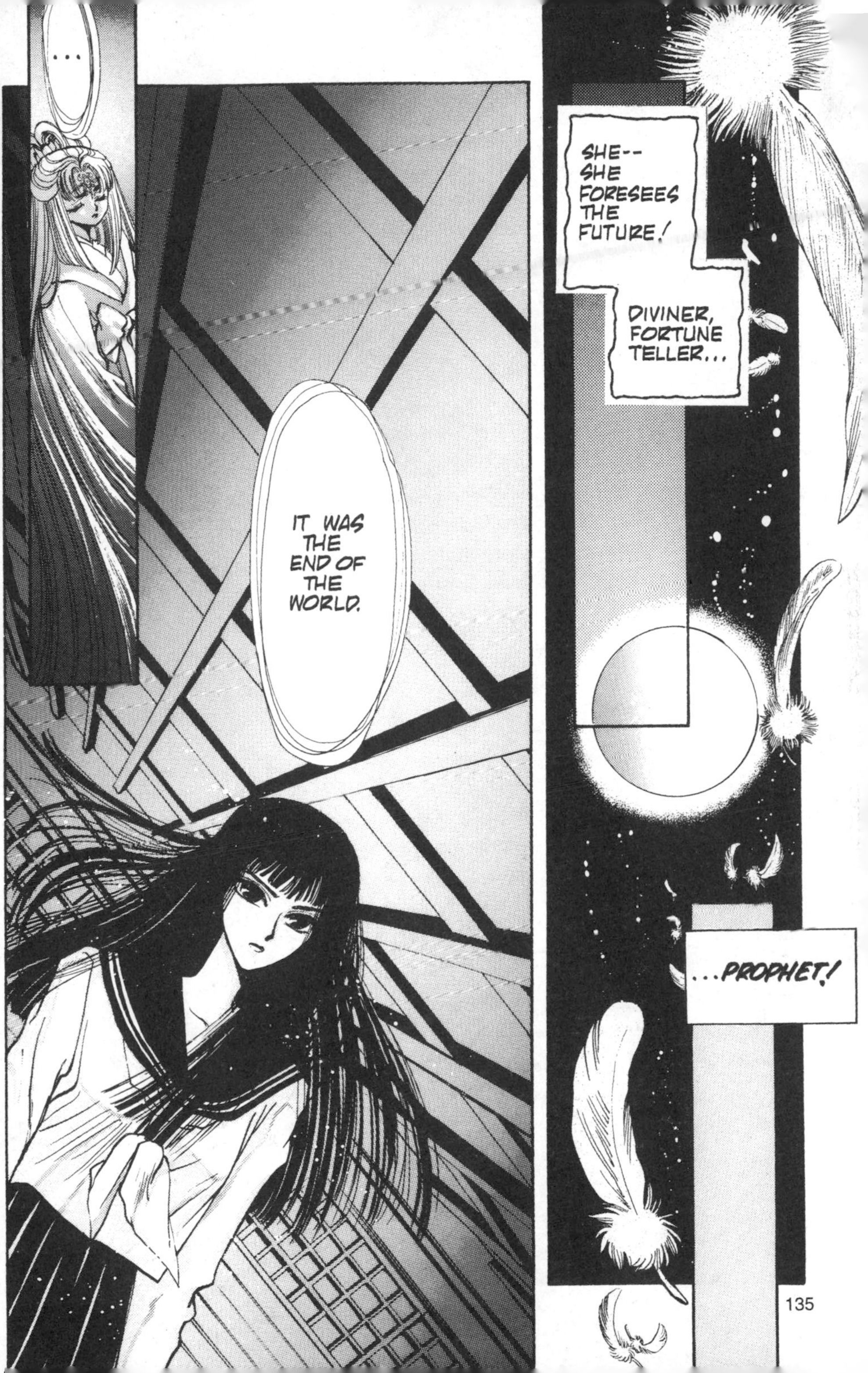
...
IT WAS THE END OF THE WORLD.
SHE-- SHE FORESEES THE FUTURE!
DIVINER, FORTUNE TELLER...
...PROPHET!

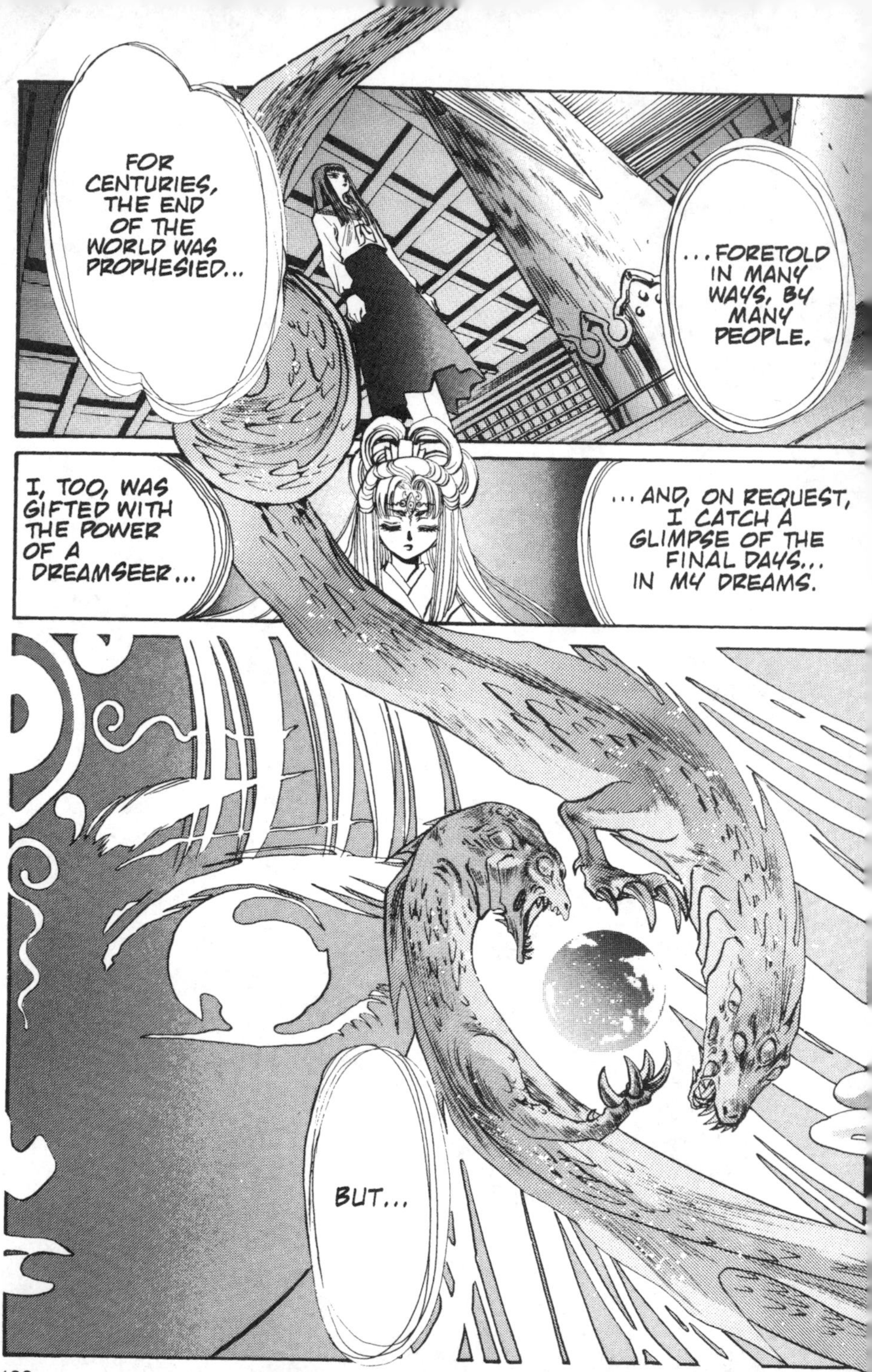
FOR CENTURIES, THE END OF THE WORLD WAS PROPHESIED...
...FORETOLD IN MANY WAYS, BY MANY PEOPLE.
I, TOO, WAS GIFTED WITH THE POWER OF A DREAMSEER...
...AND, ON REQUEST, I CATCH A GLIMPSE OF THE FINAL DAYS... IN MY DREAMS.
BUT...

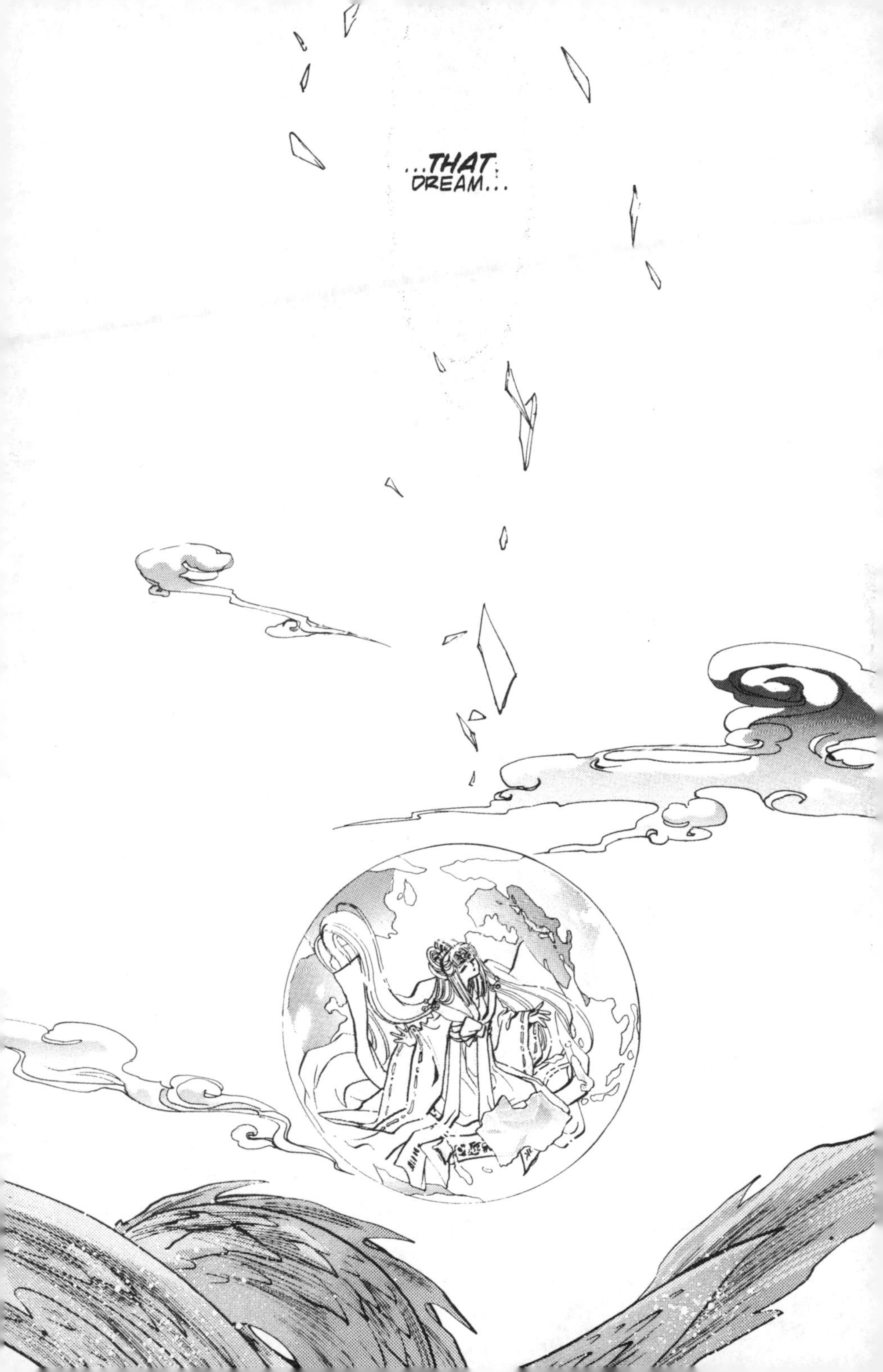
...THAT DREAM...

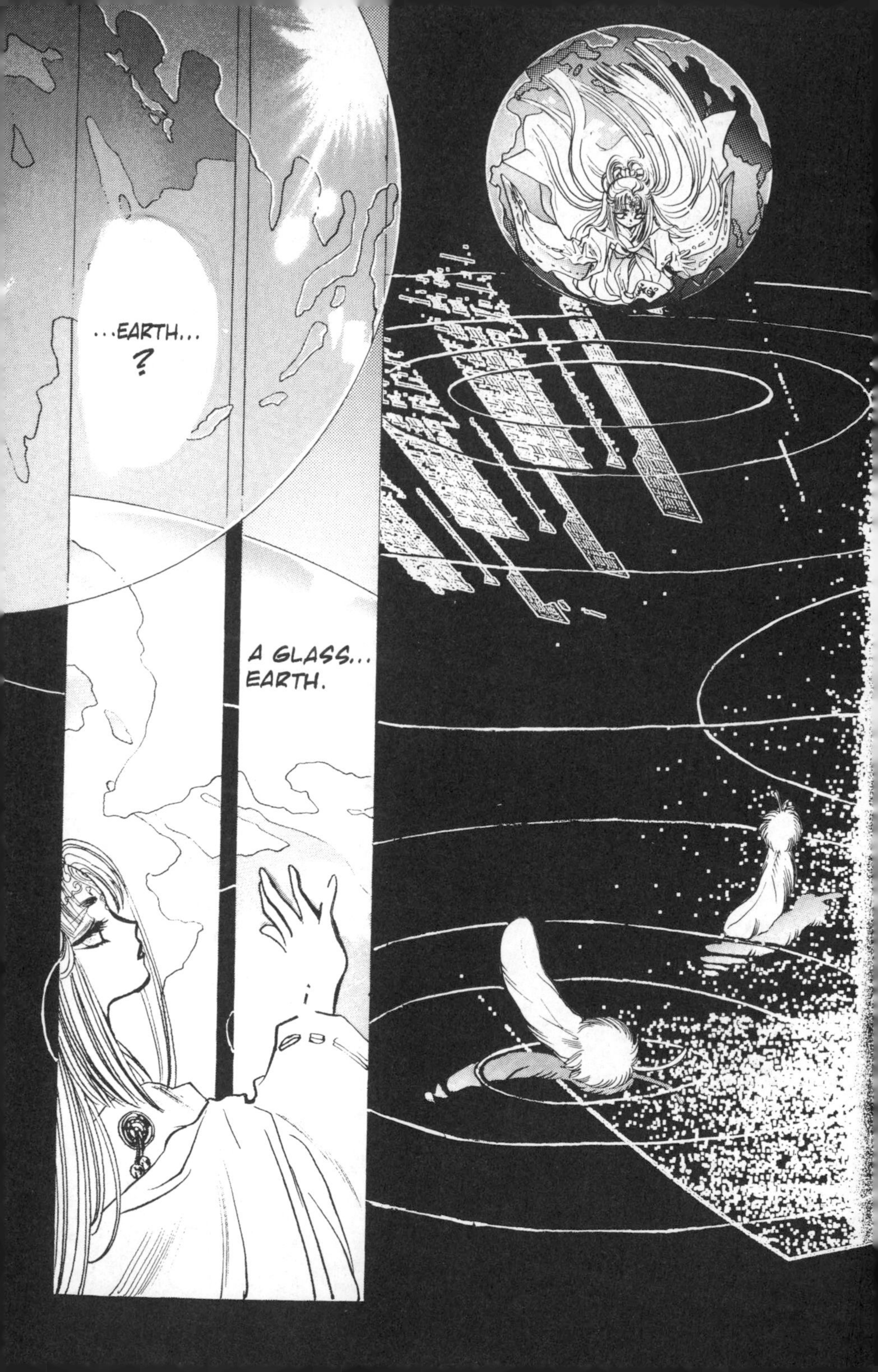
...EARTH...
?
A GLASS...
EARTH.

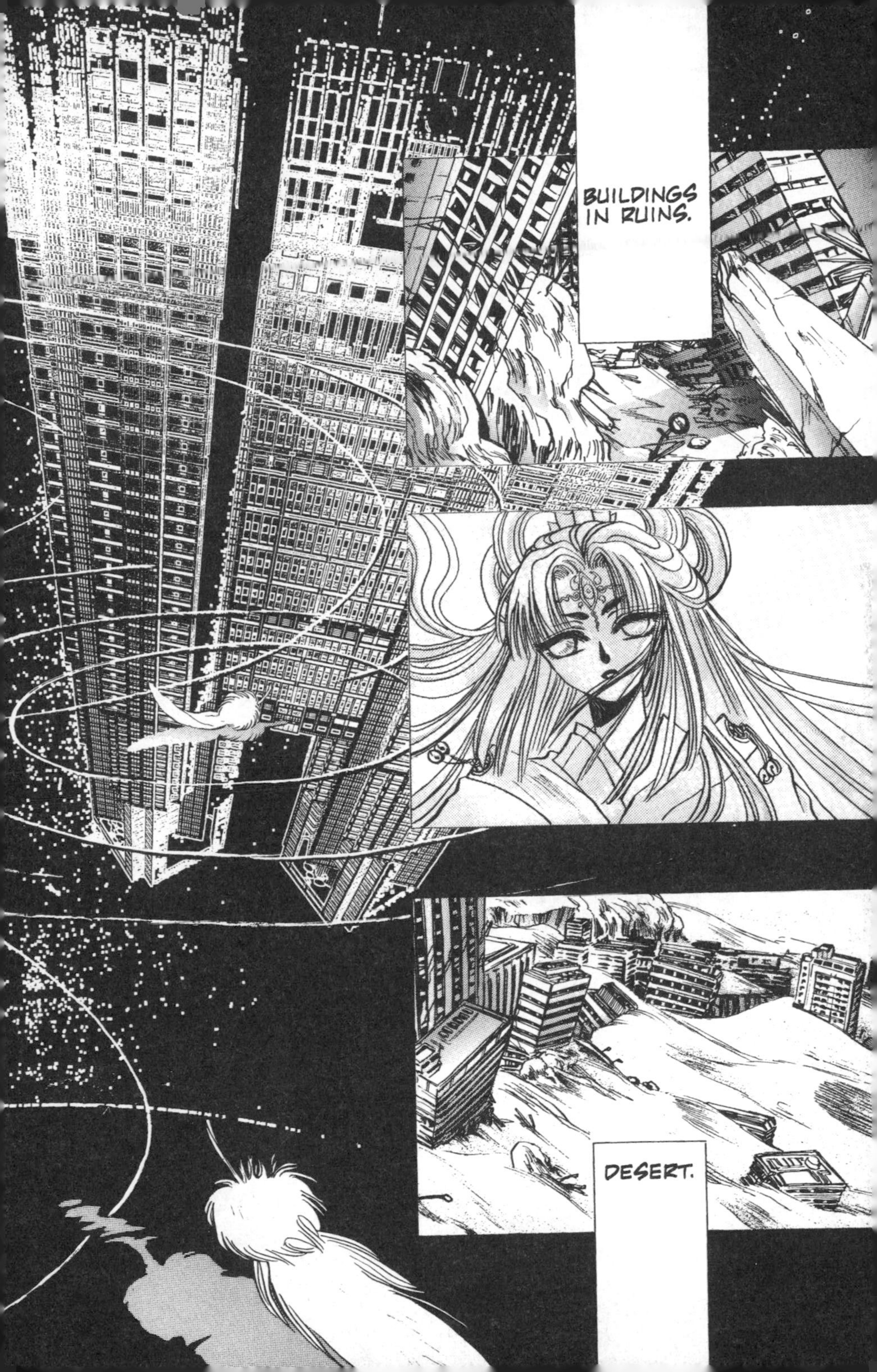
BUILDINGS IN RUINS.
DESERT.

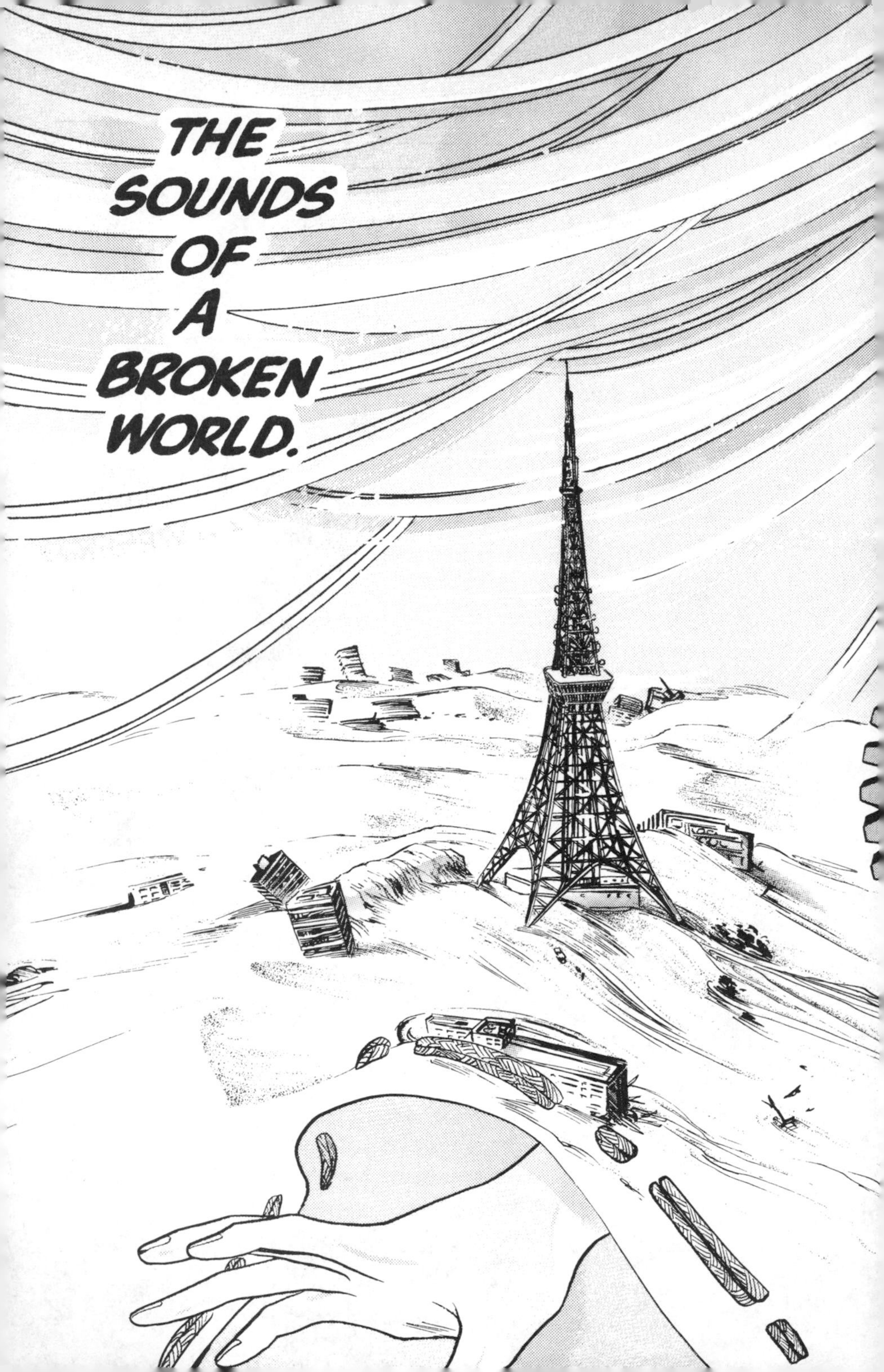
THE SOUNDS OF A BROKEN WORLD.

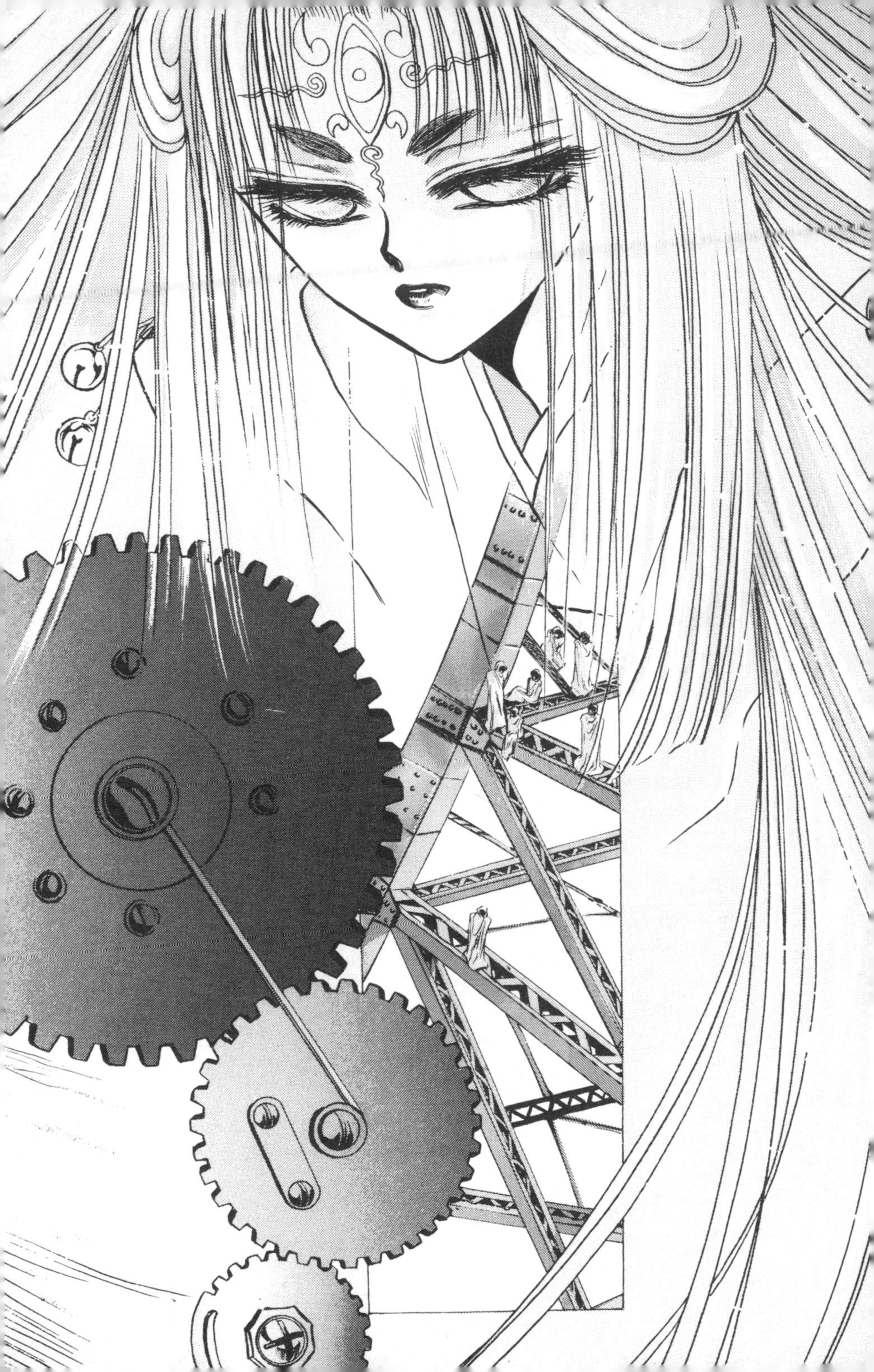

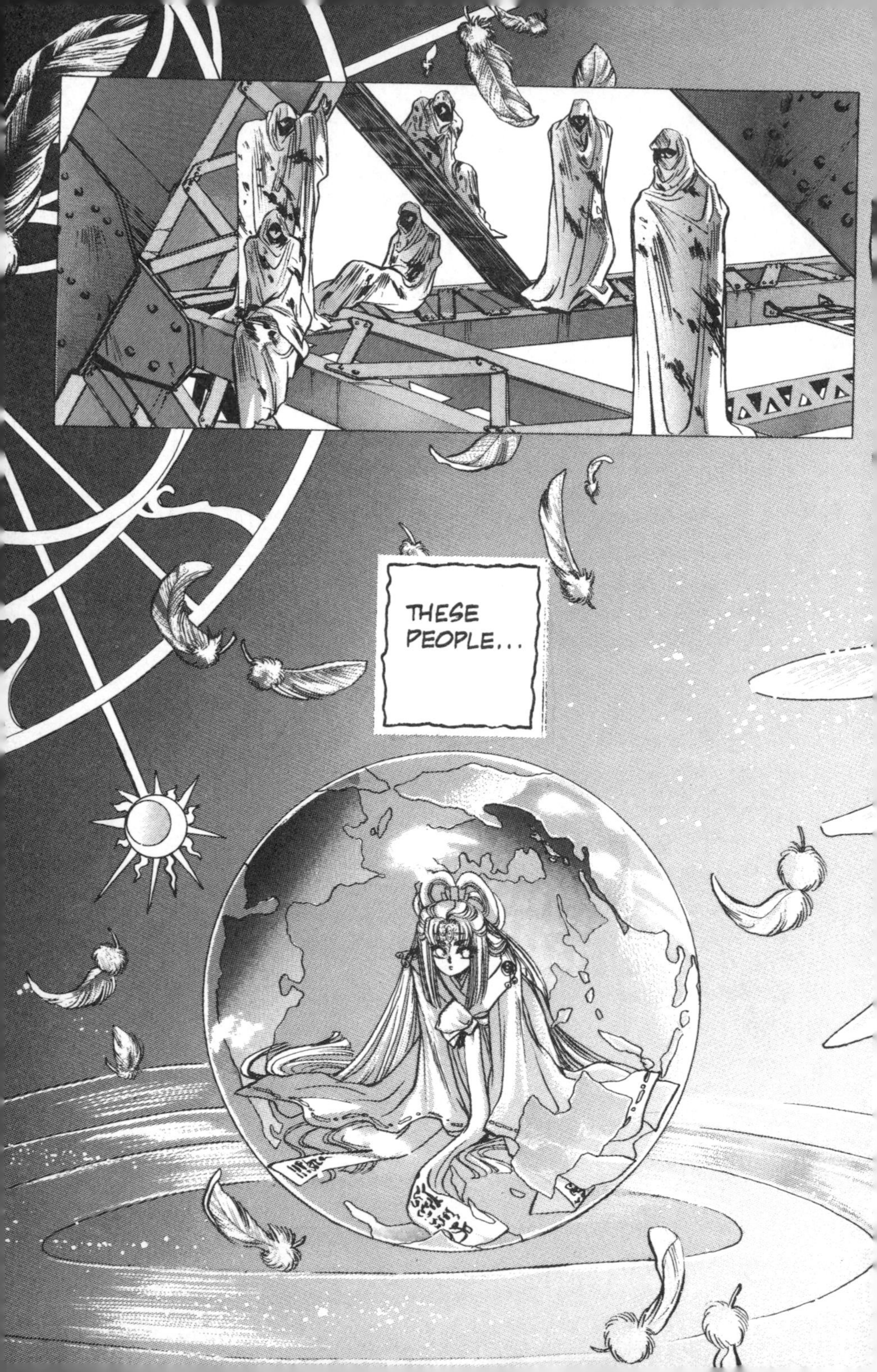
THESE PEOPLE...

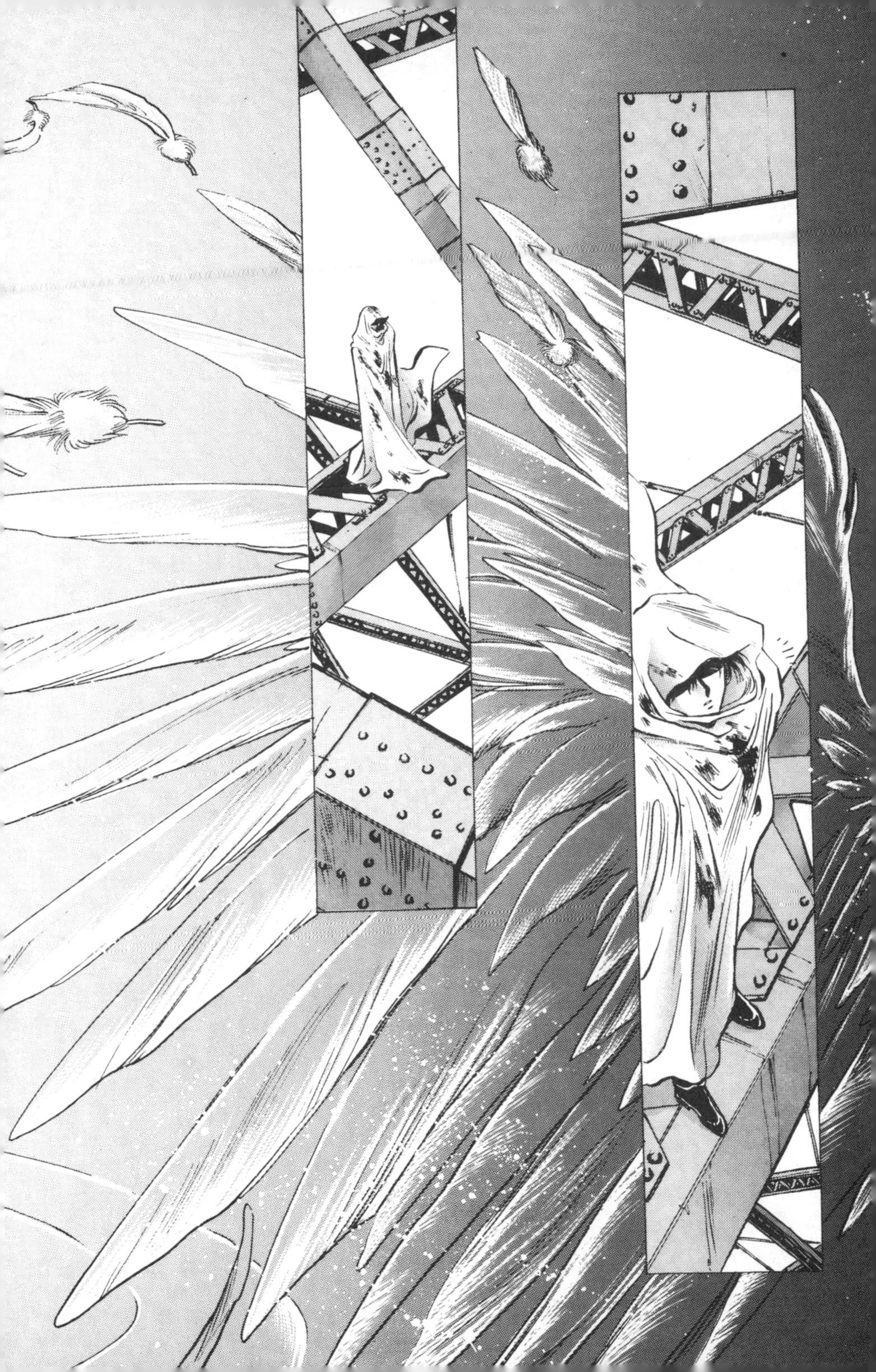

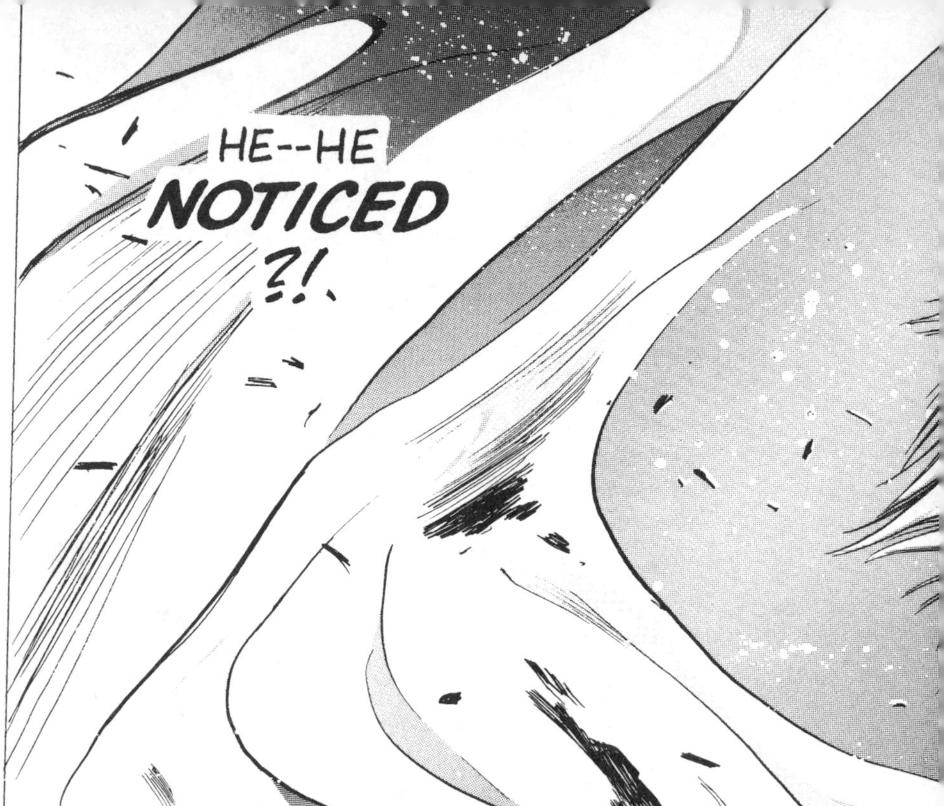
HE--HE NOTICED ?!

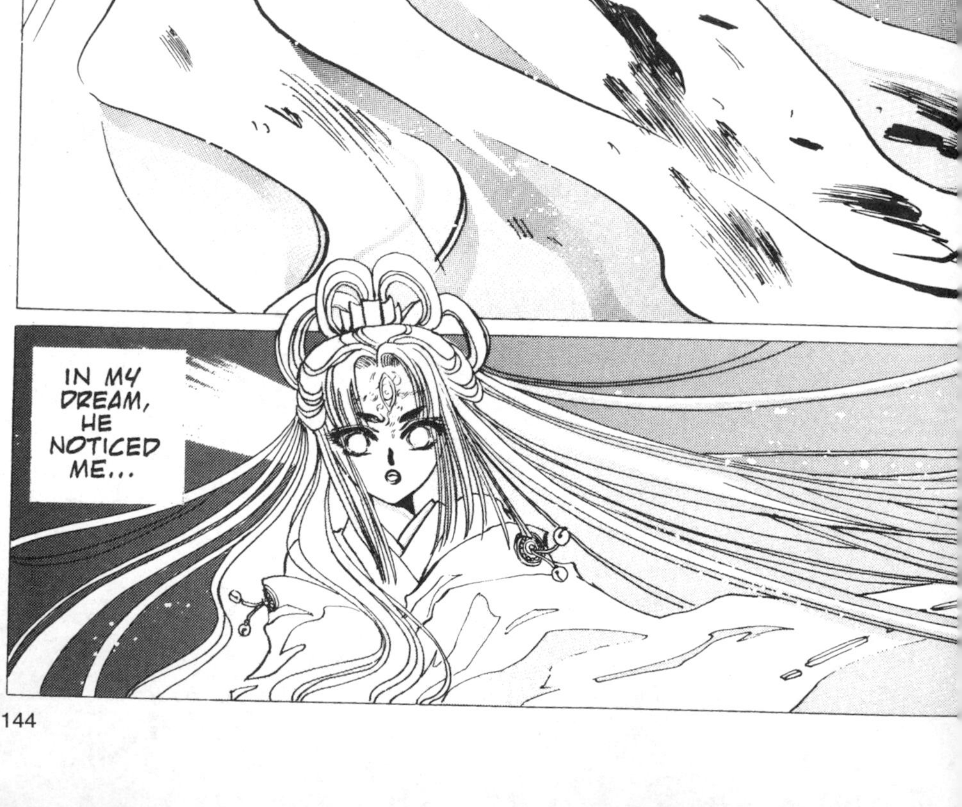
IN MY DREAM, HE NOTICED ME...

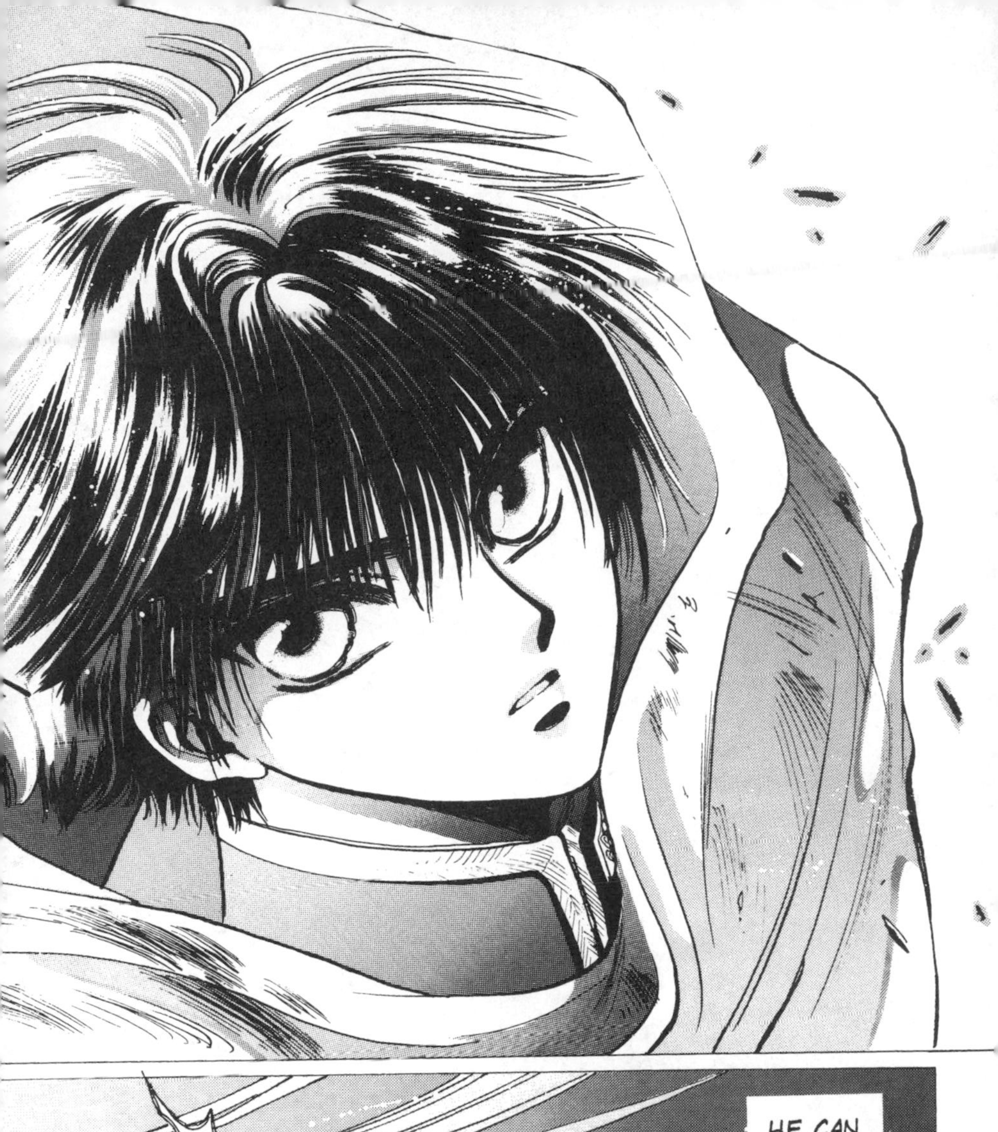

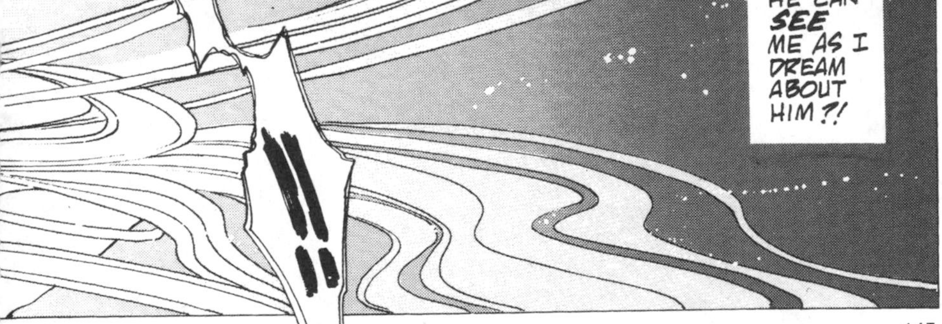
HE CAN SEE ME AS I DREAM ABOUT HIM?!

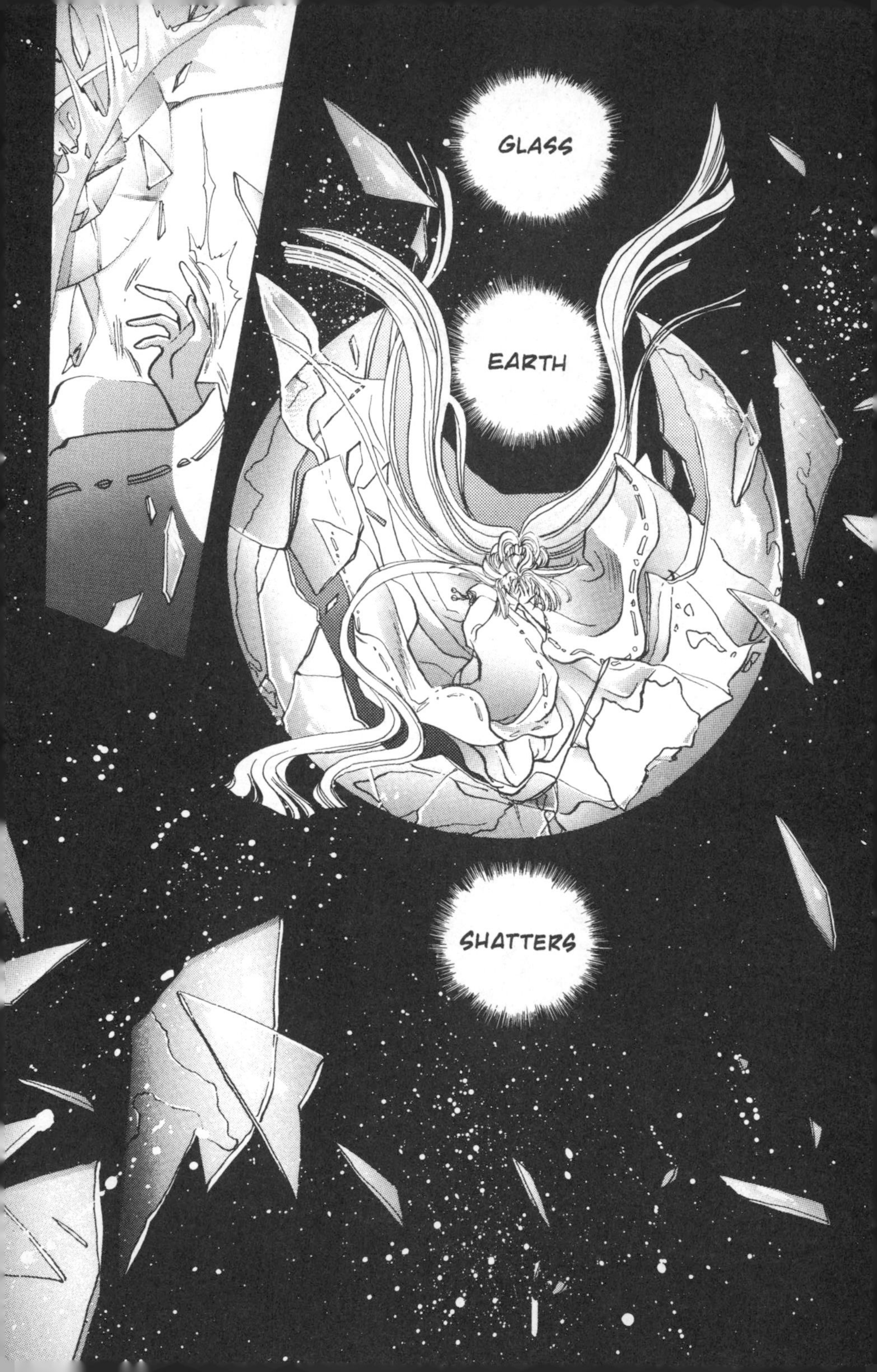
GLASS
EARTH
SHATTERS

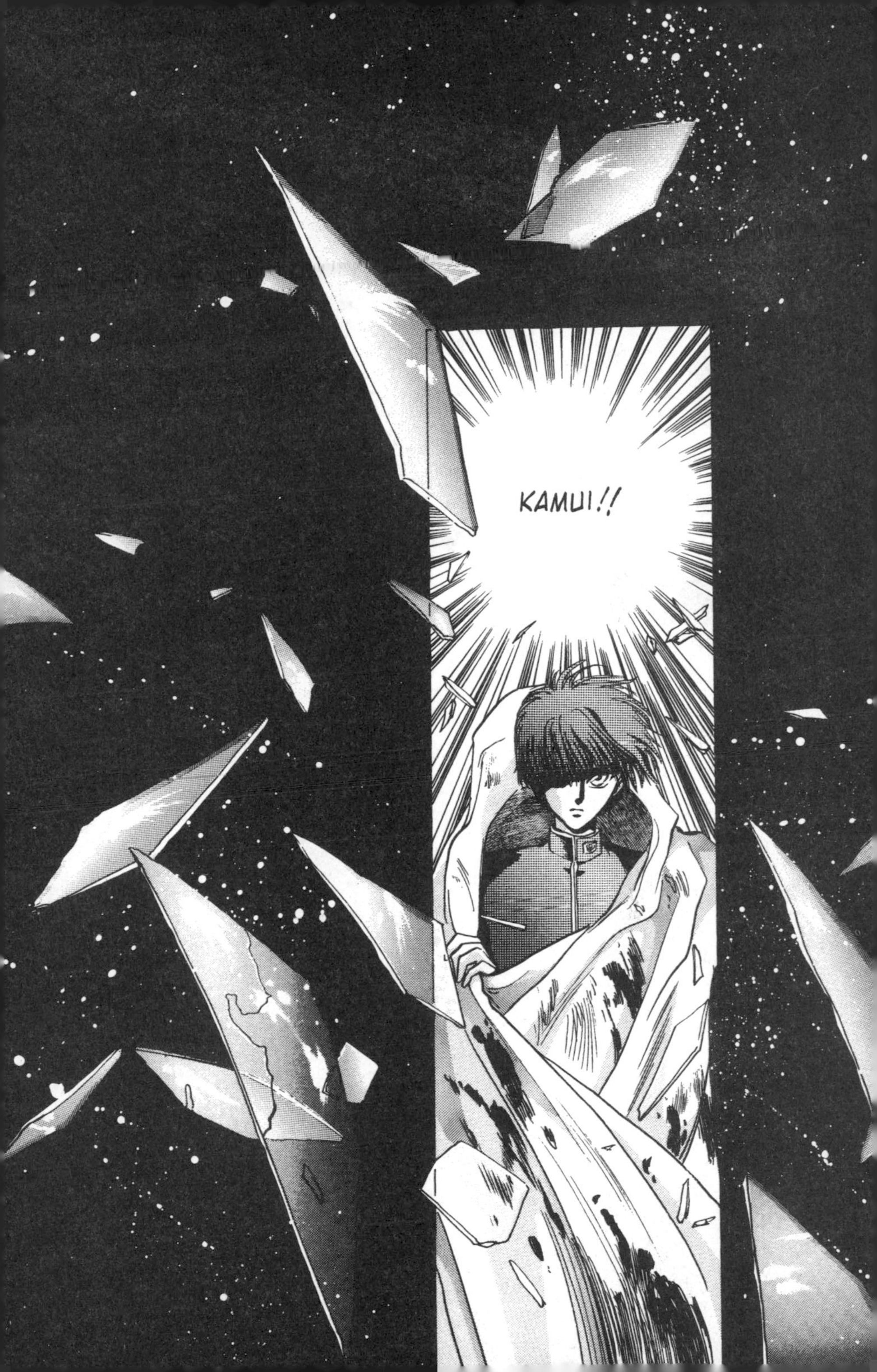
KAMUI!!

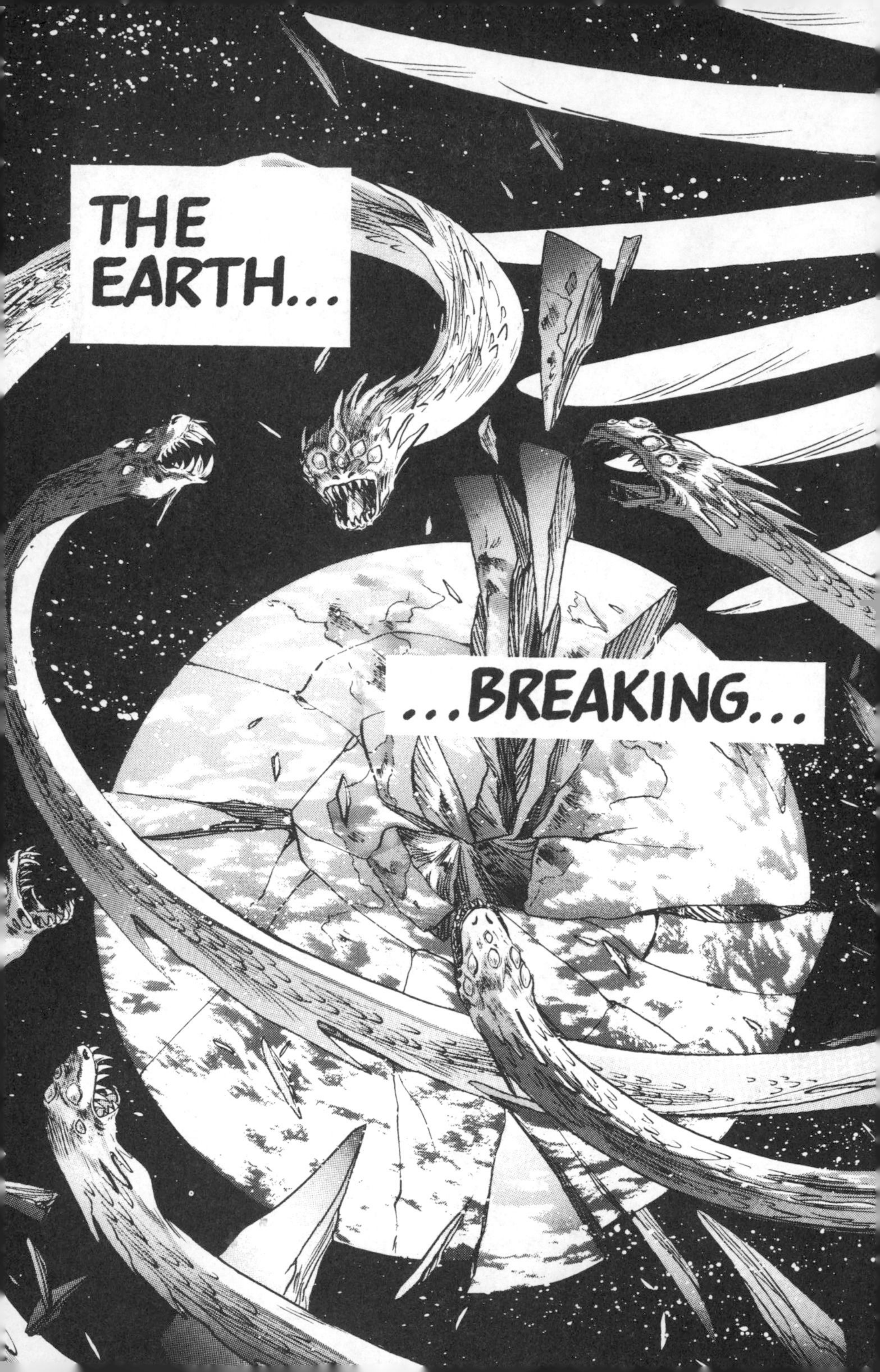
THE EARTH...
...BREAKING...

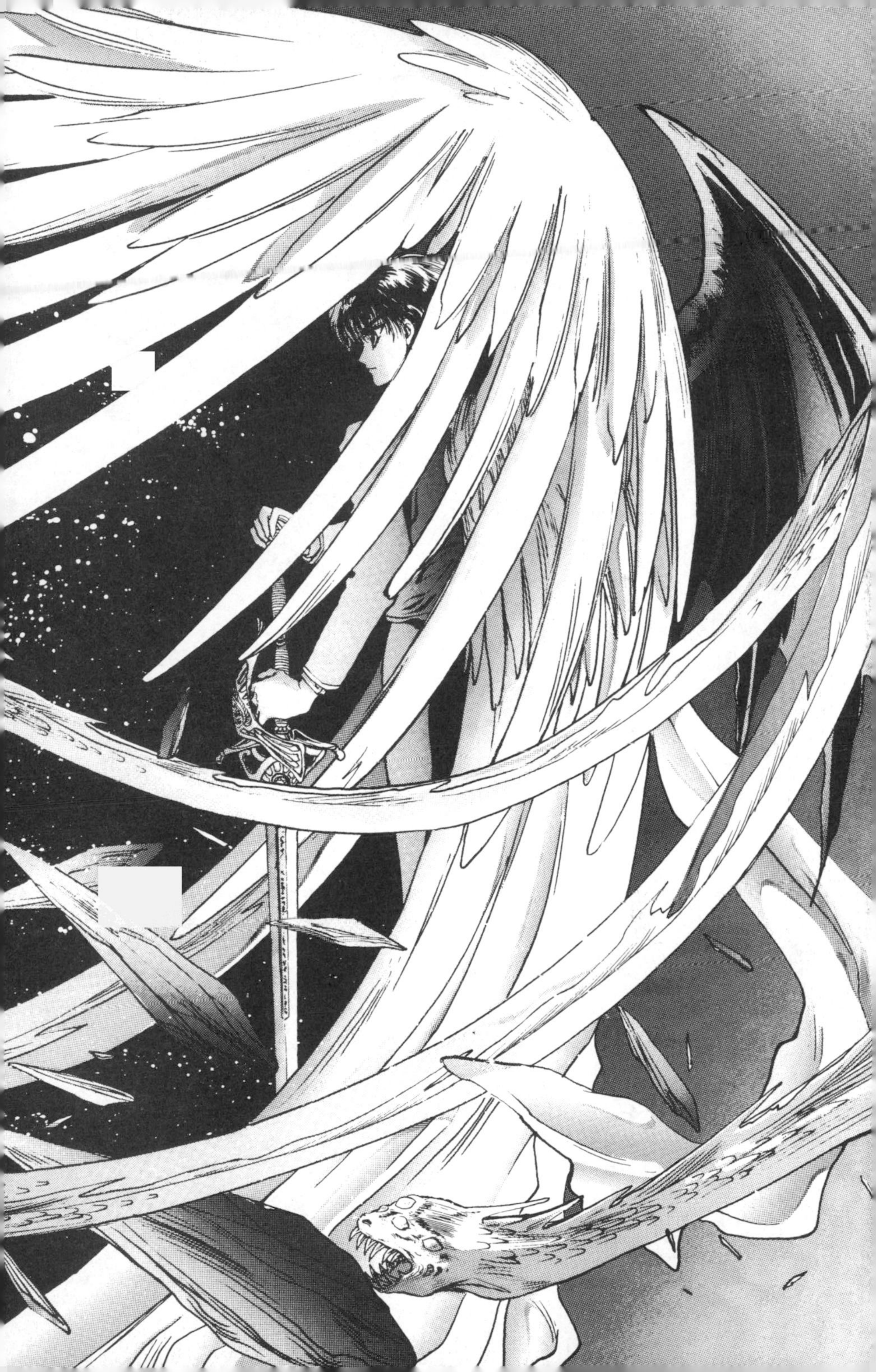

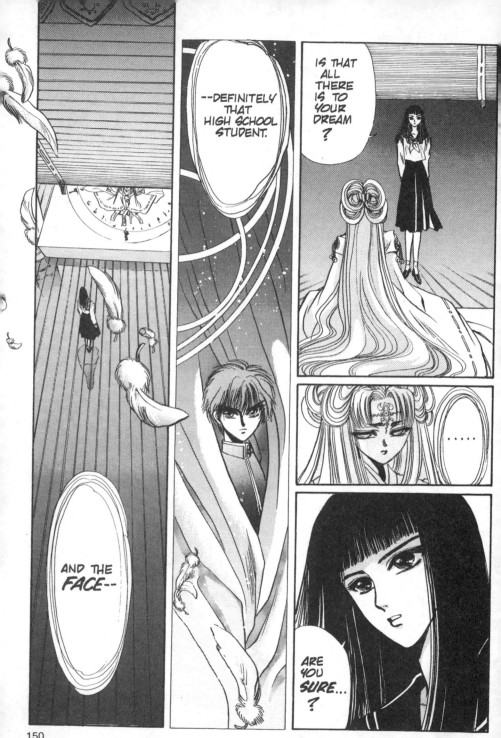

--DEFINITELY THAT HIGH SCHOOL STUDENT.

IS THAT ALL THERE IS TO YOUR DREAM?

. . . . .

ARE YOU SURE...?

AND THE *FACE*--

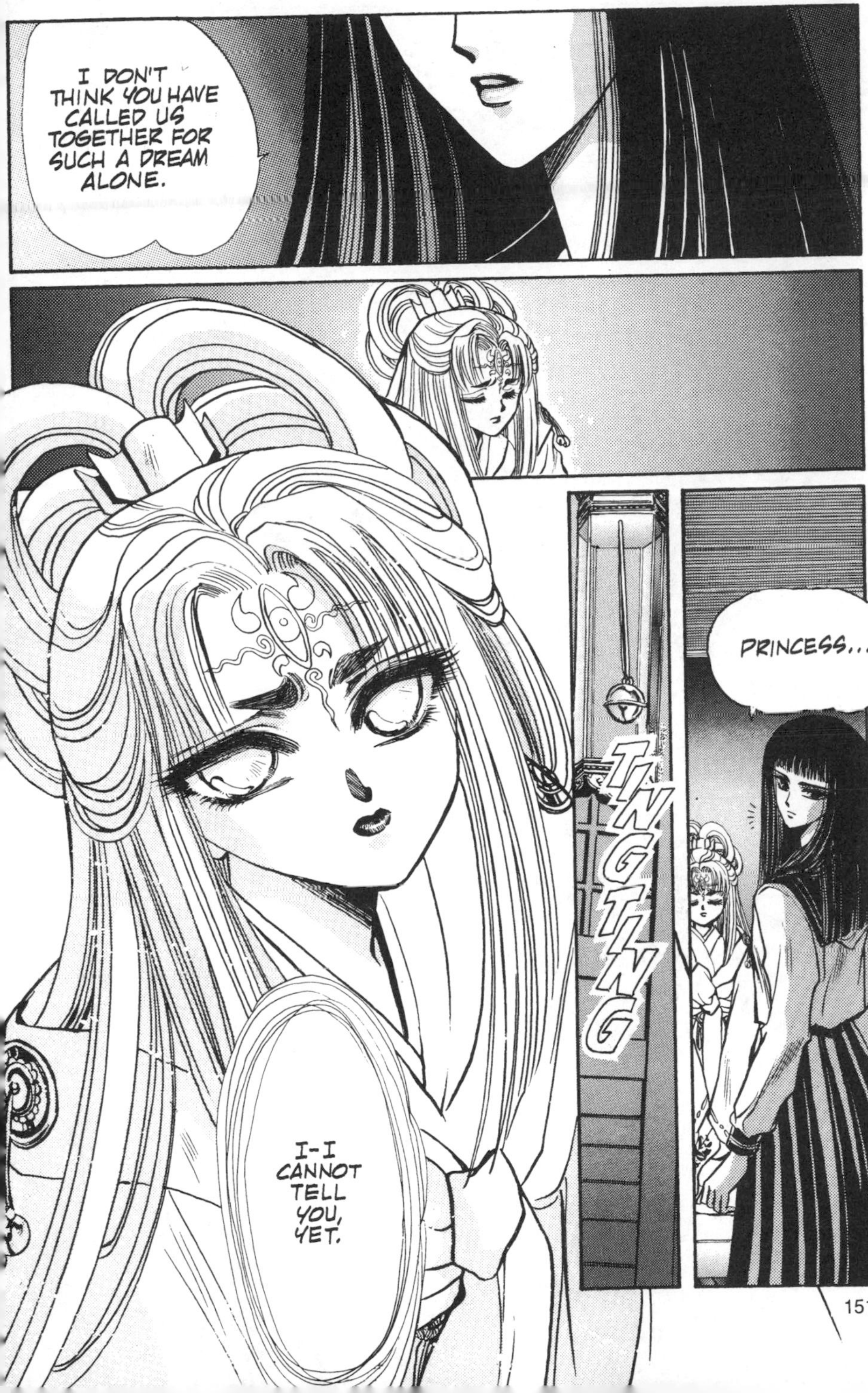
I DON'T THINK YOU HAVE CALLED US TOGETHER FOR SUCH A DREAM ALONE.
PRINCESS...
TINGTING
I-I CANNOT TELL YOU, YET.

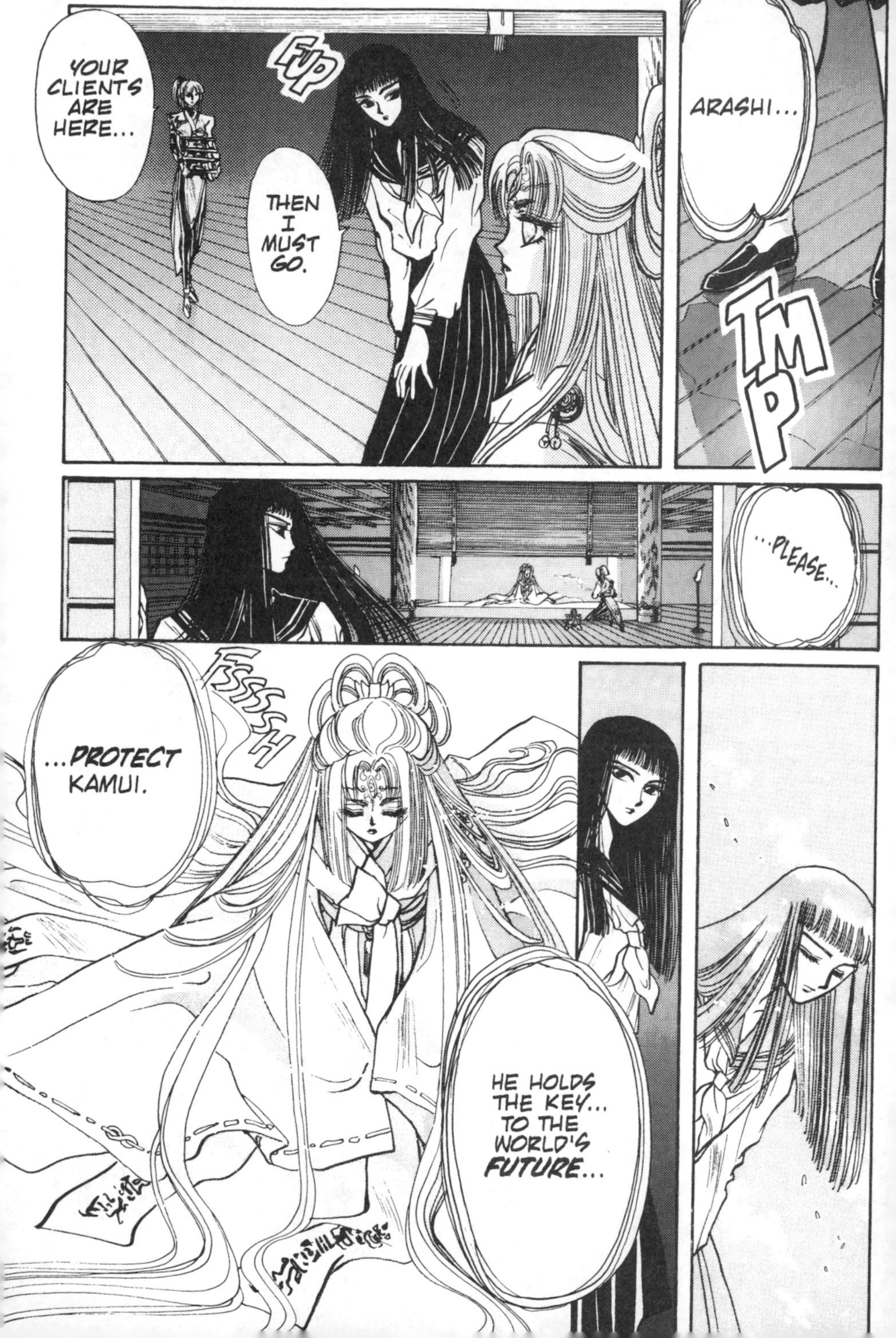

YOUR CLIENTS ARE HERE...
FUP
THEN I MUST GO.
ARASHI...
TMP
...PLEASE...
...PROTECT KAMUI.
FSSSSH
HE HOLDS THE KEY... TO THE WORLD'S FUTURE...

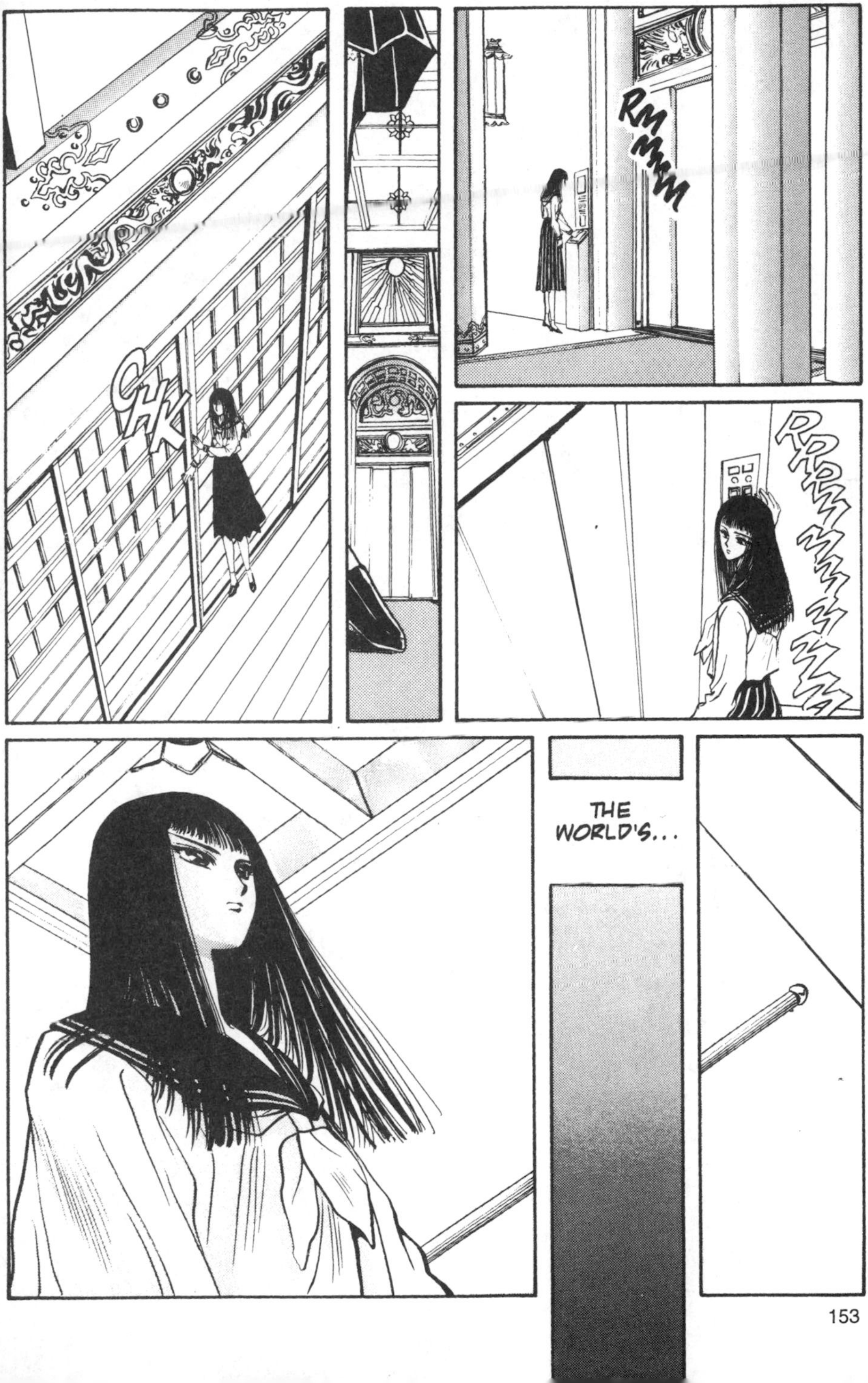
CHK
RMMMM
RRRMMMMMMMM
THE WORLD'S...

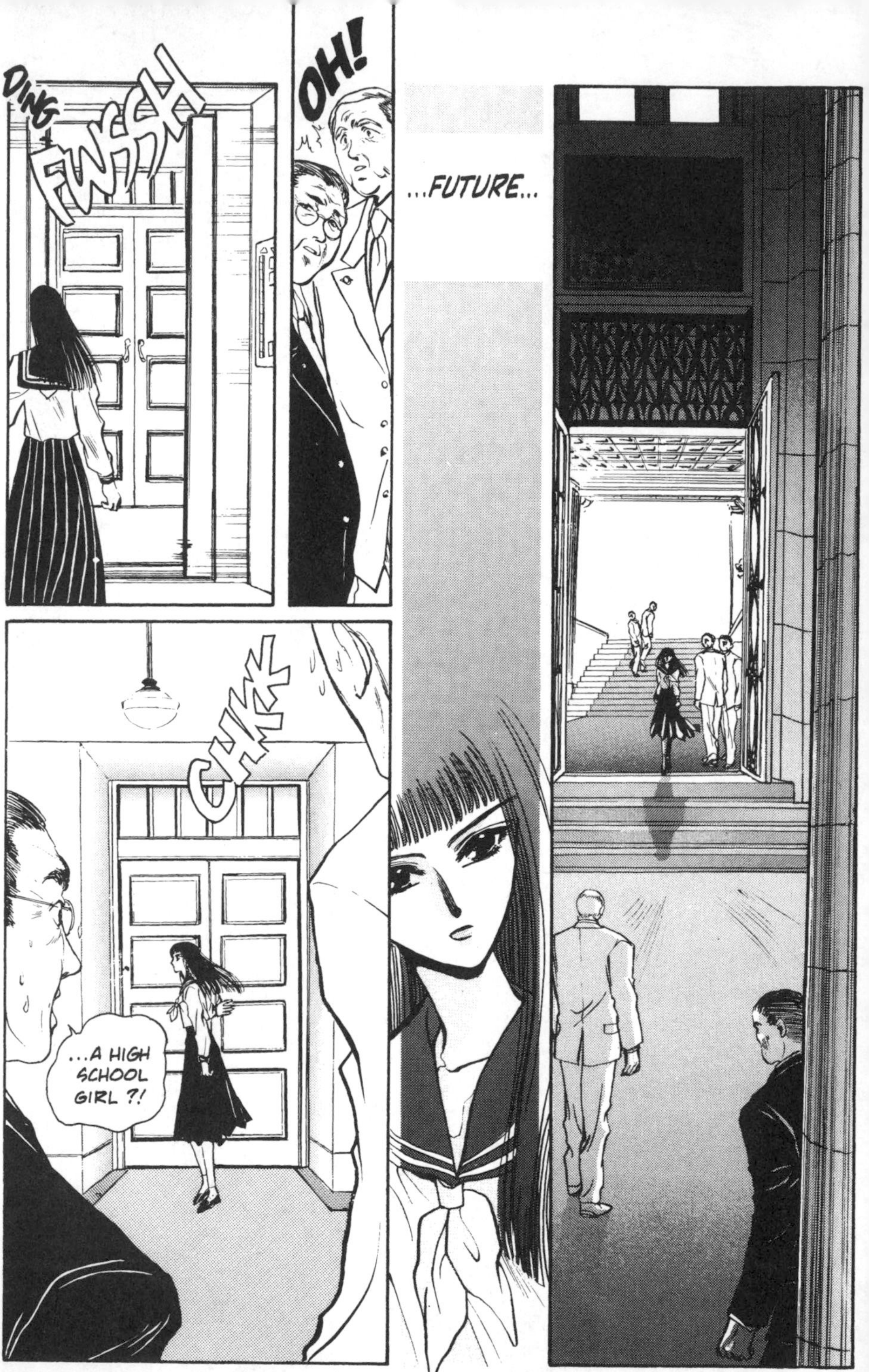
DING
FWSSH
OH!
CHKK
...A HIGH SCHOOL GIRL ?!
...FUTURE...

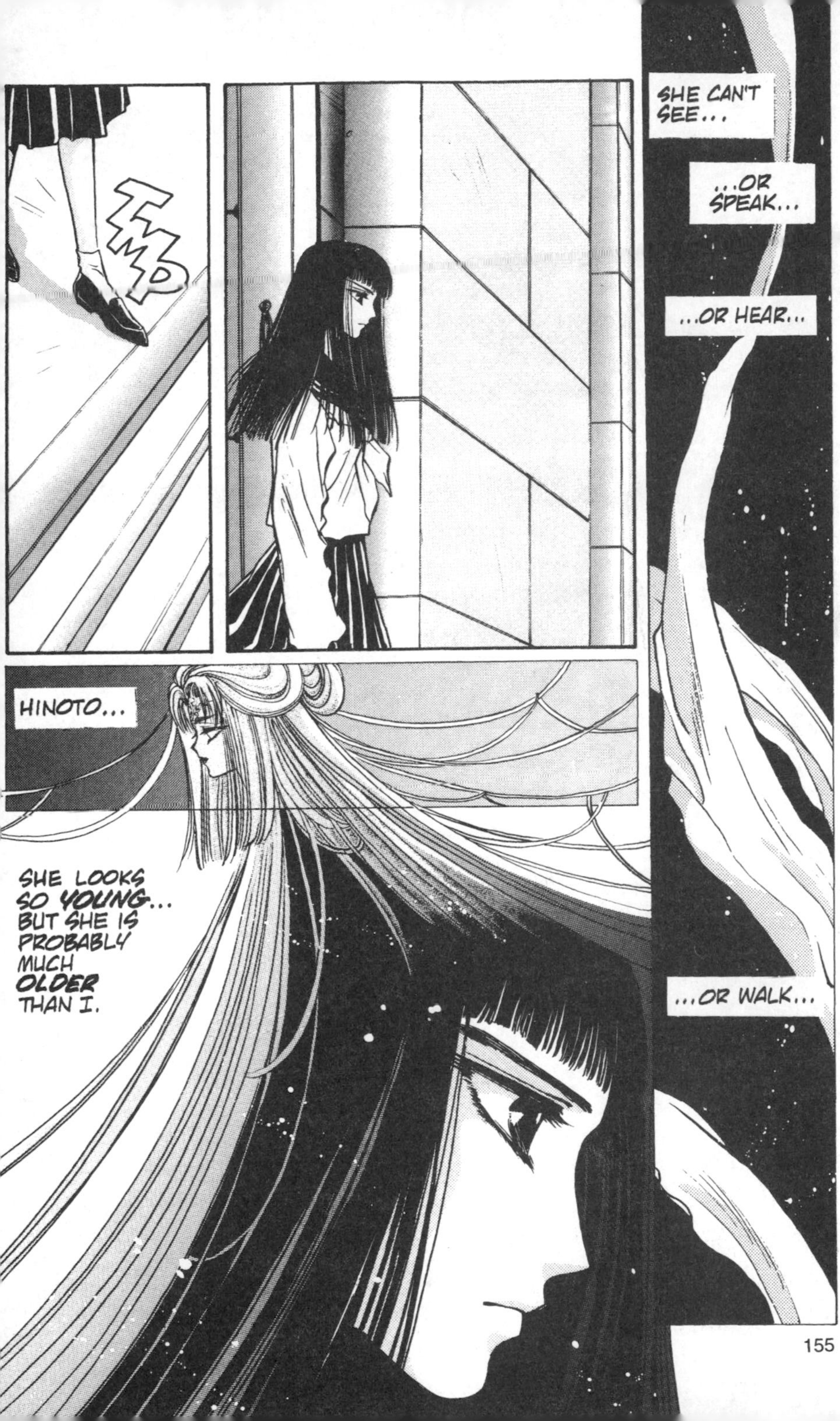
TMP
HINOTO...
SHE LOOKS SO YOUNG... BUT SHE IS PROBABLY MUCH OLDER THAN I.
SHE CAN'T SEE...
...OR SPEAK...
...OR HEAR...
...OR WALK...

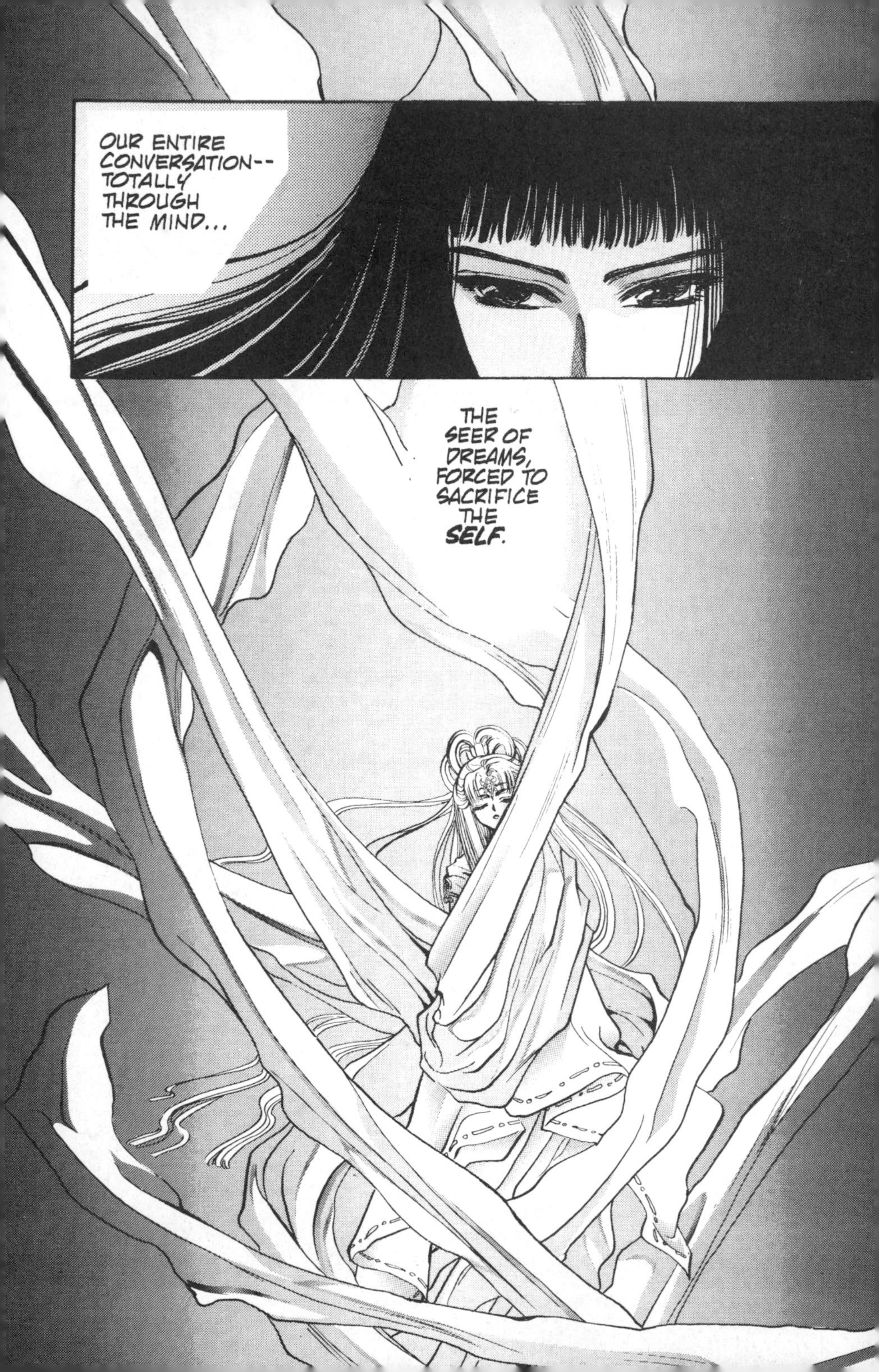
OUR ENTIRE CONVERSATION-- TOTALLY THROUGH THE MIND...
THE SEER OF DREAMS, FORCED TO SACRIFICE THE **SELF**.

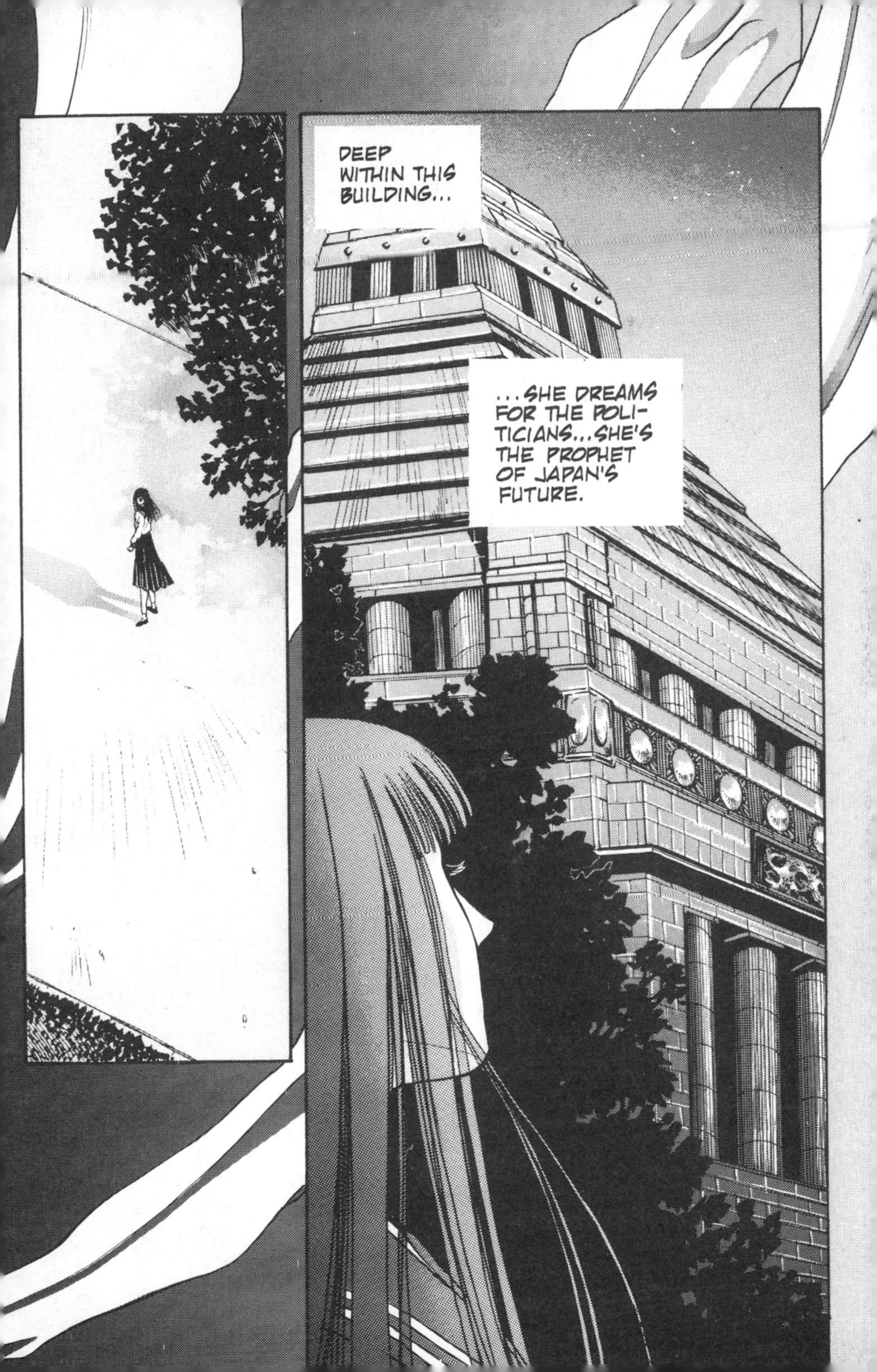
DEEP WITHIN THIS BUILDING...
...SHE DREAMS FOR THE POLI-TICIANS...SHE'S THE PROPHET OF JAPAN'S FUTURE.

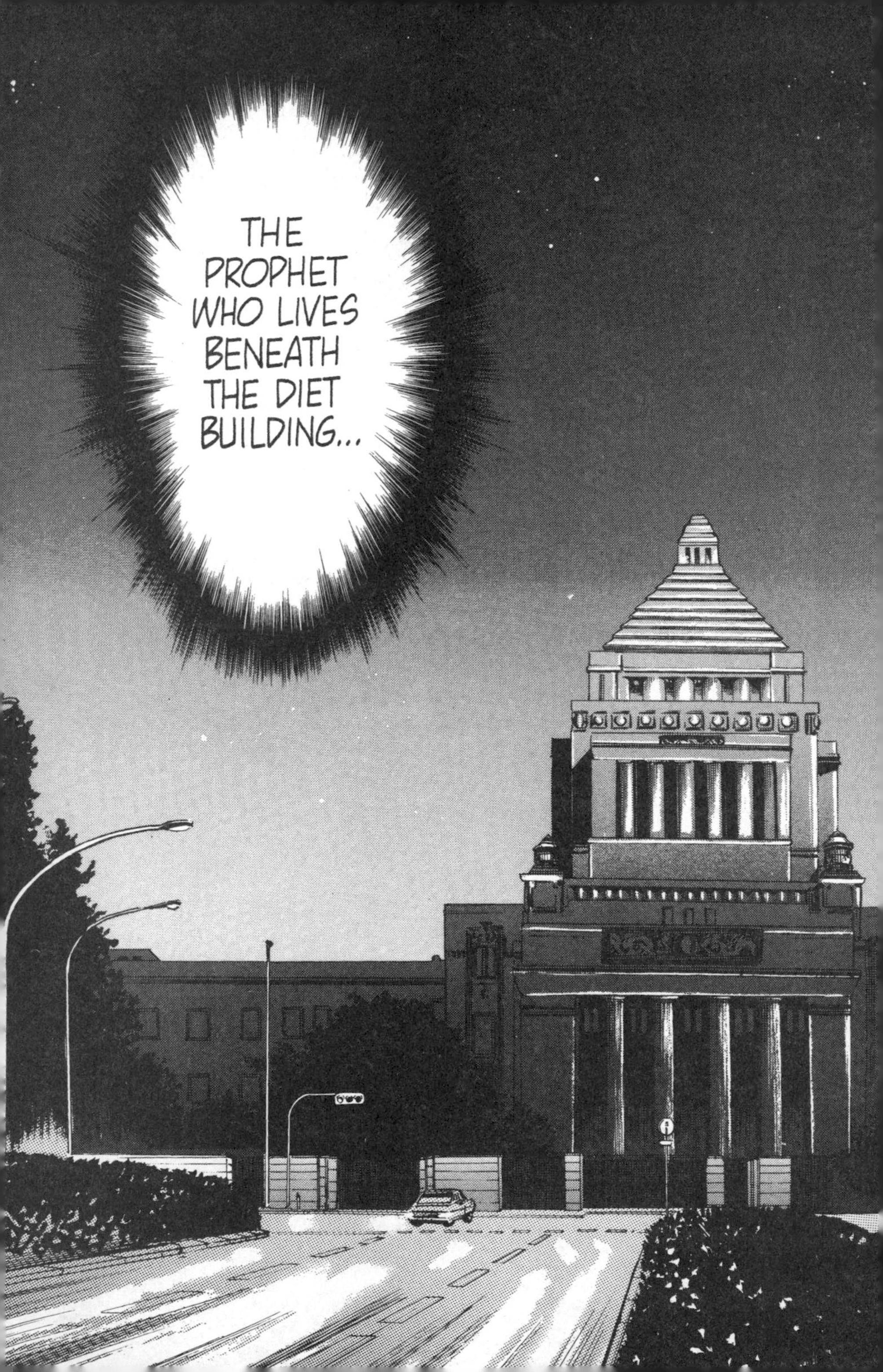
THE PROPHET WHO LIVES BENEATH THE DIET BUILDING...

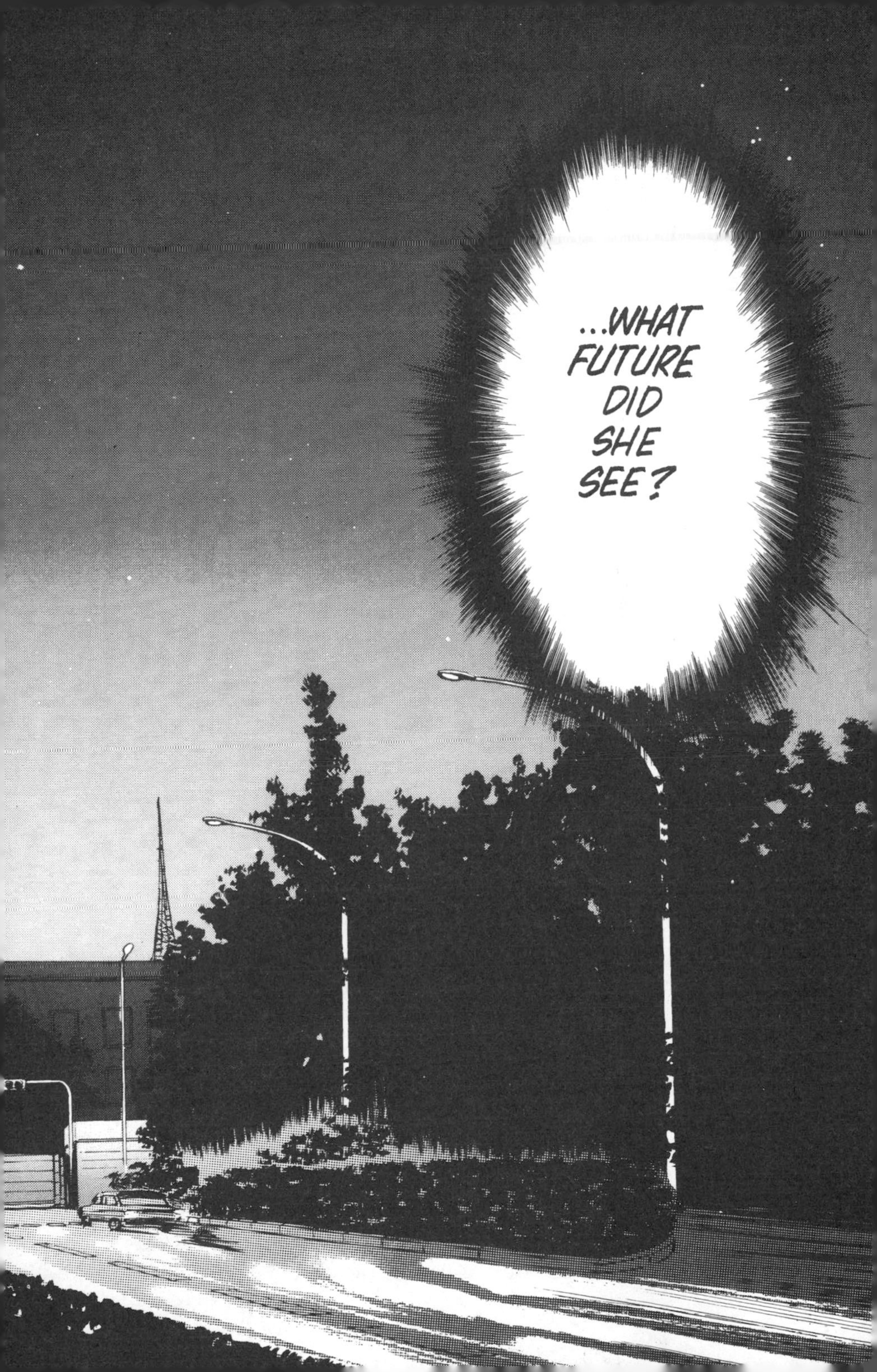
...WHAT FUTURE DID SHE SEE?

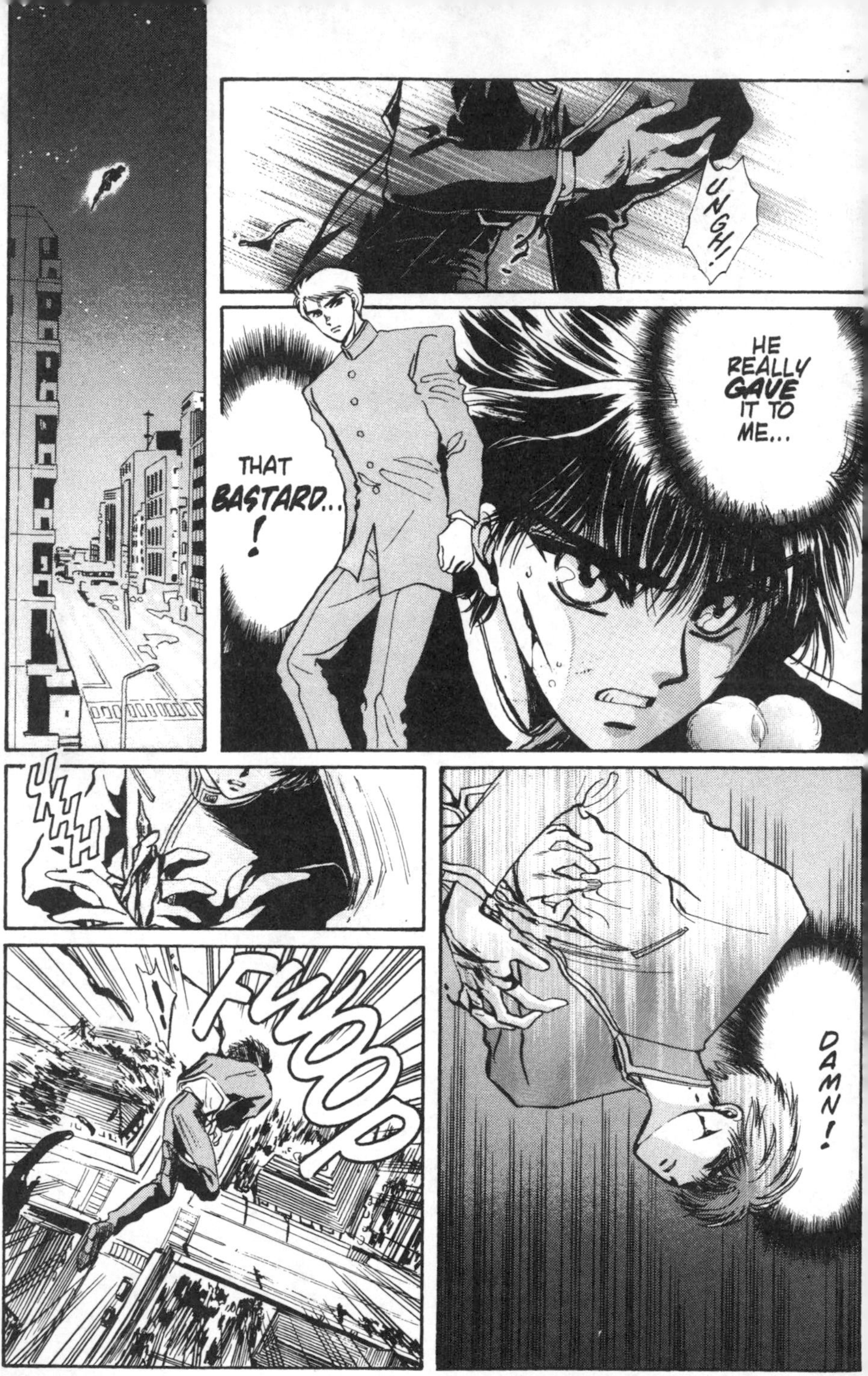
UNGH!
THAT BASTARD...!
HE REALLY GAVE IT TO ME...
FWOOP
DAMN!

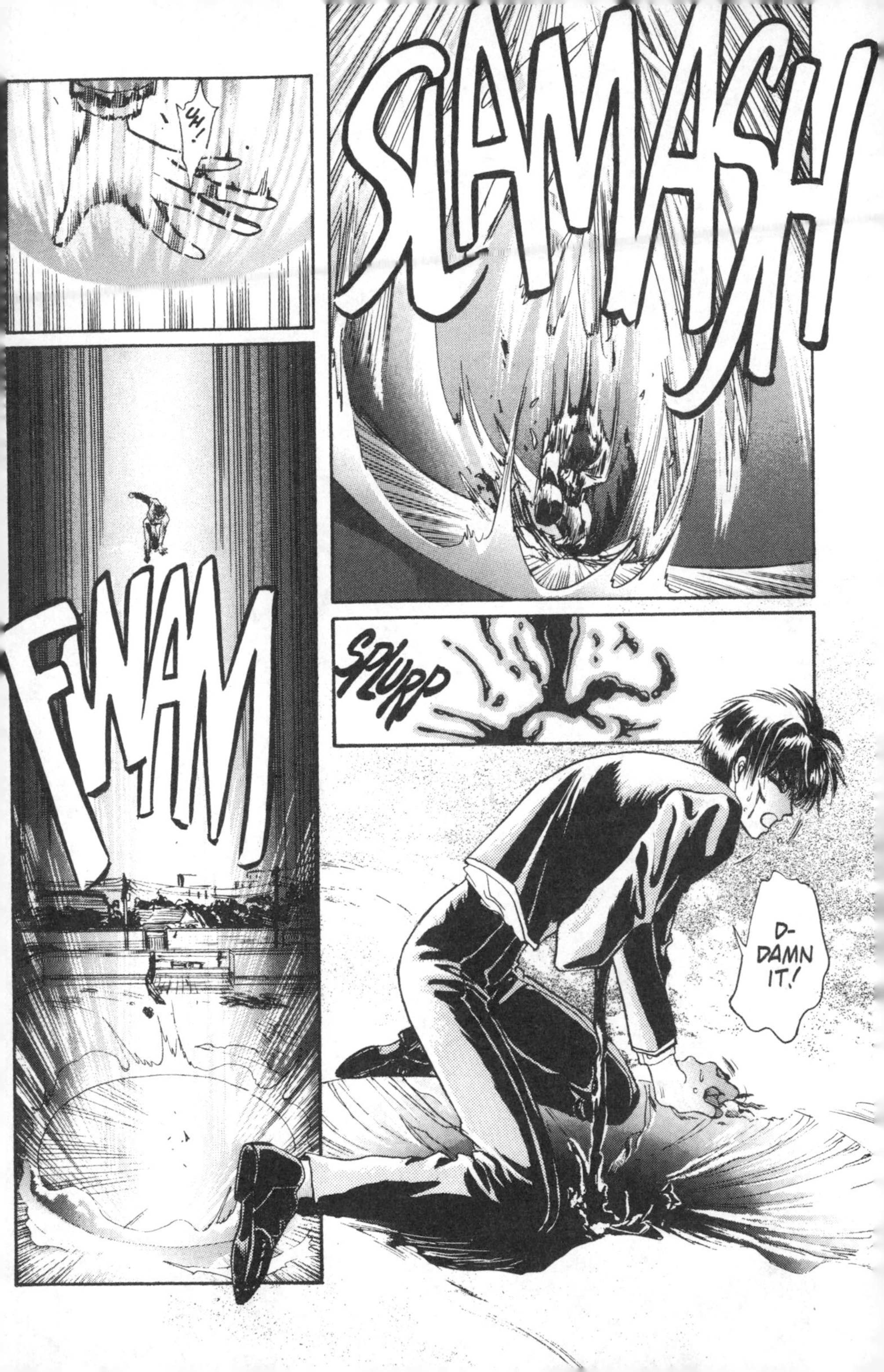
UH!
SLAMASH
FWAM
SPLURP
D-DAMN IT!

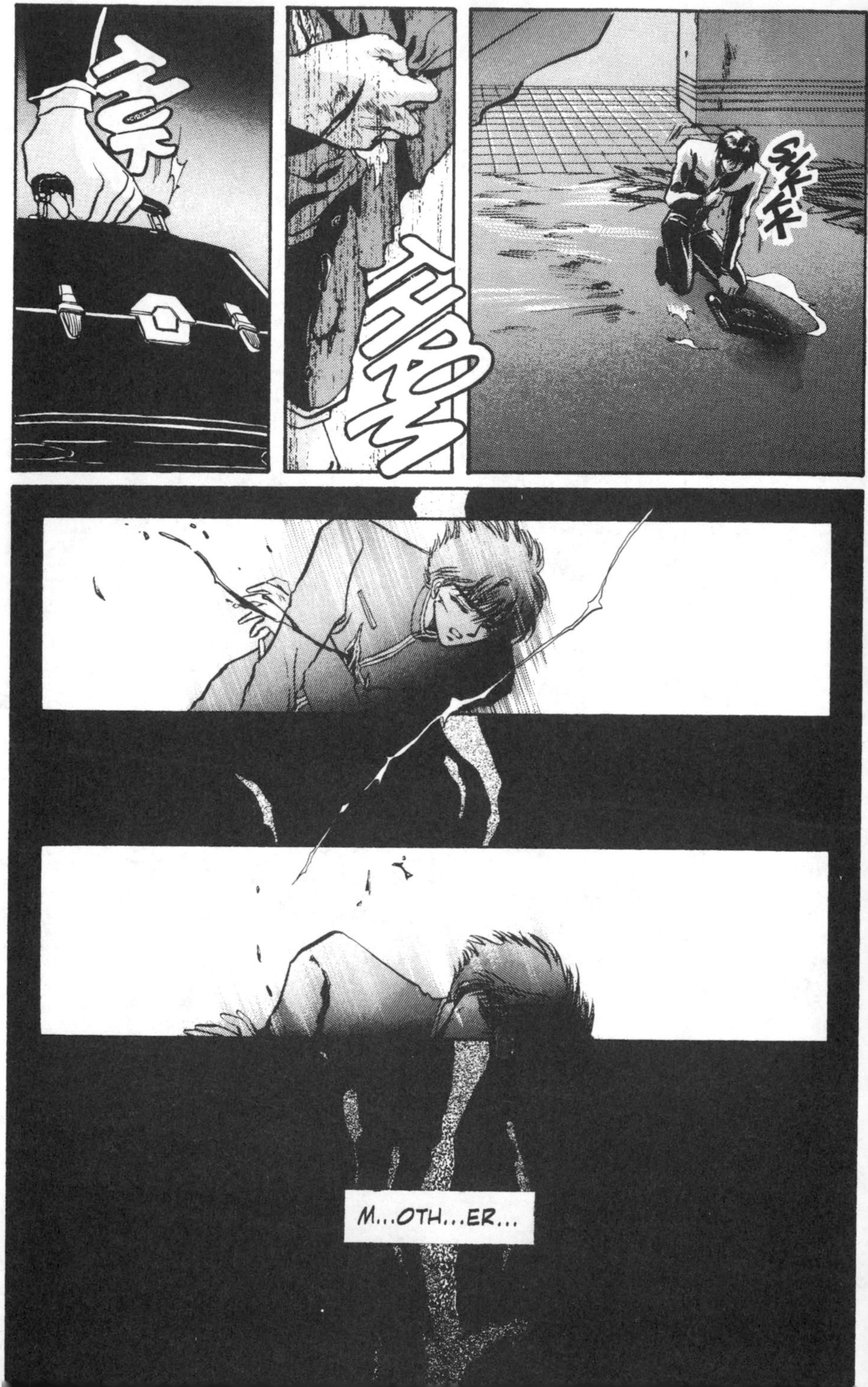
TUK
THOOM
M...OTH...ER...

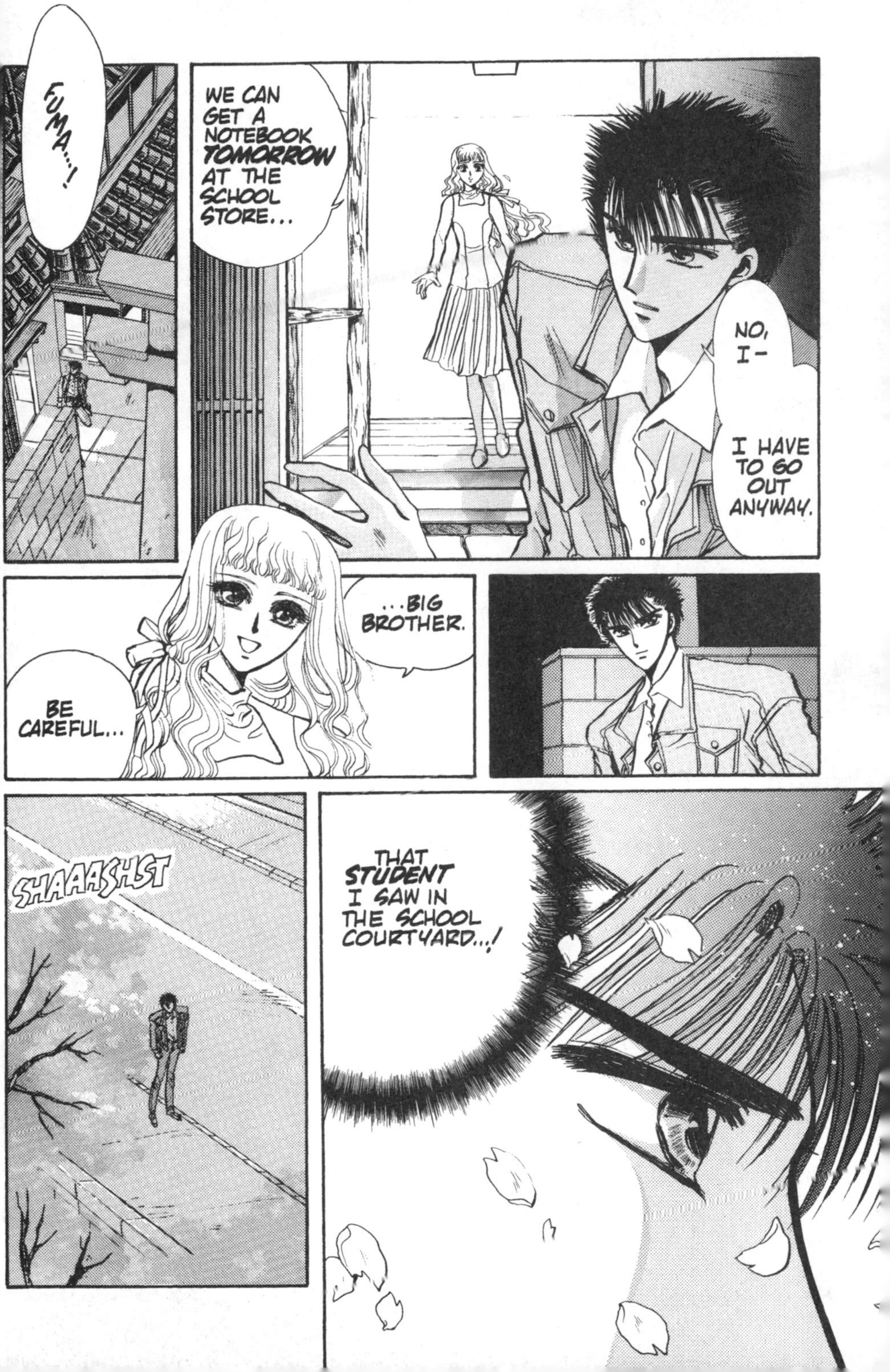
FUMA...!
WE CAN GET A NOTEBOOK TOMORROW AT THE SCHOOL STORE...
NO, I—
I HAVE TO GO OUT ANYWAY.
...BIG BROTHER.
BE CAREFUL...
SHAAASHST
THAT STUDENT I SAW IN THE SCHOOL COURTYARD...!

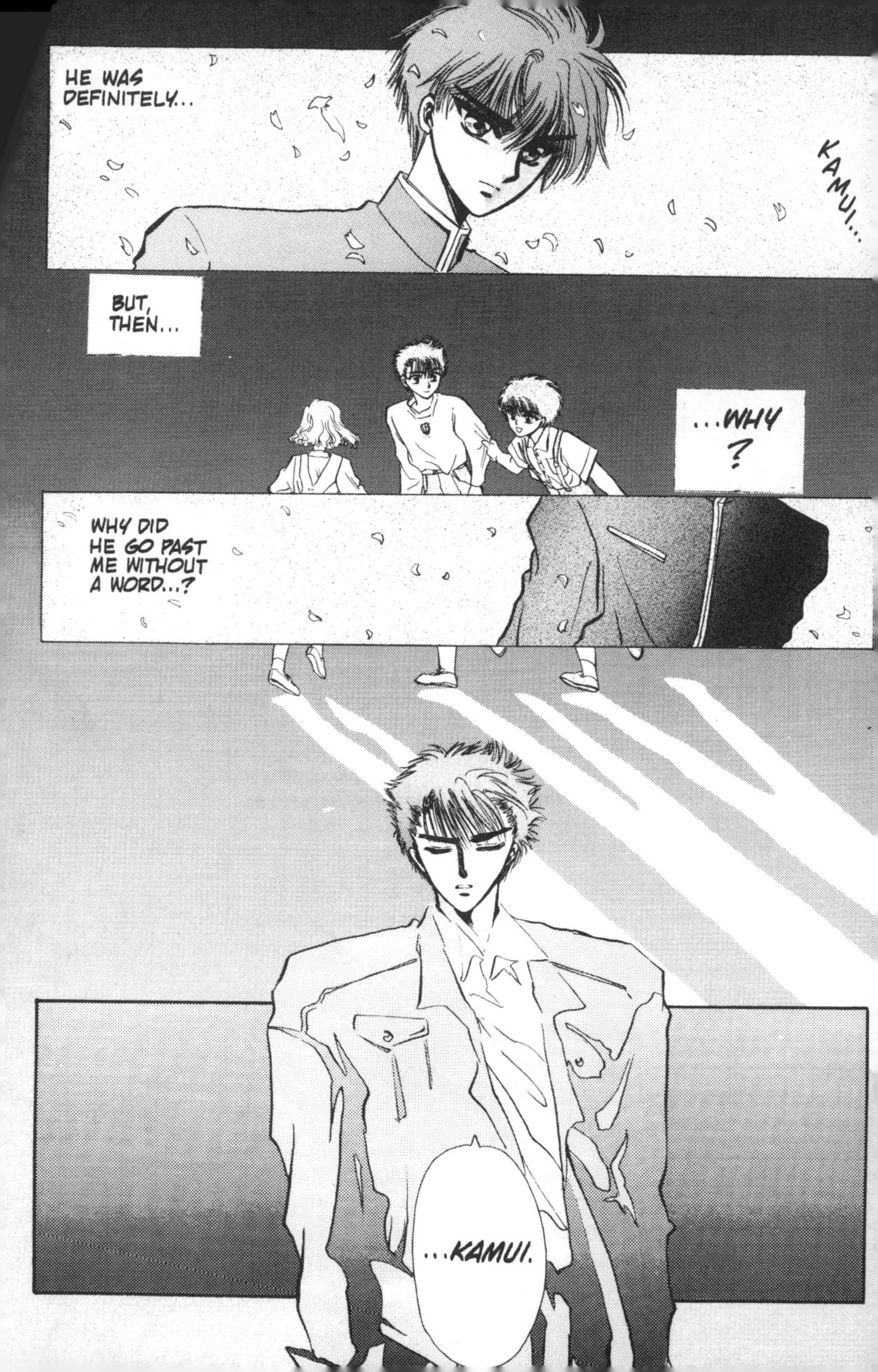
HE WAS DEFINITELY...
KAMUI...
BUT, THEN...
...WHY?
WHY DID HE GO PAST ME WITHOUT A WORD...?
...KAMUI.

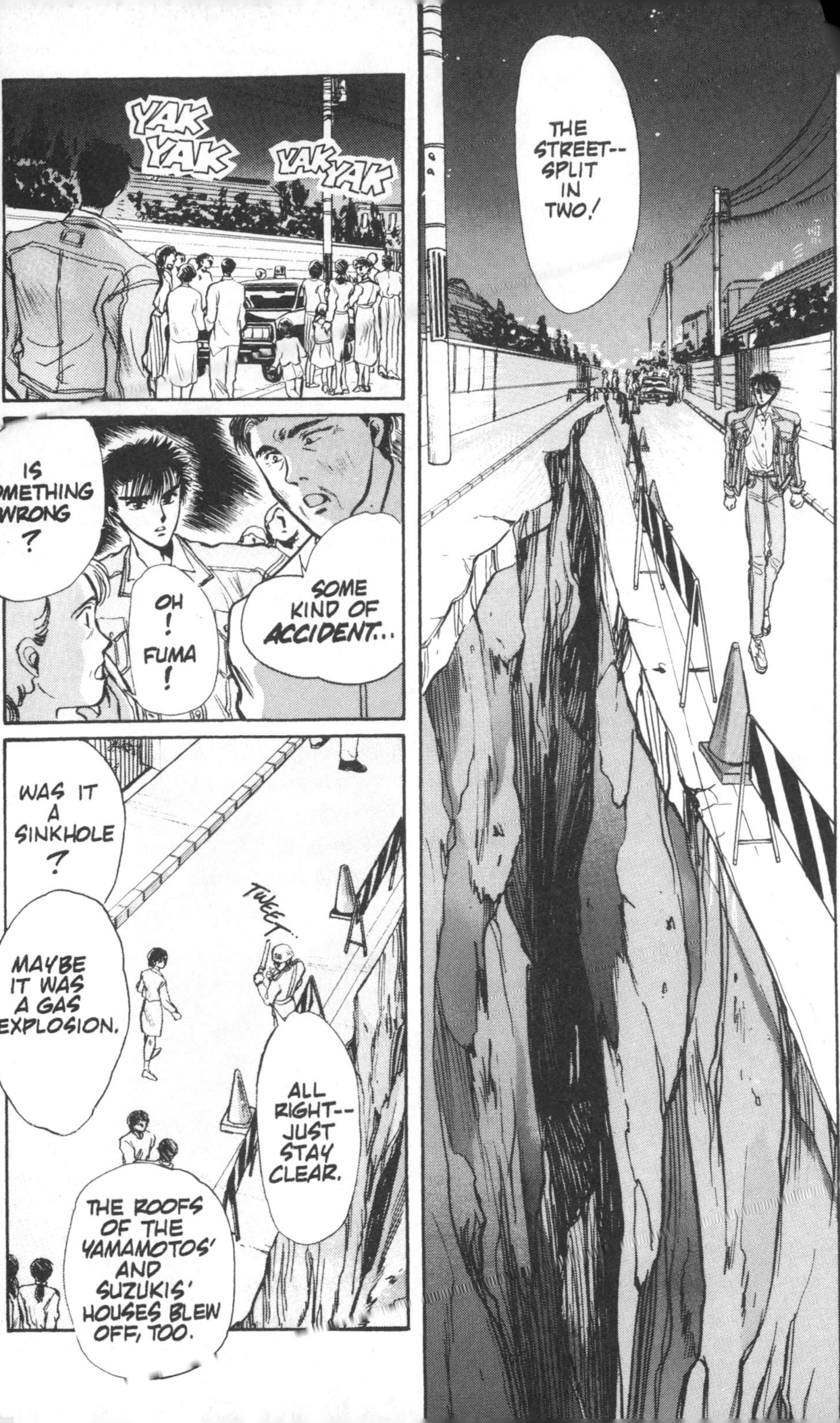
YAK YAK
YAK YAK
IS OMETHING WRONG?
OH! FUMA!
SOME KIND OF ACCIDENT...
WAS IT A SINKHOLE?
MAYBE IT WAS A GAS EXPLOSION.
TWEET
ALL RIGHT--JUST STAY CLEAR.
THE ROOFS OF THE YAMAMOTOS' AND SUZUKIS' HOUSES BLEW OFF, TOO.
THE STREET--SPLIT IN TWO!

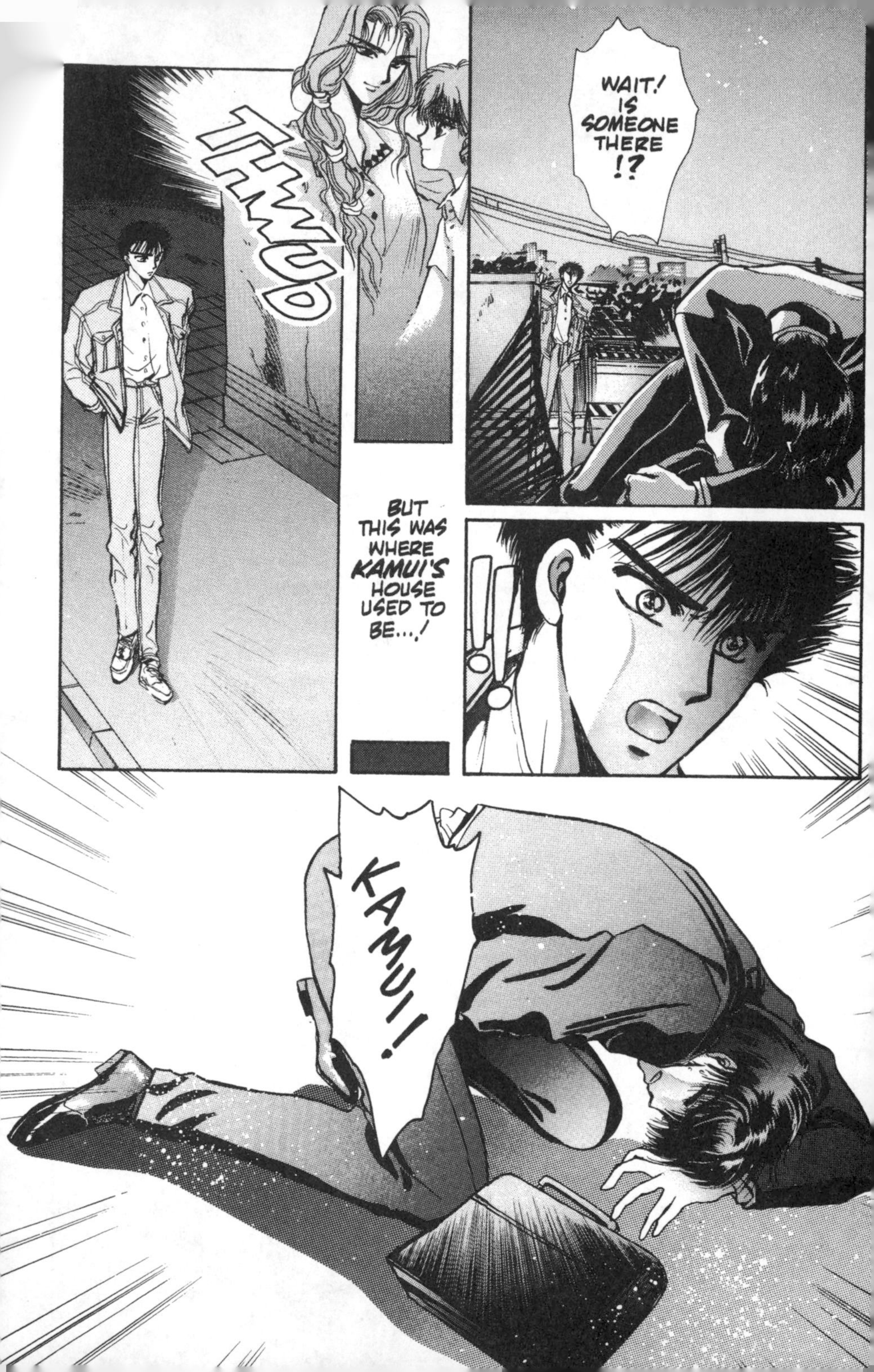
THMUD
WAIT! IS SOMEONE THERE!?
BUT THIS WAS WHERE KAMUI'S HOUSE USED TO BE...!
!!
KAMUI!!

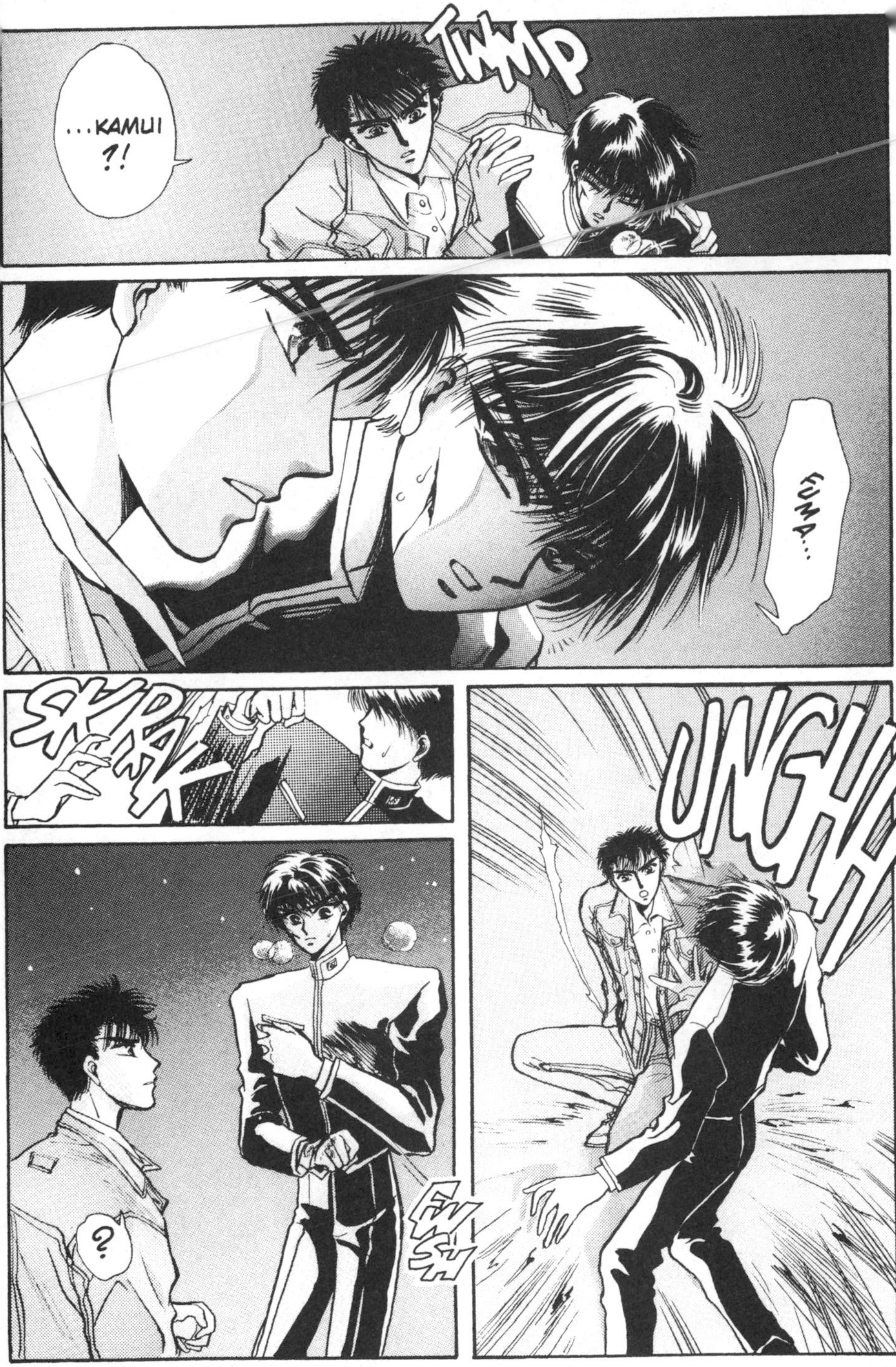
...KAMUI
?!
THMP
FUMA...
SKRAK
UNGHH
?
FWSH

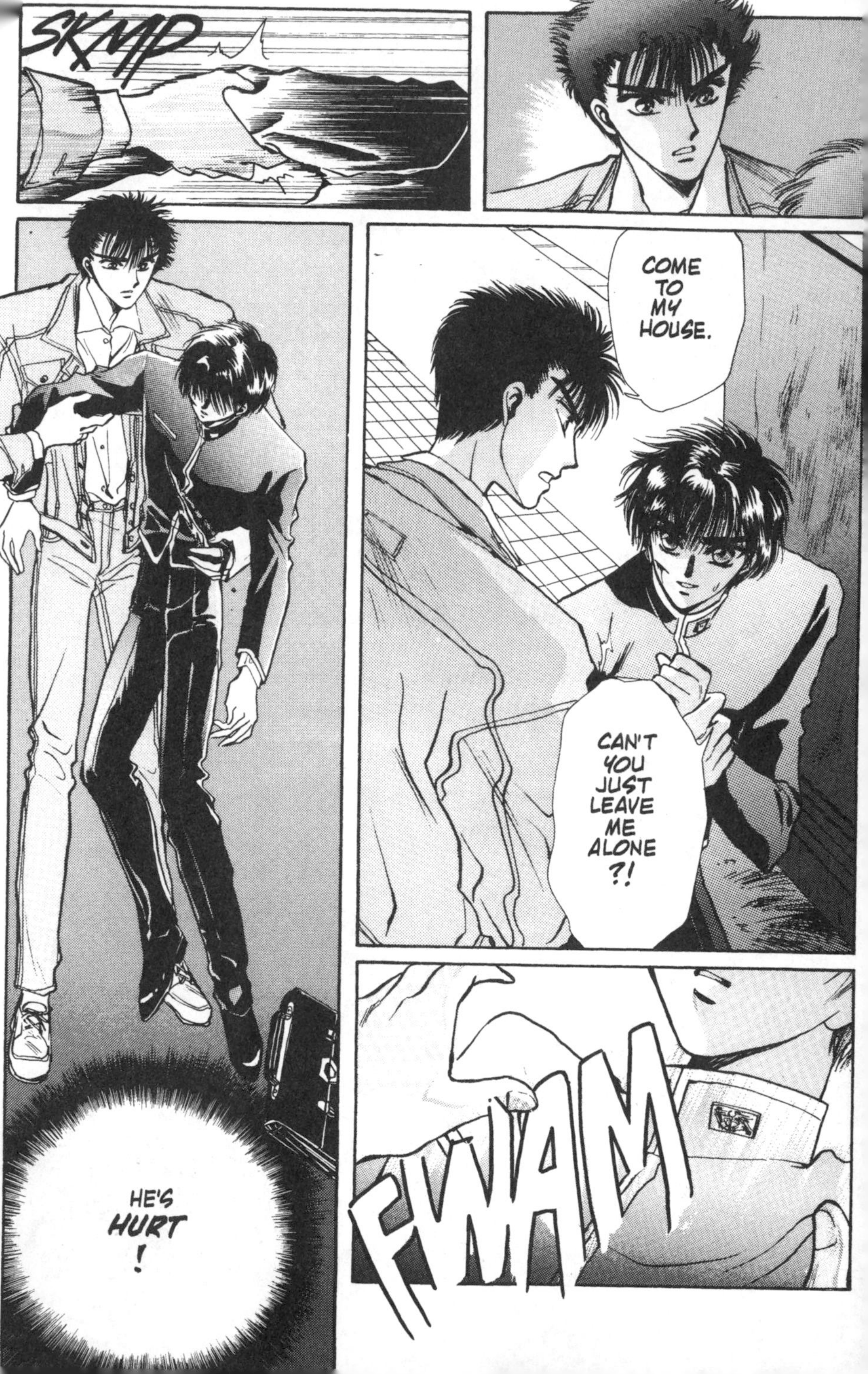
SKMP
HE'S HURT !
COME TO MY HOUSE.
CAN'T YOU JUST LEAVE ME ALONE ?!
FWAM

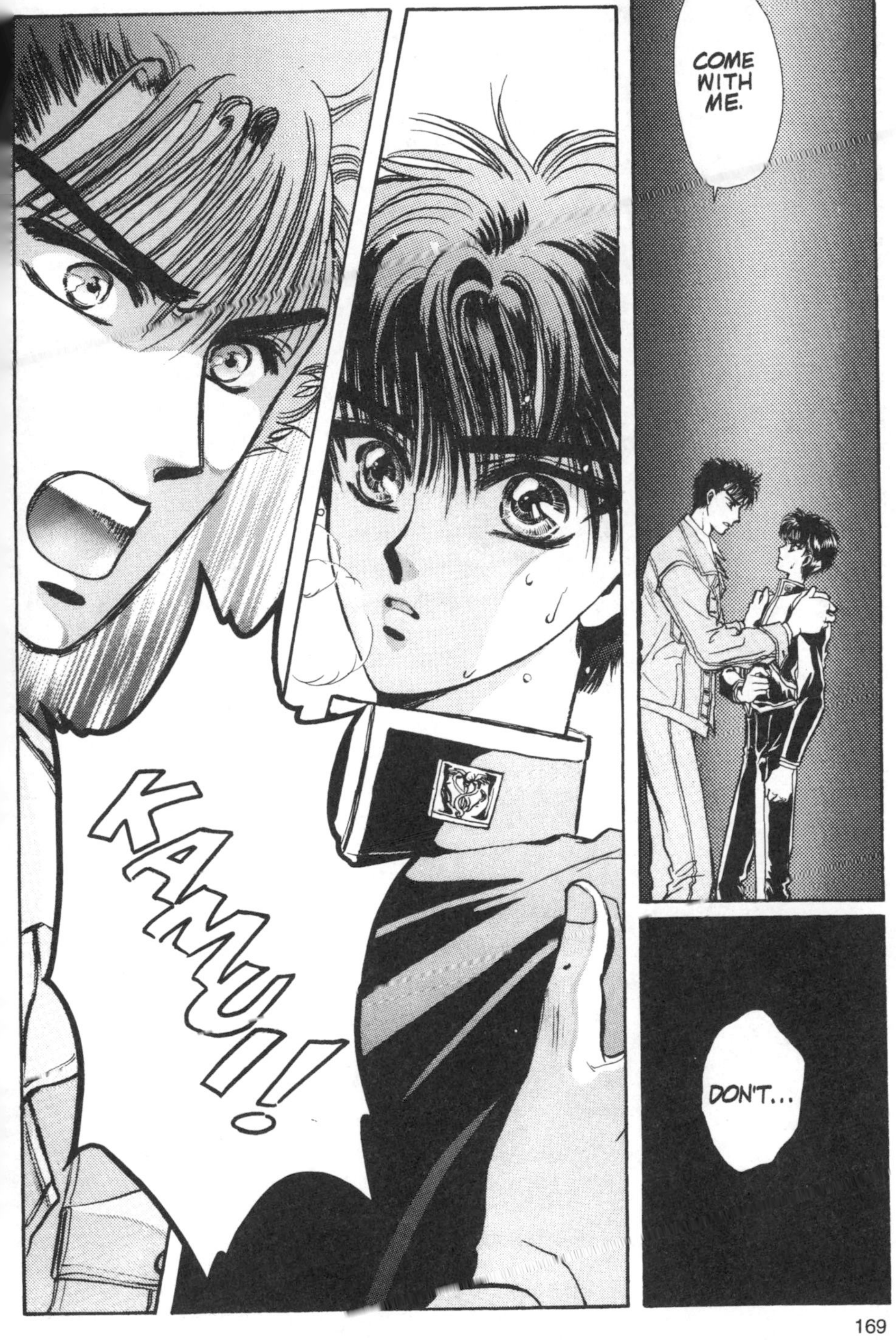
KAMUI!
COME WITH ME.
DON'T...

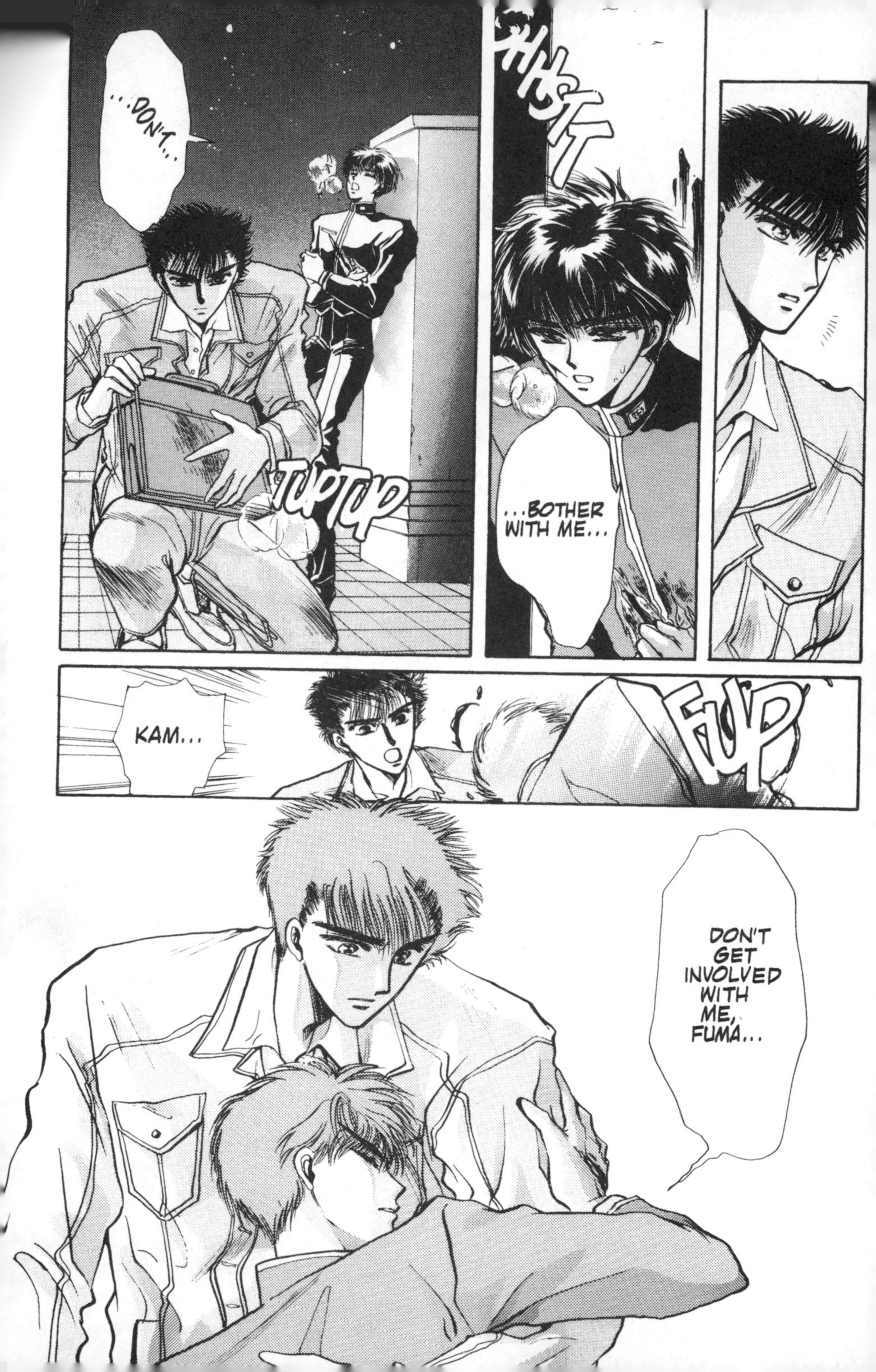
...DON'T...
TUPTUP
SHHSTT
...BOTHER WITH ME...
KAM...
FUP
DON'T GET INVOLVED WITH ME, FUMA...

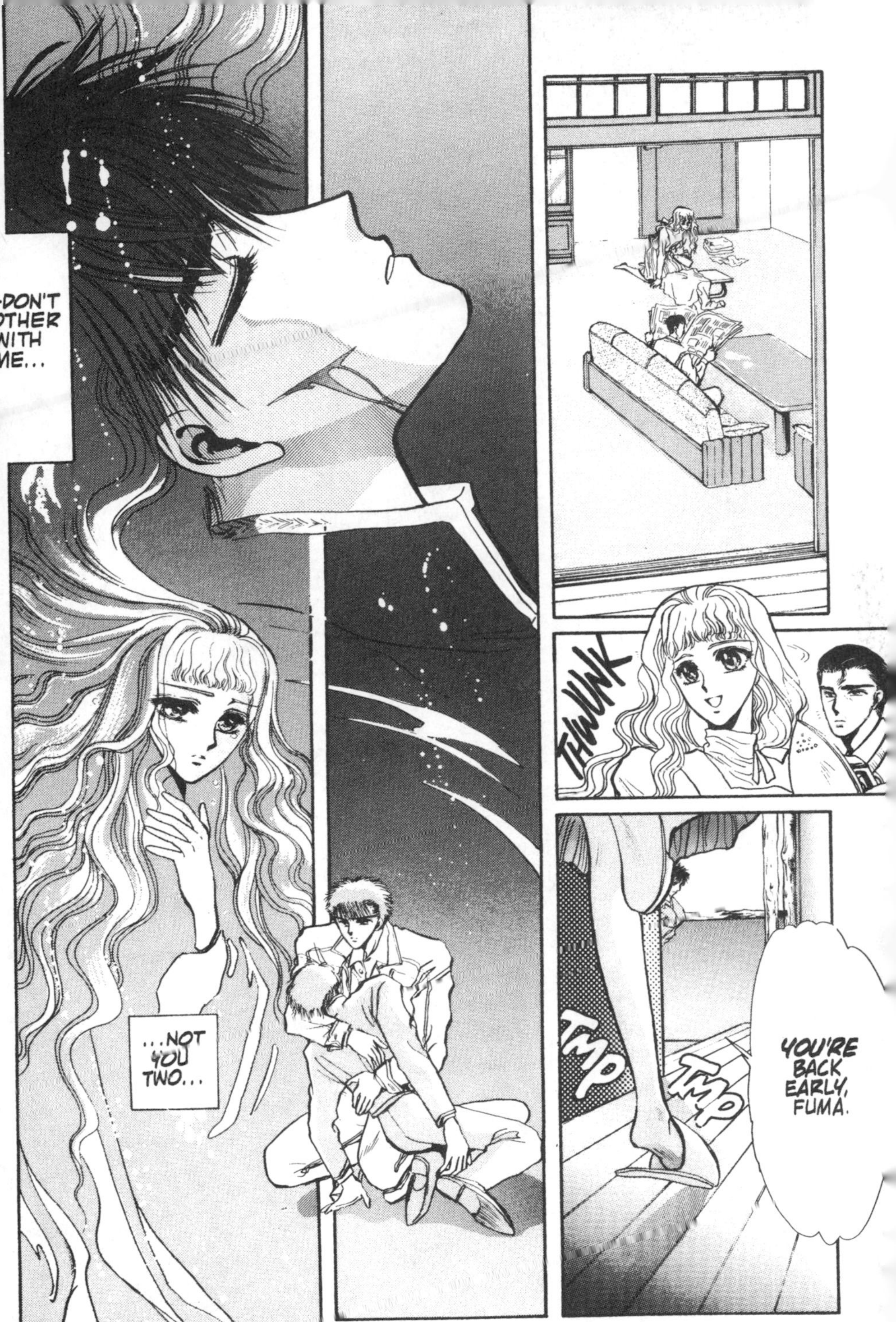
-DON'T OTHER WITH ME...
...NOT YOU TWO...
THWUNK
TMP
TMP
YOU'RE BACK EARLY, FUMA.

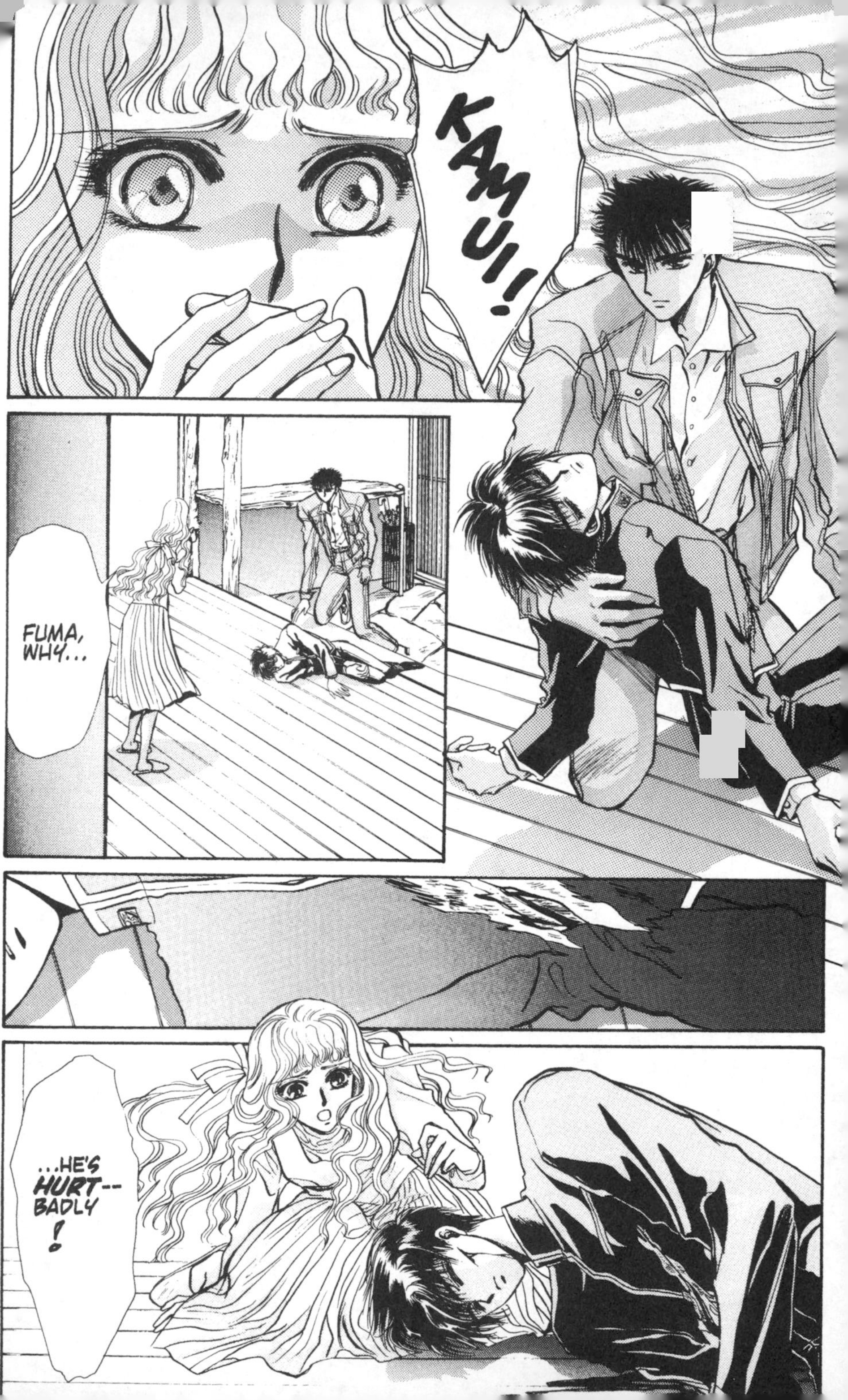
KAMUI!!
FUMA, WHY...
...HE'S HURT-- BADLY!

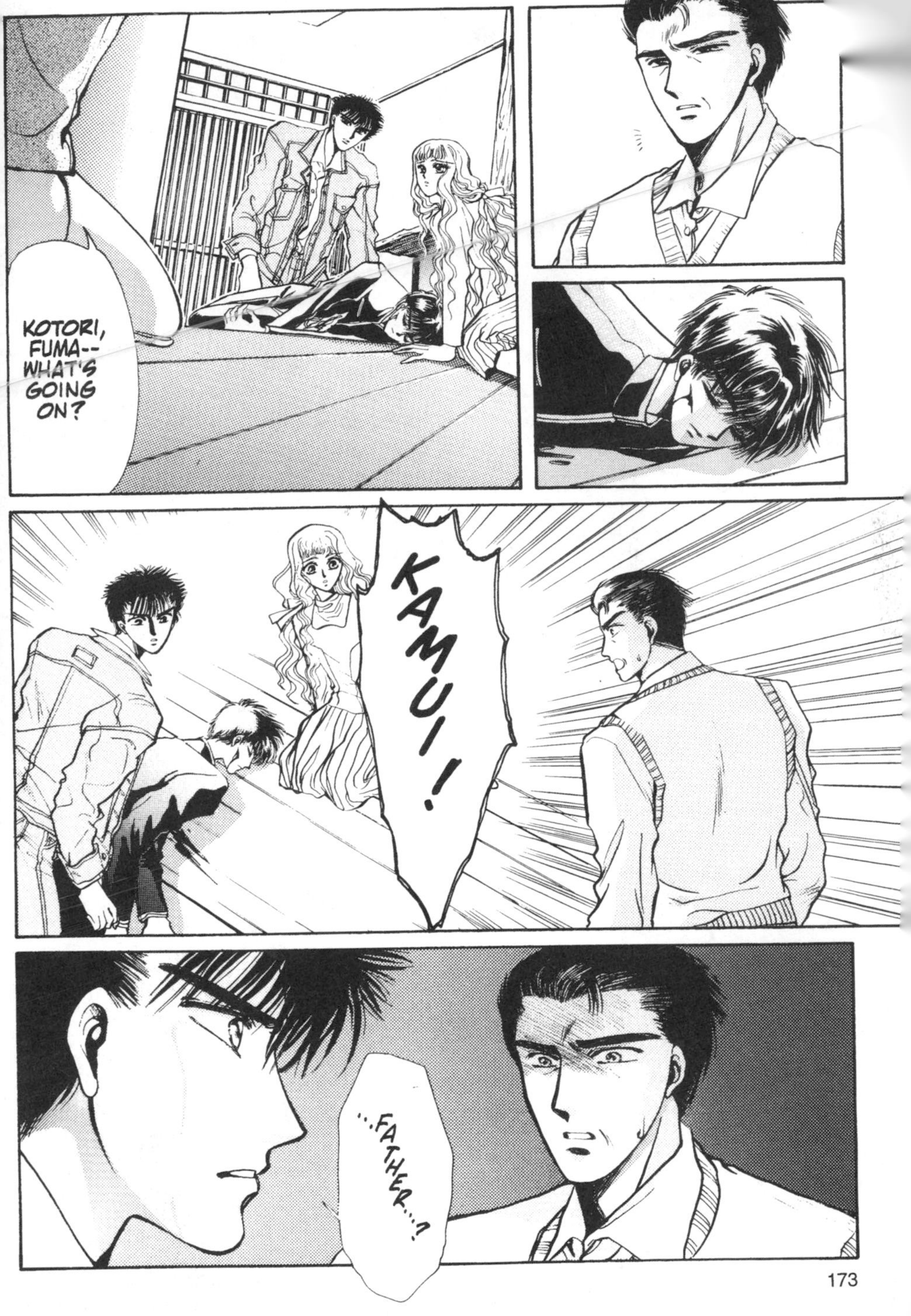
KOTORI, FUMA-- WHAT'S GOING ON?
KAMUI!
...FATHER...?

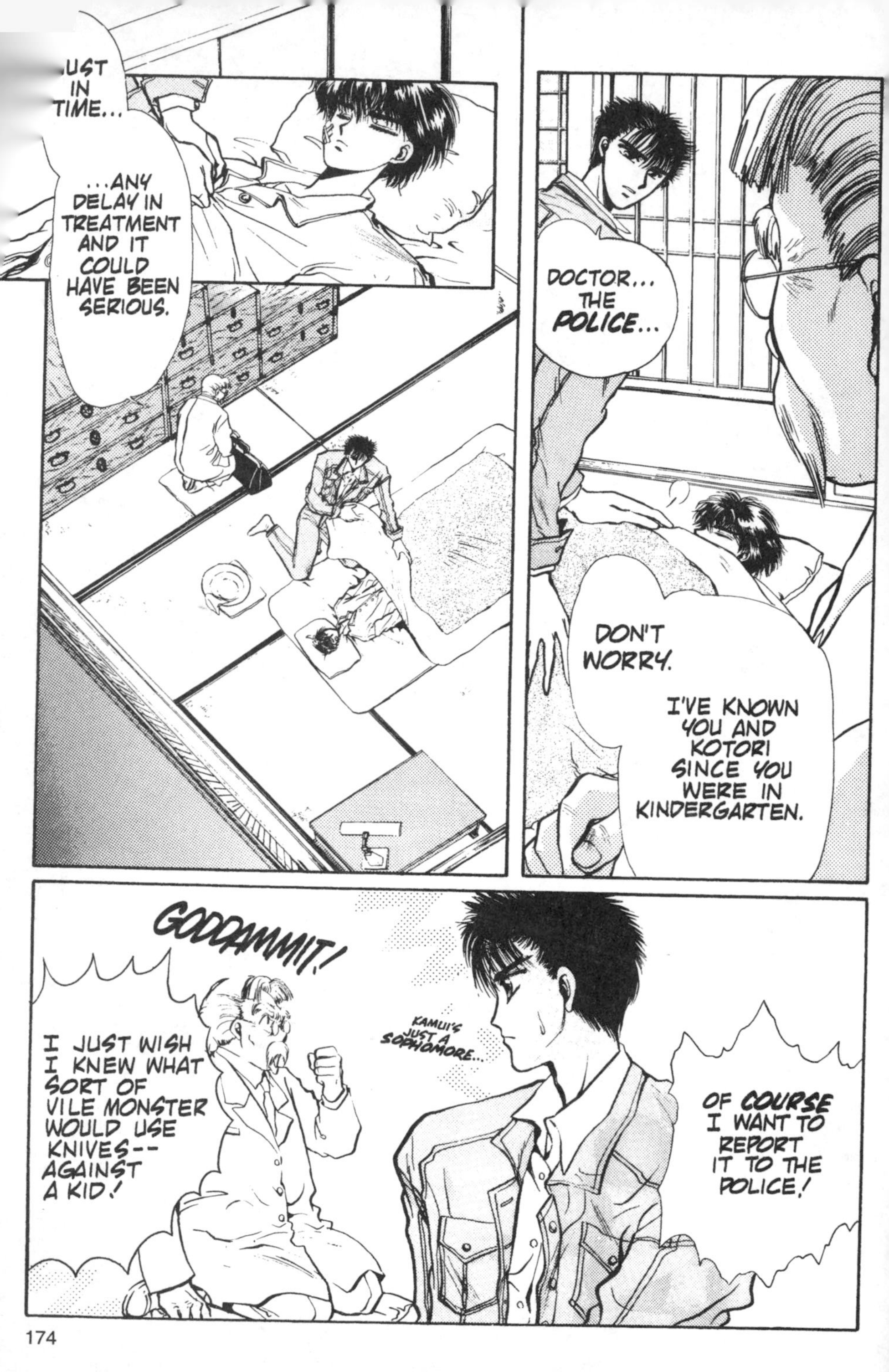
JUST IN TIME...
...ANY DELAY IN TREATMENT AND IT COULD HAVE BEEN SERIOUS.
DOCTOR... THE POLICE...
DON'T WORRY.
I'VE KNOWN YOU AND KOTORI SINCE YOU WERE IN KINDERGARTEN.
GODDAMMIT!
I JUST WISH I KNEW WHAT SORT OF VILE MONSTER WOULD USE KNIVES-- AGAINST A KID!
KAMUI'S JUST A SOPHOMORE...
OF COURSE I WANT TO REPORT IT TO THE POLICE!

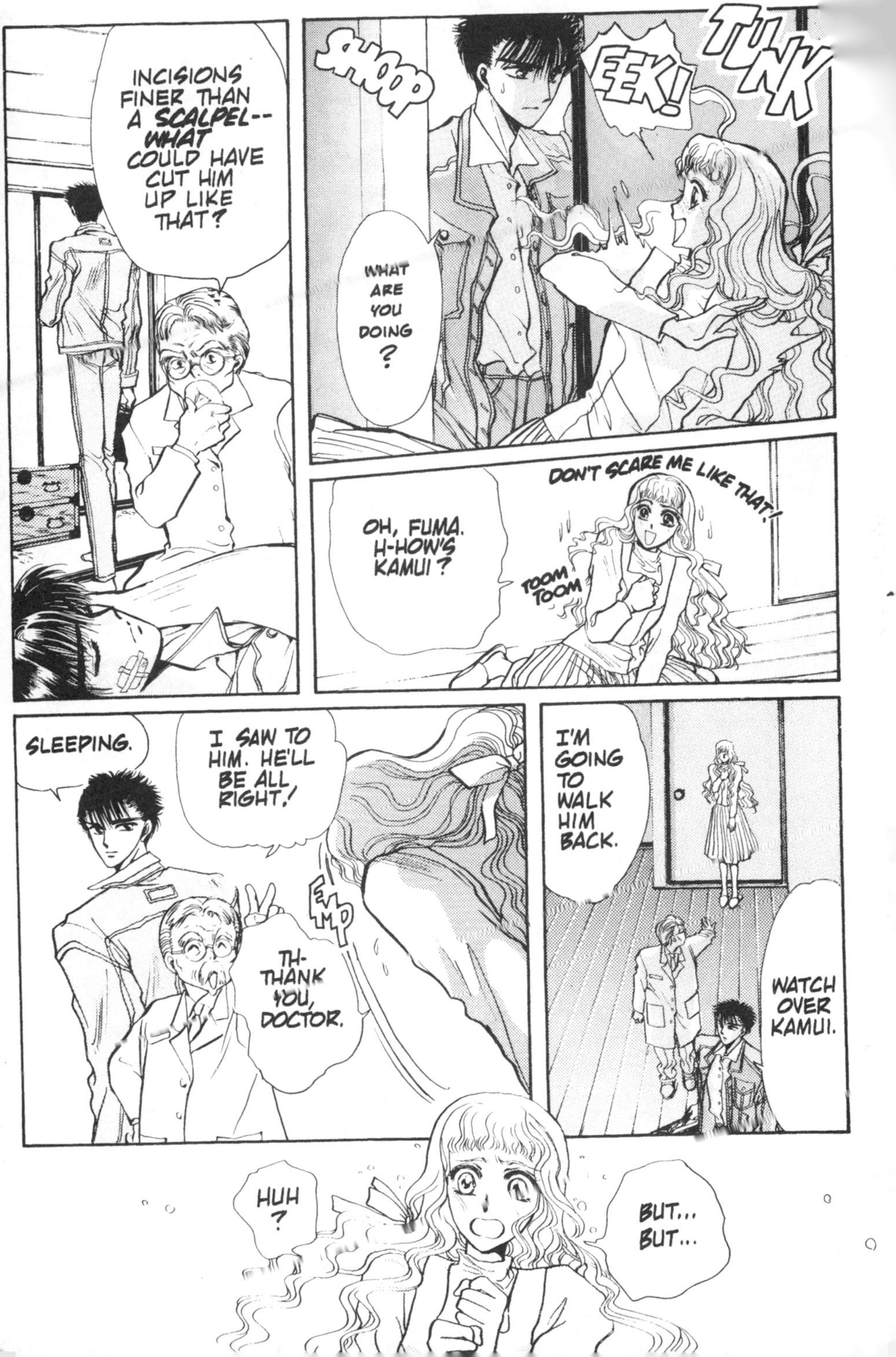
INCISIONS FINER THAN A SCALPEL-- WHAT COULD HAVE CUT HIM UP LIKE THAT?
SHOOP
EEK!
TUNK
WHAT ARE YOU DOING?
OH, FUMA. H-HOW'S KAMUI?
DON'T SCARE ME LIKE THAT!
TOOM TOOM
SLEEPING.
I SAW TO HIM. HE'LL BE ALL RIGHT!
TH-THANK YOU, DOCTOR.
FUMP
I'M GOING TO WALK HIM BACK.
WATCH OVER KAMUI.
HUH?
BUT... BUT...

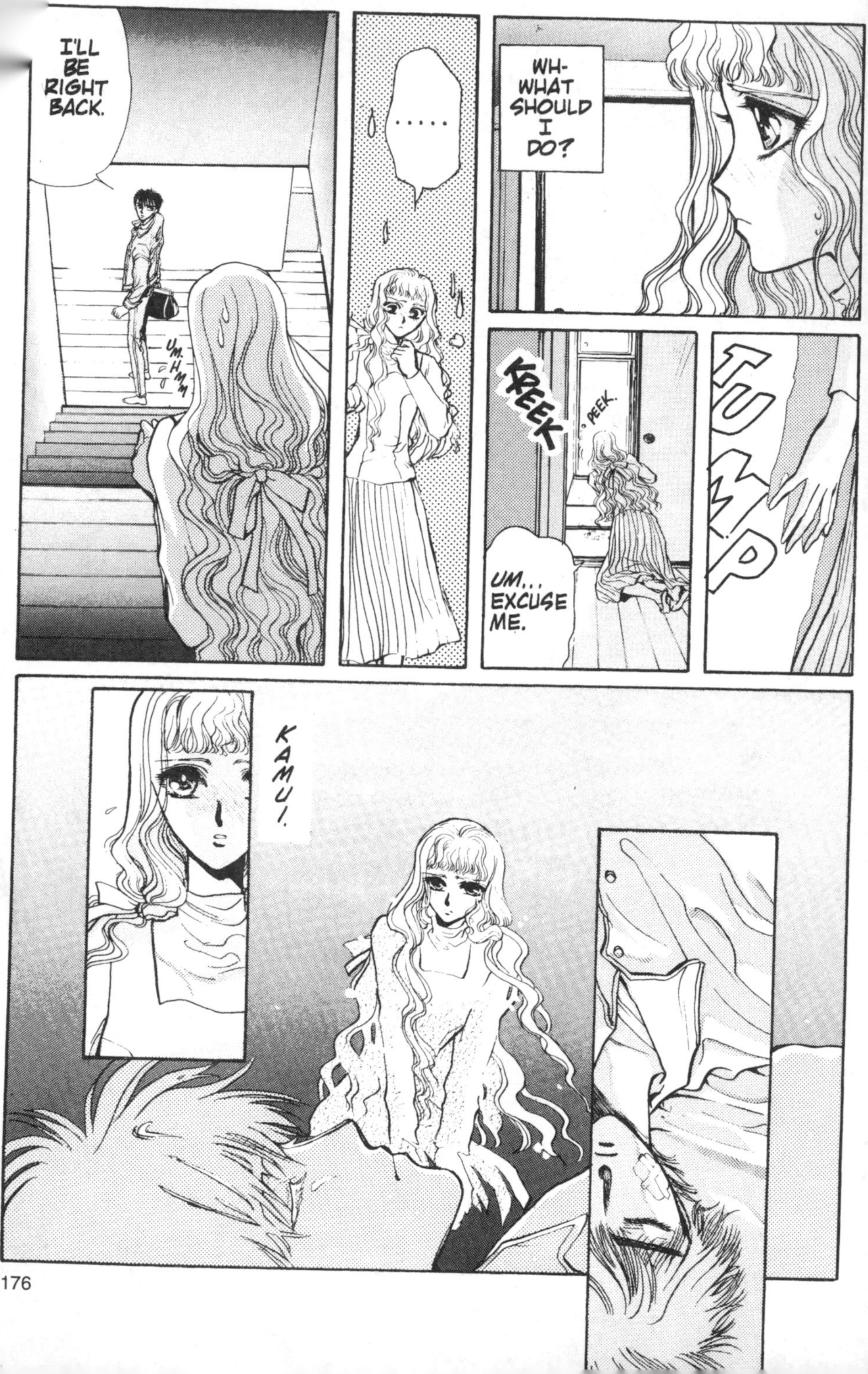
I'LL BE RIGHT BACK.
UM-HMM
......
WH-WHAT SHOULD I DO?
KREEK
PEEK.
UM... EXCUSE ME.
TUMP
KAMUI.

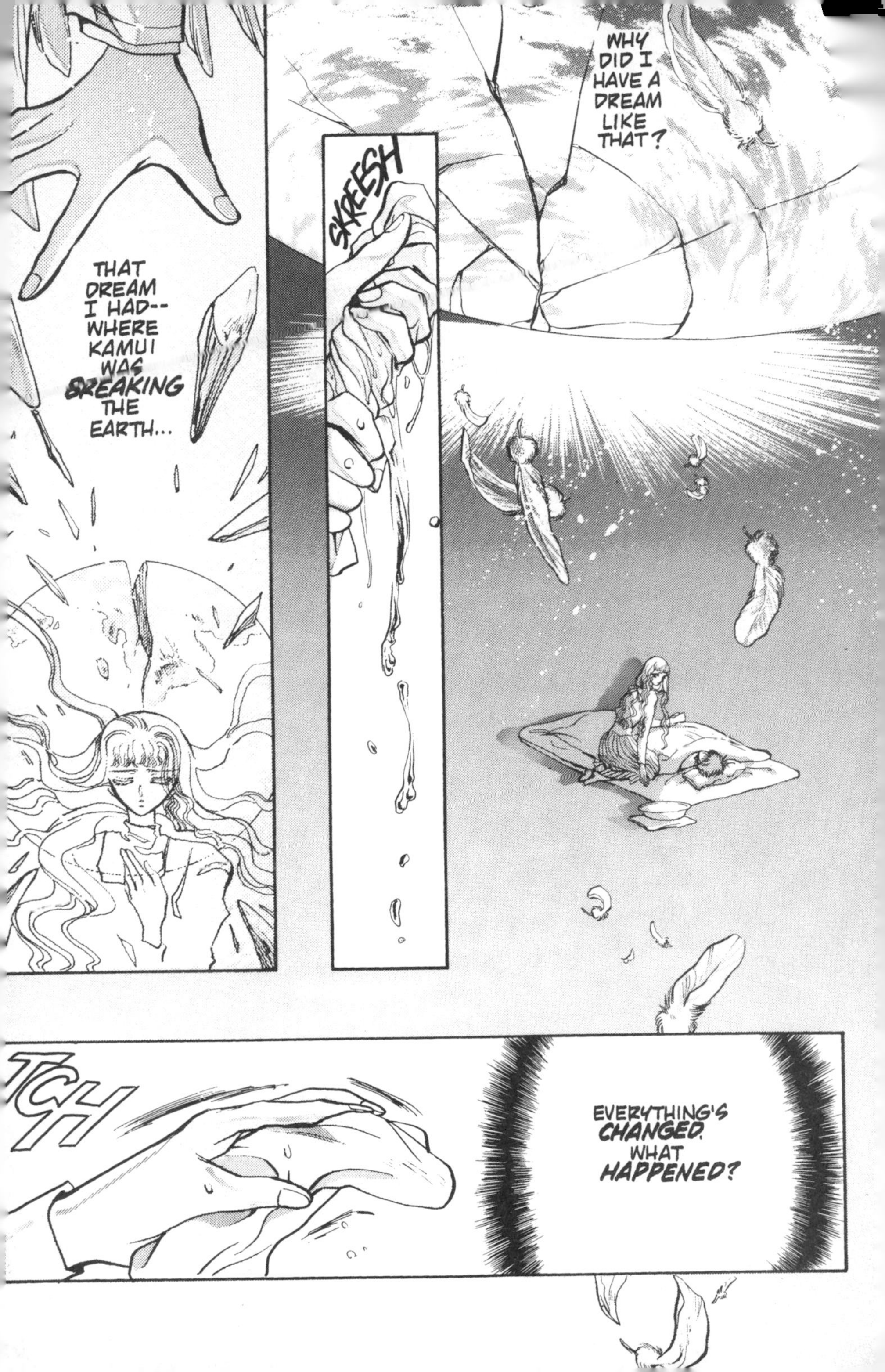
THAT DREAM I HAD-- WHERE KAMUI WAS BREAKING THE EARTH...
SKREESH
WHY DID I HAVE A DREAM LIKE THAT?
TCH
EVERYTHING'S CHANGED. WHAT HAPPENED?

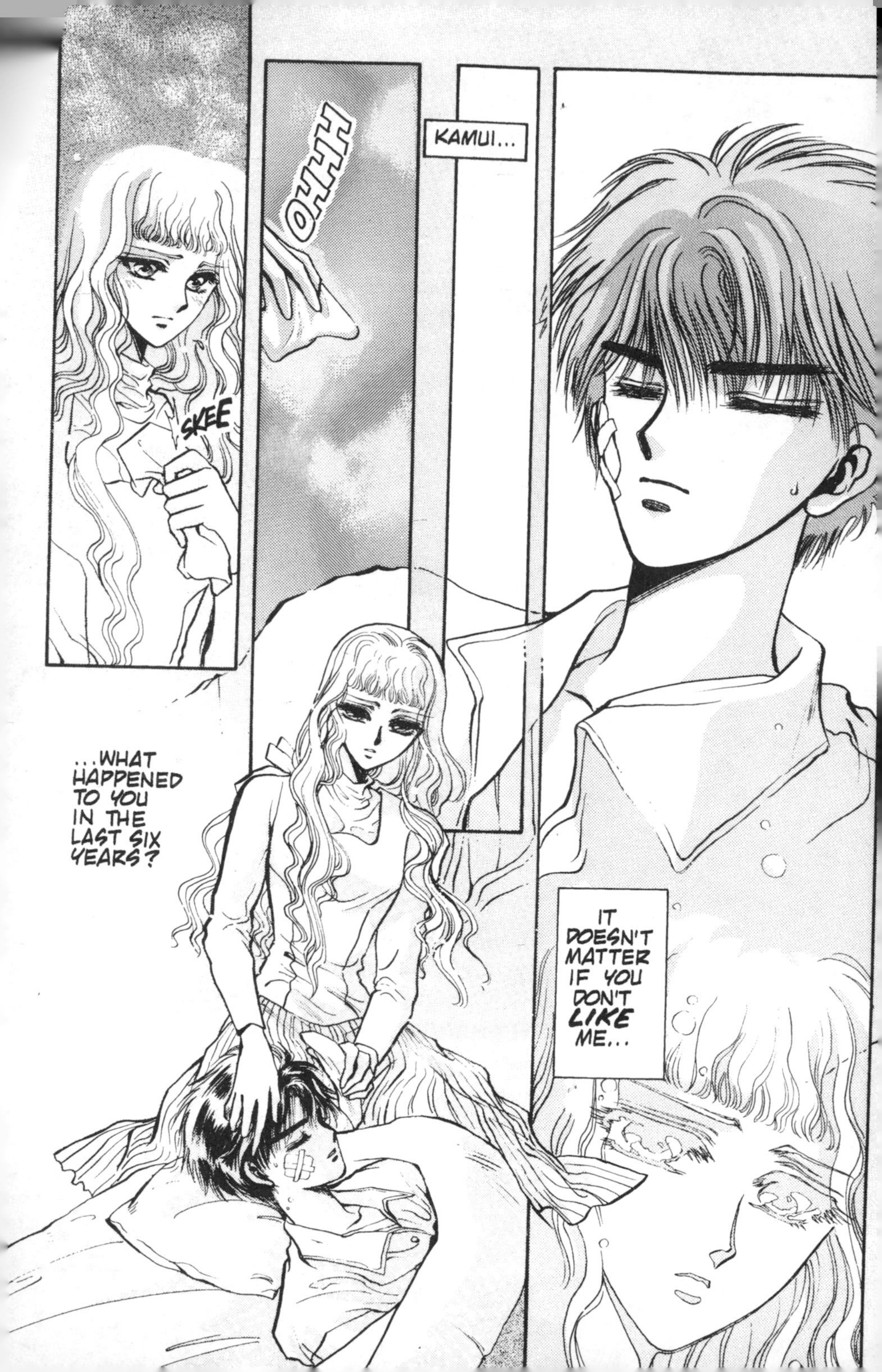
SKEE
HHHO
KAMUI...
...WHAT HAPPENED TO YOU IN THE LAST SIX YEARS?
IT DOESN'T MATTER IF YOU DON'T ***LIKE*** ME...

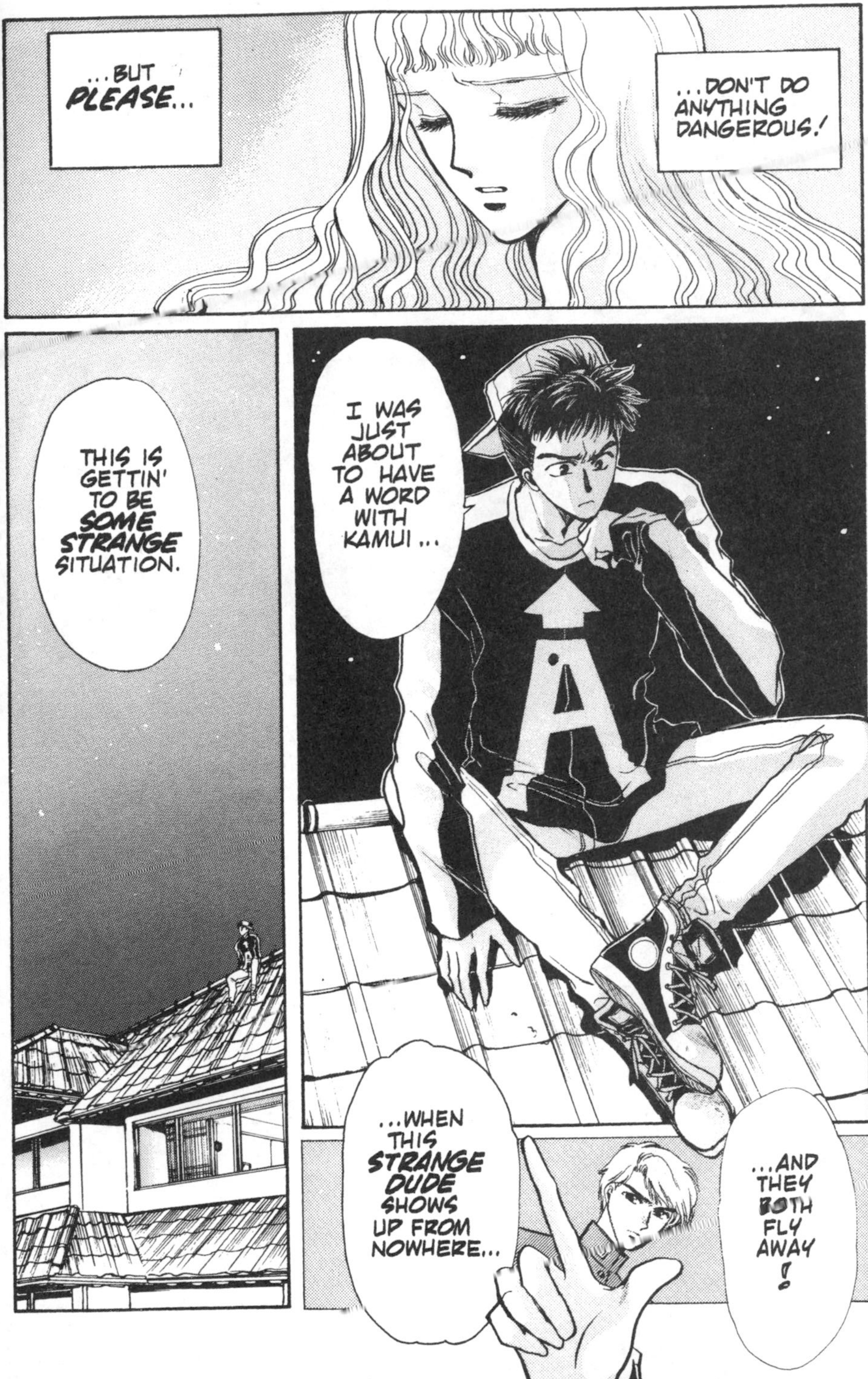

...BUT PLEASE...
...DON'T DO ANYTHING DANGEROUS!
THIS IS GETTIN' TO BE SOME STRANGE SITUATION.
I WAS JUST ABOUT TO HAVE A WORD WITH KAMUI ...
...WHEN THIS STRANGE DUDE SHOWS UP FROM NOWHERE...
...AND THEY BOTH FLY AWAY!

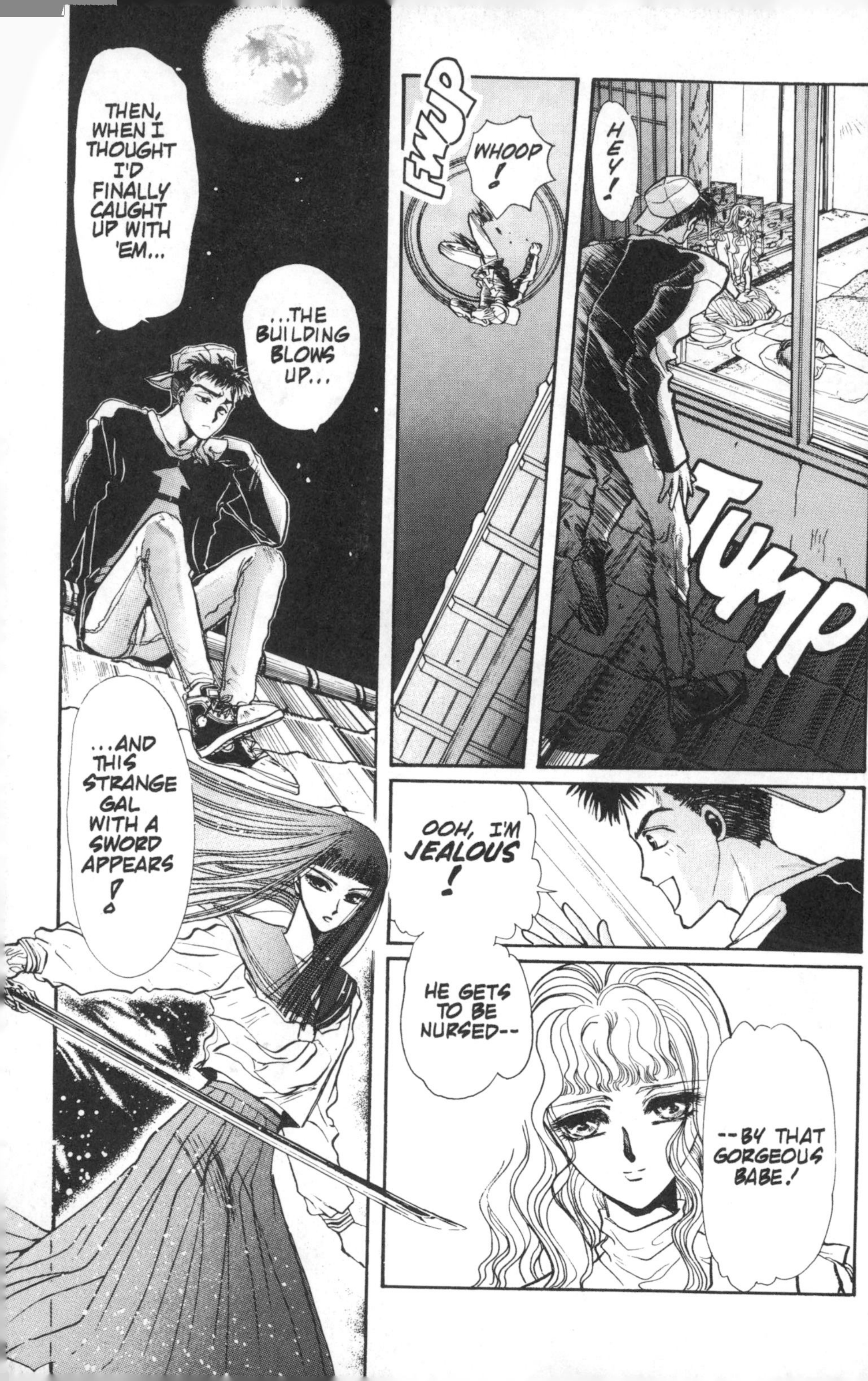
THEN, WHEN I THOUGHT I'D FINALLY CAUGHT UP WITH 'EM...
...THE BUILDING BLOWS UP...
...AND THIS STRANGE GAL WITH A SWORD APPEARS!
FWUP
WHOOP!
HEY!
TUMP
OOH, I'M JEALOUS!
HE GETS TO BE NURSED--
--BY THAT GORGEOUS BABE!

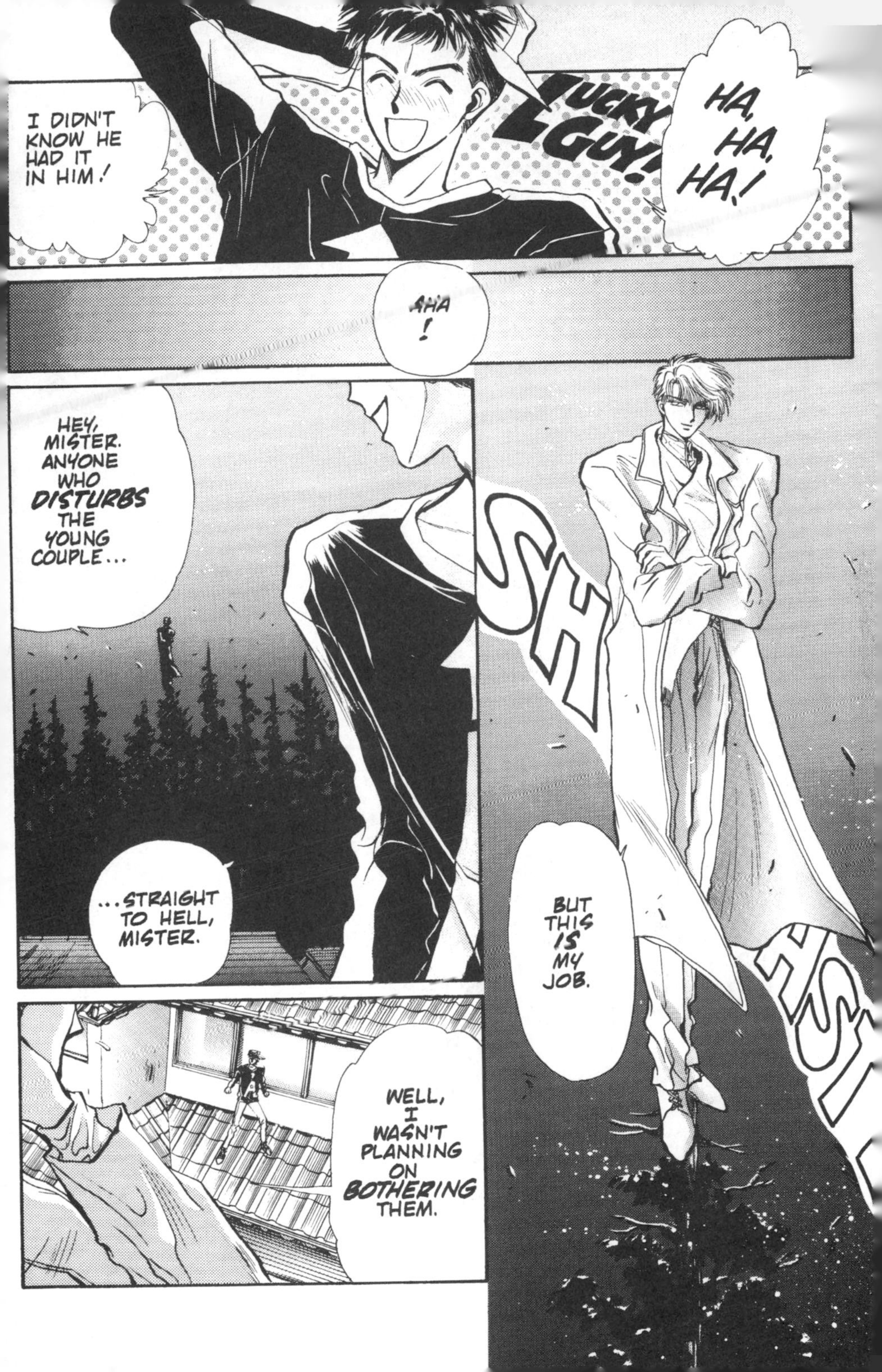
I DIDN'T KNOW HE HAD IT IN HIM!
LUCKY GUY!
HA, HA, HA!
AHA!
HEY, MISTER. ANYONE WHO DISTURBS THE YOUNG COUPLE...
...STRAIGHT TO HELL, MISTER.
WELL, I WASN'T PLANNING ON BOTHERING THEM.
SH
BUT THIS IS MY JOB.
ASH

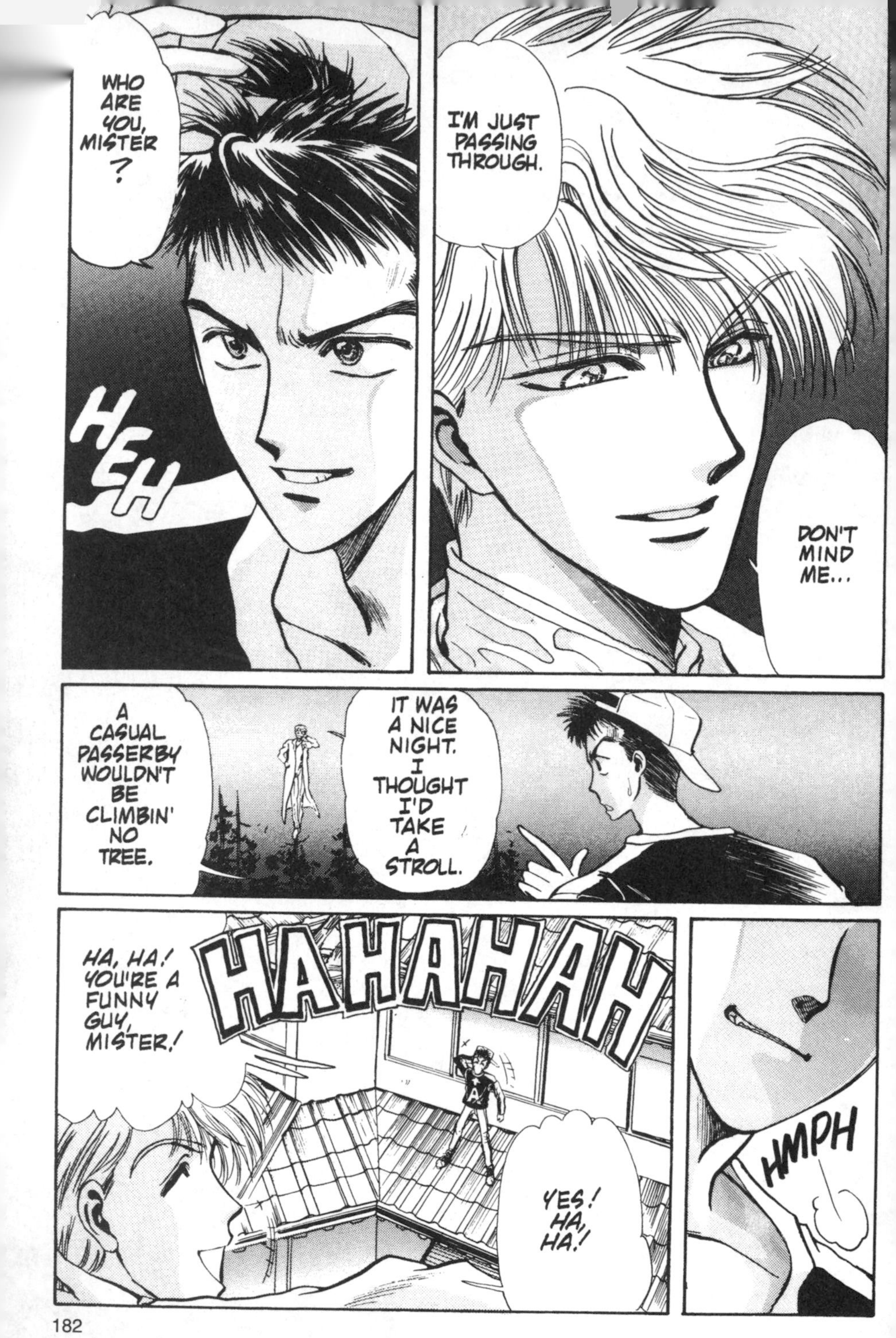
WHO ARE YOU, MISTER?
HEH
I'M JUST PASSING THROUGH.
DON'T MIND ME...
A CASUAL PASSERBY WOULDN'T BE CLIMBIN' NO TREE.
IT WAS A NICE NIGHT. I THOUGHT I'D TAKE A STROLL.
HA, HA! YOU'RE A FUNNY GUY, MISTER!
HAHAHAH
YES! HA, HA!
HMPH

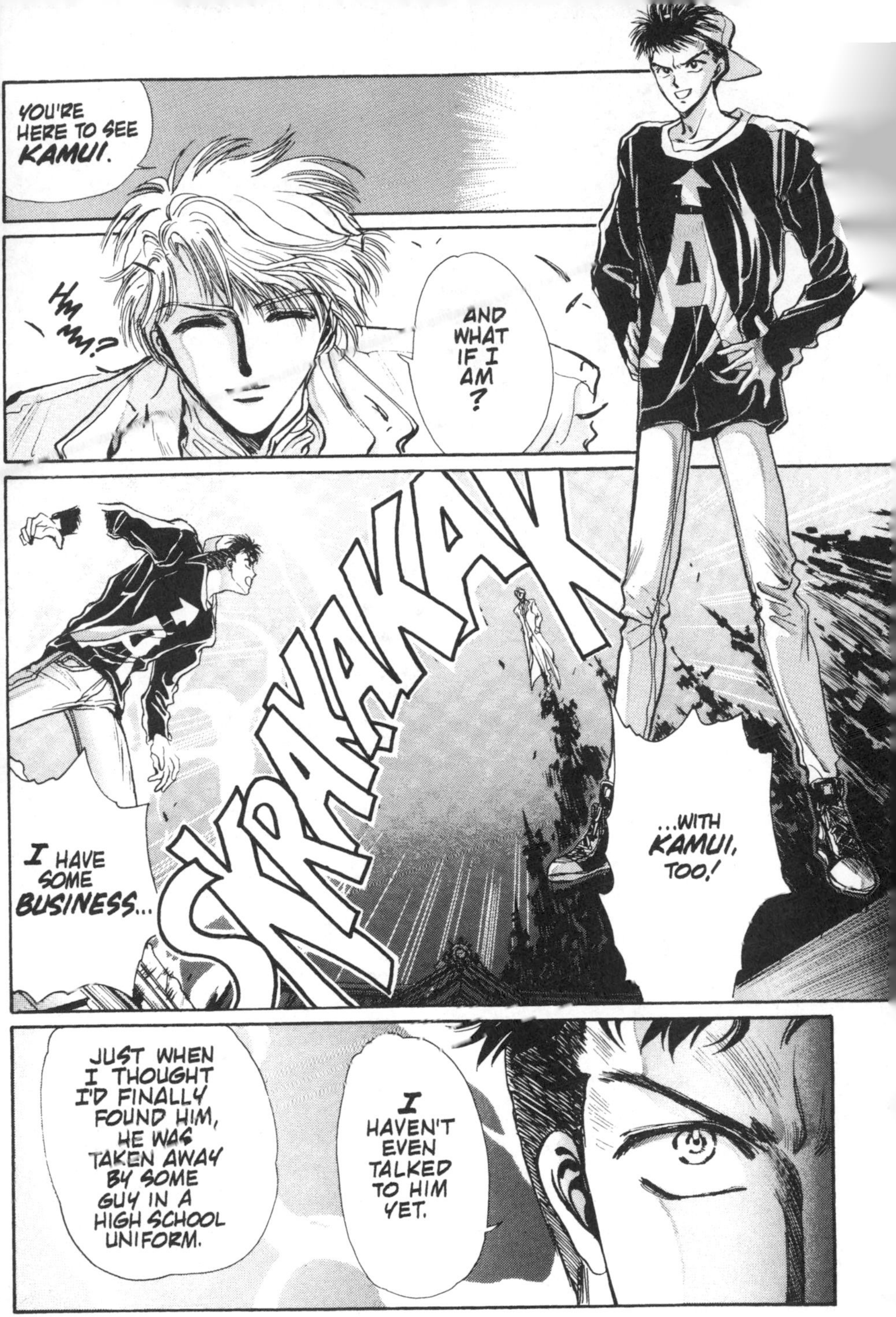

YOU'RE HERE TO SEE KAMUI.
HMMM?
AND WHAT IF I AM?
SKRAKAKAK
I HAVE SOME BUSINESS...
...WITH KAMUI, TOO!
JUST WHEN I THOUGHT I'D FINALLY FOUND HIM, HE WAS TAKEN AWAY BY SOME GUY IN A HIGH SCHOOL UNIFORM.
I HAVEN'T EVEN TALKED TO HIM YET.

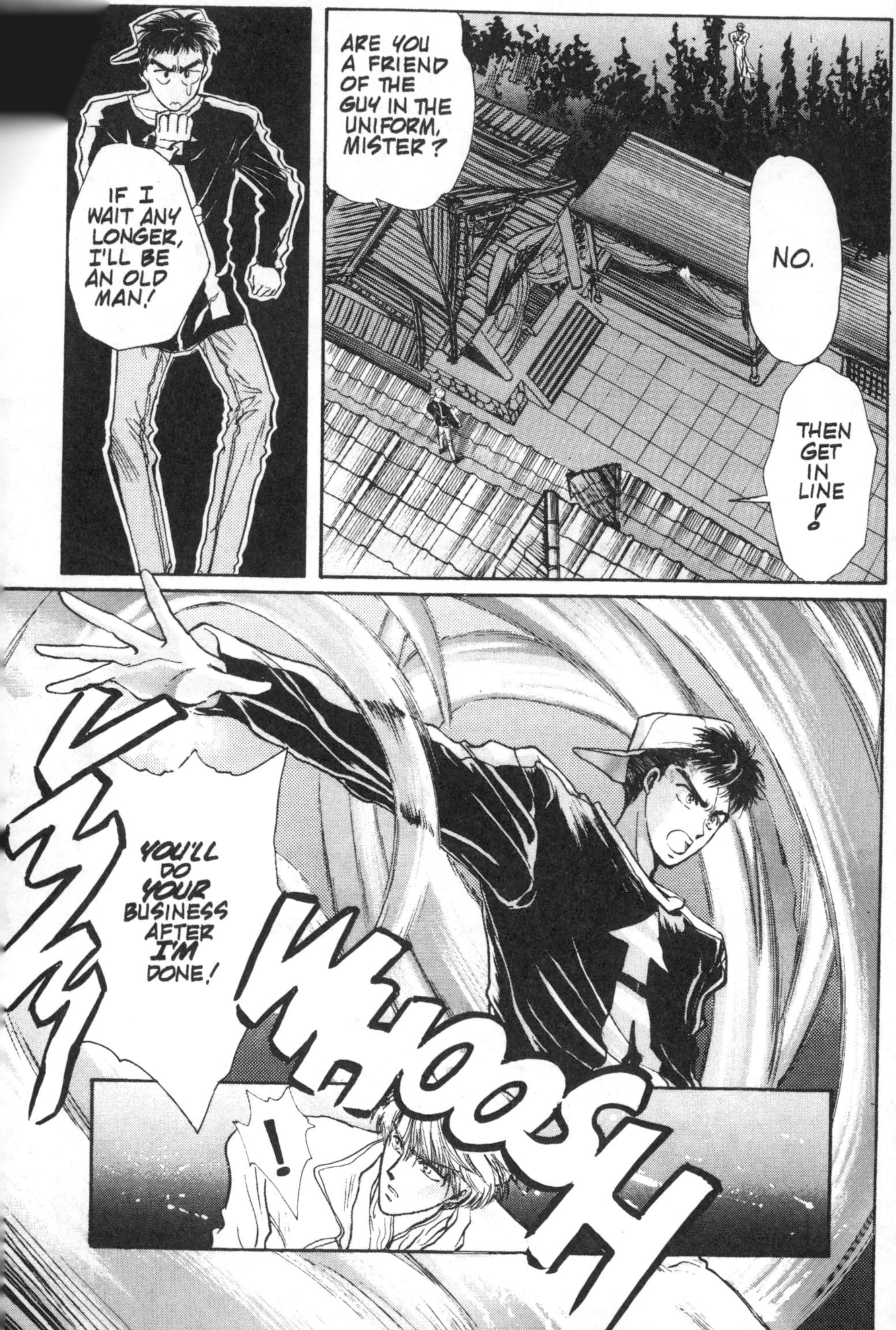
IF I WAIT ANY LONGER, I'LL BE AN OLD MAN!
ARE YOU A FRIEND OF THE GUY IN THE UNIFORM, MISTER?
NO.
THEN GET IN LINE!
YOU'LL DO YOUR BUSINESS AFTER I'M DONE!
WHOOSH
!

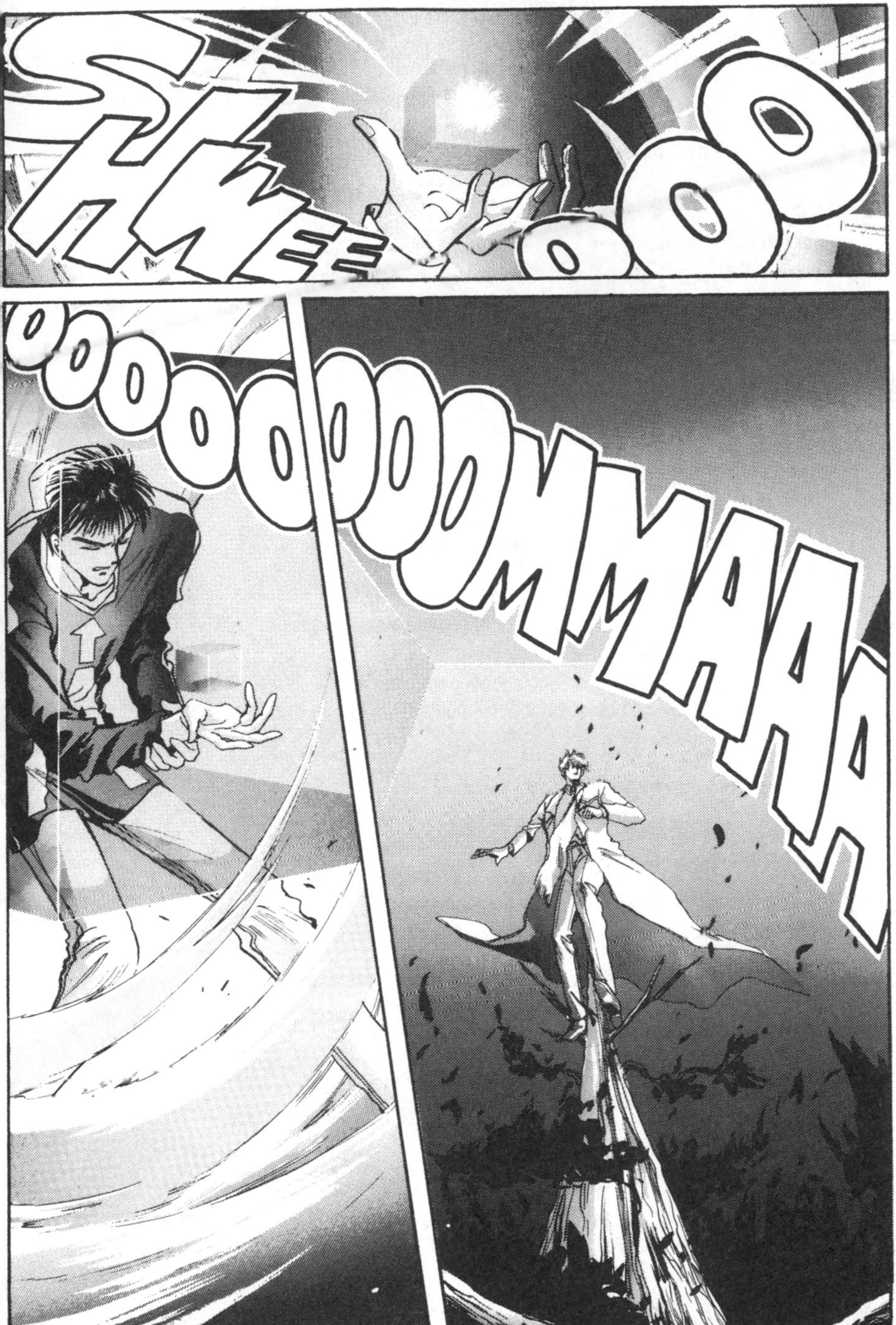
SHWEEOOOOOOOOOOOOOOMMAAAA

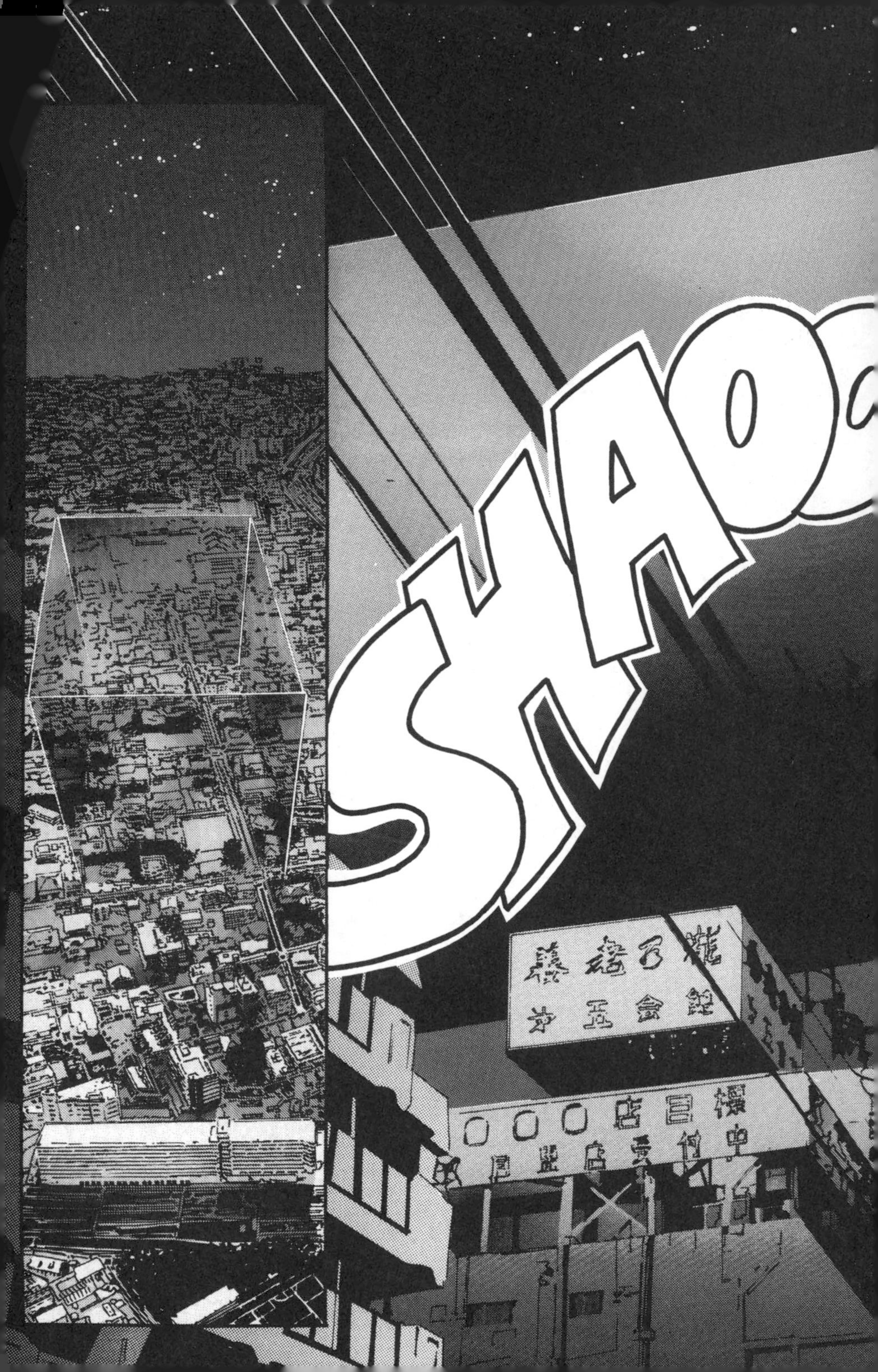
SHAO

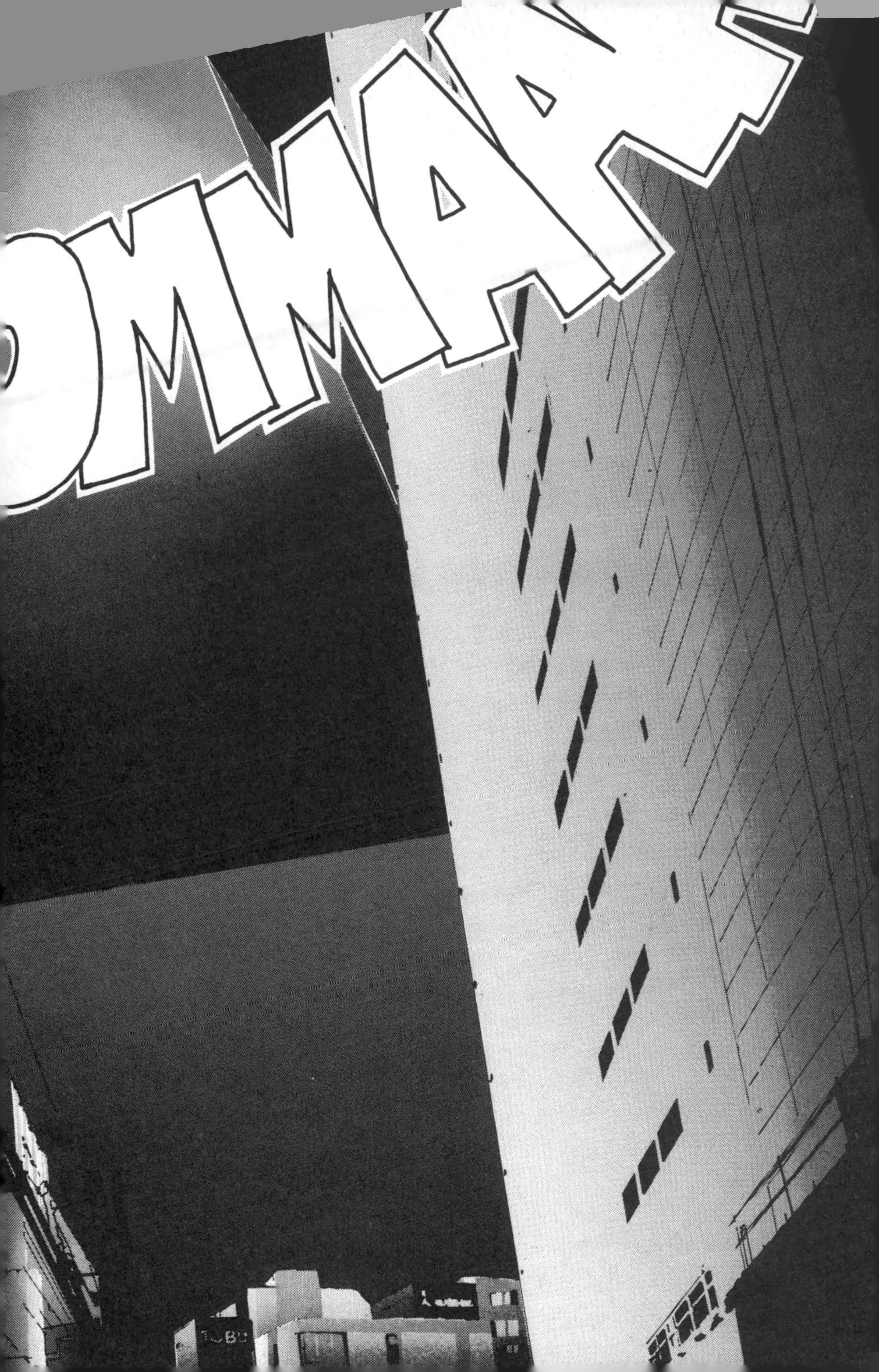
OMMA

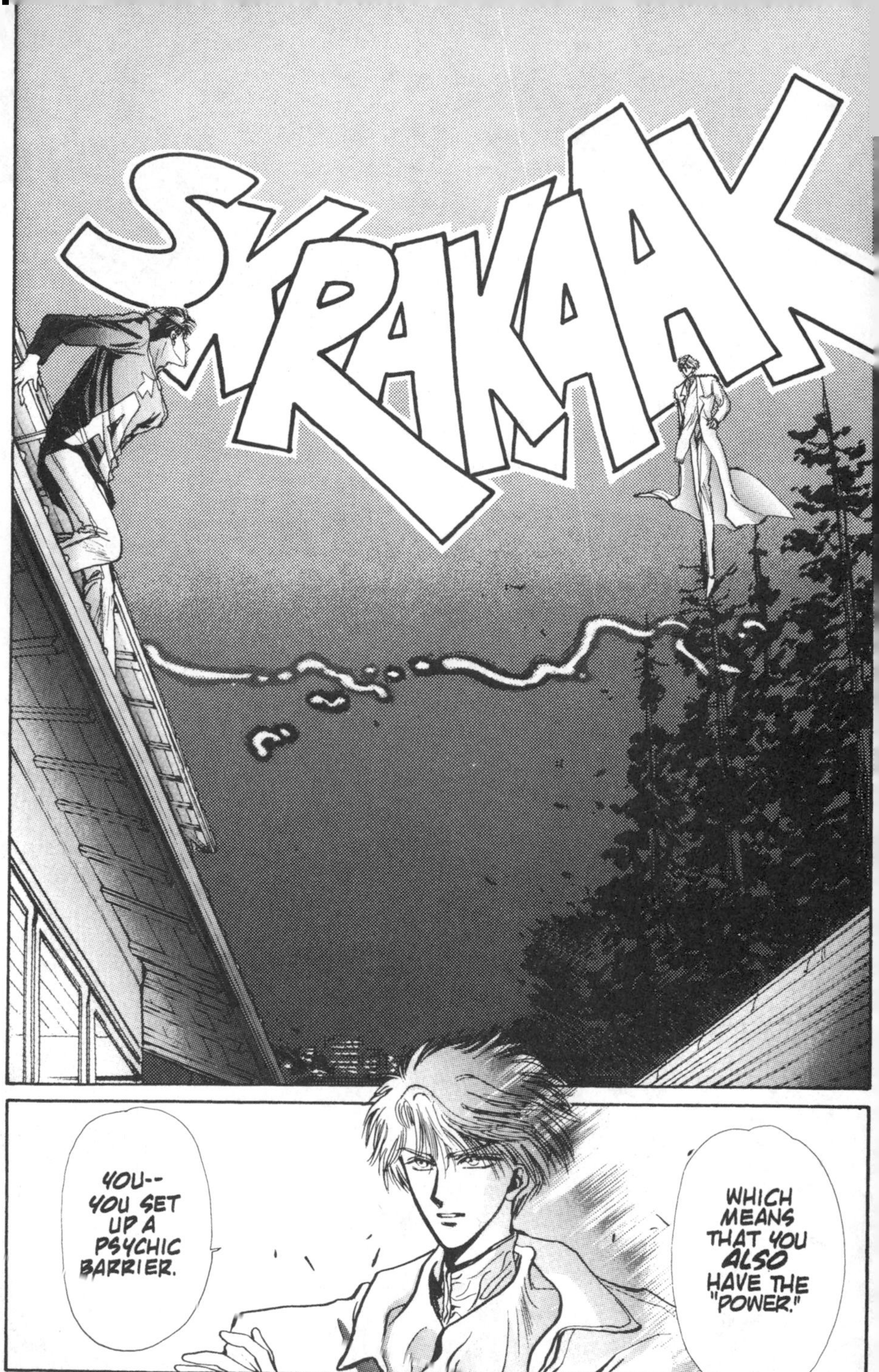
SKRAKAAK
YOU--
YOU SET
UP A
PSYCHIC
BARRIER.
WHICH
MEANS
THAT YOU
ALSO
HAVE THE
"POWER."

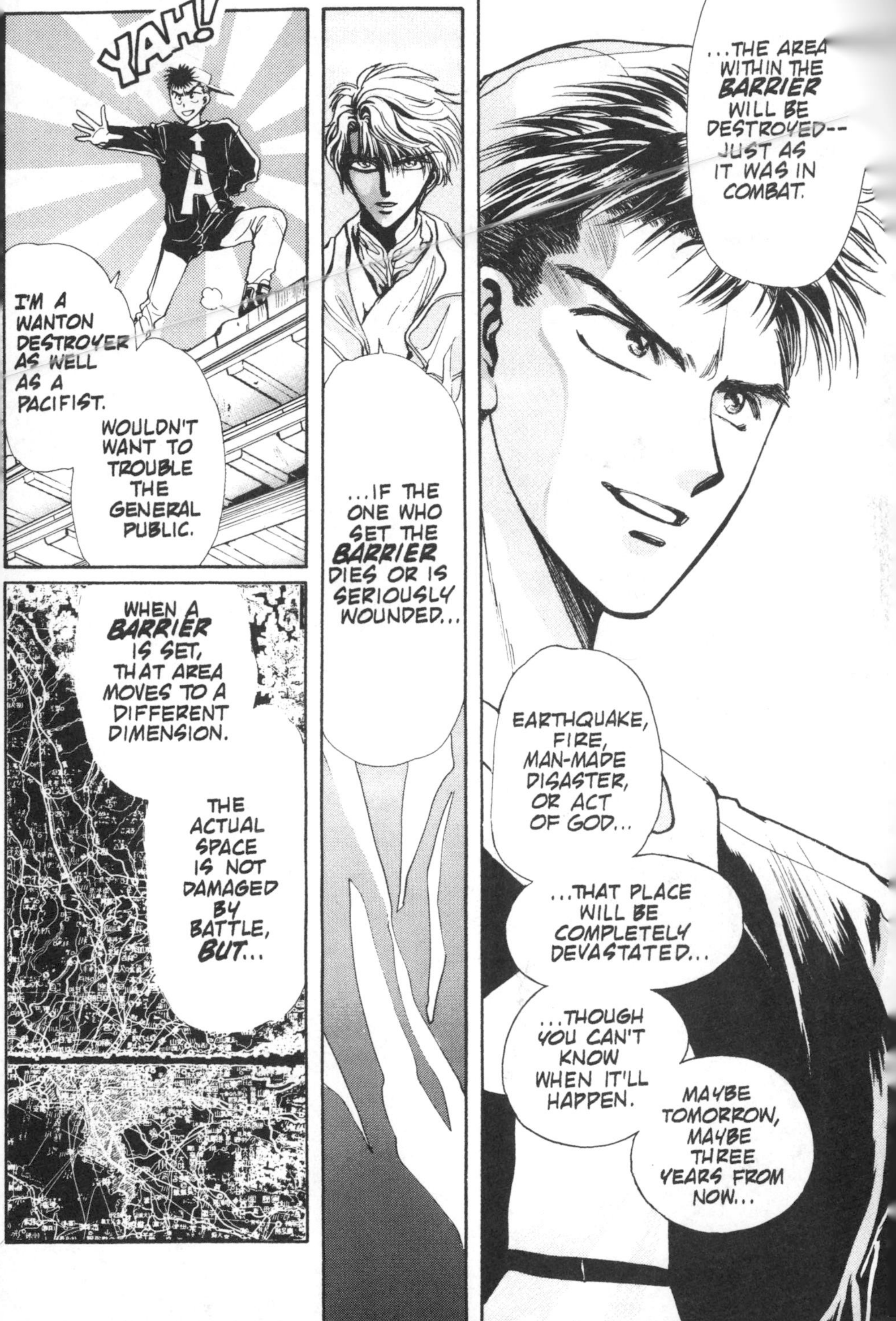
YAH!
I'M A WANTON DESTROYER AS WELL AS A PACIFIST.
WOULDN'T WANT TO TROUBLE THE GENERAL PUBLIC.
WHEN A BARRIER IS SET, THAT AREA MOVES TO A DIFFERENT DIMENSION.
THE ACTUAL SPACE IS NOT DAMAGED BY BATTLE, BUT...
...IF THE ONE WHO SET THE BARRIER DIES OR IS SERIOUSLY WOUNDED...
...THE AREA WITHIN THE BARRIER WILL BE DESTROYED-- JUST AS IT WAS IN COMBAT.
EARTHQUAKE, FIRE, MAN-MADE DISASTER, OR ACT OF GOD...
...THAT PLACE WILL BE COMPLETELY DEVASTATED...
...THOUGH YOU CAN'T KNOW WHEN IT'LL HAPPEN.
MAYBE TOMORROW, MAYBE THREE YEARS FROM NOW...

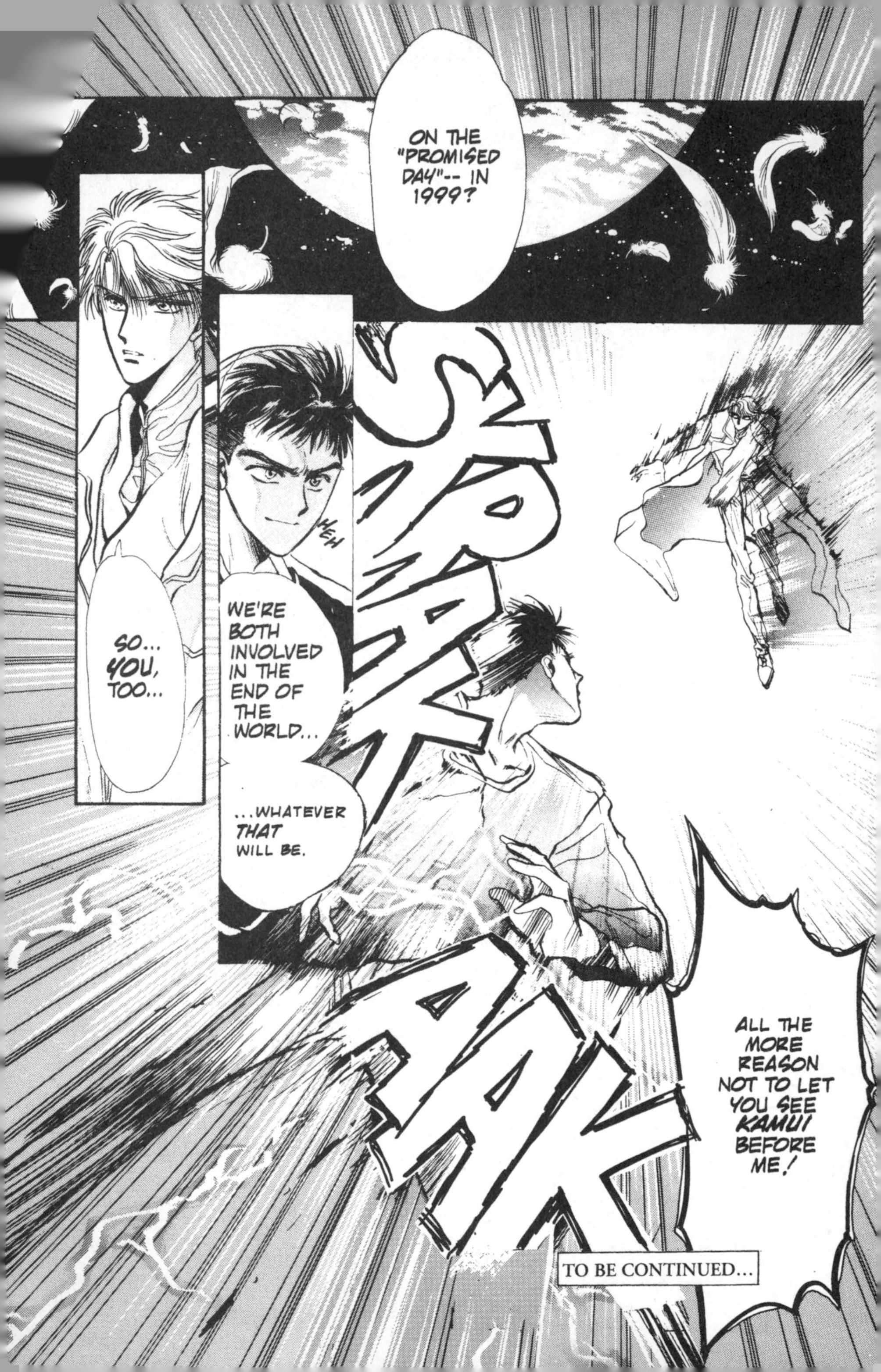
ON THE "PROMISED DAY"-- IN 1999?
SO... YOU, TOO...
HEH
WE'RE BOTH INVOLVED IN THE END OF THE WORLD...
...WHATEVER THAT WILL BE.
ALL THE MORE REASON NOT TO LET YOU SEE KAMUI BEFORE ME!
TO BE CONTINUED...